The Words and Music of Frank Zappa

THE PRAEGER SINGER-SONGWRITER COLLECTION

The Words and Music of Frank Zappa

Kelly Fisher Lowe

James E. Perone, Series Editor

PRAEGER

OCM 62393159

Westport, Connecticut
London

Library of Congress Cataloging-in-Publication Data

Lowe, Kelly Fisher.
  The words and music of Frank Zappa / Kelly Fisher Lowe.
      p. cm. — (The Praeger Singer-songwriter collection, ISSN 1553–3484)
  Includes bibliographical references, discography, and index.
  ISBN 0–275–98779–5
  1. Zappa, Frank—Criticism and interpretation. I. Title. II. Series.
ML410.Z285L68 2006
782.42166092—dc22 2005034613

British Library Cataloguing in Publication Data is available.

Library of Congress Catalog Card Number: 2005034613
ISBN: 0–275–98779–5
ISSN: 1553–3484

First published in 2006

Praeger Publishers, 88 Post Road West, Westport, CT 06881
An imprint of Greenwood Publishing Group, Inc.
www.praeger.com

Printed in the United States of America

The paper used in this book complies with the
Permanent Paper Standard issued by the National
Information Standards Organization (Z39.48–1984).

10 9 8 7 6 5 4 3 2 1

Copyright Acknowledgments

The author and the publisher gratefully acknowledge permission for use of the following material:

From *The Negative Dialects of Poodle Play* by Ben Watson. Copyright © 1995 by the author and reprinted by permission of St. Martin's Press, LLC.

For Richard Best Lowe (1943–1998), who would have delighted in the prospect of my writing a book about Frank Zappa, despite the fact that, whenever I would play Zappa records in my average middle class teenage bedroom, I was always told to "turn it down."

All you have to do is follow the example of the great masters of the world's literature, and deal with the facts of life frankly and honestly. That is what the . . . police call "obscenity."

—Upton Sinclair, "How to Be Obscene"

A person can only be offended by smuttiness if they believe in smut as a concept and believe in the concept of dirty words—which I don't. It's always something that bothered rock writers more than anybody else. I mean, who the fuck are these rock writers, anyway?

—Frank Zappa, interview in *Rolling Stone,* 1988

Contents

Series Foreword

Although the term, "Singer-songwriters," might most frequently be associated with a cadre of musicians of the early 1970s such as Paul Simon, James Taylor, Carly Simon, Joni Mitchell, and Carole King, the Praeger Singer-Songwriter Collection defines singer-songwriters more broadly, both in terms of style and in terms of time period. The series includes volumes on musicians who have been active from approximately the 1960s through the present. Musicians who write and record in folk, rock, soul, hip-hop, country, and various hybrids of these styles will be represented. Therefore, some of the early 1970s introspective singer-songwriters named above will be included.

What do the individuals included in this series have in common? Some have never collaborated as writers. But, while some have done so, they've all written and recorded commercially successful and/or historically important music and lyrics.

The authors who contribute to the series also exhibit diversity. Some are scholars who are trained primarily as musicians, while others have specialized knowledge in such areas as American studies, history, sociology, popular culture studies, literature, and rhetoric. The authors share a high level of scholarship, accessibility in their writing, and a true insight into the work of the artists they study. The authors are also focused on the output of their subjects and how it relates to their subject's biography and the society around them; however, biography in and of itself will not be a major focus of the books in this series.

Given the diversity of the musicians who are the subjects of books in this series, and given the diversity of viewpoints of the authors, volumes in the series will

differ from book to book. All, however, will primarily be organized chronologically around the compositions and recorded performances of their subjects. All of
the books in the series should also serve as listeners' guides to the music of their
subjects, making them companions to the artists' recorded output.

James E. Perone
Series Editor

Acknowledgments

This project has been more than twenty years in the making. In fall 1983 my friend Dave Mechling brought me a tape of *Joe's Garage* to play in my car as we went to lunch. I have been a fan ever since. In fact, I did not quite realize what an ongoing obsession I had with the words and music of Frank Zappa until, in an exchange of e-mails during the planning stages of this book, my old college roommate reminded me that during much of my freshmen and sophomore years I subjected him to daily doses of Zappa.

The only problem I had with the book was that right smack in the middle of writing it, I quit my excellent job as an associate professor of English and director of American studies at Mount Union College and took an excellent job with the Ellbogen Center for Teaching and Learning at the University of Wyoming. As anyone who has ever tried to move an entire household, including a wife, a child, and a menagerie of pets, 1,300 miles across I-80 can attest, it is a chore, and not something that can be done simultaneously with the writing of a scholarly book on the words and music of the aforementioned Mr. Zappa.

Several people, at both Mount Union and Wyoming, have helped with the research and writing of this book. At Mount Union College, James Perone, series editor, golfing partner, colleague in American Studies, and friend, gave me the go-ahead and encouragement to start this project. My research assistant, Mr. James DeMonte, over Christmas Break 2004–2005, created the most amazing concordance of Zappa scholarship that I have ever seen. Ms. Debi Stears, reference librarian, helped me negotiate the increasingly virtual reference materials and introduced me to a number of marvelous resources for someone attempting to do musicology who has no formal training in musicology. Gerry Wuchter, Rodney Dick, Len Epp, Andy Price, and especially Rudy Roggenkamp provided moral support above and beyond. Frank Tascone, Michael Olin-Hitt, and Bill Macauley, fellow writers and good friends, never failed to shake their heads in amazement that I was getting away with writing a book about Frank Zappa.

At Wyoming, the staff of the Ellbogen Center for Teaching and Learning has had to listen to me beat my gums about Zappa since the day I arrived; the director, Jane Nelson, gave me a lot of time neither of us could afford to finish the book. Office associate Jennifer Wade put up with all of my complaining about there not being enough hours in the day, and my excellent assistant Jessica Willford (I have never had an assistant before, and she has set the bar pretty high) read the manuscript from cover to cover to help me find and accurately credit, all of the quotes. Despite all of the help I have received, ultimately, all of the errors in the book are mine.

At Greenwood/Praeger Press, my editor, Dan Harmon, learned to dread my e-mails asking for just a *few more days* to get everything right.

Other folks who need mentioning: Mike King, Dana Mellicker, Tony Pagliaro, and Keith Norris have withstood 20 years of Zappa (and my commentaries on Zappa, his music, lyrics, and politics); my mother, Mrs. Janice Craven, and her husband, Dr. Alan Craven, are both role models and friends; my daughter, Evangeline, has amazed her friends and alarmed her teachers with her encyclopedic knowledge of Zappa's music (although, to be honest, "Who Are the Brain Police?" is a pretty appropriate anthem for Junior High School).

My wife, Lori Van Houten, who disagrees with much of my reading of Zappa's lyrics, read every word of this book several times and made more quality editorial suggestions than I can count. Her support throughout the writing of this book and the move to Wyoming has been nothing short of heroic.

Introduction: Why Study Frank Zappa?

One of the traits of genius [is] the ability to recognize your intuition and make it real in the world naturally, effortlessly and flawlessly, and Frank did that every day.[1]

In a speech he once gave about Ernest Hemingway, longtime publisher and friend Charles Scribner Jr. argued that "From the time he was a boy to the day he died, he thought of himself as a writer and nothing else. That image of himself created his ambition, directed his will, supplied his greatest satisfaction."[2] In many ways the life of Frank Vincent Zappa can be spoken about in similar terms; Zappa, like Hemingway, was that rarest of people: the truly self-made man. Without much formal training in music theory, Zappa declared himself, at the age of 14, a composer and spent the rest of his life fulfilling "that image of himself." It is a truly American story—Horitio Alger with, as Zappa writes in the song "Joe's Garage," a "Stratocaster and a Fender Camp." Raised middle class in the desert in California, Frank Zappa soon came to be seen as the very image of the smart and sophisticated rock star.

SCOPE AND PURPOSE OF THE BOOK

The question "why study Frank Zappa?" is, unfortunately, a good one; although many music and popular-culture scholars predict that his orchestral and ensemble works will more than likely be studied sometime in the future and that it is more than likely that Zappa will be considered one of the twentieth century's most important composers, his work as an American singer and songwriter presents a more difficult critical and cultural challenge.

It is precisely because of these challenges, however, that Zappa's work as a writer of pop and rock music is worth investigating. Although the rest of the book will look at these issues in depth, the challenges in studying Zappa are thus:

1. It is difficult to label his music. Stylistically, Zappa is all over the place; he is equally capable of writing the simplest blues shuffle and complex, multimodal art pieces, yet Zappa's stylistic complexity combined with a deep, varied, and extensive catalog of work, and an utter refusal to repeat himself musically while at the same time borrowing generously from his previous works (and thus creating a strange body of intertextual work), makes it difficult, especially for the novice, to access and appreciate his work. Because he was not a writer of hit singles (and indeed, he had only a handful of songs that could even be considered radio friendly), the new listener must actively seek out his work.[3] Below, I will make the case that much of Zappa's work should be considered "art rock." This distinction should, hopefully, give the novice listener a place to begin.

2. Zappa was, in one of the oldest Western artistic traditions, a master satirist. Satire is one of the most difficult of all art forms to pull off; the satirist's art is such that for every one who is amused or moved to think, another 10 are offended because they do not get the joke. And although Zappa seemed to hold little sympathy for those who did not get it, much of his professional career was spent defending himself from charges of sexism, elitism, racism, vulgarity, and just about any other -ism one can imagine. In reality, as I will argue, Zappa has had a complex and critical relationship with the American dream, and the argument that his songs make (satire is largely rhetorical in nature, and Zappa's form of satire, the rock/art song, is his vehicle for satire) is that many Americans had squandered both their rights and their responsibilities as citizens. The targets of his satire—feminists, unions, the government, and organized religion, that is, systems—seem to show, through their disapproval, that Zappa's criticism was right on the mark. Zappa, in interviews and in his autobiography, complained bitterly and at length about certain groups that seemed to be set up in order to preserve a certain image of a certain group of people (Italian Americans, unions, and so forth). It is Zappa's argument that true freedom means that one is free to screw up. That unions, for instance, for all the good that they have done, are also, especially in the postwar era, subject to corruption, dissension, and a pro-management bias that seems to be counter to their very foundational mission.

3. Although Zappa's biography is interesting in the sense that he knew, from a very young age, what he wanted to do (write music) and spent the rest of his life pursuing this dream, Zappa the personality is ultimately a frustrating subject for study because, unlike many of his peers and contemporaries, there is little scandal in his life story (thus the juicy biographical details that liven up the drugs, sex, and rock-and-roll biographies of bands like the Beatles, the Doors, the Who, the Rolling Stones, the Beach Boys, the Byrds, Buffalo Springfield, and Led Zeppelin, to name only a few, are absent in large part from Zappa's life story). In other words, Zappa lived a long and

public life that, for the most part, was, outside of what he did on stage and in the recording studio, quite boring.[4]

What I hope to accomplish in this book, then, is twofold: In the first part I will offer two ways to look at Zappa's work. I will look at him as both a writer of art songs and a satirist on par with Jonathan Swift and Lenny Bruce, two writers who, through their humor, forced their audience to take a much more critical view of the world around them.

In the second part of the book, I will look at Zappa's work, especially his rock/pop songs, and offer a cultural and rhetorical analysis of his music that makes the argument that Zappa's music offers up a fairly caustic and prophetic critique of the American dream.

It is, to say the least, ironic to attempt to write a scholarly book on the words and music of Frank Zappa; ironic in the sense that Zappa himself would have more than likely scoffed at the project. In his interesting essay on attempting to get permission to use Zappa's lyrics in his book *The Negative Dialectics of Poodle Play*, Ben Watson makes the blunt argument that Zappa was simply and openly hostile to anyone who would dare to interpret or critique his (Zappa's) work. Watson later quotes Zappa to the effect that "his [Zappa's] lyrics are so packed with arcana that he [Zappa] is the only individual capable of understanding what they mean."[5] With all due respect, this is rubbish. If Zappa's lyrics were truly that inscrutable, there would have been no need to ever release them. Indeed, the question of why Zappa sought an audience for music he felt no one but himself could understand strikes me as a fairly absurd proposition.[6] In *The Real Frank Zappa Book*, Zappa argues that "the lyrics wouldn't exist at all if it weren't for the fact that we live in a society where instrumental music is irrelevant."[7] The analysis of Zappa's lyrics, then, depends upon a number of things, two in particular: a knowledge of American culture and history and an ability to overlook Zappa's own public statements about his lyrics.

This, of course, raises a number of questions, the primary being why, if Zappa was so opposed to writing lyrics, did he not attempt to make a career out of instrumental music? Indeed, as I will argue in the subsequent chapters, Zappa's very definition of *earning a living* is what drove him toward popular music. Many of his lyrics reflect this choice he felt he had to make. I would also like to argue that, contrary to the public persona Zappa created, he had a lot to say. One needs to look no further than his first album, *Freak Out!*, to see that underneath the strange and silly and hilarious lay deep concerns with the state of the American dream. Songs such as "Hungry Freaks, Daddy," "Who Are the Brain Police?," and "Trouble Every Day" offer a devastating critique of America's major cultural revolution. And it did not stop there. Zappa's caustic social commentary, which came, for the most part, in song form, looked at the social movements in the sixties, seventies, and eighties with equal passion. So, although I think it is important to acknowledge that Zappa did not become a rock musician and songwriter/composer in order to comment upon society, the fact that his music does just that is undeniable.

A largely self-educated musician, Zappa had no real feeling for or relationship to academics, and although he seemed to understand that college towns were where some of his more loyal fans resided, he did not seem to have much sympathy for the contemporary world of academics. There is a double irony here—Zappa was very generous with his time: He seemed to know from the beginning of his career that even if he personally could not stand rock journalists and academic musicologists, for his kind of music to be heard, he would need to use both. This is the bind that all artists eventually find themselves in: the need to control the meaning of their own work while at the same time needing to get that work out into the marketplace of ideas, where it ceases to be controlled solely by the artist/author. Zappa's deep (and at least partially justified) cynicism about journalists and academics is somewhat sad (and misguided, and while I obviously have a bias here, his inability to tell the difference is a striking fact). In one of his final interviews, Zappa argued that his dislike of journalists was based on two premises: that a journalist, in general, "(a) doesn't know anything about what you do, (b) doesn't know about music in general and (c) has already made up his mind in advance before he comes to you what the answer ought to be to his precious little questions." Zappa then quotes himself as arguing that "Rock journalism is people who can't write interviewing people who can't talk in order to provide articles for people who can't read."[8]

It is in this cultural marketplace that the critic intervenes. The role of the critic, writes Barry Brummet in his book *Rhetoric and Popular Culture,* is that of "*meaning detectives;* their role is the explain what texts mean."[9] This, I know, is contradictory to Zappa's own wishes and the wishes of the Zappa family trust. In his autobiography *The Real Frank Zappa Book* as well as in the many interviews that he gave during his lifetime, Zappa argues that only he, as the artist/creator of his works, should get to decide what the meaning of his songs is. This is an argument I sympathize with, but it is one that is ultimately futile. Once a work enters the public domain—the concert hall, the record store, the art gallery, or the radio—it ceases to be under the complete control of the artist. Everyone who looks or listens or, indeed, experiences a piece of art brings his or her own feelings or experiences or understanding to the work, and once those existing emotions and ideologies absorb the work in question, the work becomes owned by the audience. That said, I do not intend to fix or provide the true meaning of the words and music of Frank Zappa. Instead, it is my intention to (1) engage in as direct a way as is possible the rock and pop recordings of Frank Zappa and (2) offer a particular *reading* of these works, a reading grounded in the traditions of rhetoric and cultural studies. The outcome of this engagement, and the subsequent purpose of this reading, is to argue that Zappa was, like Mark Twain and Lenny

Bruce before him, not just an entertainer, but one of this country's foremost social and cultural critics.

My real hope for this book is that it will get people to listen to Zappa's music and, in doing so, get them to ask the many questions that his music brings up: What is the role of the composer in contemporary America? What is the role of the government in the lives of its people? What is the proper relationship between church and state? Why are sexually aggressive women considered sluts by our culture? Why, in a democracy, do we have such a deeply class-based society? Why are the privileged so afraid of gay people, black people, and feminists? Zappa repeatedly asked all of these questions in his music and his lyrics.

In writing this book, I also understand that it exposes my own biases: toward literary analysis (I am much more at home working with lyrics than I am working with music), toward American cultural critique, toward the absurd. One of the things that has always attracted me to Zappa's work is that I understood, in hearing his music, that he loved his country enough to bother to expend the energy to try to make it a better place to live. That takes some doing. As often as he appeared to be criticizing America it was not, as might appear at first glance, because he hated it; it was because he saw the possibility of what it could become and was dismayed that so few people understood these potentials.

Visionary is a word that is used too often in our culture (as is *awesome,* but that is another book), but Zappa truly fits this definition. His extraordinary range of influences—blues, R&B, doo-wop, classical, jazz, and Eastern European folk music—led him to create music that is wholly unique in the history of American popular song.

You Call *That* Music?

Frank Zappa embodies perhaps the recording world's most radical amalgamation of popular and classical interests in a single composer.[1]

The single most important development in modern music is making a business out of it.[2]

What makes Zappa's music so interesting is that it is, according to musicologist Christopher Smith,

explicitly and intentionally situated in a referential context. It is targeted at a certain group of listeners with some range of musical experiences held in common, and it presumes that such listeners will hear allusions and make sonic connections.[3]

In other words, Zappa wrote music for people who were careful listeners. The more you listened to his music, the more you got it. The more you got it, the more in you felt. The more in you felt, the deeper your bond with Zappa. It is an intellectual project that is not an unfamiliar one: write for yourself and your friends. If they get it, great. If they do not, too bad. Zappa was, perhaps, better than anyone at this (and certainly the least willing to compromise on the matter). In this chapter, I would like to make some remarks about Frank Zappa's music (the rest of the book devotes a considerable amount of attention to his lyrics). I would like to look at a couple of intersecting ideas about his work that revolve around the same theme: that Zappa was a composer in the most traditional sense and that what he composed is easier to understand when broken down into some identifiable elements and given a vocabulary with which to discuss these elements.

In a remembrance of Frank Zappa published in *Rolling Stone,* Trey Anastasio, lead guitarist for the band Phish, describes watching Frank Zappa perform live:

> He would leave his guitar on a stand as he conducted the band. He would get the keyboard player doing a riff, get him in key while he was smoking cigarettes and drinking coffee, pacing around as he got this groove going. And he would not pick up the guitar until everything was totally together. There would be this moment—this collective breath from the audience—as he walked over, picked it up and started playing the most ripping, beautiful solo.[4]

Watching Zappa compose live, in other words, was not your ordinary rock show experience; indeed, for anyone more than a little familiar with Zappa's work, much of his live concert was in itself a satire on the modern (i.e., post–Led Zeppelin) rock concert experience (more on that later). Zappa brought to his live shows a mixture of vaudeville, Led Zeppelin, and Leonard Bernstein that is hard to describe. Beyond performing live, however, Zappa worked hard and consistently to defy expectation and categorization. This makes encountering his compositions, especially for the novice, somewhat difficult.

What kind of music does Frank Zappa make? It is a difficult and interesting question because there is no real easy answer. Zappa made just about every kind of music one could make: country, pop, punk, funk, reggae, blues, rap, techno, swing, doo-wop, and surf music. This, of course, leaves out jazz, art / progressive rock, jam band music, and orchestral music (all admittedly big and messy categories). To make matters even more complicated, Zappa often combined these various genres of music within the same song (and occasionally, as demonstrated on his various live albums, at the same time).

I would like to make the twin arguments that the category that Zappa's music falls most neatly in to is that of progressive rock and that Zappa should be considered more than a writer of pop songs; one should consider him a composer of orchestral music that happens to be made with a rock band. The reason for this distinction becomes clear as one listens to Zappa's music. Most rock or jazz or country artists have an identifiable style, and most stay with or in that style throughout their careers (thus Pink Floyd always has a Pink Floyd sound, and even a band as consciously experimental as the Beatles had, from their first album to their last, a sound that makes it easy to identify certain music as Beatles music). It is much harder to do this with Zappa's music. Much like a composer of orchestral music who might go from symphony to sonata to concerto to opera to film score, Zappa, although always working with the basic tools of the rock musician, would vary his music so wildly from one album to the next that it becomes easier to understand his work by identifying him as a composer and not just a songwriter.

I undertake these arguments with the full knowledge that Zappa himself would more than likely have me beheaded for putting such labels upon his life's work—in part because Zappa delighted in his defiance of easy categorization, in part because progressive rock, of all the excesses of the sixties and seventies, has, perhaps, the worst reputation, and declaring oneself a composer has more than a bit of arrogance associated with it. That said, there are many scholars who find that Zappa's rock and jazz work fits easily into the genre of progressive rock. For instance, in the "Preface" to the special edition on progressive rock in *Contemporary Music Review*, the editors, John Covach and Walter Everett, argue, "Though he would never have been comfortable being lumped in with progressive rockers of any kind, Frank Zappa was also a composer who carefully blended rock music with art-music techniques and sensibilities;"[5] or, put more succinctly (and more specifically), in a longer piece in the same issue,

> Zappa's ambitions were already evident in *Freak Out!* [his first major label recording], which encompassed within its four sides various "flavors" of R & B as well as white-based pop and doo-wop, combined with more experimental material (rudimentary *musique concrete,* bursts of electronically generated noise, vocal free-for-alls, imitation cool-jazz interludes, collage-style layerings and accumulations) ranging from brief interjections without the frame of fairly conventional-sounding songs…to more extensive "interference" with songs already quote unconventional in both formal structure and content…to extended pieces which could take up as much as an entire LP side.[6]

Be that as it may, if one separates the reputation of progressive rock (summed up best, perhaps, in the infamous *Rolling Stone Album Guide* entry on the band Yes: "Pointlessly intricate guitar and bass solos, [and] caterwauling keyboards") from a more scholarly/objective definition of progressive rock, a listener can begin to see that much of Zappa's pop and jazz music fits neatly inside this genre.

There are a number of interesting definitions of progressive rock. Perhaps the best way to consider it is to discuss, briefly, how musicologists have defined it and how Zappa's music might fit into this academic definition.

In the book *Progressive Rock Reconsidered,* editor and author Kevin Holm-Hudson offers the following definition of progressive rock:[7]

- Songs predominantly on the longish sides, but structure rarely improvised.
- A mixture of loud passages, soft passages, and musical crescendos to add to the dynamics of the arrangements.
- The use of a Mellotron or string synthesizer to simulate an orchestra backing.
- Extended instrumental solos, perhaps involving some improvisation.
- The inclusion of musical styles from other than a rock format.

For instance, Joseph Byrd, the main composer for the short-lived progressive rock group The United States of America, claims that, contrary to art rock, Zappa was a "cynical genius" whose musical project could be defined largely as "offend the parents." Although Byrd gives Zappa credit for outgrowing this "planned outrageousness," he (Byrd) does not feel Zappa became the musician he could have been.[8]

This is a pretty significant misunderstanding of what Zappa was up to. One only has to make a quick glance at his catalog to understand that Zappa was always trying to push the boundaries of music—both lyrically and harmonically. His earliest musical experiments on *Freak Out!* are audacious for a first album (including "Hungry Freaks, Daddy," a song that includes a number of structural changes beyond the typical verse-chorus-verse change found in most pop songs, and "The Return of the Son of Monster Magnet," a 12-minute piece of musique concrète / art rock / noise that took one look at the future and anticipated everything from Neil Young's feedback / noise explorations to Tom Waits's sound collage experiments to the New York sounds of Sonic Youth and John Zorn.

Writing about his compositional style, Zappa argued, "Composition is a process of organization, very much like architecture."[9] One of the unique features of Zappa's music is that he often borrowed extensively from himself (à la Wagner or Mahler), taking a melody from song A and a solo from song B and perhaps placing that song (call it C) in a context of other songs and creating a meaning that can be called D. This is a highly constructed piece of art. It also indicates that although Zappa thought of songs as constructions, he was also interested in the larger product, thus many of his albums feature either suites of songs (many songs addressing various aspects of a cultural or political issue; *You Are What You Is,* for instance) or entire albums of songs strung together in a narrative (*Joe's Garage, Acts I, II & III*). This aspect of Zappa's music is often the most jarring for people who have not encountered his music (or have only encountered his few radio-friendly singles, such as "Don't Eat the Yellow Snow," "Dancin' Fool," or "Valley Girl").

Toward the late seventies and through the end of his career, Zappa engaged in what has been termed *xenochrony:* the melding together of various performances to make a complete piece of music. The most jarring thing about xenochrony is the way the music sounds. Take, for instance, the song "On the Bus" (originally named "Toad-O-Line"), from the album *Joe's Garage, Acts I, II & III*. The song comes at the end of the wonderfully melodic "Wet T-Shirt Night" and is an extended instrumental break. Although the music continues in the vaguely Latin / disco theme of the previous song, the solo is from a completely different song (in this case from the song "Inca Roads") that has a different beat and different melodic structure. The solo, pasted as it is into / on top of the music, is jarring the first time one hears it, but it is such an interesting musical issue (the first time I heard it, the solo sounded wrong to me, but I could not understand how or why it was wrong and thus was forced to confront the ideas of right and wrong as they apply to basic pop song structure) that it forces you to listen all the more carefully.

Zappa biographer Barry Miles quotes Zappa in discussing his compositional ideas as saying that he liked to compose works "according to [Edgard] Varese's principles of composition with unrelated themes following in free succession."[10] This is a fine way to describe Zappa's compositional technique. Songs like "Billy the Mountain" (*Just Another Band from L.A.*) and "The Adventures of Greggry Peccery" (*Studio Tan*) show this technique to its best advantage; they are long (more than 20 minutes) songs that contain narratives that are driven by sudden shifts in structure: different beats, melodies, and instrumentation. More complex are shorter songs along the lines of "Inca Roads" (*One Size Fits All*) or "Easy Meat" (*Tinsel Town Rebellion*) that feature vastly different melodies and time structure shifts within the confines of a relatively short space. These more whiplash changes are one of the things that can make approaching Zappa's music a daunting task (one is often left asking "where is the song?" because most Americans have been trained since at least the fifties to expect very certain things from a pop song).

This idea or technique of mashing together different musical ideas is, of course, one that descends from both classical composition and progressive rock. The one thing, compositionally, that Zappa does not do that many progressive rock bands do is provide some sort of musical segue between ideas. Take the Yes song "Close to the Edge." This multipart song is full of a number of musical ideas. The difference is that "Close to the Edge" is written in typical sonata form, a musical idea that goes back at least to the work of Bach and Mozart. Sonata form is one of the most recognizable of all classical music tropes, so when Yes uses it in "Close to the Edge," it is easy to see how the song contains, "two themes, a development, and a nice stable return."[11] Zappa's songs seldom, if ever, contain these elements. One of Zappa's greatest achievements is that his songs often contain multiple parts that, musically, do not have much to do with one another; they are songs, in large part, because Zappa says they are. Zappa has repeatedly argued that one should compose largely for oneself, going so far as to tell the music journal *Telos*, "I think that if you write music, you should write for your own taste, whatever you like to hear and whatever style you want to write it in for whatever reason."[12] Although that is only feasible up to a point (the missing part of Zappa's argument is "if you want to *get paid* for what you write"), there is a sense, with Zappa more than any other popular artists, that he is willing to risk the alienation of the paying public in order to make his music his way.

In the same interview, Zappa disagrees with the author's argument that Zappa has blurred the boundaries between high and low art. Zappa responds, "Or any art at all?"[13] This rather cryptic sentiment (it is not really an answer to the stated question) is one of the keys to understanding Zappa. In framing what he does as progressive rock compositions, I am trying to reinforce the fact that for Zappa there is no difference between his orchestral works and his rock works. To call his work progressive rock is helpful in an attempt to understand what it is he is trying to accomplish, but it is not a label that is particularly comforting given the number of things Zappa has said over the years about composition in general and his compositions in particular.

One of Zappa's greatest musical techniques is that of allusion. There are two types of allusion at work in Zappa's songs: the first is direct allusion. In a song Zappa would quote another song, either one of his own, a popular song of the time, or a historical song. For instance, Zappa would often include the music from the song "Louie Louie" in his own work. He does this for a number of reasons, the primary one being that "Louie Louie" is representative of a whole set of meanings—in this case the early history of simple, dumb rock songs. Later in his career, Zappa would take to quoting popular songs of the time in order to force his audience to make extralyrical associations. The song "Tinsel Town Rebellion," for instance, often contained quotes from bands as disparate as Devo and the Scorpions. The lyrical theme of the song was, ostensibly, the decline of the popular music industry; the musical allusions then help to illustrate the argument that Zappa is trying to make. By making part of his argument musical (instead of lyrical), Zappa is increasing the likelihood that people will get the joke (and, at the same time, making the joke more complex).

The second type of allusion Zappa often worked with was the hidden allusion. He often, for instance, hid bits and pieces from his favorite classical composers inside his rock songs. In the song "Amnesia Vivace" on the album *Absolutely Free*, Zappa includes quotes from *The Rite of Spring* and *The Firebird* (Stravinsky) as well as the classic doo-wop song "Duke of Earl." These types of allusions helped Zappa build a different kind of bond with a different kind of audience; Zappa includes these works in his songs to see if anyone else can hear them, and the ones who can then become part of the in-group. Zappa's fan base was particularly fanatical and willing to follow his musical explorations wherever they might lead. To be part of his fan base was to be in the know about the various musical quotes.

Zappa would also do this kind of allusive work on a different scale, taking a texture or a tone from a certain recognizable figure in rock or pop or jazz and constructing his own music out of this generic texture. In the song "On the Bus" (discussed previously), Zappa begins the solo by directly quoting the first few notes from Toto's big hit "Hold the Line." On the song "Variations on the Carlos Santana Secret Chord Progression" (from the album *Shut Up 'N Play Yer Guitar Some More*), Zappa builds a solo around a bass and keyboard riff that sounds like the background to the Santana hit "Black Magic Woman" (itself a cover of the original Fleetwood Mac song by the same name). To make matters even more interesting, the song "Variations on the Carlos Santana Secret Chord Progression," is really an excerpted guitar solo from a performance of the Zappa song "City of Tiny Lights" and thus does not really exist as a piece of music in and of itself, except for the fact that

Zappa says it does (and he does this by excerpting it, giving it a name, and putting it on an album). Whew! Or take another, more amusing example: the song "In-A-Gadda-Stravinsky" from the album *Guitar*. This so-called song, which is really an excerpted solo from the song "Let's Move to Cleveland," taken from a November 1984 performance, features bassist Scott Thunes playing the bass line from the old protometal song "In-A-Gadda-Da-Vida," while Zappa solos (the solo is played almost entirely against the bass line); the drummer works with both Zappa and the bassist, following Zappa but not working against the very recognizable bass line. Then, partway through the song, the bassist switches and starts playing parts of Stravinsky's *The Rite of Spring*. It is a mad hybrid that works in a certain sense by defying all expectations of a contemporary song. Indeed, this is the best way to listen to Zappa—as someone who was constantly trying to defy expectation. In both his music and his lyrics, Zappa seemed comfortable in working against expectation. It is confounding, but it is also what makes him so interesting.

Satire and the Art of Frank Zappa

> Satire is a sort of glass, wherein beholders do generally discover everybody's face but their own.
>
> —Jonathan Swift, *The Battle of the Books*

> There is a strong impulse at this age to identify with these collective representations [of romantic love] and to use them as guiding fictions. Such symbolic fictions are the folklore by means of which teenagers, in part, shape and compose their mental picture of the world.[1]

Frank Zappa, American composer, arranger, and musician, is perhaps the finest satirist of the late twentieth century, certainly the finest working in the genre of music. Using both his words and his music, Zappa called attention to the social, cultural, and political trends of the time and through his art provided one of the great bodies of criticism produced during the last fifty years. By setting his critical views to music, however, he paid an enormous price, including critics who disliked him, loss of record sales, and a reputation as a mere writer of novelty songs that was at odds with his artistic and creative abilities.

Zappa, like many satirists, defended himself by arguing that he was just telling the truth. Occasionally, the truth that Zappa told hit too close to home. As historian of satire Emily Gowers argues, the satirist often must suffer for his art. The satirist, writes Gowers, has "a number of shifting roles: civic watchdog, sneering cynic, mocking or indignant observer, and social outcast."[2] Zappa was all of these. Ample evidence exists that Zappa did not want the role of cultural critic and that it was, perhaps, thrust upon him (in part because of his outspoken nature and his inability to refuse an interview). It is debatable about whether or not Zappa wanted the role of public critic. Be that as it may, he left behind, with his death in 1993, a tremendous body of critical work in the form of songs, interviews, and speeches that indicate a lifelong critique of the American dream.

Zappa was born on December 21, 1940, in Baltimore, Maryland, which is neither here nor there, except for the fact that Baltimore has produced a number of American satirists and social critics, including the writer H. L. Mencken and the filmmaker John Waters. Baltimore is an interesting place. David Simon, author of *Homicide: A Year on the Killing Streets* and *The Corner* and creator of the HBO television drama *The Wire*, all of which are set in Baltimore, writes that its defining feature is that "Baltimore is America's most northern southern city."[3] Baltimore, like all industrial cities in the United States since the Civil War, has struggled with its identity. The Zappas, as Italian immigrants, were part of this struggle, living for a time in a city that was uneasy with its new influx of citizens—black, white, brown, and so forth. The Zappa's were very aware of their place within this white hegemony. For all of the songs he has sung that might be considered critical of women, homosexuals, labor unions, and other groups, Zappa has saved the majority of his criticism, and certainly his most severe criticism, for white middle-class men. In his autobiography, Zappa describes growing up next to these kinds of folks, referring to them at times as hillbillies. It is this group of people, the white Anglo-Saxon Protestants who feel such ownership for their particular vision of the United States, who, as Zappa's satire reveals, have largely stolen, corrupted, or otherwise misplaced the American dream.

There is little proof in Zappa's music or lyrics that Baltimore had much lasting effect on Zappa's critical or cultural outlook on life beyond this rude introduction to the white majority. In reading his autobiography, as well as the work of critics and biographers, one only catches glimpses of Zappa's pre-California life in Baltimore.[4] Zappa writes sparingly about his time in Baltimore; his memories seem to be instead of his family, both immediate and extended, and the typical life of a first- or second-generation immigrant child. Zappa grew up with parents who spoke both English and Italian and grandparents who spoke nothing but Italian. In many ways, this immigrant upbringing seems to inform much of Zappa's later criticism of U.S. politics and culture. Yet his upbringing in Baltimore forced him to confront, at a young and unsuspecting age, the many ideas about social problems that some in the United States are never forced to deal with. For instance, Barry Miles writes that Zappa had three good friends, including a Panamanian boy, a crippled Irish boy, and another neighborhood boy. This diverse collection of children, at least two of whom were undoubtedly the product of fairly recent immigration to Baltimore, seems to have cemented early a sense that others are to be judged on what they can do and who they are, not by their nationality, ethnicity, or skin color. This realization would be put into practice throughout Zappa's life and work; his bands, from their earliest conceptions, were racially mixed and eventually mixed by gender as well. To be in his band you had to be good at what you did (and perhaps have a sense of humor); everything else was moot. This is Zappa's American dream in action: Work hard, play fair, and you will be rewarded.

There are a few stories from Zappa's childhood that seem to inform or indicate the kind of social critic he would turn out to be; the patriarchal nature of the Zappa family, the can-do spirit of his parents (a resourcefulness, argues Greg Russo, that was passed down to Frank), and a strange kind of generosity[5] are the constants of Zappa's early years.

There is no doubt that Zappa the bandleader, composer, arranger, and producer as well as record label executive, CEO, and film / video director was a patriarch; Zappa ran his bands and his businesses as benevolent dictatorships, much like the kind of old-school patriarchy in which he was raised. From his earliest recordings, Zappa exuded the kind of can-do-ism that has marked the best of the American entrepreneurial spirit shown in his ability to make do; to recover old, edited recordings and refashion them as something entirely new (as he did on the *Lumpy Gravy* album as well as when Warner Brothers refused to release the album *Läther*); and to use new studio technology as well as work around its limits. Further, despite arguments to the contrary, Zappa was a tremendously generous person. Throughout his career he took great pains to advance the careers of others (Alice Cooper, Captain Beefheart, the G.T.O.s) and often had people, friends, relatives, and employees living at his house for days (sometimes weeks or years) at a time, and, despite the fact that he did not seem to enjoy it all that much, Zappa was unfailingly giving to reporters and scholars. Zappa, despite much evidence to the contrary, was an optimist at heart who really seemed to believe in the foundational American dream: that if you work hard and play fair then you will be successful. Nevertheless, his life story is a long series of professional disappointments.

Zappa spent much of his career battling with record companies, management, band members, symphony orchestras, and labor unions, trying to get his music performed and recorded the way he wanted it performed and recorded. These battles, which continued throughout most of his adult life, must have made him reconsider the place of the small artist within the large and increasingly corporatized American dream. In fact, when asked about the most important development in modern music, Zappa responded, "The single most important development in modern music is making a business out of it."[6] This is not a radical thought; Thomas Jefferson's idea that we would be a nation of small business owners and small farmers has been lost to a world that seems run largely by and for the interests of big business, big government, and big religion.

Perhaps even more formative than his early upbringing in Baltimore was his move, at age 12, to California—first to Monterey and then to southern California, eventually settling in El Cajon, just east of San Diego. The move to California is an interesting one for Zappa: He started playing music (in Monterey he took up the drums), but he also started to become aware of how deeply class based U.S. society, especially in California, can be. In his autobiography, Zappa writes, "I didn't enjoy being poor. It seemed like everything that I wanted to do, that would be *fun*, cost too much money."[7] This acute awareness at an early age of the place that money plays in success and happiness drives a lot of Zappa's later criticisms of government, corporations, and white, upper-class men.

It was also around this time that Zappa discovered the two kinds of music that would inform his own compositional development: blues / doo-wop and avant-garde classical. There are interesting ideological ramifications in both of these; as Neil Slaven writes, Zappa's parents attempted to "discourage their son from finding the black stations on the radio dial, thus enhancing the pleasure of getting to hear the music."[8] Zappa's parents unwittingly, like many parents have done or are doing (rap seems to get much the same response from white suburban parents today as R&B did in Zappa's time), made black music a forbidden fruit. Zappa's love of avant-garde classical, starting with Edgard Varese's piece "Ionisation," also informs his ideological makeup in a couple of ways. First, Zappa says that he originally came to the piece because he had read a review of it in *Look* magazine that called it "dissonant and terrible; the worst music in the world."[9] Zappa's immediate response to this review was to think, "Ahh! Yes! That's for me!"[10] This shows a sort of contrariness that will inform much of Zappa's later thinking and at the same time infuriate many of his critics and fans (there are numerous stories, for instance, of Zappa refusing to endorse the politics of his fans or the politics that seemed implicit in his music because he wanted them to make their own choices). Zappa distrusted the primary social distinctions in art and culture; to profess an equal love for both blues / doo-wop and avant-garde classical, Zappa takes a hammer to any sort of line or distinction between so-called high culture and popular culture. His music would do much the same, alternating at times from inscrutable to difficult to silly to pop (often within the same song). It is this lack of boundaries that makes Zappa such an interesting cultural figure and composer; although critics often like (and often seem to need) boundaries or categories in which to describe or write about their subjects, Zappa's defiance of category seems to make critics distrust him instead of distrusting the very categories in which they place so much faith. Although this book assigns certain categories to its discussion of Zappa (progressive rock, composer, critic), it makes no assumptions that Zappa would agree with these categories; it is simply done in order to try to make the process of listening to and understanding Zappa's music that much easier.

Ben Watson, for one, seems to understand Zappa's project as a mixture of what cultural critics might call high culture and low culture, which is an interesting idea. Watson uses the word *miscegenation* in his discussion, which means the interbreeding of people of different races, and in the United States in particular it has come to mean the interbreeding of white and black. Zappa's music, in a strange way, does this. It intermixes white (classical) and black (doo-wop, blues, and R&B) to create an entirely new form of music.

In some ways this blurring of categories can be attributed to Zappa's lack of formal education. Zappa himself argues that "Since I didn't have any kind of formal training, it didn't make any difference to me if I was listening to Lightnin' Slim or a vocal group called the Jewels...or Webern or Varèse, or Stravinsky. To me it was all good music."[11] One of Zappa's most consistent critiques is that of music (and the music industry) itself; his failure to stay within the prescribed boundaries of the music business becomes a de facto critique of said boundaries. Starting with "The Return of the Son of Monster Magnet" on *Freak Out!*, through the musique concrète tape experiments on *Lumpy Gravy*, through his final recorded piece, *Civilization Phase III*, Zappa works consciously and consistently to defy any and all expectations of the traditional rock record. Zappa purposefully challenged the standard idea of rock recordings, acknowledging that part of the problem was an audience conditioned to enjoy rock and pop music only as a narrowly prescribed set of ideas: "Most of the stuff that I did between '65 and '69 was directed toward an audience that was accustomed to accepting everything that was handed to them."[12] Zappa's bitter critiques of the music industry, especially of what he considered to be manufactured pop stars (listen to *Fillmore East, June 1971* and "Tinsel Town Rebellion"), were an expression of his frustration not only with the music industry but with the music-buying public who seemed to allow the record companies to make musical decisions based on money. The idea that popular music is foisted upon an unsuspecting public by powerful corporate interests (doo-wop in the fifties; acid rock in the sixties; corporate rock, disco, and punk in the seventies; and all of the above in the eighties) is an important element of Zappa's satiric project.

Zappa's music demonstrates an understanding of both high and low culture and an acknowledgement of the relationship(s) between the two; throughout his work Zappa moves to abolish these differences, challenging his audience as well as educating them.

Lyrically, Zappa is much more straightforward in his critical project, arguing for a general sense of freedom that has deep roots in the American dream. Zappa is often criticized for turning his back on the hippie movement or being antiunion, but I feel that many critics misunderstand Zappa's disenchantment; he is not being cynical or mean, he is expressing a deep distrust of any dominant hegemony (especially one that claims to represent an underclass) and all that it has done to wreck havoc on U.S. culture and society.

Take, for instance, Zappa's aforementioned battles with the music industry. Zappa is certainly not the first artist to complain that those in power wish to dumb down music to feed simplistic pop radio expectations and that corporate decision making is questionable because the people who work at record companies are not artists and are motivated by money alone. Despite the fact that this view is something of an oversimplified generalization (and there is of course no proof that those who run record companies are not artistic or hate music or indeed that the popularity of a piece of art is inversely related to the artistic merit of said piece of art), there is a sense for many (both inside and outside the community of musicians and artists) that those who run the record companies are creating a simpleminded society. The argument that record companies are cogs in the capitalist wheel and that difficult or complex music is not allowed to come to market because it does not sell is one that goes against Zappa's sense of the American dream. This theme in Zappa's work—that artistic merit should be more important than how well a record sells—plays out in nearly all of his records.

Take, for instance, the song "Tinsel Town Rebellion" (1981). In one of his most direct attacks on the music industry, Zappa lashes out at "all those record company pricks / who come to skim the cream / of the cesspools of excitement." The theme of the corruption of the music industry in many of Zappa's songs (and on much of the album *Joe's Garage*) seems indicative of a larger critique of the corruption of the American dream itself.

Perhaps Zappa's most lasting criticism of U.S. culture is of our ability to lie to ourselves about ourselves. From the freak / hippie movement, to televangelism, to freedom of speech and gay rights, to feminism, to racism, to the Reagan Revolution, and to the way the music industry seems to lie to itself about the relationship between art and commerce, Zappa's critique of Americans' intellectual passivity and our willingness to place blind faith in leaders seems to drive much of Zappa's work. For a guy who spent only a few semesters in college, Zappa turned out to be, for a time, one of the foremost public intellectuals in the United States. In his autobiography, Zappa directly accuses Christianity as being a major cause of U.S. anti-intellectualism, writing about Adam and Eve that what they ate "wasn't *just an apple*—it was the fruit of *the Tree of the Knowledge of Good and Evil*. The subtle message? '*Get smart and I'll fuck you over—sayeth the Lord*.'"[13] It is Zappa's opinion that the government and the dominant (hegemonic) religion in the United States are in cahoots to keep you, the average citizen, from thinking too much about your place within the society and from asking silly questions like "Why do so few people have so much money?" or "Why did so few children of members of Congress fight in Viet Nam?" If one is kept busy buying records by Donovan, the Vanilla Fudge, Peter Frampton, or Culture Club, all of whom are making pretty but artistically and politically vapid music, then one has not the time to investigate how badly one is getting the shaft from the powers that be.

Zappa's critique of U.S. culture is often misunderstood because it is often indirect; only occasionally did he come out and say "this is terrible, it should change."[14] More often, Zappa would make fun of something and let the audience judge for themselves, or he would, as he often claimed, write something with a number of jokes embedded in the piece (most often musical) and hope that people would get it. In many ways this is the very essence of satire, the most difficult of all critical forms because so often the audience is not able (or is not prepared) to get the joke. Like Jonathan Swift, perhaps literature's most famous satirist, Zappa also was willing to risk public condemnation for trying to strip away the sheen of normality from society's ills.

Swift, like Zappa, spent much of his life disappointed in both his country and his countrymen. His earliest works, *The Battle of the Books* and *The Tale of a Tub,* are both satires that aim to attack "corruptions in religion and learning." As he became more public and outspoken (he was a bishop in the Roman Catholic Church and was politically active, lobbying both King William III and Queen Anne), his satire became edgier (some would say meaner), hence works such as *Argument against Abolishing Christianity* and "A Modest Proposal." Most biographies of Swift paint him as a man of the people—too often willing to bite the hand that fed him and too often willing to attack the popular authors of the day (he was disliked by both Samuel Johnson and William Thackeray)—yet Swift managed to maintain a small group of intimate friends. The same, of course, goes for Zappa: His works start off on the funny or broad side of satire and become, by *Thing Fish* and *Broadway the Hard Way,* much more angry and pointed. Zappa was, by the latter half of his career, willing to name names, singling out Donovan, Richard Nixon, Ronald Reagan, and Peter Frampton, among others, for very public scorn.

Swift's most famous piece, "A Modest Proposal," which has been read and misunderstood by generations of high school and college literature classes, is an example of the knife-edge of satire. This is the same sort of satire that makes Zappa's work so interesting: the hard edge of truth hidden in the sick joke.

Satire, especially the kind practiced by Swift and Zappa, is what contemporary literary critic James Woods calls "the comedy of correctness," the purpose of which is to lay bare "how stupid we all are." It is often written "by a writer whose comedy is often cruel" and is "obsessed with the folly and vices of bourgeois idiocy."[15] Woods later expands upon this discussion, arguing that, "in order for comedy to work we must in the end feel a pleasure at the lack of our compassion."[16] When Zappa writes and performs songs about groupies, for instance, the temptation, especially in the postfeminist United States, is to show compassion for the women; however, compassion for the women is the red herring (the thing that distracts our critical attention): it is the male band members who use groupies who are Zappa's main target. For every groupie in a song or rap by Flo & Eddie, there is a sad, desperate man who will do anything, including playing his "big hit record"[17] or "buying her a pizza"[18] to get her into bed. Although the women who are groupies are not spared criticism (see "Stevie's Spanking"), they are not seen, for the most part, as the targets of Zappa's satire. In fact, the groupies represented in Zappa's work, from Suzy Creamcheese to the groupie played by Mark Volman on *Fillmore East, June 1971* and *Just Another Band from L.A.*, are seen as perhaps deluded ("we are not groupies, we just like musicians for friends"). They are not represented as the sad, sexual playthings that they would seem to be. In all of the songs about groupies, it is the women who are in control of the sexual situation / transaction and the men who are begging for it, even to the point of having to demean themselves by playing their big hit record. Although the argument can be made that Zappa, by focusing his attention on men, was sexist, it is a difficult argument to make because the attention that is focused on these men is almost entirely negative.

This is best seen in the case of the song "Do You Like My New Car?" in which the band members end up having to play the song "Happy Together," the lame, albeit catchy, hit by the Turtles (Flo & Eddie's former band) that was antithetical to all that Zappa's music stood for. The humor on *Fillmore East, June 1971* comes from not only the groupie-band member situation but also from the hilarious musical irony of the Mothers playing a killer version of "Happy Together." Indeed, it is the men (the parodies of rock stars, especially as played by Howard Kaylan and Mark Volman) who are interrogated and found wanting.

Zappa's satirical work about the way people use their fame is comedy that walks the knife-edge of sadism and anger. It is the kind of thing that arises from a deep disappointment in the failure of others to live up to their potential. Swift's satire arose from a "vigorous, persistent, and at times almost tortured attempt to see things as they are" and "an intense idealism."[19] The work of Zappa, like many satirists, seems to come from the same sort of idealism. Although Zappa has made few public statements to this end, an examination of his satirical critiques of love songs (especially his early satires of doo-wop music) seems to indicate a dissatisfaction and frustration with the typical, middle-class teenage love songs and the supposed lies they tell about courtship.

There may be no work more deserving of satire than the traditional, syrupy love ballad of the forties, fifties, and sixties. Love songs, whether done by a crooner like Frank Sinatra or Dean Martin, the Four Preps, or early R&B groups like the Moonglows or Five Satins, were sanitized and anesthetized. Although the music is not bad, the vocal harmonies are quite often enviable, and the songs are often written, produced, performed, and recorded with a high level of technical proficiency, the lyrics of these songs are in desperate need of critique. The lyrics to these songs, and Zappa's response to them, are an important subject of study because of their intended (and unintended) effects on the listeners, especially their effects on the teenagers who were the original fans and audience of this music.

In his short history / critique of love songs, Donald Horton wrote in 1957 that "the popular song provides a conventional conversational language for use in dating and courtship, one whose highly stylized and repetitive rhetorical forms and symbols are confined to the expression and manipulation of a narrow range of values."[20] The danger that the normalization of teenage courtship rituals represents is enormous—indeed, much of the feminist revolution was based on these very premises—that love, especially as it had come to be defined by the white, male majority, was false. Love songs went a long way toward creating these false and artificial ideas about what love was and what one needed to do in order to be in love. Zappa saw right though this view of romance and realized at an early age that love had a much broader definition than, perhaps, people were willing to accept.

In many ways, Frank Zappa was following in the footsteps of U.S. satirist Lenny Bruce, who spent much of the late fifties and early sixties attempting to shock the United States by challenging what he saw as dishonesty in the way Americans viewed love and sex. In a letter written in support of Bruce, the Reverend Sidney Lanier writes, "It is never popular to be so scathingly honest," and that

> The method you use has a lot in common with most serious critics...of society. Pages of Jonathan Swift and Martin Luther are quite unprintable even now because they were forced to shatter the easy, lying language of the day into the basic, earthy, vulgar idiom of ordinary people in order to show up the emptiness and insanity of their time.[21]

Dead-honest cultural critique is the place where Swift, Bruce, and Zappa all meet: the relationship between exposing accepted values as misleading, especially in terms of looking at the world and exposing what the artist sees as its flaws. Language is used strategically to develop these ideas and make them accessible for the audience, whether that language is comedy, music, or the classical essay.

One of the great arguments of contemporary philosophy has been the need to return the language of criticism to the everyday, the use of common language (and not philosophical language) to critique the language of those in power. Philosophers have argued that capitalism, Christianity, and democracy have all worked to create a language that makes it difficult for the general public to see and understand what is being done to them by the state. It is up to the artist to help regular people see the truth.

Zappa's own words confirm his skepticism of the lyrics to contemporary rock and pop songs:

> What I think is *very cynical* about some rock and roll songs...is the way they say: *"Let's make love."*...You ought to be able to say *"Let's go fuck,"*...but you gotta say *"Let's make love"* in order to get on the radio. This creates a semantic corruption, by changing the context in which the word *"love"* is used in the song.[22]

Although your first impression might be that Zappa is arguing that there is no such thing as love (and, to be fair, he does make this argument in the song "Tell Me You Love Me"), here he is claiming that it is false for all of the sensitive singer-songwriters and R&B crooners on the radio to be talking about love all the time when what they really seem to want is sex. Zappa's larger argument is that all of the so-called love lyrics on the radio create unrealistic expectations in the minds of the listeners about what love is like and that the listener is thus unhappy when these unobtainable ideals are not reached. Zappa claims that listening to too many love lyrics "creates a desire for an imaginary situation which will never exist" and that "People who buy into that mythology [the ideas that are propagated by love songs] go through life feeling that they got cheated out of something."[23] Zappa's argument, which seems directly descended from Lenny Bruce's arguments about sex and U.S. hang-ups with it, is refreshing in its candor and is especially interesting considering the time in which he was making it (the mid-sixties through the early eighties). The kind of music and videos that are being produced today (compare, for instance, "What Kind of Girl Do You Think We Are?" with "Milkshake" or "The Thong Song") seem to owe, in part, a debt to Zappa. His career-long battle to get Americans to be more frank and forthright about sex seems to have worked; the disappointment is that much contemporary music seems unreflective and joyfully exploitive, something against which Zappa was working.

Zappa skewers the relationship between the teenage fantasy world and the manufactured pop star (and how that pop star is in return selling a false idea of love) in his between-songs monologue, performed most often with his 1976–77 bands, "Is This Guy Kidding or What?" found on the DVD *Baby Snakes* and on the album *You Can't Do That on Stage Anymore, Vol. 6.* In this monologue, Zappa directly addresses the relationship between pop songs, pop stardom, and teenage fantasy, especially as it is personified by the succulent pop star Peter Frampton. Zappa begins by telling his audience that the state of "rock has gotten entirely too preposterous." Then, getting to the central argument, Zappa asks, "how do you rationalize the appearance of an album entitled *I'm in You?*" This album, which was Peter Frampton's follow-up album to his gigantic hit record *Frampton Comes Alive,* contained the single of the same name, which was a fairly significant hit at the time. The song was a soft, deeply sensitive piano ballad. Zappa's disagreement with the song was:

> the way in which the subject of LOVE is dealt with in the lyrics of various "serious rock artists."...These people, these people are FUCKED UP.... Because see, love isn't the way they're telling you about it, you know, they're telling you wrong. I'm gonna' tell you right. [capital letters are Zappa's]

This is a theme that Zappa has been developing since his first album, *Freak Out!* It is never more apparent than it is at this point. For once, Zappa is directly stating the target of his satire. What makes Zappa's critique of "I'm in You" that much more interesting is that, after Zappa has stated his thesis, he develops it by presenting a scenario that puts into practice his theory about rock lyrics, arguing that the people who listen to these songs, especially young women, enter into a fantasy relationship with the singer (who is "Aryan and eats a lot of crumpets"). The problem with this relationship is the disappointment inherent in any sort of fantasy. As Zappa tells the audience at the end of the monologue, after the young woman has picked out her "succulent young pop star" and taken him home and undressed him, "next thing you know you hear this little voice in your ear and it says: "I'M IN YOU!" At this point in the monologue, Zappa is critiquing not only the song (or the genre of sensitive singer-songwriter music) but also the entire mood of the era.[24] The choice of "I'm in You" is perfect because the critique works on a number of levels: Zappa is able not only to critique the singer-songwriter stuff but also is able to take a shot at how beautiful Peter Frampton is (take a look at the cover of *Frampton Comes Alive* or *I'm in You*) and the way he was an obvious product of record company marketing and packaging. The argument that the singer is "really cute and Aryan and eats a lot of crumpets" is a dead giveaway that Zappa is not only concerned with a critique of love songs, he is also concerned with how pop stardom has somehow been tied to the way someone looks. As Stuart Hall and Paddy Whannel argue, "Teenage culture is a contradictory mixture of the authentic and the manufactured: it is an area of self-expression for the young and lush grazing pasture for the commercial providers," and teenagers "regard the pop singer as a kind of model, an idealized image of success, a glamorized version of themselves."[25] The fact that in most concerts Zappa's monologue would introduce the song "I Have Been in You" only makes it a more pointed piece of satire.

Zappa's song "I Have Been in You" works on both the satire and parody levels; as a parody of the sensitive love songs of the era it is right on: angelic synthesizer chords and cheesy electronic piano (Frampton's song "I'm in You" features both piano and ARP string machine) and a fine "ooh-wah" chorus in the background. The lyrics are equally stereotypical. In "I'm in You," Frampton sings, "You and I don't pretend; we make love…I'm in you—You're in me / You gave me the love, the love that I never had." This one verse, sung in an earnest, breathless manner, is a prime example of everything that Zappa has been arguing against, especially the dishonesty with which many singers seem to approach love songs. Zappa's song plays off the sentiments of Frampton's song; "I Have Been in You" takes the syrupy sentiment of Frampton and forces the listener to confront the highly sexualized nature of the song (and, coincidently, the rather one-sided nature of the relationship described in the song) by simply changing "I'm in you" to "I have been in you." The latter seems far seamier (the male narrator has gotten what he wanted or, to be frank, done his job), and the song draws attention to the fact that the act described in both songs is purely physical.

In the final verse, the lyrics become brutally straightforward and work to create a sort of punch line: "Go 'head 'n' roll over / I'm goin' in you again."

By changing the song from the spiritual ("I'm in you, you're in me") to the purely physical ("I'm going in you again"), Zappa accomplishes what he set out to do: destroy the supposedly selfless sentiment expressed in the Frampton song and challenge the industry's sanitization of the mating rituals of teenage couples. Zappa's thesis is straightforward: Songs that claim that they are about love or sentiment or holding hands are false; what boys mostly want is sex. It is refreshingly candid.

There is a fine line between satire and parody and meanness, and there were times, of course, when Zappa blurred the line. In *The Dangerous Kitchen: The Subversive World of Frank Zappa*, Kevin Courrier writes that "Zappa's parodying points to our failed concept of democracy, which doesn't allow ideas to be debated. What Zappa did in his music was to test democracy."[26] Barry Miles makes an interesting argument about this when he writes that Zappa titled one of his most sensitive instrumental compositions "I Promise Not to Come in Your Mouth" because he was "self-destructive" and had a "deep-seated insecurity."[27] It could be this or it could be simpler, that Zappa gave the song this title because he wanted to confront people with language, the same language upon which our democracy depends: Can you say the title out loud, the test goes, with a straight face? If you cannot, why not? Your answer reveals far more about you and your psychosexual hang-ups than it does about Zappa.

Zappa responded to criticism about his satire by arguing that he was just telling the truth. The argument is similar, I suppose, to the argument that rappers are keeping it real. There is truth in both; Chuck D., the lead singer for the seminal rap group Public Enemy, once argued that rap was black America's CNN, and Zappa seemed to see himself the same way, as a repressed America's CNN. Although the idea that he is just telling the truth can be an intellectual cop-out (as it seems to be with someone like Howard Stearn, who feels he can say odious things and then, because he occasionally takes a shot at himself, is an equal opportunity offender), it seems to be less so in Zappa's case because he did not shock audiences with comments unrelated to his desire to expose the false ideas of society. Classical satire has always walked the line between cynicism and anger and hate and is occasionally difficult to laugh at because of the painfulness of the laughter. In one of the most interesting theories of satire, literary critic Edward Rosenheim argues that "all satire involves, to some extent, a departure from literal truth and, in place of literal truth, a reliance upon what may be called a satiric fiction."[28]

This sense of exaggeration is what often got Zappa into trouble, even with his most sincere admirers (both Miles and Watson seem to really admire him but feel the need, at times, to distance themselves from his work). It is also this exaggeration that causes problems in interpretation; Many of Zappa's critics, in an attempt to criticize Zappa without appearing to criticize him, argue that Zappa's lyrics were playing to the dumb, frat-boy aspect of his audience; Zappa's sophisticated critique of U.S. sexuality in "Bobby Brown" or "Tittles & Beer" is lost in attacks on Zappa's audience (i.e., if they are dumb, Zappa must be dumb as well). It becomes a way of saying Zappa is bad or unimportant without having to say why or how Zappa is bad or unimportant (as was argued previously, Zappa's critics found it difficult to engage Zappa on his own terms). By saying his audience is dumb and then arguing that he was dumbing himself down in order to reach his audience, you can critique Zappa for selling out and make this argument instead of arguing with his increasingly difficult music and lyrics.

This kind of argument is rhetorically disingenuous; in making the assumption the audience is dumb (and no attempt is ever really made to prove that assumption), the critic lays bare his or her own biases and elitist tendencies. Zappa is attacked, as many satirists have been attacked throughout history, for making fun of protected groups. But the satirist's art, as Rosenheim reminds us, "is prompted not by limited and specific aversions but by a hatred of evil, however and in whomever manifested." In the same essay, Rosenheim argues that "a serious writer cannot be expected to relish the role of a mere controversialist."[29] Although Zappa was at times outrageous (often in order to sell records, something Swift never had to worry about), he would, I imagine, have liked to avoid much of the controversy. It sold records, certainly (especially his later albums), but it caused him no end of grief. He spent as much time, especially in the seventies and eighties, defending himself against a whole host of accusations—of sexism, of anti-Semitism, of homophobia—when, in reality, he was trying to force the United States to deal with the lies it was telling to itself. The satirist's road, indeed, is a lonely one.

These twin issues in approaching Zappa—his work as a satirist and critic of U.S. culture and his need to be outrageous in order to sell records—will define Zappa's musical career. His oft-stated argument, that he had to write and perform his few so-called hits ("Don't Eat the Yellow Snow," "Camarillo Brillo," and the like) in order to subsidize his desire to have his orchestral compositions performed, serves as an apt metaphor for his career. Critics tended to concentrate on Zappa's outrageous behavior, dress, attitudes, or statements in order to ignore the large, more difficult, and more complex task of writing about his music.

The Mothers of Invention

This chapter and the four that follow are informed by two caveats: first, Zappa himself did not really differentiate between pop, orchestral, and jazz music, and many of his jazz and orchestral works are rerecorded or revised versions of songs or themes that first appeared on his rock records. Second, Zappa, despite his many public political statements, would cringe at being read by someone other than himself. Indeed, Zappa was crystal clear in his disdain for the academic study of his music, writing in his book *Them or Us*, "Think of the miserable creatures in the university libraries who study this shit. Why? Who the fuck cares?" Be that as it may, not only do people care, but Zappa's work stands alone in its intense challenge to the ethos of the sixties, seventies, and eighties, and Zappa's importance, not only as a composer but also as a social critic, can not be denied.

That said, there are more than 40 albums of original rock and pop music recorded by Zappa with and without the Mothers of Invention. For a number of reasons, this chapter does not analyze the six albums' worth of excerpted guitar solos (*Shut Up N' Play Your Guitar* and *Guitar*), the album of Synclavier/jazz compositions *Jazz from Hell*, and several albums featuring Zappa's orchestra compositions, including *Orchestral Favorites, Boulez Conducts Zappa, London Symphony Orchestra, Vols. I & II, The Yellow Shark,* and *Francesco Zappa*.

These are admittedly subjective categorizations: *Hot Rats* and *The Grand Wazoo* (and perhaps even *Waka/Jawaka*) are primarily what we might now call jazz fusion. (Critics and musicians both spent a lot of energy in the late sixties and early seventies trying to invent a new form of music that would fuse jazz and rock. Miles Davis's album *Bitches Brew* along with the work of the jazz band Weather Report and the rock bands Three Dog Night and Chicago all represent this genre.) For continuity's sake, this chapter will deal with the fusion albums as part of Zappa's rock catalog.

There is one final complication when writing about Zappa's significant output: There are many, many bootleg and unofficial recordings in existence, and many of which are poorly recorded concerts[1] or recordings of pre-*Freak Out!* recordings. This chapter sticks closely to the official Zappa releases as certified by the Zappa Family Trust and listed at the Official Frank Zappa Web site, http://www.zappa.com / spifnificent.html.[2]

The albums that are discussed in this book are the most recently released versions. This is an issue that has given collectors and fans years of angst; there were, until very recently, usually at least three versions of each album available: the original release (put out by the record company Zappa was working with at the time); the original 1987–91 Rykodisc releases (Ryko bought most of the Zappa catalog and gave them all deluxe packaging and excellent digital remastering); and then a series of so-called official remasters starting in 1995 (again released on the Rykodisc label), with many additions and revisions done by Zappa himself. Unless otherwise noted, I am working from these official releases. Several Zappa biographers and Web sites have detailed information on the differences between the vinyl, original label CD, 1991, and 1995 releases; for the purposes of this project, it is less important to note these differences (many of them are along the lines of "the solo on song X is 3 seconds shorter on the remaster" variety; if this interests you, the best place to start is the Web site *The Frank Zappa Album Versions Guide*, http://www.lukpac.org /~handmade / patio / vinylvscds).

ZAPPA AND RHETORIC

Rhetoric, according to the Greek philosopher Aristotle, "is the study of the available means of argument." Rhetoric, like satire, is an important way of understanding Zappa's art; in short, Zappa's recordings make an argument about something. Although I have tried to justify the importance of Zappa as a musician and a cultural critic elsewhere in this book (see Chapters 1 and 2), this chapter and the three that follow offer an in-depth reading of Zappa's music in order to argue that Zappa was one of the foremost social critics in the United States. All of Zappa's critical themes, including the corporatization of the music business, the eroding separation between church and state, the unwillingness of the people to take control of democracy, drug abuse, and the greed of unions, seem to be parts of a larger argument that Zappa is making against systems, against privilege, against elitism, and against falsity.

Barry Brummett, author of *Rhetoric in Popular Culture*, explains that a rhetorical analysis "wants to know about *meaning*. It asks, what does a text, an experience, an object, an action, and so forth mean to different people"[3] A rhetorical analysis does three things: looks for a text's meaning(s), attempts to portray the complexity of texts, and offers an evaluation of a text.[4] The aim of these chapters is to look at Zappa's work and contextualize it both by individual album (looking at the what the album says about the time in which it was recorded and released) and as a totality of experience—in other words, looking at the arguments that Zappa's work makes in toto, across the entirety of his career.

Plenty of books exist that offer standard, plot-based readings of Zappa's songs (i.e., " 'Wet T-Shirt Contest' is about a wet T-shirt contest"); these chapters offers a more critical reading of Zappa's work. Once one digs below the surface of his songs and begins to understand the, at times, elaborate musical and lyrical jokes, one can see that Zappa was working on a much more complex ideological project. Indeed, the many supposedly simple songs that Zappa wrote with lyrics that the composer himself called stupid hide a complex argument that comments on the very nature of simplicity and stupidity.

Throughout much of his career, Zappa has been accused, by various ideological interest groups, of racism, sexism, and many other isms. Many of these accusations are unfair and shortsighted. In my readings of his work, I will argue that Zappa was not the shallow misogynist that he is often portrayed as being but was a keen social critic who, in the tradition of the satirist, called attention to things that many would prefer remain hidden.

Song Choice

The readings offered of certain songs on Zappa's albums coincide with a continuing argument about Zappa's work as a satirist and his growing ability as a composer and arranger of increasing sophistication (and the relationship between these two skills or abilities). It would be impossible to discuss every song Zappa ever wrote in a one-volume book, and although Zappa wrote very little filler, there are songs in his catalog that are less politically consequential or provide few clues to his development as a musician and social critic. I have tried to avoid the classical Aristotelian fallacy of leaving out information simply because it does not help my argument, but I will leave out songs that do not seem to add much to an understanding of the words and music of Frank Zappa.

Freak Out!

"Their Clothes are dreadful.... Their hair and beards are filthy. They smell bad."[5] *Freak Out!* (recorded February–March 1966; released on June 27, 1966, on the Verve label; currently available as Rykodisc RCD 10501). Highest *Billboard* chart position: No. 130. Personnel: Frank Zappa, Ray Collins, Roy Estrada, Jimmy Carl Black, and Elliot Ingber. "What freaks sound like when you turn them loose in a recording studio at one o' clock in the morning on $500 worth of rented percussion equipment."[6]

It is an oft-repeated cliché in the music business that you have your entire life to write your first album. This is perhaps nowhere more true than with *Freak Out!* Much of the material on this album was written in the years that Zappa was working as a bandleader and studio musician in and around Los Angeles in the early sixties. According to Zappa's autobiography, many of the songs started taking shape in 1964 when Zappa was invited to join the Soul Giants, a local cover band working around Southern California. For two years before the album was recorded, Zappa and the Mothers of Invention played around the same Los Angeles music scene that would produce the Doors, Buffalo Springfield, and the Byrds, to name just a few.

The album is a real product of the Los Angeles / Southern California sound. In his autobiography, Zappa takes great pains to differentiate the music (and art and social) scene in Los Angeles from the scene in San Francisco. Contrary to popular belief, the San Francisco scene (which has been passed down to us through film, television, and books as the heart of the counterculture) was only one of many places where new and original art and culture were being produced.

Freak Out! is very representative of this Los Angeles scene, one that Zappa called "more bizarre" and "more random and outlandish" than the San Francisco scene.[7] Zappa was deeply embedded in this cultural scene. At the same time, a larger movement was taking place in the music world in general. Todd Gitlin, in his provocative history *Sixties: Years of Hope, Days of Rage,* writes, "Coupled-up love had long been a staple of pop music. Now, for the first time, the normal culture of teenagers was becoming infiltrated by grander ideals: freedom, license, religiosity, loving community."[8] This is the Zeitgeist that Zappa had discovered in the L.A. scene. In a number of interviews and in his autobiography, Zappa exclaims disgust for what Gitlin terms *coupled-up love. Freak Out!* challenges this existing sentiment in a number of ways.

The album begins with the most typically sixties song on the album, at least musically. With a basic guitar, bass, and drum riff reminiscent of the Rolling Stones' "Satisfaction," the song "Hungry Freaks, Daddy" begins in this style but soon takes a tremendous left turn, adding percussion, keyboards, and that most satirical of all instruments, the kazoo. As well, any expectation of standard 4/4 time goes out the window as the song starts, stops, and mutates throughout. The lyrics seem influenced by Allen Ginsburg's protest poems "Howl" and "Amerika," with a strong message for "the left behinds of the Great Society." By unleashing this sentiment on the first song on his first album, Zappa makes a pretty formal statement about what his political and ideological project is and will be. The Great Society is a less-than-subtle reference to the presidency of Lyndon Johnson, who had since 1963–64 watched as a number of his social programs, including civil rights, increased funding for education, and the war on poverty, crumbled as more and more government money was funneled toward the growing war in Vietnam. The left-behinds of this would encompass a large number of folks, the biggest group of whom were the young.

The song begins with the bold statement, "Mr. America Walk on by, your schools that do not teach." It continues with a litany of other social problems that the government social and cultural programs of the sixties failed to solve.

Right away we start to see, with the first song on the first record, that one of Zappa's overriding concerns as an artist and social critic is going to be the false hope that society (often defined as "the government") holds out from its citizens.

A simple analysis of this and many of Zappa's so-called protest songs exposes a deeply ingrained us-against-them mentality wherein Zappa and the freaks or teens are *us* and the establishment or government or believers in the Great Society are *them*. A closer investigation of all of Zappa's albums reveals that Zappa is both antagonistic and ambivalent to much of the freak / hippie / counterculture movement. This is indicated in both the music (there is nothing more antirock than the kazoo and the vibes) and the lyrics.

The second song on the album, "I Ain't Got No Heart," was a perennial favorite of Zappa's and was performed by many of his bands for many years. It is, however, one of the most antilove love songs in the repertoire. This song seems to demonstrate Zappa's own distaste for what he called love lyrics. In one of the most interesting chapters of his autobiography, Zappa argues that teenagers were getting "the bulk of [their] behavior norms mapped out for [them] in the lyrics to some dumb fucking love song. It's a subconscious training that creates a desire for an imaginary situation which will *never exist for [them]*."[9] In "I Ain't Got No Heart," Zappa creates an antilove song that defies a lot of expectations. The brilliance of the song is that, musically, it fits a lot of the most tried and true genre conventions of the fifties and sixties (something Zappa would do again and again: set deeply ideological lyrics against deeply conventional music, or vice versa). The musical setting for the song is straightforward, reminding one of any number of Burt Bacharach-Hal David songs: lots of trumpet and cocktail electronic piano in straight-ahead 4/4 time. In contrast, the lyrics are a direct attack on standard love song conventions. Zappa sings, "I sit and laugh at fools in love / there ain't no such thing as love / no angels singing up above today." This is, of course, a direct challenge to expectations of conventional teenage love relationships. Traditional ideas of courtship and marriage are challenged by Zappa's argument that settling down with one woman seems at odds with the male urge. In the same song, Zappa writes about throwing away the groovy life that he had been leading. The argument is that a relationship, at least the kind of monogamous boy-girl relationships that contemporary pop songs were describing, is false. Boys, especially teenage boys, in Zappa's world are crude, hormonal beasts who do not want to give flowers and candy and engage in hand-holding. They want to lead a groovy life of sex and rock and roll. This

Eyes Are Nothing Like the Sun," which lists all of the bad physical characteristics of a woman and yet how much the narrator still loves her). Zappa,
throughout his career, would raise questions of hygiene as one of his attacks
on the counterculture, and they became one of his standard targets.[12]

"You Didn't Try to Call Me" returns to the male-centered themes of cars
and girls and teenage love. It again exposes some of the cultural icons of
white, male teenageness that Zappa would use again and again to point out
the stupidity of the Hollywood/pop-radio portrayal of teenage love. The
music is a parody of sensitive love songs, with a crystal-clear acoustic guitar
introduction and a chorus featuring flutes, tympanis, and a full horn section. The lyrics are an indictment of yet another stupid teenage male who is
obsessed with a woman who is not in love with him and who can not understand why someone would not be impressed with his absolute fabulousness.
As the song fades out, we find that this character feels that girls should be
impressed with him because he's fixed the upholstery in his car and has had
it washed and wants to take her to the root beer stand because they have
"been going steady for six weeks." Including these same icons again (the car,
the upholstery) seems to indicate that part of Zappa's ideological project was
going to be a critique of middle-class norms. By establishing these gender
roles as silly or stupid, all he has to do is mention them in subsequent songs,
and the devoted listener gets a wealth of contextual meaning.[13]

Zappa would establish the same sort of contextual clues with musical cues,
especially as he started touring constantly, referencing the songs "Louie
Louie," "Wooly Bully," and, later in the eighties, "Do You Really Want to
Hurt Me?" and "Whip It," to name only a few. The references made certain points, often about the state of popular music at the time or about the
mindless repetition and disposability of pop music. Zappa's fascination with
doo-wop (I might call it a love-hate relationship, but I am not sure that does
justice to the complex nature of Zappa's relationship with the form) seems
to fall, at least in part, into this category, except that he often played, in concert, doo-wop covers and would play them straight. (At one point during a
performance of the old doo-wop song "The Closer You Are," on *You Can't
Do That on Stage Anymore, Vol. 4*, Zappa is heard telling his band, "no, we'll
do it straight.") In some ways, of course, doo-wop music was an easy vehicle
for Zappa's critique of stupid love songs, but his attention to craft and detail
(it would have been easier for the songs to be sloppy and poorly sung, but
the harmonies and instrumentation in all of these songs are tight and well
constructed) makes any argument that he was just making fun of doo-wop
suspect.

In many ways, Zappa's strength as a satirist is at war with Zappa's strength
as an arranger and composer. As Zappa matured and surrounded himself
with studio pros, not the bar-band players of the early Mothers, this struggle
(parody and satire versus composition and arrangement) made for some very
sophisticated musical adventures.

"I'm Not Satisfied" is the first of Zappa's many attacks on the bored, middle-class, white teenage male (he comes back to this theme in "Teen Age Wind" and "Suicide Chump" on *You Are What You Is*). In this song, the main character has "Got no place to go . . . No love left for me to give" and responds to this dilemma with the suggestion, "Maybe I'll just kill myself / I just don't care no more." This absurdist argument (I'm going to kill myself because I'm so bored with the excesses of our white, plastic, automated world) is one that Zappa would come back to, especially in relationship to his critique of the counterculture: the idea that the people involved in the counterculture were fake and were involved in the lifestyle, not for some noble political reasons but because they simply needed something to do. The very fact that Zappa could walk this razor's edge, wanting (and needing) the countercultural audience and credibility that was necessary for musical and critical success in the mid- to late sixties but also being highly critical of the very same group of people draws such strong reactions from critics and politicians. It is hard to be a satirist while at the same time wanting those whom you are satirizing to buy your products.

In fact, many critics write this off as cheap cynicism. Lester Bangs, for instance, once wrote that Frank Zappa was "a despicable wretch morons actually call 'composer' instead of 'rip-off artist,' walking human offal if such matter ever lived."[14] Bangs dislikes Zappa for the most part because he dared to question the authenticity of the self-proclaimed hipsters and countercultural leaders (which Bangs, along with *Rolling Stone* and *Cream* magazine, felt they were). The hatred that many critics had for Zappa springs from the central contradiction that the counterculture always faced: How does one run a movement that questions authority yet at the same time demand that one's own authority not be questioned? One can not, of course, and in pointing out this hypocrisy, Zappa saw the counterculture turn on him, exulting figures like Donovan and the Byrds instead of listening to his critiques and questioning their own inherent contradictions. In many ways (as will be discussed later) Zappa is making the postmodern argument in favor of self-reflexivity; Zappa is simply arguing that the leaders of the so-called revolution needed to look at themselves with the same critical eye with which they looked at the rest of society.

Contradictions like the one just mentioned are part of the fabric of Zappa's entire artistic project. David Walley writes, for instance, that Zappa had to deal with the tremendous (and amusing) fact that although "the Mothers have traditionally drawn most of their audience from those imbibing psychedelic drugs," Zappa was himself very antidrug.[15]

Lest one think that *Freak Out!* is made up entirely of gentle doo-wop parodies and teen-angst lyrics, the first of Zappa's great political masterpieces, "Trouble Every Day," is worth the wait. The song, which became known as the Watts riots song in large part because Zappa is supposed to have written it while watching the riots on TV, is a fine example of Zappa's more straightforward social critique. According to Zappa, it is nothing more or less than a piece of journalism,[16] which is an interesting term for something as ideologically loaded as this song, which features, among other things, the lines "I'm not black / But there's a whole lots a times / I wish I could say I'm not white." It is interesting to imagine now, in the early twenty-first century, how politically charged this statement might have been to an audience of white, middle-class, record-buying Americans in 1966. It is also difficult to consider the lyrics mere journalism, because they (the sentiment and the song) are far from objective.

The music in "Trouble Every Day" is far more blues based than the other pieces on the album, perhaps a nod to the fact that African Americans, the primary participants in the riots, were far more familiar with the blues than the Caucasian characters in the other songs on the album. The song also is devoid of a lot of flourishes we see in the other songs: no percussion, trumpet, and so forth. The song features multiple guitar tracks, bass, drums, and harmonica (very reminiscent of the Animals, the excellent English band that Zappa would work with briefly). It is a straight-ahead blues-rock groove, a great example of Zappa's theory that when he had something important to say he would not let the music get in the way (although, if one follows the theory that Zappa based this song in the blues, then it is possible to see Zappa using the history of music to make his point).

Lyrically, "Trouble Every Day" is probably the most important song on the album. It makes an outright statement instead of hiding inside parody or satire. It is both a commentary on the cause of the riots as well as a more trenchant commentary on the televised coverage and media exploitation of the event, another theme that Zappa would return to again and again (most famously in "I'm the Slime" from *Over-Nite Sensation*).

The song begins as a rather straightforward protest song, decrying the behavior of the cops and worrying that "there's no way to delay / that trouble coming every day." The song changes, however, and starts to focus on the media and their obsession with things like sports and hair and clothing (i.e., the looks of the broadcasters are more important than the news they are covering). The song becomes a critique of the competitive nature of local news and its exploitation of the riot for ratings; Zappa claims that the press is more concerned with who gets the news out faster than it is with fairness or accuracy. This argument, that getting the scoop is more important than getting the information correct, is a critique of media that are driven only by ratings and advertising.[17] Of course, Zappa was largely correct, although he could not have known it then, that the sixties, of which the Watts Riots were a signal event, would become nothing more than "haze and myth... a collage of fragments scooped together as if a whole decade took place in an instant."[18]

"Trouble Every Day" stands in direct defiance of those who accuse Zappa of nothing but cynicism. Barry Miles, for instance, accuses Zappa of focusing "not on the right wing in power, but upon liberal hypocrisies and lifestyle."[19] Zappa's attacks on cops and the car culture, both of which are representative of the right-wing power structure, are both far more critical of mainstream conservative views than they are of the counterculture. In fact, if one were to count the number of attacks on freaks or hippies, on *Freak Out!* or other albums, one would find the numbers pale in comparison to the number of criticisms of the things near and dear to mainstream, conservative, middle America: cars, guns, religion, and the police state. In fact, Miles's argument that Zappa did not really start a project of social criticism until later in his life is without evidence. As further discussion of the albums will indicate, Zappa was engaged in a sophisticated critique not of the counterculture but of those who joined the counterculture under false pretenses—to drop out or disengage. Zappa's true enemy was ennui, not freakdom.

Immediately following "Trouble Every Day" are the most overtly experimental pieces on the album: "Help, I'm a Rock," "It Can't Happen Here," and "The Return of the Son of Monster Magnet." These three songs are a result, it seems, of two things: Zappa's desire to experiment with avant-garde / orchestral compositional techniques and his previous work as a film composer.[20] All three of these songs are deliberately experimental: they feature repeated figures, lack of melodies, random noise, spoken-word texts, and processed vocals. Perhaps more important, all three songs are heavily edited and are the product of an increasingly sophisticated studio technique, something Zappa would continue to do throughout his career. This technique of editing is one of the primary ideas around which musique concrète is built. Musique concrète is a technique in which "sounds that were previously ephemeral can be captured, and environmental phenomena can be imported into music. Moreover, close exploration of sounding bodies (including instruments) with microphones magnifies and reveals the internal detail of sounds, sometimes with surprising results."[21] This radical experimentation (radical in terms of rock and pop music) on his very first album leads one to believe that Zappa, from the very genesis of his career, was interested in ideas and forms that went far beyond the three-minute pop song. Although "Monster Magnet" does not really hold up to repeated listenings, as a precursor to *Absolutely Free* and *We're Only in It for the Money*, it is a marvelous rough draft.

Freak Out! did not, to no one's surprise (except perhaps for Zappa and MGM), do very well by traditional measure (it is not, of course, a traditional record). It did spend a respectable 23 weeks on the *Billboard* charts and peaked at No. 130, but it did not, until much later, make Verve / MGM their money back. Reviews for the album, reports Neil Slaven, were almost uniformly bad, although *Cash Box* saw the band's potential.

The years have been particularly kind to *Freak Out!* In some ways this album could have been written off as a rough sketch for what Zappa would try to do later in his career (once he surrounded himself with better musicians and more advanced technology). Contemporary critics see this album as one of Zappa's masterpieces. *Musichound Rock* calls it "The most audacious debut album in rock history,"[22] whereas *The New Rolling Stone Album Guide* claims that "the record's antilove songs and daft non sequiturs raised the rebel flag for the misfit clowns and underdogs Zappa and the Mothers would henceforth champion."[23] The *All Music Guide* (http://www.allmusic.com) argues that "few of Zappa's records can match its excitement over its own sense of possibility."[24] The most insightful reflection on the power of the album comes from Amazon.com's review. In it, Andrew Boscardan writes:

> The recording debut of the Frank Zappa and the Mothers of Invention is a brilliantly wicked counter-strike to the flower power sensibilities prevalent at the time of it's [*sic*] release in 1966. Arguably rock music's first true "concept album," Zappa's aural collage mashes together chunks of psychedelic guitars, outspoken political commentary, cultural satire, and avant-garde musical sensibilities, and then hides it all under cleverly crafted pop melodies. Not diminished in the slightest by the passage of time, *Freak Out!* remains as vital and relevant today as it was in the 1960's.[25]

What all of the contemporary assessments of the album have in common is the luxury of time. It is clear now, 39 years after the album was released, that it was the starting point of a lifelong political project; it could not have been clear then. At the time, the album was written off by contemporaries as a passing part of the freak movement. How wrong they were.

Absolutely Free

"Upward and onward to teenage stardom."[26] *Absolutely Free* (originally released on June 27, 1967, on the Verve label; currently available as Rykodisc RCD 10502). Highest *Billboard* chart position, No. 41. Personnel: Frank Zappa, Ray Collins, Roy Estrada, Jimmy Carl Black, James "Motorhead" Sherwood, Billy Mundi, Don Preston, Bunk Gardner. "If *Freak Out!* announced the arrival of the Mothers of Invention and their sublimely subversive intentions, *Absolutely Free* was the fulfillment of those ambitions."[27]

According to Billy James, *Absolutely Free* was recorded in "am amazingly brief 25 hours over 4 sessions" in and around November 1966.[28] Technically, conceptually, and compositionally, this album is a giant leap forward, in part because of two new musicians, Bunk Gardner and Don Preston, both of whom were classically trained and able to execute more of Zappa's ideas.

The title of the album is open to examination. Neil Slavan reports that Zappa was quoted in the *Los Angeles Free Press* as saying "We [the Mothers] play the new free music, music as absolutely free...unencumbered by American cultural suppression."[29] Taken in that vein, the album itself is an execution of that very idea.

Among other things, the album calls into question the very idea of songs, especially the idea of the album as a collection of radio-friendly singles; although the Beatles were starting to move in the same direction (and would take a big leap with *Sgt. Pepper's Lonely Heart Club Band*), there was really no one defying traditional expectations like Zappa was. In many ways, Zappa should be seen as what art and literary critics would call postmodern. Although this is not a book on contemporary music, literary, or critical theory, I think it is important to discuss two particular aspects of postmodernism as they relate to Zappa's work, especially as it became apparent with *Absolutely Free*.[30] Zappa does two things with this album that are hallmarks of postmodernism: (1) he quite often quotes other types of music in order both to pay homage to the older forms of music (doo-wop, avant-garde composition, and blues) as well as to point out the exhaustion of originality; and, (2) he calls attention to the very constructedness of the music. From the very beginning, so much of Zappa's work was purely a studio creation, and many, many overdubs and editorial constructions make the music very much a technical construction and not an organic thing.[31] Further discussions of Zappa albums will reveal that Zappa was at the forefront of this kind of studio technology.

Zappa subdivides the album into two parts, calling part one "'Absolutely Free' (the first in a series of underground oratorios)" and part two "'The M.O.I. American Pageant' (the second in a series of underground oratorios)." An oratorio is a large work for orchestra, vocalists, and ensemble. The purpose of an oratorio is to essay a particularly large theme, and the classical oratorio is one of the oldest forms of sacred music. In calling his works oratorios, Zappa is both thumbing his nose at the serious nature of music (indeed, an oratorio that uses "Louie Louie" as its primary leitmotif is a serious finger in the eye of musical convention) and at the same time calling attention to the fact that this music is serious in its political project.

The first song on the album, "Plastic People," was written in response to a clash between the police and the Los Angeles street freaks outside of the L.A. restaurant Pandora's Box.[32] In the song, Zappa presents a challenging narrative in a complex musical setting that starts with a direct quote of "Louie Louie" and then evolves into a piece of music that changes time signatures at will and moves from spoken word to singing to instrumental breaks. One interesting story about the genesis of "Plastic People" is related by Barry Miles, who claims Zappa wrote the song in response to a number of Los Angeles club owners wanting him to play the kinds of songs that would allow the audience to dance. When he asked one club owner what kind of music this might be, the owner cited "Louie Louie" as a good song. According to Miles, "Zappa told the band [the Mothers of Invention], 'Ok, we'll give them 'Louie Louie' for 45 minutes.'"[33]

The lyrics are, as usual, confounding because they refuse to let anyone off the hook. The song starts with a snide reference to President Lyndon Johnson but quickly calls into question the more local events surrounding the riots. Although the lyrics do call into question the actions of the police, they are also very unsympathetic to the freaks who were there, again arguing that many freaks were not part of the politics but were far more interested in going to the riot in the same way they would go to a movie—that the riots, in Zappa's opinion, were not a political action but some sort of activity. Zappa writes in the song about "plastic people," identifying girls who paint their faces with plastic goo and wreck their hair with shampoo as the worst kind of offenders, the kind of people who would "dress for a riot."

What distinguishes this song, and many of the songs on the album, is the extensive use of spoken-word interludes and commentaries. Not only does Zappa introduce the songs and have others speak while music and singing are happening, he also, at times, comments upon the compositions themselves, at one point telling the listener, "This is the exciting part.... It's like the SUPREMES...See the way it *builds up*/BABY BABY." This countertextual aspect of the album places it squarely in the postmodern. The political project is thus: by calling attention to the very recordedness of the album,[34] Zappa is letting the audience into a world that is all their own; listeners are divided into those who get the jokes (and the ironic stance) and those who do not. This irony was not lost on Zappa (nor was it lost on his various biographers). Although several biographers argue that Zappa should have felt weird or apologetic for creating, in essence, a soundtrack for drug use, Zappa himself simply felt disappointed, telling Frank Kofsky, "it breaks my heart when people don't dig into [the songs] and see all the levels that I put into them."[35]

The next several pieces on the album, "The Duke of Prunes," "Amnesia Vivace," and "The Duke Regains His Chops," are all part of the same song. This is Zappa at his mocking best. "The Duke of Prunes" begins with a very serious piece of music featuring spacey woodwind sounds and nice, distortion-free, electric guitar. This very serious music is then juxtaposed with completely nonsensical lyrics about the Duke, who intones, very seriously, about "A moonbeam through the prune / In June." The *moonbeam-June* rhyme seems to argue, as Zappa would do regularly, about the thorough stupidity of rock lyrics. Band member Ray Collins seems to agree, arguing "Frank had this beautiful tune called 'And Very True,' and when we went in to record it . . . I [Collins] just ad libbed on the spot...and I changed it to 'Moonbeam through the prune, in June.'"[36]

This same argument continues in the next two parts of the song, contrasting the very serious art music with extraordinarily silly lyrics. Zappa does, however, at the beginning of "The Duke Regains His Chops," take yet another shot at standard fifties music when he starts chanting "Duke, Duke, Duke, Duke of Prunes" to the music in the melody of fifties chestnut "Duke of Earl." Zappa accounts for this lyrical silliness, arguing that his lyrics can be placed into three categories: "some of them [the lyrics] are truly stupid, some are slightly less stupid and a few of them are sort of funny."[37] Zappa was always sort of put out that, in order to get record companies to release his records and radio stations to play them and people to buy them, he had to write songs that at least had a nodding acquaintance with the conventions of popular music, and this meant lyrics. In many interviews as well as in his autobiography, Zappa argued that the only reason he wrote lyrics to most of his songs (he does admit to liking the snide political stuff) was that "we live in a society where instrumental music is irrelevant."[38]

Contrary to Zappa's own statement, however, comes the next two songs, "Call Any Vegetable" and "Invocation & Ritual Dance of the Young Pumpkin." Although the lyrics to "Call Any Vegetable" are indeed nonsensical, beginning with "This is a song about vegetables / They keep you regular" and featuring some fine yodeling by singer Ray Collins, the music is intensely melodic, featuring some incredible soprano sax work by Bunk Gardner. The song leads into a seven-minute blues vamp featuring some fine guitar and saxophone soloing, much of it recorded live and in one or two takes. Gardner relates that "the band was really cooking" in the studio and that he was pleased with his solo.[39] It really is, upon repeated listenings, an incredible tune. As fine an example of extended progressive rock soloing as exists, it also features a neat quote from the Holst tone poem "The Planets," neither the first nor the last time Zappa would directly quote classical composers.[40]

Side one of the album ends with the song "Soft-Sell Conclusion," which continues the argument begun on *Freak Out!* about the dangers of advertising. Spoken and sung over a standard rock beat (it features some of the fullest chords that Zappa, who was not really known as a rhythm guitarist, would ever play), the lyrics begin with a spoken-word section that sounds just like an advertising pitch; this one happens to argue that one will be a better, more fulfilled person if one only calls and talks to the vegetable of his or her choice. The song ends with an increasingly frantic salesperson / televangelist rant about vegetables and organized religion, two of Zappa's favorite themes.

The second side of the album again offers a song cycle instead of individual tunes.[41] The side begins with "America Drinks," a satire of the kinds of music Zappa played in lounge bands, including Joe Perrino and the Mellow Tones, which Zappa describes as "sit on the stool, strum four chords to a bar...one twist number per night, don't turn it up. All that kind of crap."[42] Beginning with Zappa counting off the band with "One two, buckle my shoe" and the hi-hat keeping a standard burlesque beat, the song, as might be expected, quickly derivates into weirdness, with different vocalists offering their takes on the sort of hipster jazz scatting; this then evolves into a singer doing a true faux-jazz / beat-type vocalization. The irony here, of course, is that the lyrics are of the stupid variety as described previously, so although the music itself is interesting, the lyrics include "With your fast car / And your *class ring* ... I fell for the whole thing" variety. Even though the song only lasts 1:53, it sets the tone for the entire second half of the album: the variety of musical settings and the fairly free movement between classical, rock, jazz, and R&B genres would take up the rest of the album.

Even though "America Drinks" features another stab and antilove lyrics, the next song on the album, "Status Back Baby," is a direct attack on high school and the traditions of the American teen. Musically, it is one of Zappa's songs that wear the time (1966–67) most consciously; it features a melody and instrumentation that would not sound out of place on a Sonny and Cher record.[43] Ironically upbeat and featuring a wonderful wandering soprano sax line in background, the song is really an attack on the social status games that high school students play. The song is the first appearance (although there are many allusions to this character on *Freak Out!*) of one of the great stock characters in Zappa's writing: the popular, white, male high school star. "Status Back Baby" concerns the trials and tribulations of the typical American high school stud: "Everyone in town knows I'm a hand-some football star / I sing & dance & spray my hair and drive a shiny car." This stereotypical character would show up repeatedly in Zappa's work, most famously in the song "Bobby Brown"; it indicates both Zappa's delight in tweaking tradition and status (what could be more ephemeral and, in the long run, meaning-less than any sort of high school popularity) as well as a revulsion with the kinds of traditions that high school seems to reinforce.[44] The song eventually breaks down, as many of Zappa's songs of this era do, into a sort of acid / jam freak-out music (all the better to dance to) and then, just when it is beyond reclamation, segues into "Uncle Bernie's Farm."

According to Ben Watson, "Uncle Bernie's Farm" "attacks the war toys that are promoted at Christmas and compares authority and parents to robot simulacra."[45] Certainly beginning the song with a drunken quote of "White Christmas," the most successful (and thus, in capitalist terms, most popular) song in U.S. popular music, does not hurt this thesis. The song also harkens back to the beginning of the album, referring to parents and politicians as plastic. Further, the verse about the father is impressive in what it can convey in a short space. Zappa writes, "There's a doll that looks like daddy ... / Push a button & ask for money / there's a dollar in his hand." This is truly indicative of the sense of suburban alienation that would dominate U.S. pop-ular culture in the coming decades; the complete absence of parents from the lives of children that is only hinted at in Zappa's work will become, by the eighties, simply a given.

"Son of Suzy Creamcheese" not only revisits the famous character of the same name who was featured on *Freak Out!* but also adds a layer of satire to the already satirical notion of the good girl gone bad / groupie Suzy. The music reminds me intensely of the music played during a lot of television shows of the late sixties and early seventies (and mimicked so successfully as segues in the *Austin Powers* films), specifically *Rowan & Martin's Laugh-In* and *Love, American Style*. In a lot of ways, the musical setting of "Son of Suzy Creamcheese" is critiquing the point to which pop and rock music had been co-opted by other, more popular, and more banal forms of entertainment. The lyrics only reinforce this idea.

The first we hear of Suzy Creamcheese is as a character in "The Return of the Son of Monster Magnet," when Zappa asks, "Suzy Creamcheese, honey? What's got into you?" This, of course, is an easy-to-decipher double entendre that, although probably pretty risqué for 1966, seems kind of juvenile today. Regardless, between the time of the first and second albums, Zappa invented a much more well-rounded mythology for Suzy Creamcheese, including letters from her to the *Los Angeles Free Press* in which she tried to explain the band.[46] Her return on *Absolutely Free* shows the kind of progress that Zappa envisioned for the naive girl from Salt Lake City: she is into acid ("Blew your mind on too much Kool Aid"), is a thief ("Took my stash and left me lonely"), and is known by the cops ("Heard The Heat knows where you are"). Unfortunately, Zappa knew this kind of person; he was surrounded for much of his professional life by people who had started as naive and perhaps well-intentioned folks but who had, after coming to Los Angeles and entering the freak scene, been transformed. In many ways, this reinforces Zappa's argument that there were only a few true freaks, and Zappa refers to one of them, Vito, later in the same song (Vito was Vito Paulekas, an old freak and one of the folks who seemed a central part of the Los Angeles freak/hippie scene).[47] Suzy, in many ways, seems representative of the poseur, the fake hippie wannabe.

Zappa's disgust and delight with groupies is another manifestation of this same ideology that girls should not have to be groupies. I am not sure he wrote about groupies in a misogynist manner; I feel that his real enemy was sloth, and that for many of these girls being a groupie was an easier route to supposed success than putting in the hard work of being in a band.[48] The last we see of Suzy in the song is that she has gone to Berkeley to protest marching Styrofoam. Again, this is a thinly veiled attack on what Zappa thought was the hypocrisy of the hippie movement; Berkley, the home of the free-speech movement was also home, Zappa felt, to a gigantic wave of false hippiedom (so false it was made out of Styrofoam). It would be a theme he would return to on his next album.

The album's masterpiece follows. The 7:30 miniopus "Brown Shoes Don't Make It" is social commentary at its most arch and satire at its most deadly. The song begins as dirty blues, galloping along at breakneck speed. Although the music will change a number of times during the piece, it stays fairly rooted in basic blues. The song was difficult to record and perform and is a fine example of Zappa the progressive rocker.

At its heart, "Brown Shoes Don't Make It" is about Zappa's favorite subject: the conformist bent in U.S. culture. The song starts with the narrator urging Americans to "shine up your shoes and cut your hair" and to quit school and go to work. This ideal—that education is for the elite and work is virtuous—is important to remember in any discussion of Zappa's ideology; he has discussed a number of times how useless he feels education is, especially secondary and postsecondary education, and his workaholic attitude makes clear that he sought both comfort and virtue in the surprisingly Calvinist attitude he brought toward his professional life.

Halfway through the song, however, it changes rather dramatically from a critique of youth and youth culture[49] to a much more savage critique of white male hegemony. Soon, after a chugging bridge that urges the listener to "be a jerk, go to work," we meet another of Zappa's satirical characters, old City Hall Fred. In many ways Fred is the personification of the privileged white male predator: obviously some sort of city official ("A world of secret hungers, perverting the men who make your laws"), Fred spends valuable work time thinking up ways to sexually molest his 13-year-old girlfriend. While his wife is out of town at a flower show, Fred is "rocking and rolling and acting obscene" with his mistress/victim.

The reading of this song is complicated by Zappa's insistence that the girl is somehow a willing participant in these events: "She's nasty! She's nasty! She digs it in bed!" Although many critics cite the beginning of the song, all are fairly silent about the almost pedophiliac relationship between Fred and the girl. Ben Watson, for instance, argues that the song "draws a parallel between repression and authoritarian government,"[50] but this leaves the question of the pedophilia unasked.

Lest one think it is easy, the song then takes another twist when Zappa himself enters the narrative. Zappa asks, "If she were my daughter, I'd ..." and leaves the question hanging. Zappa's manager at the time, Herb Cohen, lent Zappa his daughter, who asks in a tiny, girlish voice in one of the most chilling pieces of music ever recorded, "what would you do daddy ... ?" After this repeats several times, Zappa lists a number of things he would do to the girl, all of which are socially unacceptable.

There is simply no way around the fact that these are profoundly unsettling lyrics. The fact that a 13-year-old girl is considered a teenager, able to carry on a consensual relationship with a man in power over her (whether father or employer or older male role model) is difficult to grasp, especially in light of 30 years of feminism. The glee with which they are sung (they are staged in an almost big-band setting) adds to the absurdity of the situation.

So what are they mocking? Where is the humor? There are two possible arguments that can be made about this song. The first is that this is an indictment of male power. Zappa is deeply critical of the abuse of power by the white male hegemony (he would return to this theme time and time again, especially as he watched and commented upon the growing hypocrisy of televangelists caught up in sex scandals) and that this abuse of power is in fact the sort of ultimate abuse; City Hall Fred is so powerful he can have sex with a 13-year-old girl without consequence. Zappa's own commentary in the song, that he would do the same thing (and to his daughter no less), takes the song, in my opinion, into the realm of absurdity. According to the *Grolier Encyclopedia,* the absurd, at least as an artistic statement, is defined by "the images...[that] tend to assume the quality of fantasy, dream, and nightmare."[51] This absurd dreamscape, where a father can cover his daughter in chocolate syrup and "strap her on again" can only be attributed to a large ideological project of Zappa's, the critique of U.S. culture that had seen the promise of freedom and had somehow missed the mark.[52] That, and missing the mark was dangerous because it left people like City Hall Fred in charge.

Another argument can be made, and has been made by both Ben Watson and Kevin Courrier, that "Brown Shoes Don't Make It" is a song about sexual repression and Zappa's growing awareness that, although he thought sexual freedom was the be-all and end-all of the freak movement, it was not going to happen like that, and in place of writing thoughtful critiques of the social mores of the Americans, Zappa started to believe in shock as a vehicle for his argument. Watson makes the argument that Zappa's increasing use of sexually charged language in his songs was an attempt to conspicuously push the boundaries of both society and the audience (i.e., Zappa is making the argument that if you want freedom, here you go, I will give you freedom). Again, you either get it or you do not.

The album, although recorded in 1966, was not released until 1967. It did marginally better than *Freak Out!*, reaching No. 41 on the *Billboard* charts. The album was, and remains, a favorite of Zappa fans and friends. Bunk Gardner claims that *Absolutely Free* "represented some of Frank's most creative and original writing."[53] *The New Rolling Stone Album Guide* argues, like many, that the album took the raw material of *Freak Out!* and "pushed the envelope even further."[54] Others are more skeptical, arguing, for instance, that although the album is "by turns hilarious, inscrutable, and virtuosically complex, *Absolutely Free* is more difficult to make sense of than *Freak Out!*"[55] Others seek to solve the dilemma of the album, including arguing the fact that, because it comes between the debut *(Freak Out!)* and the masterpiece *(We're Only in It for the Money)*, it has been lost in the shuffle.[56] It is, of course, all of those things. It is a transitional album and at the same time a fuller flowering of the lyrical themes and musical ideas begun on *Freak Out!* It is with *Absolutely Free* that one begins to get a sense of just what Zappa is up to—that to listen to Zappa, to really hear him, one must hear and understand all of what is going on. With his next three albums, all recorded in New York while waiting for *Absolutely Free* to be released from the evil clutches of the record company, Zappa would reach what for many would be his creative zenith. In other words, he was just getting started.

WE'RE ONLY IN IT FOR THE MONEY

Requiem for the Summer of Love. *We're Only in It for the Money* (originally released on March 4, 1968, on the MGM / Verve record label; currently available as Rykodisc RCD 10504 or as RCD 40024).[57] Highest *Billboard* chart position: No. 30. Personnel: Frank Zappa, Ray Collins,[58] Roy Estrada, Jimmy

Carl Black, James "Motorhead" Sherwood, Billy Mundi, Don Preston, and Bunk Gardner. The First Masterpiece.[59]

We're Only in It for the Money comes at an interesting time in Zappa's career. The Mothers of Invention have recorded two albums that have not garnered a lot of acclaim (or money), and although their live performances are being fairly well received at the time, they are not, as a band, making a lot as performers. Biographies of Zappa paint this period as a sort of crossroads; the band, which is made up entirely of Los Angelinos, decides to decamp to New York for an extended period of time, eventually taking up residency in the Garrick Theater. What this does, other than create a place of fairly significant artistic freedom (many of the urban legends about Zappa seem to come from this era), is make the band incredibly tight; many of the songs that would be on later Zappa albums, including "Son of Mr. Green Genes," "King Kong," and "Oh No," were written, rehearsed, and performed during these Garrick Theater shows. Billy James argues that "Much of the music recorded for *We're Only in It for the Money* benefited from the new found tightness the band had acquired from their residency at The Garrick."[60]

Zappa is also, at the time, working on his first solo project (he had been signed to Capitol Records as a solo performer / arranger / composer) during the times when the band is not recording. These are, as many of the biographies point out, both the best of times and the worst of times for the band: Zappa the workaholic starts to drive the other members of the band crazy, and although many of them thought that they were not getting the kind of acclaim they would like, they were able to live the life of the carefree rock star, experimenting with drugs and sex to a fairly significant level. This also starts to drive a wedge between band and its leader. Zappa was, for his entire life, very much against the use of drugs, especially by his band, and the music was so demanding that there was no way they could play it while out of their heads. The band members, who are left in New York with little money while Zappa is in the studio or with his live-in girlfriend (and soon-to-be wife) Gail, are incensed that Zappa would, as he did, simply tell them not to do drugs. Throughout his life, culminating in his autobiography, Zappa urged people not to do drugs. His reasons are fairly simple: First, they did not work for him; he also had a more philosophical argument that had to do with dulling the senses. Zappa's musical and artistic project is difficult and complex, and he wanted his audience to be able to experience it in an unaltered state. Zappa writes, "Americans use drugs as if consumption bestowed a '*special license*' to be an *asshole*."[61] Zappa's music, like any avant-garde composition, demands that it be listened to; it can not be put on as background music because too many things are happening with the music and lyrics and the overall structure of the pieces. It is hard to do this while high. People get the surface stuff but fail to see what is happening within the piece or fail to see the connections between the pieces.

Related to the drug issue was the issue of the politics of the time. *We're Only in It for the Money* is both a journalistic and anthropological look at what has come to be called the Summer of Love. This time (although it is hard to fathom that the people who were living in it at the time really knew what it was all about) was, as Gitlin describes, one of high drama and turmoil, even within the counterculture:

> At the risk of oversimplifying the currents of 1967: There were tensions galore between the radical idea of a political strategy—with discipline, organization, commitment to results *out there* at a distance—and the countercultural idea of living life to the fullest, *right here,* for oneself, or for the part of the universe embodied in oneself.[62]

Related to this political and cultural division was the fact that, by 1967, the freak / hippie movement was, for many of the originals and true believers, dead; it had instead been taken over by dropouts, publicity-hungry kids, and slick opportunists. Historian William Manchester argues that by 1967, "many of the charter members of the movement had quit, disgusted by the exhibitionists who were giving colorful interviews to newspapermen and television columnists."[63] Zappa, too, shared this disgust, that the promised freedom of the sixties—freedom from the conformity of his high school days—was being co-opted by middle- and upper-class kids from the suburbs who were interested mainly in easy sex and cheap weed. As proof of this co-optation, in 1967 you could take a bus tour of the San Francisco hippie scene and perhaps see a real freak.[64]

According to Manchester, Gitlin, and others, the Summer of Love began on Easter Sunday 1967 with simultaneous events in New York and San Francisco.[65] If this is the case (and trying to fix a certain date to a movement is difficult), then Zappa was right in the thick of things, playing in the Garrick Theater and working at various recording studios around New York.

Unlike the first two albums, which featured songs written during much of Zappa's early years (some going back to the late fifties), most, if not all, of *We're Only in It for the Money* was brand new. "Many of the songs on the album were actually adaptations from instrumental sections that the band played live, Zappa only adding the lyrics and vocals in the studio after the instrumental was recorded."[66]

The album was recorded mainly during fall 1967 in New York. It features several of Zappa's most overt attacks on what he saw as the disintegration of the counterculture. The album begins with the spoken-word / sound collage "Are You Hung Up?" Much like the earlier question, "Suzy Creamcheese, what's got into you?" are you hung up was both a real question and a satirical attack on the way that hippie language was making its way into the mainstream. The piece, which ends with Mother Jimmie Carl Black announcing that he is "the Indian in the group," segues neatly into "Who Needs the Peace

Corps," one of the most straightforward and hilarious pieces of social criticism ever recorded. It is effective because of its musical complexity, its wicked humor, and its incisiveness. The music is, at least in the beginning, a basic shuffle, featuring guitar, bass, and drums as well as woodwinds. There is extensive use of written guitar lines in this piece, something that would come to define Zappa's work in the future. As the song develops, you find Zappa working in his usual vein of odd and varying time signatures. The song starts and stops and segues quite unexpectedly. It finally ends up with a marvelous light jazz outro with Zappa speaking over it.

But it is the words that made the song famous. Zappa, the counterculture icon, had turned his back on the counterculture. At least that is how the argument went. What is really going on, however, is more interesting. Although Zappa has been, on the records up to now, critical of the white, male privilege that he saw everywhere he looked, his disappointment with those around him was less apparent (it shows up in "Hungry Freaks, Daddy" and "Plastic People"). There had simply not been this kind of direct attack upon the freak kingdom.

But what is Zappa attacking? The song begins with the question, "Who needs the Peace Corps?" In many ways, this sets up the argument that Zappa seems to be making; this song is about his disappointment. The song, in general, argues that the ultimate failure of the freak/hippie movement was in the fact that it seemed to encourage or collect those who would, instead of some following a great cause, be content with dropping out of society. For Zappa, this failure is indicated in his rage that the hippie movement, especially in San Francisco, was a commodity, something for sale. The commodification of art or politics (something Zappa would critique when he got around to speaking about contemporary classical music) was something that was anathema to Zappa's ideas about freedom. In his autobiography Zappa addresses the issue of the selling of the freak movement, albeit looking backward from 1989, when he argues that the San Francisco scene was fake from the start (his major beef with *Rolling Stone* magazine seemed to be that, because they were based in San Francisco, they helped to promote the fiction that San Francisco was the capital of the counterculture) and that, for all of its grounding in capitalism (all the major record companies were based in Los Angeles), the L.A. freak scene was somehow more authentic than the San Francisco scene.[67] (For Zappa, authenticity was one of the better compliments, although, to be honest, if one studies Zappa for any length of time, one finds that authenticity is often something of a judgment call by Zappa.) This would be why in the middle of "Who Needs the Peace Corps?" Zappa directs his attack squarely on San Francisco, singing, "Every town must have a place where phony hippies meet." The song then shifts into a show tune reminiscent of nothing less than *The Jazz Singer*, singing "how I love ya, how I love ya, how I love ya, how I love ya...Frisco!" He repeats the verse, adding at the end, "oh my hair is getting good in the back," a comment Zappa once heard a "fake hippie" utter; again, the criticism is directed more at the people who adopt the hippie lifestyle but not the commitment. The song then ends with a hilariously funny spoken-word section, told in the first person by one of these kids: right off the bus, the narrator is trying extra hard to get the full San Francisco experience, which includes smoking dope, getting the crabs, and asking the chamber of commerce how to get to the capital of the freak kingdom, Haight Street.

The argument is clear: a real freak does not stop off at the chamber of commerce to pick up a map. Hunter Thompson, one of the great chroniclers of the sixties, makes much the same argument. In an essay written for the *New York Times Magazine* in 1967, Thompson argues that the hippie movement was counterproductive to the counterculture because, "Students who once were angry activists were content to lie back in their pads and smile at the world through a fog of marijuana smoke—or, worse, to dress like clowns or American Indians and stay zonked for days at a time on LSD."[68] Sound familiar? They (Zappa and Thompson) are working on the same thesis, and although they both seemed to see different causes, the end result is roughly the same. Clothes and dress were one way that the hippies identified themselves, and it would be a recurring theme in Zappa's music (smell becomes a special obsession in Zappa's work in the seventies). Of course, Zappa was not the only one noticing this trend: Ronald Reagan, newly elected governor of California, was heard to have said at the time that "a hippie was someone who dresses like Tarzan, has hair like Jane, and smells like Cheetah."[69] The attitudes of the government and parents toward the hippie kids would become the next avenue of attack on the album.

Lest Zappa be accused of attacking only the hippies or kids, the very next song on the album takes on one of the oddest subjects / urban legends from the sixties: the idea that then-governor of California Ronald Regan was going to use the old internment camps that held the Japanese during World War II to house hippies. "Concentration Moon" tells this story in a silly, beer-hall sing-along style, complete with player-piano stylings and a pseudo brass band playing in the background. Again, Zappa juxtaposes against this lighthearted music very serious lyrics. In the song, Zappa turns the tables 180 degrees and goes after the creeping totalitarianism of the state, arguing that they were putting (or going to put?) the hippies away for no reason at all: "Drag a few creeps away in a bus / AMERICAN WAY / SMASH EVERY CREEP IN THE FACE WITH A ROCK." The interesting thing about this criticism is that, unlike much of Zappa's work, it is overt and to the point; Zappa is not pulling his punches or hiding behind a satirical stance. His song is a direct statement on what he saw as a creeping authoritarian state. The idea that people could be pulled off the street and put in concentrations camps simply for exercising their constitutional rights to free speech and free assembly ran counter to every part of Zappa's ideological makeup.

This argument continues in the next song, "Mom & Dad," in which Zappa continues not only his indictment of the police / government but also of the parents (a group that had been conspicuously absent from criticism in his first two albums). The musical setting is hilarious in and of itself, a parody of the serious hippie music of the day (one biographer compares it to the oh-so-serious music of Donovan, which makes perfect sense because Zappa would take shots at Donovan a couple of times in his career), complete with flutes and vaguely Eastern percussion instruments.

It is the lyrics, however, that are so unusual and stunning: Zappa writes, "Someone said they made some noise / The cops have shot some girls & boys / You'll sit home & drink all night." Although this is a subject Zappa alluded to on the songs "America Drinks" and "America Drinks and Goes Home," his overt reference to the fact that the parents seemingly did not care that their children were being abused by the cops is a big change in both tone and subject. It is important to remember, however, that at this time the clash between hippies and cops had also started to involve parents as well. Although there is little room in this book to get into it, the history of the teenager in 1967 was actually relatively recent, indeed, the children who were 14 to 21 in the late sixties were really only the second generation of teenagers the United States had ever known.[70] The parents at this time were scared and reacted in the ways that parents most often do. William Manchester writes that "parents of the late 1960s could not grasp that the country had become so prosperous it could afford to support tramps, or that their own children would want to be among the tramps."[71] "Mom & Dad," as brief as it is, is devastating in its criticism of parents and their lack of understanding for their kids. There has not been a time, at least according to most cultural historians, when the rift of misunderstanding between parents and children was so huge. Zappa cuts right to the heart of this rift when he accuses parents of being the worst things that one could be in the sixties: plastic.

There is a lot going on in this short song. Several themes that Zappa had been developing and would continue to develop coalesce: The competing ideas of falsity (moisture cream and facial lotion), the failure of independent thinking (not thinking, whatever its causes, is the number one crime for Zappa), and the return of *plastic* as an invective all combine for a devastating critique of the middle-class American family from whence most of the hippies came. William Manchester reports that what made this parent-child divide so unusual is that, despite the fact that the children often "looked like bums ... but they were no ordinary bums. Most had spent their lives in middle-class surroundings, finishing high school, often graduating from college—the American dream."[72] An interesting final note on this song: It ends with an argument that children were being beaten and killed by the cops for just looking like freaks. Zappa argues that the daughter of the parents in the song got shot because she was lying next to a hippie and, in an interesting turn, also blames the hippies for getting the poor girl shot (she is shot both for her lack of commitment to the movement and for letting herself get sucked into the false world of the hippies). This song was written three years before Kent State and two years before Altamont. Zappa saw the inherent danger (and the unintended consequences) of the strange and sad mixture of hippies and drugs with uninvolved parents and overzealous police.

"Bow Tie Daddy" follows a strange recorded piece called "Telephone Conversation." "Conversation" has an odd place in the Zappa oeuvre because, despite the fact that it is not a song, much as been written about it. It is actually a recorded telephone conversation between a friend of Zappa's (Pamela Zarubica, who at one point played Suzy Creamcheese on the Mothers of Invention's first European tour) and her sister. Ben Watson cites Jonathan Jones's argument that Zappa, in taping people (sometimes with and sometimes without their knowledge), becomes an "organizing intelligence."[73] These tapes of conversations would show up on numerous Zappa albums, and looking for meaning in them is difficult, in part because, as we find out in Zappa's discussion of *Lumpy Gravy,* many of the people he taped were given cues or scripts from which to read. Part of this whole project is the musique concrète idea, that Zappa, by taping people (backstage, on the phone, etc.), is calling attention to the very nature of conversation.

An alternate reading, of course, and the one that detractors are quick to make, is that Zappa saw himself as somehow apart from the rest of the people with whom he surrounded himself—something that Zappa's biography seems to support (you find Zappa, especially after the breakup of the Mothers, taking great pains to refer to his band members as employees)—and that the taping of these folks is somehow an abuse of that power. The people seem to know that they were being taped, however (no one seems to have complained), and, especially for the later band members, could not have imagined that they would not be taped. So while it is an interesting issue, it strikes me as one that is a nonstarter. As I discuss later in this chapter and in another chapter, the habit of taping his band members and friends was one that Zappa would continue to mine throughout his career.[74]

"Bow Tie Daddy" is a natural companion to "Mom and Dad," which is, despite the title, addressed only to mom. "Bow Tie Daddy" tells the story of an even more disaffected parent than in the previous song. The main character has lost himself in a world completely separate from his family, a man who is upset with what has been happening in the world (upset with what we do not know—the rise of the counterculture? Feminism? The War? The National Debt?) but is able to deal with the stress through drinking and material goods ("Don't try to do no thinkin' / Just go on with your drinkin' . . . Then drive home in your Lincoln"). The music, much like "Concentration Moon," is performed in a Tin Pan Ally style, featuring a player-piano–style riff and what sounds like a banjo (more than likely, it is a guitar played in its upper register). Kevin Courrier calls it "innocuous Rudy Vallee sounding," which is a fine description of the song.[75] The song is very short and serves as a nice segue into several songs that would cause critics and fans years of interpretive difficulty: "Harry, You're a Beast," "What's the Ugliest Part of Your Body," and "Absolutely Free."

"Harry, You're a Beast," because of the line "that's you, American Womanhood," after a series of fairly derogatory statements, becomes the first of many songs in which Zappa is accused of misogyny or something worse. I think the song has been misread, however, sometimes on purpose, in order to support this or that thesis about Zappa. Looked at from beginning to end, the song is much more an indictment of white, male privilege and an acknowledgement of the growing sense of frustration that many women had with the role(s) that society had proscribed for them. Telling women that "the life you lead is completely empty" should not be shocking—it is the same thing they would be told later in *Ms.* Magazine—that the lives they were leading were unfulfilling. What is missing is the malice that seems to be attributed to Zappa. What he is saying in this song, much like his attacks on the pseudohippies, is that sitting around the house waiting for hubby to come home is a lousy way to live, and that if you are not really into it, do something about it; it is the same argument and impulse that would make up the early (second-generation) feminist movement. One critic of Zappa's writes, "The aggression that runs right through Zappa's lyrics manifests itself . . . in a particularly repellent kind of male chauvinism" in which "the men, even the straight men, are people with a potential for redemption, women are objects, the ugliest part of whose bodies are their minds."[76] Unfortunately, this is a sloppy argument. Both Karl Dallas, the critic cited previously, and Ben Watson, who uses Dallas's argument in the building of his own argument, conflate the two songs "Harry, You're a Beast" and "What's the Ugliest Part of Your Body?" It is important to note that these are two different songs; both Dallas and, to an extent, Watson want to argue that there is some sort of relationship between the lines "American Womanhood" and "your mind" (as an answer to the question "what's the ugliest part of your body"). The argument then gets made that somehow Zappa felt a woman with a mind of her own was ugly (that American womanhood should not use their brains). I simply fail to see how this argument operates. If the two songs are kept separate, one has to rejudge them, and I think a new argument can be made that sees Zappa as professing a much more enlightened and progressive politics than critics have given him credit for in the past. Zappa's criticism of women in "Harry, You're a Beast" is not a rant so much as a plea, much more in tune with Zappa's meta-argument about sexual freedom. The key to the song is toward the end when Zappa writes, "You're phony on top / You're phony underneath / You lay in bed & grit your teeth." This line is making the quintessential Zappa argument: Women had been intentionally misled to think that sex was bad and that only men were allowed to enjoy it (an argument that many feminists would make). If American womanhood was to be indicted for anything, it was for playing along with the dubious sexual double standards created by the male hegemony. The title of the song, "Harry, You're a Beast," is spoken by the female character, Madge (Madge is one of those great stereotypical American middle-class-wife names), in response to her husband's (Harry) plea that their relationship is "not merely physical." The song finishes with the controversial chorus "Don't come in me" repeated several times. Originally these lines were censored at the request of MGM. Zappa was not pleased.[77]

The next song on the album, "What's the Ugliest Part of Your Body," is another song that has been misread. It is actually a fairly straightforward critique of what Zappa saw as the dumbing down of the United States. The musical setting returns the Mothers to their old fallback position of doo-wop. This shifts fairly quickly to a more dissonant rhythmic setting in which Zappa speaks over it. The song's argument is that a mind unused is ugly. The lyric, that the ugliest part of one's body is the mind, needs to be heard or read in the context of the song: When Zappa speaks the following, "All your children are poor unfortunate victims of lies you believe a plague upon your ignorance that keeps the young from the truth they deserve." So, although many critics seem to think Zappa is calling his audience dumb, or women dumb, he is really staying rather true to form: A mind, especially one subjugated within the public school system, a repressive government, and ignorant parents, is a pretty ugly thing.

"Absolutely Free" and "Flower Punk," the next two songs on the album, are more overtly a return to the themes of the first two albums: the silliness of the pseudo-countercultural revolution. "Absolutely Free" is funny in the sense that Zappa is making fun of the trippy lyrics that many bands were foisting upon an unsuspecting public. In the first verse he writes, "Shifting; drifting / Cloudless; starless / velvet valleys and a sapphire sea." This is just the sort of nonsensical poetry that was passing for lyrics in 1967. As the song goes on, Zappa becomes more specific, mentioning the licking of stamps (a reference to S&H Green Stamps) and even name checking "Mello Yello," the famous Donavan song that he would mock throughout his career. This song moves right into something that Zappa rarely did, an outright parody song.

"Flower Punk" is a fairly straight-up rewriting of the Jimi Hendrix song "Hey Joe."[78] The music is a sort of sped-up version of the Hendrix classic, with double-time drumming. The lyrics are a fairly absurdist account of someone deeply involved in the flower power movement. Instead of the original lyrics, "Hey Joe, where you goin' with that gun in your hand?", the Mothers ask a series of questions addressed to "hey punk, where you goin' with that flower in your hand?" The punk answers variously that he is "goin' up to Frisco to join a psychedelic band," "goin' to the love-in to sit & play my bongos in the dirt," and "goin' to the dance to get some action, then I'm goin' home to bed." Zappa's theme here, like it is for much of the album, is a critique of people who joined the counterculture in order to be part of a scene. The song ends with another of Zappa's studio masterpieces: three different speakers (one on the left channel, one on the right, and one in the center), all speaking about the joys of making a rock-and-roll record.

An interesting juxtaposition then occurs (interesting in the sense that it comes just after Zappa has extolled the virtue of making a rock record); the two songs that follow are very traditional musique concrète. Both "Hot Poop" and "Nasal Retentive Calliope Music" are cut-and-paste / tape-edited creations featuring a variety of white noises and recorded voices (including the very famous Eric Clapton playing on the rumors swirling around England at the time that "Clapton is God" was found spray-painted on various buildings; Clapton tells the listener, "Beautiful God, I see God").

For some reason, the next song on the album, "Let's Make the Water Turn Black," became a controversial piece in the Zappa repertoire, perhaps because one of the lines, "And I still remember Mama, / With her Apron and her pad, / Feeding all the boys at Ed's Café," caused much consternation at MGM. Apparently someone at MGM thought that the pad in the song was a sanitary napkin when, in fact, it was simply part of the true story of Zappa's childhood friends Ronnie and Kenny Williams whose mom, as luck would have it, was a waitress (which just goes to show the assumptions that people made, even at the beginning, about Zappa's intentions).[79] Controversy aside, the song is one of Zappa's more carefully arranged pieces, showing, even at this early stage in his development, his clear compositional abilities. In subsequent years, the piece would be performed as an instrumental (often with "Harry, You're a Beast" and "The Orange County Lumber Truck" from the *Weasels Ripped My Flesh* album), and as Zappa varied the players in the band (often, from tour to tour, varying the number of woodwind and brass players), the songs would take on radically different forms.[80] The music is very approachable and listenable; it gallops along with a nice Sunday matinee feeling (many of Zappa's songs, once the lyrics are taken away, seem influenced by fifties and sixties film music).

"Idiot Bastard Son" starts with a verse that makes it sound like Creedence Clearwater Revival's "Fortunate Son," but it quickly devolves into another story about Zappa's boyhood friends Kenny and Ronnie Williams.[81] The music is far more interesting (in fact, this may well be one of the better examples of Zappa's own philosophy of not obscuring his more difficult music with lyrics that demand attention; this song's lyrics are certainly within Zappa's own definition of stupid). The music is very avant-garde in nature, rapidly shifting tone, key, and meter from a basic march to a spoken-word accompaniment. The song would be performed by a number of different bands. A good representation of the song in its later incarnation can be found on *You Can't Do That on Stage Anymore, Vol. 2*, which reveals the more hardcore jazz influences in the song.[82]

"Lonely Little Girl" and "Take Your Clothes off When You Dance" follow and return the album to its counterculture politics. Both songs are about freedom, and a case can be made that they are more about the oppression occasionally play, as well as the melodies to the songs "Oh No" and "King Kong," both of which would show up on a later albums). Zappa himself remarks that "It's more of an event than it is a collection of tunes."[97]

The album would also cause Zappa no small amount of grief. Immediately after the release of *Freak Out!* and while *Absolutely Free* was being argued over by Zappa and his record company, Zappa was signed to a solo contract with Capitol Records as a composer and arranger, although his current record company, MGM, did not seem to know it at the time. The music on the album was recorded in late 1966 at Capitol studios in Los Angeles; the vocal and spoken-word parts were recorded in New York at the same time Zappa was working on *We're Only in It for the Money* (as well as *Cruising with Ruben & the Jets* and *Uncle Meat*). *Lumpy Gravy* would spend more than a year-and-a-half on the shelf while Zappa litigated and negotiated with Capitol and MGM. When he finally did get the master tapes from Capitol, he found that the album had already been cut and mastered at Capitol (which had its own way of doing things), and he had to literally take it apart and recut the entire album, piece by piece.

Lumpy Gravy is an incredibly ambitious musical project. It ultimately involved more than 50 musicians (labeled the Abnuceals Emukka Electric Symphony Orchestra and Chorus) and includes spoken-word sections, surf music, Dixieland jazz, electronic noise, and random percussion and symphonic bits all woven together through the magic of tape and razor blades.

In the liner notes to the album *Civilization, Phase III,* Zappa explains how *Lumpy Gravy* was conceived:

> One day I decided to stuff a pair of U-87s [microphones] in the piano, cover it with a heavy drape, put a sand bag on the sustain pedal and invite anybody in the vicinity to stick their head inside and ramble incoherently about the various topics I would suggest to them via the studio talk-back system.... In *Lumpy Gravy*, the spoken material was intercut with sound effects, electronic textures, and orchestral recordings of short pieces, recorded at Capitol Studios, Hollywood, autumn 1966.... The process took about 9 months.

The album cover for *Lumpy Gravy* features the rather cryptic question, "Is this phase 2 of *We're Only in It for the Money?*" It is an interesting question. In a lot of ways, *Lumpy Gravy* is the direction Zappa had been headed since *Freak Out!*; it is the fullest realization of his musical ideas to date. On the other hand, it does not seem to share much, thematically or conceptually, with the work that Zappa was doing on *We're Only in It for the Money* and *Absolutely Free.*

There are a couple of very interesting point-by-point analyses of *Lumpy Gravy.* Ben Watson's take on it in *The Negative Dialectics of Poodle Play* is a fascinating attempt to make a linear narrative out of what might be seen as an exercise in absurdism or Dadaism. Watson is aware of this danger and

and repression that women were feeling at the time and Zappa's proposed solution to the issue. "Lonely Little Girl" starts with a recording of Zappa's engineer complaining about working with Zappa and then segues into an interesting song that takes up the argument, once again, that the culture itself is ruining our children.

Musically, it starts as a straightforward rock song (of the sort that one might call acid rock today), but it quickly mutates, with the addition of a great trumpet part, giving it a vaguely Mexican flavor (the trumpet chart seems very influenced by the stock music that you would hear in the Westerns of the fifties and sixties). Then, if that is not enough, the song virtually stops in its tracks while Zappa pulls the first of many Charles Ives moves: He has different singers singing different parts of different songs at the same time. In this case, two different parts of "What's the Ugliest Part of Your Body" are sung simultaneously to great effect.

The answer to what the lonely little girl feels, of course, is absolute freedom of the kind advocated in "Take Your Clothes off When You Dance." This song, which was another staple of many touring bands, was a marvelous parody of the superhappy, peppy tunes of the day (as well as harkening back to the golden age of fifties pop).[83] Kevin Courrier relates that this is one of the oldest songs in Zappa's catalog, dating back to the early sixties.[84] The song is probably the most optimistic on the album (and perhaps one of the more optimistic that Zappa ever wrote); a case can be made that it is satirizing the sort of superoptimism that flower power was engendering, but there is, more than likely, a simpler explanation: It is what Zappa believed. He is on record in a number of places as being in favor of complete freedom and in favor of what we would call today tolerance. Take, for instance, the line "we know that hair ain't where it's at." Hair was very important in the sixties as a demarcation of who was part of the movement and who was not. Zappa's argument (hair was, after all, simply an affectation and not an indication of one's true self) stakes out some very particular ground. The song goes on to argue that total freedom will be achieved when one is free to take off their clothes when they dance. Of course, with Zappa, nothing is too easy, and his sentiment that one day we will all be free enough to take off our clothes when we dance is in response to the sentiment: "Who cares if you're so poor you can't afford / To buy a pair of Mod A Go-Go stretch-elastic pants." So the philosophical question must be asked: Is Zappa saying that the ultimate freedom will be the ability to dance naked under the moonlight, or is this a sop to the poor poseurs who are sad that they can not afford to buy the hep costumery of the counterculture?

The last two songs on the album are of note for two very different reasons: the first, "Mother People," is often cited as Zappa's so-called philosophy song. (Courrier cites it as his "manifesto.")[85] Musically, "Mother People" is all over the map; there are elements of doo-wop, spoken word, jazz, and the high melodrama of film music. It seems to be recorded in order for the listener to hear the lyrics, which are certainly trying to make a specific argument. Zappa argues that he and his band and his followers (and his fans?) are "the other people" and that their message is getting out ("found a way to get to you"). Zappa, who, until he started actively touring the United States, had spent most of his life in either California or New York (with, during the recording of this album, stops in London, Amsterdam, and other European hot spots). He seemed to have a fascination with his carefully constructed stereotype of the Midwestern teenager. The idea that the Mothers were insinuating themselves into the minds of their teenage fans was one that would delight Zappa throughout his career. Like the best satirists, Zappa seems to enjoy it most when unsuspecting listeners are exposed to his music and change their ideas or ideals based upon hearing it. The entire album *We're Only in It for the Money* presents a tremendous challenge to white, middle-class cultural and social standards: the standard line on flower power, the standards of popular music, sex, drug use, and relationships.

The album's closing "song," "The Chrome Plated Megaphone of Destiny,"[86] is another of Zappa's experiments in both avant-garde composition and musique concrète. Much more fully realized than "The Return of the Son of Monster Magnet" on *Freak Out!*, this song shows Zappa's progress as a composer of serious symphonic music. In many ways this song is reminiscent of late-nineteenth- and early-twentieth-century program music, a term that comes from Hungarian composer Franz Liszt. According to Liszt, "In programme music...the return, change, modification, and modulation of the motifs are conditioned by their relation to a poetic idea.... All exclusively musical considerations, though they should not be neglected, have to be subordinated to the action of the given subject."[87] This is an important concept to keep in mind when trying to understand "The Chrome Plated Megaphone of Destiny." In the liner notes to the album, Zappa recommends that, in order to fully understand the piece, one needs to have read Kafka's *The Penal Colony*, in which unsuspecting and innocent victims of a totalitarian state are captured and put away in an institution and have their crimes tattooed upon their backs. In what ostensibly counts as the program for this piece, Zappa writes, "As you listen, think of the concentration camps in California constructed during World War II...as part of the final solution to the non-conformist (hippy) problem today."[88] This scary scenario (played out in Anthony Burgess's *A Clockwork Orange*, among other works) comes as a small surprise: Zappa has spent much of the album attacking the hippie lifestyle, and yet he reserves his most powerful and serious composition as a means to warn the same hippies he has critiqued on the album's first 18 cuts that they could be hauled off and put in "Camp Reagan" if they are not careful.

Ben Watson's description of the piece is the best: "Speeded-up laughter and notes struck from inside the piano all pursue each other with a unique energy."[89] It is certainly a unique piece, but it is the kind of piece that made

Zappa such a unique personality. Here was a guy with two credit who could have used a big hit but instead delivers an antihippie and antidrug messages and concludes with a six-and-a piece of avant-garde program music that could be about sexual the concentration camp, both, or neither.

The album did better on the charts than the previous two M. Invention albums, eventually rising as high as No. 30. This cons minor hit record. It also managed to win the Dutch equivalent of a [...] Award. Contemporary critics see this album as the central moment of [...] career; *The New Rolling Stone Album Guide* calls it his masterpiece; [...] Durchholz calls it "a savage attack on all things smelling of patchouli [...] argues that "the music...scores a direct hit on the America that so de[...] ately wanted to be hip."[90] Andrew Boscardan calls it "quite simply on[...] the best rock albums of all time."[91] It is also a fan favorite. The many Za[...] fan Web sites as well as the reviews at Amazon.com, CDNow.com, and oth[...] Web sites are gushing in their praise. In his critical appreciation of the album[...] Kevin Courrier argues that the album represents Zappa at his most ambiva-lent, "leveling with every strata of society as he documents the cultural war of the '60s."[92] This is an interesting summation of the album. I would agree with Courrier except for the word *ambivalent*. Zappa is anything but ambivalent; he is seething with rage at a dream gone wrong. Where, the album asks over and over again, is the promise of the sixties? Where is the society that was glimpsed on the streets of Los Angeles in 1964–65? The answer is that is has been destroyed—by advertising, government, drink, parents, television, and, indeed, ambivalence—in fact, the album is a frontal assault, from beginning to end, on the ambivalence of the cultural warriors.

Lumpy Gravy

The soundtrack to the sixties. *Lumpy Gravy* (originally released in December 1968 on the Verve label; currently available as Rykodisc RCD 10504).[93] Highest *Billboard* chart position: No. 159. Personnel: various (the Mothers, plus a 50-person orchestra, plus spoken-word performances by various folks who visited the studio while Zappa was recording). "The way I see it, Barry, this should be a dynamite show."[94]

The best way to listen to this album is to hear it as the soundtrack to the most twisted film imaginable; it is an energetic attempt to meld rock and roll, musique concrète, and avant-garde symphonic composition into an entirely new and shocking form of recorded entertainment. Courrier calls it "contemporary audio collage art,"[95] whereas Watson refers to it as "a grating, contradictory work which mocks artists tied to single genres."[96] It is a problematic album for many fans, especially contemporary fans, because it does not really contain any songs (although it does have a theme that Zappa's bands would

takes great pains to work around this potential fault. Watson's most engaging comment on the piece is when he writes that what makes *Lumpy Gravy* so interesting, especially in terms of Zappa's expanding musical ability, is that it places several kinds of music "in a new context, freeing them from the pall of art music that reserves so much musical exploration for a high brow elite.[98]

What Zappa was trying to do with *Lumpy Gravy* was to create something new; while it is easy to look back and make informed critical analyses of the piece, I am uncertain that Zappa had the piece as theoretically worked out as Watson claims he did. For Zappa, the idea of *new* was more tangible and less theoretical.

Kevin Courrier, in *The Dangerous Kitchen: The Subversive World of Frank Zappa,* argues that the album works the same ground that U.S. composer John Cage was working and places the album squarely in the genre of the avant-garde. Courrier quotes Zappa as telling Sally Kempton, a writer for the *Village Voice,* that "Cage is a big influence."[99] Courrier, like Watson, sees Zappa as having a terrific master plan with *Lumpy Gravy,* arguing that Zappa "was after a philosophical grasp of the meaning of music."[100] Zappa himself, in a number of different venues, has tried to explain what the album might mean and how it might fit, philosophically, within his works.

Although I agree with both Watson and Courrier and find their readings of *Lumpy Gravy* to be both interesting and valid, I tend to see the piece as more developmental. I am troubled by the desire to see Zappa's craft as Athena-like—that he was, by 1966–67, a fully developed composer and that *Lumpy Gravy* is the work of a young rock Mozart.

The way to view *Lumpy Gravy* is to see it as the response to an accident. There is no evidence to be found that this is the album that Zappa actually wanted to make. On the contrary, all evidence points to the fact that Zappa wanted to do a series of orchestral compositions and, because of time, budget, and contractual pressures, was unable to make the record he wanted to make. It then sat, half-finished, for close to a year while Zappa, MGM, and Capitol Records argued about it. By the time the tapes got to Zappa, he was a very different composer. The tape editing that he had done on *Freak Out!* and *Absolutely Free* had given him a direction; the way *Absolutely Free* was constructed, not as individual songs but each song as a movement of a larger work, gave Zappa the idea and courage to make *Lumpy Gravy* something bigger than he had perhaps intended it to be.

The album is also interesting when placed into the context of what Zappa was working on at the same time. Both *Cruising with Ruben & the Jets* and *Uncle Meat* were more song-oriented albums, and, perhaps, if Zappa had been willing to work on one album at a time, the elements of *Lumpy Gravy* would have been rolled into these other albums (*Uncle Meat,* for instance, is a genuine reflection of what Zappa had learned in making *Lumpy Gravy*). Zappa's success and his creative drive and focus, however, gave him the opportunity to work on all of these projects simultaneously and thus compartmentalize some of his musical experiments.

The album, as one might guess, did not do too well (indeed, there were no singles released and, consequently, no airplay). It spent one week on the *Billboard* charts, entering and exiting at No. 159. Contemporary reaction to the album is mixed. *The New Rolling Stone Album Guide* calls *Lumpy Gravy* a "sometimes surprisingly lovely record of John Cage-ish modern music,"[101] whereas Durchholz ignores it completely. On the *All Music Guide* Web site, Francois Couture writes that the album "suffers from a lack of coherence, but it remains historically important and contains many conceptual continuity clues for the fan."[102]

CRUISING WITH RUBEN & THE JETS

The doo-wop album. *Cruising with Ruben & the Jets* (originally released in November 1968[103] on the MGM / Verve Label; currently available as Rykodisc RCD 10505). Highest *Billboard* chart position: No. 110. Personnel: Frank Zappa, Ian Underwood, Don Preston, Jim "Motorhead" Sherwood, Roy Estrada, Bunk Gardner, Jimmy Carl Black, Art Tripp, and Ray Collins. "Is this the Mothers of Invention recording under a different name in a last ditch attempt to get their cruddy music on the radio?"[104]

According to musicologist John Rockwell, doo-wop music is defined as "A style of vocal rock and roll popular in America in the 1950s and early 60s. It was essentially an unaccompanied type of close-harmony singing by groups of four or five members; if an accompaniment was added it functioned as a restrained background, largely obscured by the voices." Rockwell continues, defining the differences between black doo-wop (the original) and white doo-wop: "Their style differed from that of the black groups in that their sound was closer to Tin Pan Alley, and their lyrics correspondingly more escapist and less sexually suggestive."[105] The Mothers of Invention album *Cruising with Ruben & the Jets* is satire and parody working at the highest level; not only does it critique some of Zappa's standard targets (white, middle-class, high school kids; love songs; cliques; cars; dropouts; capitalism), it also critiques the white appropriation of black music.

Critics, fans, and band members alike have spent more than 30 years debating this album. Is it a hoax? Is it an homage? Is it a cynical attempt to garner radio airplay? Is it a send-up of doo-wop? Is it one of the most carefully constructed satires ever? Or is it all of the above? It is an interesting album, one that really holds up over time and proves the timeless nature of doo-wop music. It also demonstrates the rather effortless virtuosity of the Mothers of Invention and the increasing studio mastery of Zappa. It is also, unfortunately, the swan song of original Mother of Invention Ray Collins, who cowrote several of the songs on the album and seems to be the member of the band with the deepest ties to this kind of music.

The album has an interesting history that highlights a number of things about the Mothers: since their founding in 1965, they had improved immeasurably as musicians. Although the album is, on the surface, simple to a fault, repeated listening gives the listener a sense of the incredibly complex set of musical ideas going on underneath the music. What makes the album even more interesting is how it was made in the first place. According to recording engineer Richard Kunc,

> During a break at a session for some other album, we were sitting around talking about old high school days and doo-wop tunes. Ray Collins and some other people just started singing them. Then someone sat down at the piano, someone else played drums, and so forth. All of a sudden Frank said, "Hey, let's make an album of this stuff!" Right then and there *Cruising With Ruben and the Jets* was born. He [Frank] came in the next day with charts for the whole album.[106]

This is both virtuosity and flexibility. In the ensuing years, Zappa seems to have added to the mythology of the album, arguing, for instance, that he had a much larger theoretical project in mind with the creation of *Cruising with Ruben & the Jets*. Michael Gray argues that Zappa "had several reasons" for doing the album, including, "the challenge of combining fragments from a whole wealth of genuine fifties r' n' b' numbers, and mixing them up with Fragments of Stravinsky."[107] In an interview with Gray, Zappa also argues that *Cruising* was supposed to be educative, that it was an album of doo-wop and R&B, specifically intended to remind the record buyers of the late sixties where music had been.[108]

Stravinsky is an interesting point of reference here. According to a number of biographers, Zappa was trying to do on *Cruising* what Stravinsky was trying to do in his neoclassical period. According to *The Grove Dictionary of Music and Musicians,* neoclassicism is "a movement of style in the works of certain 20th-century composers, who, particularly during the period between the two world wars, revived the balanced forms and clearly perceptible thematic processes of earlier styles to replace what were, to them, the increasingly exaggerated gestures and formlessness of late Romanticism."[109] What makes *Cruising with Ruben & the Jets* so interesting is that, in many ways, Zappa is reacting to his own music. On his first four albums, *Freak Out!, Absolutely Free, Lumpy Gravy,* and *We're Only in It for the Money,* Zappa had become a writer and producer of increasingly complex musical ideas. To create an album of neoclassical rock is a brilliant strategic move.

Listening to the album is a rewarding experience because it is not simple at all. There are a number of interesting musical ideas going on in many of the songs. Lyrically, although many of the songs are full of the kind of stupid lyrics Zappa decries in his autobiography, they are also subtly critiquing these kinds of songs in the same way that many of the stupid lyrics on *Freak Out!* were doing. Zappa argues that, on this album, he was experimenting with what he called cliché collages and that these were important because the kind of music on *Cruising* "was just riddled with stereotyped motifs that made it sound the way it did."[110] This combination of clichéd lyrics and stereotypical music makes for an album that seems simple on the surface but, with some examination, is as complex as many of the other records.

For listeners, especially those who were worried about the decreasing number of songs on recent Mothers of Invention albums, this album must come as a relief. It is nothing but one pop song after another. The album starts with the song "Cheap Thrills," featuring very nice harmonies and, on the remaster, some very tasty upright bass.[111] The lyrics are hilariously subversive. After an angelic beginning, the narrator repeatedly argues that what he wants from his date are a variety of cheap thrills up and down his spine, in the back of his car, all over the place. Right off the bat, then, the album is challenging our expectations: in a doo-wop setting, Zappa is arguing, not so subtly, for emotionless sexual gratification. The next song is a true return to *Freak Out!* form. "Love of My Life," which would be a concert favorite for most of Zappa's career, is full of the silliest of lyrics, starting with "I love you so...don't ever go," and moves on to "Stars in the sky...they never lie." It simply does not get more banal than this. Musically, however, this song is astonishing. The harmonies are incredible, with separate bass, high tenor, and tenor parts all, at times, working three different themes simultaniously.[112] When Zappa tells Barry Miles that the album should be seen as "careful conglomerates of archetypal cliches,"[113] he seems to be talking about songs like this.

"How Could I Be Such a Fool," a song originally on the *Freak Out!* album, is given a thorough rewrite, placing it much more in the doo-wop genre (on *Freak Out!* it is intensely melodramatic, featuring a great trumpet chart as well as some glorious percussion). On *Cruising* the song retains some of its great melodrama, but it is sped up and simplified (the accompaniment is mainly piano, bass, drums, and guitar, gone are the trumpet and marimba). What is substituted are voices, especially during the chorus; what was done by instruments on *Freak Out!* is done with voices on *Cruising*.

"Deseri," written by Ray Collins and Paul Buff, is closer, in some respects, to the kind of close harmonies that the Beach Boys were doing (surprisingly, despite their popularity, the Beach Boys never really seem to be a target of Zappa's satire). The song is a sunny, major-chord romp that features typically silly lyrics. The middle of the song has a hilarious spoken-word section that features such complex rhymes as "I saw you walking down the street / And my heart skipped a beat."

"I'm Not Satisfied," another remake from *Freak Out!,* is much more closely related to the blues than other songs on the album. Borrowing a wandering bass line from, among other places, the Clyde Otis and Nancy Lee song "The

Stroll," the song features some interesting guitar work (buried in the mix) and another set of complex vocals. What makes this remake so interesting is how different it is from the original *Freak Out!* version. On that album, it is a very Byrds-like rock song, with jangly guitars and rockin' Jerry Lee Lewis–style piano. On *Cruising*, it is a much darker R&B-based song. Much like the paring of "How Could I Be Such a Fool" (dark) with "Deseri" (light), the album pairs "I'm Not Satisfied" (dark/slow/blues/R&B) with the next song, the light, sunny, funny "Jelly Roll Gum Drop."

"Jelly Roll" starts off with an almost direct quote of "I Can't Help Myself" (Sugar Pie, Honey Bunch), a Holland-Dozier-Holland song made famous by the Four Tops in 1965; it was certainly as close to Motown as Zappa would ever come. The song soon moves out of this genre and into a more straight-ahead rock genre. The song itself refers to a number of dances that were popular at the time, "The Pachuco Hop and the L.A. Slop," and also seems to refer to a general style of the times. On the album's liner notes were instruction on "How to Comb & Set a Jellyroll," a popular men's hairstyle in the fifties (Zappa is seen wearing one in what is ostensibly his high school picture, on the back of the album). The idea of "jellyroll gum drop" seems to have a similarity with "sugar pie, honey bunch" or "Candy Girl," a 1963 song by Frankie Valli and the Four Seasons, both of which equate and objectify women with overly sweet confection (and confirming Zappa's theory that love songs gave people the wrong ideas about love).

"Anything," the next song on the album, is unique in the sense that it is not a Frank Zappa song. Written by Ray Collins, it is a far more serious attempt to create an authentic doo-wop song. It is well written, well sung, and well played, but it is not a Zappa song, and it is apparent that it is not really trying to do more than it appears to be doing on the surface.

"Later That Night" features some of the more interesting vocal harmonies on the album. As well, it seems to be chock full of references to other songs and bands and carries with it, because of these references, some of the more complex subtexts you will find on the album. Ben Watson, Greg Russo, and the obsessive completist Web site *ARF* (http://www.arf.ru/Notes/Ruben/ltn.html) have all gone into great detail about the song and its references to other songs and cultural icons. Especially important is the quotation from the song "The Glory of Love" by the Velvetones (Zappa likens them to Lawrence Welk, the symbol of all that is lowbrow and middle class). This is, perhaps, where those who are cynical about Zappa's intentions with this album get their ammunition. There is disagreement among band members and fans about Zappa's dedication to this kind of music. At least two, Art Tripp (who had just joined the band as a drummer/percussionist) and Lowell George (who would join the band in the coming year for a short time and then go on to found the Dixie rock band Little Feat), argue that Zappa had a real disdain for this kind of music. Zappa has, over the years, repeatedly disagreed with his old band members, telling Barry Miles, "I like that kind of music, I'm very fond of close harmony group vocal."[114] But even Watson, perhaps his most die-hard defender, disagrees, arguing that the album as a whole is somewhat artificial and hard to like, especially in terms of the wild musical experiments Zappa had been doing up to this point.[115] It is an interesting question, of course, one that is central to the question of satire. (Can you really satirize something you loathe? Swift thought so.) The number of musical quotes and references in "Later That Night" certainly add to the discussion.

Another way to look at this issue is much more musicologically. Jonathan Bernard, for instance, writing in *Contemporary Music Review*, argues that "Parody in Zappa's work often involves a complex of chain of associations, not merely the listener's grasping that a specific style or song is being given satirical treatment."[116] This is the very issue the Velvetones reference brings up. You need to do more than recognize the reference to "I hold in my hand three letters from the stages of your fine, fine, super-fine career" as a direct quote from the song "Glory of Love"; you then need to understand Zappa's connection between them and Lawrence Welk; you then need to understand Lawrence Welk as a cultural icon who represents the sort of white, middle-class cheesiness that much of Zappa's work interrogates. With Zappa, nothing is easy, and nothing is as it seems.

Concert favorite "You Didn't Try to Call Me" is next. This is an interesting song insomuch as it is a very complex piece of music masquerading as a simple doo-wop song. This is the third of the songs on the album that also appeared on *Freak Out!* On that album, the song is a straight-ahead 1965-style love song, with nice, high guitars and a sweet brass and woodwind chart in the background, very much a Bacharach / David type of song. On *Cruising*, it becomes much more a doo-wop standard, with a repetitive piano triplet and three-part vocal harmonies.

"Fountain of Love," cowritten with Ray Collins and dating to Zappa's earliest original work, is a surprisingly complex song, featuring various key changes, quotations from famous songs (including Stravinsky's *The Rite of Spring* and the Moonglows' "Sincerely"),[117] and an interesting melodic through-structure that is very reminiscent of the song "Tears on My Pillow" by Little Anthony and the Imperials. The cut starts with a voice-over from someone in the studio (an engineer? Zappa?), announcing, in a very happy and enthusiastic voice, "Fountain! Of! Love!" The lyrics are pretty straightforward, continuing the great fountain imagery in American popular song, including "Three Coins in the Fountain" and at least two nineteenth-century religious songs entitled "Fountain of Love." Fountain imagery would reappear throughout Zappa's career; the rather basic (and silly) sexual double entendre of the fountain would provide many bands with song lyrics.

From this point on, the album starts to move away, at least a bit, from standard doo-wop and much more into blues and R&B. It is almost as if Zappa is telling us "enough, you get the joke, now let's do something more interesting." "No. No. No." takes Zappa's ideas about the stupidity of love lyrics to a new height. This is one of the most repetitive songs on the album. Repeatedly, the singers sing "No no no no no no no-o-o-oo-oh /(Boppa dooayyydoo Boppa dooayyydoo / Boppa dooayyydoo Boppa dooayyydoo) / Makes me cry to see you go-o-o-oo-oh." Musically, the song is much closer to R&B and blues, with some interesting basic blues piano work (still playing triplets, but much faster and in a minor key). This extraordinary repetitive-ness as a representation of stupidity is something that would show up in many Zappa songs of the late seventies and early eighties.

"Any Way the Wind Blows," another remake from *Freak Out!,* is given a fairly radical revision. On *Freak Out!,* the song is a peppy, early sixties, straight-ahead rock song. On *Cruising,* it is radically slowed and given some interesting and intricate backing vocals. By slowing it, Zappa has managed to turn it much more introspective and blues based, although it still retains much of its silliness from *Freak Out!*

The final song on the album is a great contradiction: a doo-wop song about the singer's suicide, with an absolutely stinging guitar solo. As disturb-ing as this is, it is another great Zappa social critique of teenage love and love songs. Musically, it is not quite doo-wop; the rhythm sort of lurches along in a blues shuffle, although the piano and rhythm guitar are still playing stan-dard triplets. Lyrically, the song features the grand narrative of male teenage love: "If you decide to leave me, it's all over."

What does one make of *Cruising with Ruben & the Jets?* Contemporary critical responses to the album are almost nonexistent. *The New Rolling Stone Album Guide* gives it three-and-a-half stars but does not say anything about it; *Musichound* ignores it altogether. Francois Couture seems to like the album but, in final judgment, argues, "Unless listeners are particularly fond of Doo Wop music, this album is definitely not the best place to start in Zappa's catalog."[118] Fan sites and reviews on Amazon.com, CDNow.com, and other Web sites tend to run the gamut from loving the album and the remixes to hating the remixes enough to let it cloud their love of the entire album. The album reached No. 110 on the *Billboard* charts, although, the story goes, it could have gone higher; many Zappa biographers report that the album, upon release, started to get some good airplay, especially in the Midwest, then, as fans and disc jockeys started to realize that it was a Frank Zappa album, they stopped playing it, supposedly outraged that the Moth-ers of Invention would try to trick people into listening to them. This, of course, seems absurd in light of the cover art, which features the statement, "Is this the Mothers of Invention recording under a different name in a last ditch attempt to get their cruddy music on the radio?" It turns out to be an interesting moment in Zappa's catalog; it has provided several songs that were concert favorites, especially as performed with the bands in the late sev-enties and throughout the eighties (many of the bands in the late sixties and early seventies, except for the Flo & Eddie years, lacked the vocalists capable of singing these songs) but is less intellectually serious than some of Zappa's other albums of the time. Coming, as it does, sandwiched between *We're Only in It for the Money, Lumpy Gravy*, and *Uncle Meat*, it does seem sort of tossed off, and the joke, as it were, seems to only really hit one note (i.e., "doo-wop lyrics are stupid and the music is simplistic"; by the 12th song, you get the joke). Nevertheless, it is an interesting record.[119]

UNCLE MEAT

The High Water Mark of musique concrète. *Uncle Meat* (Originally released on the Bizarre/Reprise label in March 1969; currently available as Rykodisc RCD 10506/07).[120] Highest *Billboard* chart position: No. 43. Personnel: Frank Zappa, Ian Underwood, Don Preston, James "Motorhead" Sherwood, Roy Estrada, Bunk Gardner, Jimmy Carl Black, Art Tripp, Ray Collins, Buzz Gardner, and Lowell George.[121] "Revolution is just this year's flower power."[122]

If *We're Only in It for the Money* is the first real masterpiece, the first real flowering of Zappa's totalizing vision for the capabilities (both musically and ideologically) of recorded music, and *Lumpy Gravy* is the first real attempt to do something truly different with the standard rock LP, then *Uncle Meat* is the apotheosis; it is Zappa's doctoral dissertation on how far one can push the limits of the rock audience. It is an astounding album, one that defies all expectations. It is smart, challenging, and, in places, exasperating. It contains some of the music Zappa would use in concert for the rest of his career (especially "King Kong" but also "Cruising for Burgers" and "Mr. Green Genes") and some band mythology. It also contains, for the first time, a mixture of studio and live recordings, something that Zappa would do for the rest of his career.

Zappa, by late 1968, was fully bent on making and releasing music of incredible variety. The two albums that preceded *Uncle Meat* were, as Billy James writes, "two very different extremes of the musical spectrum."[123] In some ways, *Uncle Meat* seems to be a finale (Zappa's albums would never be, with the exception of some of his orchestral music, as challenging again); in some ways the album is an artfully constructed argument against the complacency of the contemporary music fan. Zappa has been quoted often as saying, about the people who bought his albums in the sixties, that they were

> accustomed to accepting everything that was handed to them.... It was amazing: politically, musically, socially—everything. Somebody would just hand it to them and they wouldn't question it. It was my campaign in those days to do things that would shake people out of that complacency, or that ignorance and make them question things[124]

even if it were his music. *Uncle Meat,* with its mixture of tape, symphonic scoring, free jazz improvisation, blues, doo-wop, and everything in between, challenges all preconceived notions about your typical rock-and-roll record.

The album started as a soundtrack to a film to be titled *Uncle Meat*. Zappa had always been interested, since his high school days, in film and would face a lifelong series of disappointments in trying to bring his films to the screen (although he had started and even filmed a number of things, ultimately only *200 Motels* and *Baby Snakes* ever made it to the screen, and neither did very well at the box office or with the critics). The plot was typical Zappa, an almost incomprehensible mixture of fifties science fiction film clichés and road stories (i.e., the sexual escapades of the various members of the Mothers of Invention). The liner notes to *Uncle Meat* try to clarify for the listeners just what they are hearing; to try to summarize them is nearly impossible: each line contains a scenario even weirder than the last (see Watson for the best, most complete attempt at a summary of the story; that said, knowing the story is not all that important to understanding the album).

Even band members were mystified about the meaning of the film. According to Billy James, band member Bunk Gardner only "vaguely remembers the filming of the *Uncle Meat* movie." James quotes Gardner as saying, "I don't know what it was all about. I remember Frank shooting a lot of film in the woods of Vienna and other locations. Also he used some of the live footage from the concert we did in 1968 at the Royal Festival Hall."[125]

The movie, like many of Zappa's nonmusical projects (and a few of his more ambitious musical projects), was never really finished (a version of the film was finally constructed and released on video in 1989). The album, which may be the strangest soundtrack ever created, is subtitled "Most of the music from the Mother's movie of the same name which we haven't got enough money to finish yet."[126]

Most Zappa critics and biographers leave *Uncle Meat* alone. There is little written, outside of Watson and Courrier, on either the history of the project or attempts to fix a meaning to the album. One reason for this is simply that the album really is that weird. It takes what Zappa learned in *Lumpy Gravy* and applies it in a much more thoughtful and artful manner. In the liner notes to the album, Zappa takes great pains to describe, in some detail, the recording techniques used to realize his vision: an incredible number of overdubs and complete mastery of the, at the time, new 12-track recording technology as well as lots of studio tricks and techniques, including speeding up and slowing down the tape, playing unusual instruments through studio effects, and so forth. If *Lumpy Gravy* was an attempt to rescue existing music, *Uncle Meat* seems much more deliberate in its pacing and overall structure. The album is as fine a representation of the postmodern theory of pastiche as one can get. Of course, nothing with Zappa is that easy. Postmodernists see pastiche, the idea that art is a collection of things (images, ideas, fragments) borrowed from elsewhere that, when put together, form something new, as a result of an artistic exhaustion brought on by the end of the twentieth century.[127] What makes this album so fascinating is that Zappa creates a pastiche out of his own music; he borrows fragments of soundtrack music (a lovely orchestral score, pseudocarnival music) along with dialogue, rock music, concert recordings (including a famous recording of Don Preston playing "Louie Louie" on the pipe organ at Royal Albert Hall in London), and a series of free jazz workouts.

Unlike his previous albums *Absolutely Free* and *Lumpy Gravy,* both of which began with a spoken prologue, *Uncle Meat* jumps right into things. The "Main Title Theme" is a wonderfully melodic and upbeat piece of music that really walks the line between classical symphonic film scoring and rock instrumentals. The song showcases the fine percussion work of Art Tripp and Ruth Komanoff and emphasizes Zappa's increasing strengths as composer and arranger. Zappa, whose first instrument was the drums, would come to write increasingly intricate percussion parts in much of his music. The "Main Title" is one of the first Zappa pieces to feature an intricate percussion melody realized almost entirely on marimba and xylophone (and, in the case of the "Main Title," doubled on the drums). Twenty years later would find Zappa writing strikingly similar pieces; indeed, much of the music on Zappa's all-Synclavier album *Jazz from Hell* sounds as if it were cut from much of the same cloth as "Main Title."[128] The song lopes along at an impressive clip for about one minute and then stops on a dime and resolves itself with a lush, romantic theme played on the harpsichord (an instrument that was, unfortunately, seeing some resurgence in some of the more baroque art and progressive music of the sixties). After some electronic noise, we get, for the final time, the return of Suzy Creamcheese, who greets the listener with "Hello teenage America" and tells us that, after a series of misadventures and disappointments, she has finally "come home to my mothers." Soon after this album, the woman who had provided the voice of Suzy Creamcheese on two albums would be out of Zappa's life. Many things at the time of *Uncle Meat* were coming to an end.

"Nine Types of Industrial Pollution" is one of Zappa's most far-out compositions. In some ways it is as if he were making fun of free jazz; it is a melodically formless piece that is rooted in a strong percussion chart. Over the top of this theoretical mess is an intense guitar solo that was part inspiration and part studio wizardry; it was recorded and then sped up in the tape player to create a unique, somewhat irreproducible, sound effect. Interestingly enough, "Nine Types" is a precursor to the kind of music Zappa would make in the future. His live shows, which would increasingly become showcases for extended guitar soloing, would often feature a strong relationship between guitar and drums/percussion, the kind of which is evident here. Immediately following is the short (54-second) piece, "Zolar Czakl," which is also reminiscent of the kind of work Zappa would do in the eighties.

"Dog Breath, in the Year of the Plague" is, on the surface at least, a funky, straight-ahead folk-rock song, featuring a pleasant reminiscence of the stupid kinds of stuff in which teenagers would have been interested. The same verse is sung three times, once straight, once with the help of opera singer

Nelcy Walker, and once with the tape sped up (à la the Chipmunks). What is interesting about the song is that, after the third verse, it evolves, without the listener realizing, into an interesting piece of avant-garde orchestral funk, all trumpets and percussion and synthesizer. This leads into a more traditionally avant-garde (pun intended) piece of music, "The Legend of the Golden Arches," which takes advantage of Ian Underwood's abilities as a woodwind player. The melody starts off sounding a bit like a German beer-hall sing-along and ends with a Satie-like harpsichord piece. Musically, the song covers a lot of ground and seems indicative of the music Zappa was considering for the film.

One of Zappa's great musical jokes follows: a recording of Don Preston playing "Louie Louie" on the Royal Albert Hall pipe organ. It is one of the great ironic juxtapositions in music: that most staid of all instruments (one can imagine, especially if one were British, composers Vaughn Williams or Benjamin Britten playing this organ) playing that most staid of rock songs. It is marvelous. After a short instrumental break of nonsense music, Zappa introduces the horribly played music as being performed by "The London Symphony Orchestra." This is one of Zappa's first-of-many attacks on the classical community, a group of folks he felt an incredible disdain for and would battle throughout his life, going so far as to tell an interviewer, "The difference between classical and rock musicians is that classical musicians are interested in money and pensions. And rock musicians are interested in money and getting laid."[129] His refusal to take serious music seriously (and to, gasp, mix it up with rock and roll) would continue to get him into trouble with the symphony establishment, leading Zappa, toward the end of his career, to simply pay for performances of his symphonic music himself.

"Dog Breath Variations," a song that would become a favorite symphonic piece (rearranged and recorded by Ensemble Modern and available on *The Yellow Shark*), takes the "Dog Breath" theme, without lyrics, and makes it into a beautiful melody for acoustic guitar, synthesizer (Zappa seems fascinated by the sounds Don Preston is able to get out of his keyboards, many of which, including the Moog, were brand new at the time; Zappa's fascination with new seems to spill over into sounds and tones), and percussion (there is some excellent vibe / marimba work on this piece). Zappa would do the same thing with the piece "The Uncle Meat Variations" later on the same album (and would combine them as one continuous piece on his orchestral album *The Yellow Shark*). "The Uncle Meat Variations" again shows a strong influence of German beer-hall music, vaudeville and Tin Pan Alley songwriting, and avant-garde symphonic composition. Peter Rundel, the conductor of Ensemble Modern, likens the pieces ("Dog Breath" and "Uncle Meat") to "much of Stravinsky, with its irregular patterns."[130] Toward the halfway point, Zappa starts including voices in the piece, repeating some of the lyrics, specifically *fuzzy dice*, from "Dog Breath, in the Year of the Plague," again, a juxtaposition of classical / symphonic form with stupid rock lyrics. From that point, the song turns more toward rock, with a guitar-based outro that stops suddenly and leads into "Electric Aunt Jemima."

A lot has been written about "Electric Aunt Jemima." Zappa's racial politics, always provocative, take a beating because of his explanation of this piece. Ostensibly written about Zappa's guitar amplifier, it is a problematic explanation in two ways. The first is that the amplifier, which is squat and black, is equated with Aunt Jemima, a horrific turn-of-the-century racist creation of two white businessmen who were selling pancake mix. The fact that the character of Aunt Jemima was short and black and serviced the white folks, just like the guitar amplifier, is difficult to play off or down, as Zappa does, by arguing that it was just a funny nickname.

The second, and more troubling, explanation is found in Zappa's comments to Barry Miles, "I get kind of laugh out of the fact that other people are going to try to interpret that stuff and come up with some grotesque interpretations of it. It gives me a certain amount of satisfaction."[131] This is a disappointing sentiment because it displays the kind of arrogance of which Zappa would increasingly be accused; this sort of "fuck 'em if they can't take a joke" attitude works when things are funny, but, as rhetorical theory reminds us again and again, once you have sent your argument out into the world for the audience to hear, it is no longer entirely up to you as to how it gets interpreted, and the sort of casual racism that "Electric Aunt Jemima" exhibits is difficult to defend. As well, the argument that the song is simply about his amplifier is belied by the lyrics, which state, in part, "Please hear my plea / Electric Aunt Jemima / Cook a bunch for me." The fact that the song places the character in the stereotypical role of cooking for whitey makes Zappa's argument more of a cop-out than an explanation and / or counterargument.

That said, 1968 was a different time than 2005, and it is unfair to hold Zappa to a standard that was, in 1968, only beginning to be set. The callousness of "Electric Aunt Jemima" is, more than likely, simply indicative of an age in which casual racism was still supposedly acceptable, even within the Left.[132] Another argument is that one of Zappa's projects from the beginning of his career is an interrogation of the white appropriation of black music. Zappa does this by making the musical setting of "Electric Aunt Jemima" the whitest and squarest of all of the doo-wop sounds. Zappa also uses the sped-up tape trick to have the lead singer sound, again, like a chipmunk, referring to, perhaps, the superlame pseudoband the Chipmunks, who had a number of huge-selling (million-plus) hits in the late fifties, including "Witch Doctor" and "The Chipmunk Song." These were some of the squarest, whitest music one could imagine. Zappa's tape manipulations are, in a strange way, a savage commentary on the Chipmunks. The fact that the voices in "Dog Breath, in the Year of the Plague" and "Electric Aunt Jemima" are sped up and then counterposed against fairly sophisticated music is a reminder, perhaps, that all doo-wop music was stolen from black music and are a pale (pun intended) imitation.

As if sensing that things got too simplistic with "Electric Aunt Jemima," Zappa pulls out all the stops for the rest of the album, featuring a number of extraordinary instrumental workouts, including one of the great showstoppers of his career, "King Kong," and a great piece of band mythology (and a tasty piece of music) with "Ian Underwood Whips It Out (Live Onstage in Copenhagen)."

"King Kong" is first heard, very briefly, as a theme on *Lumpy Gravy;* it is then heard as a triple-time, free-jazz workout (very reminiscent of the work Ornette Coleman was doing on *The Shape of Jazz to Come*) on "Prelude to King Kong." It is hard to capture in words the technical virtuosity that goes in to "Prelude." Although there would be numerous other versions of the song (especially interesting is the 25-minute version found on *You Can't Do That on Stage Anymore, Vol. 3,* which features, in a typically maniacal bit of editing, a melded version of the song as performed by the 1982 band, featuring Ed Mann on percussion and Steve Vai on stunt guitar, and the famous 1971 band featuring Flo & Eddie and a sax solo from Ian Underwood that is still talked about on fan Web sites and in the biographies), the version of "King Kong" and its variations, as set down on *Uncle Meat,* is a minor masterpiece.

The song, which appears on the album as a six-part set of variations, is based on a very simple, catchy, descending-scale melody (spelled out in the first movement, "King Kong Itself"). In many ways it is a standard jazz setting, perfect for improvising over (it reminds one, for better or worse, of John Coletrane's version of "My Favorite Things," which takes a catchy, easy melody and turns it into a great vehicle for extended soloing). This quickly moves into a moody electric piano-organ-synthesizer solo by Don Preston ("King Kong, Its Magnificence As Interpreted by Dom DeWild"), the frenetic sax stylings of Motorhead Sherwood[133] ("King Kong, As Motorhead Explains It"). The song reaches its zenith with the 6:17 workout "King Kong, the Gardner Varieties," which features an incredible bit of extended soloing by Bunk Gardner that, according to Gardner, was done on a clarinet and played through various studio effects and not done on a saxophone as others assume.[134] The song then continues with two more movements. The first is a manipulated tape version of the song ("King Kong, As Played by 3 Deranged Good Humor Trucks"), built to sound like a toy instrument version; it is actually very guitar heavy and serves as a nice segue into the final piece, "King Kong, Live on a Flat Bed Diesel in the Middle of a Race Track at a Miami Pop Festival...the Underwood Ramifications," which is a recording from a year earlier. (Billy James reports that "King Kong" had been part of the band's live show from "late 1965, early 1966.")[135]

"King Kong" is a nice clue to Zappa's development; it is the direction his music would take in the near future (Zappa would move much more toward jazz and rock and away from orchestral composition). His live shows would increasingly become showcases for extended soloing, originally by the whole band and later by Zappa alone, and its relative simplicity suggests an exhaustion on Zappa's part with his educational project. Zappa's albums in the future, although always interesting, would, with the possible exception of *Civilization Phase III* (released more than 20 years later), never be as musically challenging.

There are a few other songs on the album worth mentioning. "Mr. Green Genes" is funny because it started the rumor that Zappa was the son of the man who played Mr. Green Jeans on the old *Captain Kangaroo* television show. It is such a rumor that Zappa addresses it on the first page of his autobiography. Suffice it to say that it is not true.[136] The song is a continuation of the themes developed on "Call Any Vegetable" and is interesting insomuch as it is a smartly developed half-time waltz sung in a very serious manner. This leads into several interesting short pieces, including a hilarious recording of drummer Jimmy Carl Black complaining about Zappa as bandleader and business manager, which leads into a great straight-ahead rock song, "The Air," a nice piece of psuedo-doo-wop about waking up next to your loved one "in a chevy at the beach" and finding out that they do not look (or smell) as great in the morning. It then devolves into an interesting fantasy about getting busted for trying to bring some tapes across the border, a possibly veiled reference to an incident in Zappa's youth in which he was set up by a local vice cop and had to surrender several tapes and pieces of recording equipment, allegedly because he (Zappa) was making pornography.

"Project X" is an interesting instrumental that starts off with a very delicate acoustic guitar riff (very similar to the Sixpence None the Richer song "Kiss Me"). Over this lovely major chord strumming first comes some dissonant percussion and then a full-blown orchestral / ensemble setting (somewhere in the middle the guitar is lost so it just becomes orchestral).

The non-"King Kong" part of the album ends with perennial concert favorite "Cruising for Burgers," which is yet another comment on the stupidness of white, male, teenage behavior. Cruising, as Zappa's many attacks on car culture make clear, is a silly male ritual set up to waste time, waste gas, and waste money. The music is a surprisingly complex band-oriented piece with several tempo and melody changes (at one point it sounds strikingly like the Simon and Garfunkel song "Hazy Shade of Winter"). Lyrically it hits many of Zappa's favorite teenage targets: "Cruising for burgers in daddy's new car / My phony freedom card / Brings to me, instantly, ecstasy." Zappa, who did not really like or understand people's need to alter themselves chemically and did not really like or understand typical male teenage culture (or he could understand it but simply found it wanting), seems to find the whole concept of the fake ID hilarious (he would take up this issue 20 years later in "Teen Age Wind" on the album *You Are What You Is*). The song's musical setting builds to a screamingly funny bit of pomposity before fading out and ending the side of the record.

Uncle Meat did surprisingly well for an experimental record, rising to as high as No. 43 on the *Billboard* charts. Contemporary reaction to the album has been kind, recognizing *Uncle Meat* for its place as both masterpiece and blueprint. Daniel Durchholz writes that *Uncle Meat* is "Zappa's most demanding opus outside of his strictly classical work."[137] *The New Rolling Stone Album Guide* calls it an "inspired monstrosity" and argues that it is an "assault of glorious noise."[138] Steve Huey writes, in a fairly dead-on critique, that "despite the absence of a conceptual framework, the unfocused sprawl of *Uncle Meat* is actually a big part of its appeal. It's exciting to hear one of the most creatively fertile minds in rock pushing restlessly into new territory, even if he isn't always quite sure where he's going."[139]

Sadly, *Uncle Meat* was the end of a period of creativity that seems unrivaled in contemporary music. Zappa would go on to record more than 30 more albums (several of which were groundbreaking in their own right) and would write complex and achingly beautiful music for the rest of his life, but never again would he create albums as documents as challenging and interesting and weird as *Lumpy Gravy* and *Uncle Meat*. There seems to be a sense, looking back with the gift of hindsight, that *Uncle Meat* is the mythical high-water mark. That it would be good in the future, but never this good. *Rolling Stone* seems to hit the mark when they write of *Uncle Meat* that it seems as if Zappa were "the cryptic prophet howling in the wilderness."[140] With his next full album of original music, *Hot Rats,* on its way, the next several years would see a growth in Zappa in some unusual and unexpected directions.

MOTHERMANIA

Originally released in March 1969 on the Verve label as an attempt to recoup money the label felt they lost on the original Mothers albums (it was also, Zappa feels on purpose, released less than a month before *Uncle Meat*). Zappa has disowned the album, although he was involved, at the time, in the remixing and packaging of it and, according to Slaven, "slipped in an uncensored version of 'Mother People',...and 'The Idiot Bastard Son' was a radically different mix."[141] The first of many repackagings of the Mothers, this Zappa-overseen greatest hits package includes the songs "Brown Shoes Don't Make it," "Mother People," "Duke of Prunes," "Call Any Vegetable," "The Idiot Bastard Son," "It Can't Happen Here," "You're Probably Wondering Why I'm Here," "Who Are the Brain Police," "Plastic People," "Hungry Freaks, Daddy," and "America Drinks and Goes Home." The album is unusual only insomuch as it takes many of the songs out of their original context(s) (i.e., "Duke of Prunes" was originally part of a multimovement piece, as was "America Drinks and Goes Home"). The album is currently unavailable on CD, and there are, at present, no plans to make it available.

4

Hot Rats, the Last Two Mothers Albums, Flo & Eddie, and the Jazz-Rock Albums

HOT RATS

The Jazz Album: *Hot Rats* (originally released on the Bizarre / Straight label in October 1969; currently available as Rykodisc CD RCD 10508). Highest *Billboard* chart position: No. 173. Personnel: Frank Zappa, Ian Underwood, Captain Beefheart, Don "Sugarcaine" Harris, Jean-Luc Ponty, John Guerin, Paul Humphry, Ron Selico, Max Bennett, and Shuggy Otis. "An all-instrumental album, except for one vocal cut.... Why are you wasting America's precious time with this, you asshole!"[1]

The year 1969 turns out to be the first of many turning-point years for Zappa. Although the Mothers of Invention are terminally close to breaking up (which they would do, officially, for the first time, in October), Zappa finds himself gaining a measure of critical, cultural, and popular success and respect. In April 1969, Zappa and the Mothers played the Boston Globe Jazz Festival. During the show, Zappa invited the respected jazz saxophonist Rahsaan Roland Kirk to play with the band, and, if the reviews are to be believed, they created some spectacular music. Zappa would go on to expand upon the ideas he seemed to be developing in Boston with his album *Hot Rats*. This album, although never all that popular in the United States, would be the first to launch Zappa into international acclaim, climbing to number 9 on the British album charts and staying on the charts for more than six months. The album is important for a number of reasons: It is Zappa's first real break from the Mothers of Invention (only Ian Underwood comes along for the ride); it is the first album in a while to feature nothing but music (there are no pieces of musique concrète or spoken-word sections); and it is really the first, outside perhaps "King Kong," to feature several extended jams.

Zappa, in his autobiography, writes, of *Hot Rats,* "I happened to like [it] a lot, [and it] sneaked onto the *Billboard* charts somewhere around 99 and vanished immediately."[2] To be fair, however, it did extremely well in Europe.

The album is, in many ways, a trendsetter; more than one critic has called it the first jazz fusion album (coming, as it does, at around the same time as Miles Davis's *Bitches' Brew,* often acknowledged as the first fusion record), although it is much closer to the blues that it is to jazz. Concert favorites "Willie the Pimp," "Peaches En Regalia," and "Son of Mr. Green Genes" all flirt with jazz, rock, and blues, making the album a far more forward-looking piece of work than many of Zappa's earlier records (it is the first album of Zappa's, for instance, to feature no doo-wop songs or parodies).

Unfortunately, many fans see the early / original Mothers of Invention albums as the only worthwhile records. *Hot Rats* shows a musician and composer who was really developing as an arranger. The complexity of the pop / rock songs on this album is far beyond what Zappa had been doing up to this point. (Although it is perhaps not as complex as some of the orchestral work Zappa was doing, it is much more complex than the doo-wop song parodies that were the staple of the first five albums).

The album is also striking because Zappa does not sing on it. Only one song has lyrics, "Willie the Pimp," in which the lyrics are largely inconsequential to the extended (9:00) blues / rock jam. The rest of the album is made up of extended instrumental jams that feature lots of guitar and woodwind soloing.

The album begins with one of Zappa's most enduring songs, "Peaches en Regalia."[3] Unlike many of the songs on the album, "Peaches" is a tightly structured melodic theme (as opposed to a loosely structured avenue for extended improvisation). "Peaches" is almost like an overture or an introduction; it is short and tight and resolves itself without really challenging the listener.[4] The music is dramatic and forceful, filled with piano trills, synthesizer runs, and a deep drum sound that is very much at the center of the mix. Zappa, who in later years would return to this kind of music quite often, especially on *Jazz from Hell* (the so-called beautiful theme as opposed to the vamp for improvisation), seemed to have an ability to knock out these kinds of catchy themes. *Uncle Meat* and *Lumpy Gravy* abound in them, as does *200 Motels.*

"Willie the Pimp" is a supposedly true story told to Zappa by two women (Zappa recorded the story and later released the recording on the album *Mystery Disc* as "The True Story of Willie the Pimp") as interpreted by his boyhood friend Don Van Vliet (also known, of course, as Captain Beefheart). The song is one of the greasiest blues songs Zappa ever recorded, with a blistering guitar solo that lasts for several minutes. The song is also interesting because it features some great blues violin playing by Don Harris, which gives the piece a really unusual atmosphere. Lyrically it is a hilarious song about a wannabe pimp named Willie (indeed, it is almost too bad that Zappa never made it to the gangsta rap era; "Willie the Pimp" would fit in well with the tales of bling and excess that are common on hip-hop radio today) who works the lobby of the Lido Hotel (according to one of the women in the interview, the Lido was a "perverted hotel on Coney Island"). The song features a terrific vocal from Beefheart, who has a much more authentic blues voice than does Zappa, and thus makes the song that much more telling (live it often would be performed by Ike Willis, Zappa's best vocalist, who would imbue the piece with some real blues). Despite the lyrics and vocals, the song is really a vehicle, as are all the songs on the album, for Zappa's pent-up musical creativity. The guitar solo is a masterpiece of blues soloing that indicates the direction in which Zappa is going to take his music in the future (indeed, it is my thesis that *Hot Rats* indicates in general where Zappa is going to go, much more toward popular song structure and toward the music being a background for extended guitar soloing).

"Willie the Pimp" is followed by "Son of Mr. Green Genes," which takes the musical theme from the song "Mr. Green Genes" (from the *Lumpy Gravy* album) and becomes another excuse for extended soloing by Zappa and Ian Underwood. Zappa would increasingly do this to his older music: strip the theme from something and use it as material to solo over. It is an interesting premise, one that falls very much into the postmodern. The idea is that Zappa is expressing the ennui and exhaustion of the late twentieth century through the constant recycling of his own themes. This is debatable, but it raises a valid point, one that *Hot Rats* seems to generally raise: that Zappa's increasingly avant-garde works (*Lumpy Gravy* and *Uncle Meat*, in particular) were not finding success commensurate with the work that was being put into them, and therefore *Hot Rats* is, in some ways, a strategic retreat into music that is understandable. The view of the album as a retreat can account for the lack of critical focus on it (it is virtually ignored by Zappa's biographers), and even Watson, who usually has a lot to say about all of Zappa's works, only devotes a few pages to it in *The Negative Dialectics of Poodle Play*. I tend to agree with Watson's argument that *Hot Rats* was so popular (especially in Europe) because of its "professional, straight-ahead sound," and that it was a hit because there was "no musique concrète, no live chaos, no Suzy Creamcheese, no nonsense."[5] What neither Watson nor the other biographers seems to question is why this album at this time? Zappa had been on an unprecedented artistic roll, to the point that *Hot Rats* seems like a disappointment. "The Son of Mr. Green Genes" represents this disappointment in many ways: Zappa's disappointment with the record-buying public, his disappointment with the failed promise of the sixties, his disappointment with the Mothers of Invention, and all seem represented in this album. Zappa seems to be saying "here, if you want a regular 'rock record,' you got it." The fact that Zappa never really produced anything like a rock record is part of the irony. *Hot Rats* is considered good because people can understand it; it is not full of inside jokes or band anthropology, just easily identifiable themes played in an easy-to-understand setting.

Immediately following "Son of Mr. Green Genes" is a short interlude piece named "Little Umbrellas." It is fairly unremarkable except for the fact that, much like "Peaches en Regalia," it is another in a long line of sweet and lovely melodies that Zappa created. Unlike "Peaches," there is little evidence that this song was performed by any of Zappa's bands, although Bill Lantz writes that "this is a popular ensemble piece today for the tribute projects that have proliferated since his passing."[6] The song also features one of the few recorder solos on a rock/jazz record.[7] Perhaps it is heretical to say, but "Little Umbrellas" is as close to either a song by the band Chicago or cocktail jazz as Zappa ever got.

As if to redeem himself, the next song on the album serves as a compositional centerpiece. "The Gumbo Variations" clocks in at just less than 17 minutes.[8] It is a marvelous piece of late sixties funk/jazz, with a stinging horn section and a set of solos, first from Ian Underwood (on sax) and then from Zappa (guitar) and Don Harris (violin), that take one's breath away. Although Zappa did not return to this piece very often, he did compose many others like it, including "Waka/Jawka," "Big Swifty," and "The Grand Wazoo"; it shows his ability to work in an incredibly wide range of genres and his generosity as a band leader, allowing the sax and violin parts to really stretch out on what was ostensibly a Zappa solo record.

The album ends with "It Must Be a Camel," a much more free-form piece that centers around various percussion sounds and an interesting piano melody. There are a couple of interesting features of the song that must be noted: The first is the interesting overdubbed horn arrangements; as Zappa would demonstrate with his work on both *The Grand Wazoo* and with the various recordings of the 1988 big band, he was an ace arranger of horn parts. The fact that Zappa and Ian Underwood are creating the horn charts by themselves is one part instrumental mastery and one part studio wizardry. The second interesting feature of this song is that it features a short violin solo by Jean-Luc Ponty, a rising jazz star who would be in and out of Zappa's world for the next several years.[9]

Hot Rats is a difficult album because in many ways it seems like a holding pattern or an admission of exhaustion or a result of too many years on planes, buses, and in dressing rooms with the same folks. It could be, too, a result of a larger cultural fatigue that was enveloping the United States at the same time.

The summer of 1969 was not the summer of love. Many, including Joan Didion, cite the summer of 1969 as the end of the sixties and with it the death of the American dream. The deaths of Martin Luther King Jr. and Robert Kennedy in 1968 and the Manson family killings in 1969 made the idea of summer of love laughable, and *Hot Rats* seems, at least in terms of Zappa's critical project, to say the same thing. Zappa, who has been arguing since 1965 that the whole hippie/summer of love thing was not working, finds himself in the embarrassing position of having been right all along. What do you do? You put out an album of almost all instrumental music, break up your band, busy yourself with film and production projects, and wait for the seventies.

That said, *Hot Rats* is an album that is beloved by contemporary critics and fans. It is one of the few albums that *Rolling Stone* liked upon release, and that critical appreciation is evident almost 30 years later in their review in *The New Rolling Stone Album Guide,* in which they write that with *Hot Rats* "Zappa the composer reached a majestic peak."[10] The All Music Guide writes that *Hot Rats* "is a classic of the genre. *Hot Rats'* genius lies in the way it fuses the compositional sophistication of jazz with rock's down-and-dirty attitude."[11] Many of the fan reviews on Amazon.com cite the album as a favorite, liking it for its accessibility. Indeed, the marketing materials from the publisher even call it "probably the first FZ album that Most-Folks-Who-Don't-Even-Like-Frank Zappa ever bought, and the one that began to establish him as a virtuoso musician and composer."

Ultimately, the album maintains an odd place in Zappa's catalog. For someone who had put so many voices on all of his previous records, it is a surprisingly voiceless album. For someone who wanted to be taken seriously as a composer of avant-garde symphonic music, it is a retreat into popular song form. For someone who had something to say about U.S. culture, it is a puzzle. In the final analysis, it captures a specific moment in both Zappa's career and in U.S. music. By late 1969, almost all of the bands that had been Zappa's contemporaries were defunct: the Beatles and the Byrds were no more, Brian Jones was dead, and Janis Joplin and Jim Morrison were in the last gasps of their careers. It is interesting to note that while many of the bands that were working the Sunset Strip at the same time as the Mothers of Invention were winding down, Zappa was just getting started.

BURNT WEENY SANDWICH AND WEASELS RIPPED MY FLESH

The death of the original Mother of Invention. *Burnt Weeny Sandwich* (originally released in February 1970 on the Bizarre / Reprise label; currently available as Rykodisc RCD 10509). Highest *Billboard* chart position: No. 94.

Weasels Ripped My Flesh (originally released in August 1970 on the Bizarre / Reprise label; currently available as Rykodisc RCD 10510). Highest *Billboard* chart position: No. 189.

Personnel who played on both albums include Ian Underwood, Bunk Gardner, Motorhead Sherwood, Buzz Gardner, Roy Estrada, Jimmy Carl Black, Art Tripp, Don Preston, Ray Collins, Don "Sugarcane" Harris, and Lowell George. "I didn't think of them [the original Mothers] so much as musicians than as people. It was their idiosyncrasies that made the group, not their musicianship."[12]

Although many feel that these two albums form some sort of apotheosis of the original Mothers, they are, in many ways, placeholder albums. Both

they are available on some often-bootlegged recordings) that refer to the riots: "See the student leader / He's fucked up / He's still a Nazi like his mom and dad." This would not be the last time Zappa took a cheap shot at the Germans (his opinion seems to be that the Germans could not even do riots correctly).[18] As has been established on several earlier albums, Zappa had little patience for student protests (indeed, the 1968 European student protests must have seemed somewhat silly to Zappa; after having lived through the civil rights protests and riots in the United States, he arrived in Europe to find that students were, in essence, rioting in favor of a socialist educational policy).

The major and most memorable song on the record is "The Little House I Used to Live In," which continued the trend toward blues / jazz based jamming that started with "King Kong" and was perfected on *Hot Rats*. The song begins with a lovely jazz piano prelude by Ian Underwood and segues into an 18-minute jam featuring some fine guitar work by Zappa and a violin solo by Don Harris that sounds as close to blues harmonica as one can get. It is a song that requires repeated listening, in which each listening reveals a number of different musical things happening in the work. It is one of the many pieces of Zappa's that can be categorized as progressive rock; it has a number of clearly defined movements (more than likely patched together in the studio) that vary in tempo, tone, and genre.[19] In his analysis of the song, Román García Albertos has gone so far as to identify which members of Zappa's multiple incarnations of the Mothers are responsible for which parts of the song.[20] It is clear from Albertos's analysis that the song has at least four different bands contributing parts to it.

Burnt Weeny Sandwich ends with the song "Valerie," another doo-wop hit clearly representing an older iteration of the Mothers (the engineering and recording of the song have a very different sound than the rest of the album, a lot more treble and a much thinner drum sound). According to Zappa, the song was recorded in yet another desperate bid to get their music on the radio. This argument is strange because, by 1970, the U.S. music scene had moved away from doo-wop (although, had Zappa kept creating and releasing doo-wop music, he more than likely would have scored a few hits in the late seventies during the brief fifties revival).

Released immediately on the heels of *Burnt Weeny Sandwich* was *Weasels Ripped My Flesh* an album that stands as part of a larger project. If *Burnt Weeny* is a collection of blues and jazz pieces, then *Weasels* is a collection of symphonic and avant-garde pieces, with some mean blues and a few rock singles (including concert favorites "My Guitar Wants to Kill Your Mama" and "Oh No") thrown into the mix. The album is the last to feature the original (or semioriginal as it were, because the original Mothers had ended with the departure of Ray Collins) Mothers lineup. In some ways Zappa seems to be scraping the bottom of the barrel; the songs, including "Didja Get Any Onya" and "Prelude to the Afternoon of a Sexually Aroused Gas Mask" are both aural experiments in noise and instrumentation. Unfortunately, by this point in Zappa's career, they are old hat, sounding like any number of experimental pieces off of any of the first five albums.

One exception to this is "The Eric Dolphy Memorial Barbecue," which is as close to hard-core jazz as Zappa ever got. Musicologist Barry Kernfeld describes what made Dolphy so original:

> Dolphy was a highly versatile musician, playing jazz but also performing third-stream music by Gunther Schuller and pieces such as Edgard Varèse's *Density 21.5* at the Ojai (California) Music Festival in 1962. This close link to 20th-century art music influenced his fondness for dissonant harmonies in jazz, while his strident, trebly timbre and nervous, skittering lines on alto saxophone are perhaps best understood as a personalized intensification of bop melody.[21]

What makes Kernfeld's description so resonant is that Ian Underwood, throughout *Weasels,* plays in much the same manner ascribed to Dolphy.

Another unusual departure for Zappa is that the song is neither parody nor tribute (fan Web sites devote a lot of space to this question); despite the reference to Dolphy in the title, the song is not a tribute in the sense of Zappa doing a Dolphy-esque piece. It is a tribute, however, from one avant-garde composer to another. According to Zappa, "I used to listen to Eric Dolphy albums and I really liked 'em."[22] Like Zappa, Dolphy spent much of his career feeling abused and misunderstood by the record-buying public, although he was highly respected by his peers and by serious fans of a certain kind of avant-bop jazz. Zappa can be described in much the same way. The song begins in a fairly straightforward manner (in fact, the early melody seems close to "Mr. Green Genes"); however, it quickly veers off into a series of instrumental explorations (many of which are accomplished with the drummer playing in a straightforward waltz time / beat). Halfway through the song, the melodic line disintegrates into a free-form set of explorations and variations, including what sounds like a New Orleans funeral march, a slow keyboard dirge, laughter, drum solos, bass clarinet (or bassoon, undoubtedly a tribute to Dolphy who was thought to be the first bass clarinet player in jazz), and wah-wah laden blues guitar, often all played at the same time. It is a complex piece and demands the listener's attention.

The album ends with three blazing rock songs (and a fourth so-called song that consists of nothing but several minutes of guitar feedback and noise named, appropriately, "Weasels Ripped My Flesh"). After nearly an entire album of aural experiments (with the exception of the wonderful down and dirty blues of "Directly from My Heart to You," an old Little Richard song sung by Don Harris, a fantastic piece of music with one of the dirtiest violin solos ever committed to record), the listener is rewarded with "My Guitar Wants to Kill Your Mama," a straightforward rock song about teen rebellion and generational clashing. Although not nearly as funny as his other songs, the music is the Mothers as rock band at its best, a groovy rock song with a great horn chart and a series of short, focused solos in the middle (keyboards, woodwinds, acoustic guitar). The song, however, indicates, yet again, that these two albums are stopgaps; Zappa is reusing the same ideas, themes, and concepts again and again (antiauthoritarianism, blues covers, bop/symphonic/rock hybrids) and seems to be clearing out the catalog backlog in order to get on with some new stuff.

The album ends with the songs "Oh No" and "The Orange County Lumber Truck." "Oh No" had already appeared in instrumental form on *Lumpy Gravy* and had been (and would remain) a concert favorite for years. Ben Watson devotes a lot of space to an analysis of the lyrics, drawing a connection between the line "I think you're probably out to lunch" and the Eric Dolphy album *Out to Lunch* (Watson used the nom de plume "out to lunch" in his earlier writing). It is an interesting, albeit pretty far-fetched, argument. The song seems to be, in large part, taking a shot at the Beatles, whose argument "all you need is love" was counter to the arguments Zappa would make about love. Zappa writes, "You say love is all we need . . . / I think you're probably out to lunch."

Watson, however, is one of the few biographers and critics to devote much space at all to the album as a whole. Most critics tend to see the album, as I do here, as filler (not to say it is bad filler, just that there is little new on these albums, especially if you had been following Zappa's live shows; many of these pieces, especially the pieces on *Weasels Ripped My Flesh,* had been performed live since as far back as 1965). Michael Gray, for instance, a usually reliable chronicler of Zappa's early years, writes off the album as "a ragbag of odds and ends from here, there and everywhere," although he considers it "evidence of Zappa's editing skill at its height."[23] Barry Miles devotes two paragraphs to the album, most of which is a discussion of the (admittedly cool) cover art, which shows a Roy Lichtenstein-ian cover of a typical fifties businessman shaving his face with a rabid weasel. Billy James goes one better and writes *Weasels* off in one paragraph. David Walley skips it altogether. Kevin Courrier offers an interesting song-by-song reading of the record, including a nice breakdown of when and where each song was recorded. Courrier also offers an alternate reading of "Oh No" that clashes significantly with Watson's. Courrier furthers the argument that the song was "written in response to John Lennon's 'All You Need is Love.' "[24]

It is an interesting album and one of the Zappa albums that rewards careful and repeated listening. It is not a funny album, and it is not a statement. It is a fitting swan song for the original Mothers of Invention, reminding people of what Zappa and the Mothers were capable of.

Contemporary critical reaction for both albums is good. *The New Rolling Stone Album Guide* lumps the two albums together and proclaims them to be evidence that Zappa was working at the height of his abilities.[25] Daniel Durchholz calls the two albums "the most consistently great albums" of

Zappa's career.[26] Fan reviewer "Samhot" at Amazon.com writes, "This album [*Weasels*] is not for purist, close-minded or faint-hearted listeners. However, if you're a fan of jazz-fusion and / or challenging, experimental, cerebral and adventurous music, take a risk and pick up this album. You may just find a new favorite artist, and / or appreciate music in a whole new way."[27] Steve Huey argues that the album ultimately succeeds because "there is a certain logic behind the band's accomplished genre-bending and Zappa's gleefully abrupt veering between musical extremes; without pretension, Zappa blurs the normally sharp line between intellectual concept music and the visceral immediacy of rock and R&B."[28]

It is my opinion that these albums are loved in retrospect because they are the last by the original group (for which people felt a lot of love and feel a lot of nostalgia). They also represent, at least for a good while, the last of Zappa's most far-out, experimental work. His next several albums would make him much more popular but would deeply divide, for some time, his fans and provide much ammunition for his enemies.

CHUNGA'S REVENGE; FILLMORE EAST, JUNE 1971; 200 MOTELS; AND JUST ANOTHER BAND FROM L.A.

The Flo & Eddie Years. *Chunga's Revenge* (originally released in October 1970 on the Bizarre / Reprise label; currently available as Rykodisc RCD 10511). *Billboard* chart position: No. 113. Personnel: Ian Underwood, Max Bennett, Aynsley Dunbar, Jeff Simmons, George Duke, John Guerin, Don "Sugarcane" Harris, Howard Kaylan, and Mark Volman.

Fillmore East, June 1971 (originally released in August 1971 on the Bizarre / Reprise label; currently available as Rykodisc RCD 10512). Highest *Billboard* chart position: No. 38. Personnel: Ian Underwood, Aynsley Dunbar, Jim Pons, Bob Harris, Don Preston, Howard Kaylan, and Mark Volman.

200 Motels (originally released in October 1971 on United Artists Records; currently available as Rykodisc RCD 10513 / 14). Highest *Billboard* chart position: No. 59. Personnel: Ian Underwood, Aynsley Dunbar, George Duke, Howard Kaylan, Mark Volman, and the Royal Philharmonic Orchestra.

Just Another Band from L.A. (originally released in March 1972 on the Bizarre / Reprise label; currently available as Rykodisc RCD 10515). Highest *Billboard* chart position: No. 85. Personnel: Ian Underwood, Aynsley Dunbar, Don Preston, Jim Pons, Mark Volman, and Howard Kaylan. "I'm interested in things of a glandular nature."[29]

Two months after the release of *Weasels Ripped My Flesh*, Zappa released *Chunga's Revenge*, supposedly a sort-of-solo album, although one with portents of things to come. The liner notes indicate, for instance, that "All the vocals in this album are a preview of the story from *200 Motels*." In this case, the vocals were by the 22- and 23-year-old ex-lead singers of the Turtles, Mark Volman and Howard Kaylan, otherwise known as Flo & Eddie.

These four albums, the collected output of the Flo & Eddie years, represent a radical departure for Zappa. They are difficult albums for fans and critics and have taken, unfairly I think, a pretty severe beating over the years (see following paragraphs for more on contemporary critical reactions). This reaction comes from a couple of places: (1) these albums represent a definitive break with the old Mothers of Invention. Some fans and critics simply can not get over the breakup of that band. Billy James, for instance, argues that "Zappa's recorded output through the early 70s remained notoriously prolific and innovative as ever but in some people's eyes never really recaptured the spirit of his original band."[30] (2) There is a (not so) subtle change in attitude. Although the lyrics are still gleefully antiauthoritarian, the albums are, for lack of a better term, smuttier. It is difficult work to understand and place these albums in their proper historical and cultural context, and it is work that many do not approve of. There is, upon hearing these albums for the first time, a grand tendency to rush to judgment on the shockingly sexual lyrics, but when one considers the time in which the albums appeared, they present a real challenge to U.S. ideals of authority, rock and roll, capitalism, sex, love, and culture.

Chunga's Revenge is a nice starting point to discuss this change because it, like the two previous albums, is a transition piece; some of the songs on the album were recorded at the same time as *Hot Rats,* whereas others were recorded quickly in Los Angeles and England immediately after Kaylan and Volman joined the group.[31] Indeed, the listener is not introduced to Flo & Eddie until after the song "Transylvania Boogie," which opens the album. "Boogie" is what many had come to expect from Zappa. It is a song that would not be out of place on either *Hot Rats* or *Burnt Weeny Sandwich,* an extended acid rock jam that shows off the evolving nature of Zappa's guitar playing (which was ever more often straying from the blues and moving toward something entirely different). It also introduces listeners to English drummer Aynsley Dunbar, a much more accomplished rock drummer than Jimmy Carl Black.[32] The next song, "Road Ladies," starts a two-year period of songs about the sex lives of the band members, starring Flo, Eddie, Frank, and the band. It is an interesting song for a couple of reasons: It is one of the first rock songs about the (supposed) downside of being in a rock band (something Jackson Browne would perfect with *Running on Empty*), and it is the first of many controversial songs about groupies and sex and band members. It is also the first of many songs in which the band members would adopt larger-than-life personas (i.e., Flo & Eddie were to become caricatures of rock stars, and they would play these characters well, creating a rich tableau of silliness that would take Zappa fairly far away from his original work of subtle critique and into the world of absurdity, parody, caricature, and satire).

Musically, the song is a basic blues vamp that would reappear in a slightly different form in the song "What Kind of Girl Do You Think We Are?" on

Fillmore East, June 1971. It makes the argument that life on the road is a horrible torture; over this basic blues (featuring a hilariously clichéd organ intro), Zappa sings, in the style of an old bluesman, a litany of things that are wrong with being on the road, including the loneliness of having only groupies and employees to hang around with, the piles of dirty laundry that abound, and the crappy places one has to play. Zappa also laments, "When the P.A. system eats it, / And the band plays some of the most terriblest shit you've ever known." These are legitimate symbols of life without the comforts of home. They potentially alienate the band's fans, however. It is always a mystery as to why bands do this. Touring is undoubtedly exhausting and difficult work, but it is not like the exhausting and difficult work that many, if not most, of the people in the audience are doing every day. It is one of those sticking points that gets Zappa into trouble; one has to assume that Zappa knows that he is lucky (and the song indicates that he knows this) and that this complaining is part of the rock star persona that he and the band had adopted.

One way to read this song is that it is not just a collection of gripes by Zappa but is a setup for Zappa's continuing exploration and critique of male privilege. The so-called answer to all of the perceived troubles that Zappa sings about in the first two verses is sex with groupies; the interesting thing is that it is not Zappa who sings about this solution, it is Flo & Eddie, the rock stars of the band. This change in dynamic is important. Zappa's complaints about the road—the alienation and exhaustion, the fact that you do not really have any friends (only sycophants and employees), that the band that bears your name can not play, and that the halls you are booked into can not take the time to set up the sound systems correctly—are the same kinds of complaints any worker would have about missing all of the comforts of home. Flo & Eddie sing in the chorus about missing the girls back home and the downside of the road, having to get a shot from the doctor because of "what the road ladies done to you." Much like his indictment of teenage lust and the silliness of pop songs, Zappa is critiquing the privilege that the men in his band assume (that your stature as a pop star makes you extradeserving of female attention); although there is some evidence that Zappa, in his younger days, partook in the groupie scene to some extent, he seems to have stayed away from the kinds of insane antics that some of his band members proudly engaged in with great frequency (and which are revealed on the next several albums). Mark Volman seems to indicate that Zappa understood the satire he was creating: "He [Zappa] always had this idea to do a satire of an anti-pop band and now [because of the addition of Flo & Eddie] he had the ability to mock pop through the faces of a pop band. It became a satire on satire."[33]

It is also important to remember the time in which these songs were being written and performed: It is 1970, pre-AIDS, post-sexual revolution United States. Ideas about sex, at least by those in Zappa's generation, were radically different than they were 10 years before or would be 10 years later. The ideology that one could go on the road, get the clap, get a shot, and be well is, in this era of AIDS, an unheard-of and unhealthy attitude and one that is easy to condemn in retrospect. In fact, what is much more surprising than the frank discussion of sex on the album (and on the subsequent albums) is the complete lack of discussion about the disintegration of the student movement, something upon which Zappa had cast, from time to time, a critical eye. Perhaps Zappa did not want to gloat or was burned out by the whole thing; whatever the reason, the fact that much of what Zappa had predicted in 1965–67 had come true, in a far more horrible fashion than anyone could have predicted.

Chunga's Revenge was released in October 1970. Five months prior to this, the National Guard had fired 61 shots at 13 unarmed students, killing 4 of them, at Kent State University in Kent, Ohio.[34] The reaction to this event by many Americans was "they got what was coming to them," and Zappa's lack of comment—song after song about groupies, sex, and life on the road—was both a retreat and a diversion. Riots and protests, as Zappa has said previously, are not going to work. All that is left is sex.

This turn away from protest toward sex should not be all that surprising. According to historian William Manchester, late 1970 and early 1971 saw Americans fondly looking backward: "nostalgia became big business."[35] The people were scared and tired and wary. The monumental changes of the past 10 to 20 years had worn people down; fewer and fewer people lived on farms or in small towns, gas prices (related, of course, to gas consumption) were rising with great rapidity, and the number of shopping centers in the United States had increased by 13,000 in 10 years. It was an alienating time.

The year 1970 also saw many Americans realize that there was money to be made off of Americans' interest in sex. Soft-core porn director Russ Meyer was celebrated in 1970 for making his 21st successful film in a row (a record no mainstream director could ever approach). Meyer was quoted as saying that his films made money because "I don't play games with an audience."[36] New York had more than 200 adult bookstores, and one X-rated film, *What Do You Say to a Naked Lady* (directed by Allen "Candid Camera" Funt) was grossing more than $7,000 a day in San Francisco alone. Manchester writes of 1970 that "curiosity about sex seemed to be insatiable" and that much of the writing, talking, looking, listening, and thinking about sex "was rooted in the era, in the sexual revolution and the mini-micro-bikini-topless-bottomless mood of the times."[37] It was simply a different time. The year 1970 saw the beginning of the debate over sex education (one that has not abated), with one pro-sex-ed national spokesperson arguing that children should be taught about sex "not as something you do but as something you are."[38] Although Zappa likely agreed with the statement, the more brutal truth was the fact that the very same year, right-wing antisex crusaders in Racine, Wisconsin, succeeded in convincing people that sex ed in the schools "was a Communist plot to undermine the morals of the pupils."[39]

The year 1970, of course, is also the year of feminism. It had been around, of course, forever, but 1970 saw the first flowering of a powerful and unique ideological movement by and for women. It is important to remember that feminism was different in 1970 than it is now; it was both newer and more of a challenge to accepted cultural and social norms. There was much political theater, including the famous incident of former child actress Robin Morgan disrupting the 1968 Miss America Pageant and informing the world that she had started an organization calling itself the Women's International Terrorist Conspiracy from Hell (or WITCH for short). This is the same year that Abby Rockefeller, granddaughter of business giant John D. Rockefeller, informed the world, in a phrase that had to be dear to Zappa's heart, that "romantic love between men and women was 'counter-revolutionary.' "[40]

Against this backdrop of revolutionary anger, *Chunga's Revenge* is a tame statement, not the horrible and reactionary piece of misogyny it often is accused of being. Accusations of sexism by critics of Zappa do not fit in light of the concurrent cultural revolution.[41] Often, lyrics that on the surface seem misogynistic actually critique the system, not the women trapped within the system. "Road Ladies," which is as smutty as *Chunga's* gets, is a relatively tame piece of work, and although the albums would get dirtier (*Fillmore East, June 1971,* discussed later, is admittedly a joyously filthy album), they would never fail to signify and critique the cultural revolution of the times. In many ways, in fact, Zappa seems to have predicted this tumultuous time in the history of male-female relationships; one of the primary themes in his music since the founding of the Mothers in 1965 was the falseness of boy-girl relationships.

Ironically, "Road Ladies" is followed by one of Zappa's most beautiful songs, the instrumental "Twenty Small Cigars." A leftover from the *Hot Rats* session, its acoustic bass and brushed drums place it squarely in the jazz idiom.[42] The song lasts only 2:17 and segues immediately (through a fairly harsh edit) into "The Nancy and Mary Music," an attempt, it seems, by Zappa to have the current band pull off one of the long instrumental improvisations/experiments for which the Mothers were so famous. "The Nancy and Mary Music" is not to everyone's taste, although Watson argues that it is interesting because it involved the use of the audience as a musical instrument and introduced George Duke's ability to work within "Zappa's freaky-funk concept."[43]

The next two songs, more traditional vocal pieces, feature the comic stylings of Flo & Eddie. "Tell Me You Love Me," which would be performed by nearly all of Zappa's future groups, is a typical Zappa antilove song. The primary difference is the more complex vocals Zappa was able to get with his new lead singers. Lyrically it is no different from earlier songs like "Love of My Life" or "I Ain't Got No Heart."

"Would You Go All the Way" is in some ways more interesting. It deals with themes that seemed to amuse Zappa: the cliché-ridden horror movies of the fifties, the desperation of servicemen (again, the theme of what men will do to get sex from women seems to inform this song), and the wretchedness of adolescent sex. Musically it is another parody of early sixties happy rock (it is a perfect Turtles song, undoubtedly mocking the former employers of Flo & Eddie) that, as it progresses, becomes a heavier blues workout (featuring, of all instruments, a trumpet). The lyrics are a mélange of clichés about the fifties, including white socks and black pants, a rolled up T-shirt, and "A '55 Chevy that his brother just stoled." What this typical fella wants, of course, is a date, "An' he asks you for a date / To the servicemen's dance!"

When the two eventually go to the servicemen's dance, we find that it is really just a brothel. As it moves out of the poppy sounds of the first two verses, the song becomes both bluesier and sleazier, ending with a repeated chant, "would you go all the way for the USO / would you go all the way for the USA?" In light of what was going on at the time (Vietnam) and the era in which Zappa had been raised (the immediate aftermath of World War II), the sort of argument he makes in the out choruses of this song are particularly poignant: the girls are encouraged to go all the way to show their patriotic fervor, another example of male privilege at its finest.

Following these two songs is the fine instrumental title track, "Chunga's Revenge." Another leftover from the *Hot Rats* album, it is a much more blues-based piece, with a tremendous guitar solo and an infamous wah-wah sax solo by Ian Underwood.[44]

The funniest song on the album, and one that has given critics and fans fits for years, is the song "Rudy Wants to Buy Yez a Drink," a ditty about a union boss. Zappa's relationship with unions, like his relationships with sex, the counterculture, and religion, is a complicated one. Musically it stands out; mixing beer hall clichés (trombone and tuba) with show-tune phrasing and surf guitar, it immediately sounds old fashioned, which is exactly the point. Zappa sees unions as atavistic—old fashioned. It is a complex argument, however, one that critics seem to want to avoid. In one sense, Zappa seems to be against systems—religion, political parties, public education, unions, and so forth. Zappa was the quintessential small businessman and quasi-libertarian. He wanted the role of the government to be to create a space where anyone (in his case the artist) was free to do what he or she needed to do (in his case create). The things that Zappa seemed most interested in critiquing are all systems of some sort: the way things are sold to people, the way art has been turned into a business (Zappa's complaint is that record companies are more interested in making money than in releasing good or interesting music). Seen in this light, Zappa's antiunion stance is not out of place. It is a surprising stance to some, especially because Zappa seemed, at times at least, sympathetic to leftist causes. Zappa's caustic critique of flower power and student demonstrations should indicate to all that he is contrary by nature and hostile to groupthink, and to expect him to have a regimented ideological position that endorses a particular group is expecting something of him that he certainly never promised.[45]

The album ends with the heartbreaking soul / doo-wop song "Sharleena."[46] In many ways this song seems calculated to show the listener, despite all of the silliness that has ensued on the rest of the album, that the new guys can sing; the falsettos and harmonies of Flo & Eddie take the song into another place. It is no wonder that Zappa would return to the song several times on several albums, especially with bands that had great singers (Ike Willis and Ray White, perhaps Zappa's best singers, handle the vocals on the versions recorded on *Them or Us* and *You Can't Do That on Stage Anymore, Vol. 3*). It is a fitting and deceptive end to *Chunga's Revenge;* no one had any idea what they were in for next.

Contemporary critical reaction to the album has been mixed. Watson writes that it is "generally dismissed as 'transitional'"; *The New Rolling Stone Album Guide* simply lumps it in with *Hot Rats, Burnt Weeny,* and *Weasels;* Steve Huey writes that "while there are plenty of fine moments, *Chunga's Revenge* is in the end more of a hodgepodge transitional album, with less coherence than Zappa's other 1969–70 works."[47]

Chunga's Revenge has a thrown-together feel, and there is little on the album that might hint at where Zappa and the new Mothers were going next. Although Zappa had on previous albums included live material, *Fillmore East, June 1971* was the first entirely live album of his career (Zappa had included, up to this point, live recordings of individual songs, including the famous version of "Louie Louie" on *Uncle Meat* and "The Nancy and Mary Music" on *Chunga's Revenge*), and he had in fact always planned to release a recording of the infamous 1968 Albert Hall concert, which was finally released in 1993 as *Ahead of Their Time*. Fans who had been accustomed to musical adventurousness and lyrical weirdness with *Uncle Meat* or *Hot Rats* had another thing coming.

There are a number of interesting historical notes about the album. *Fillmore East, June 1971* was recorded in June 1971 on the occasion of the closing of the Fillmore East, the New York version of the venerable Fillmore Ballroom, the San Francisco hippie headquarters that was the place to play in the sixties.[48] Both were owned and booked by Bill Graham, perhaps the most famous promoter of the era. Zappa seems to have admired Graham; more than likely they were kindred souls, both self-made and successful small businessmen. There is another interesting story about the album: Sometime before the day of the show, Zappa was introduced to John Lennon and Yoko Ono, who both ended up performing with the Mothers at that evening's concert.[49] By all accounts, Lennon was a real fan, telling *Village Voice* reporter Howard Smith that Zappa was "at least *trying* to do something different with the form."[50] All in all, the shows at the Fillmore were fraught with meaning and importance. It was, by all accounts, a pretty great set of performances.

The concerts with this particular band (the same band that would be recorded two months later for *Just Another Band from L.A.*) were very different from the shows by the original Mothers of Invention. The new shows were tightly rehearsed, with few variations in set lists from night to night; they were less theatrical and closer to traditional concerts (no costume changes, props, etc.). The singers, along with Zappa, had worked out a number of 30-minute set pieces that would vary from night to night, depending upon what city they were playing in, to incorporate local scenery and / or the adventures of the band members. Ben Watson argues that with these extended set pieces Zappa was drawing attention to the absurdity of the popular rock opera or progressive rock blowout (the Who's *Tommy* or Yes's *Tales from Topographic Oceans*); although it is an interesting argument, these set pieces were less about a critique of *Tommy* than about trying to break away from the Mothers and to continue the arguments Zappa had been making about male privilege and the ridiculousness of people in love.[51] Mark Volman argues that Zappa "created music, during our time with him, specifically designed for us and our capabilities."[52] The music was less theater of the absurd and more vaudeville.

The album begins innocently enough with a hyperactive remake of "The Little House I Used to Live In" from *Burnt Weeny Sandwich,* featuring some interesting vocalizations by Flo & Eddie and showcasing the musical abilities of the (relatively) new band. This song leads into Zappa's extended monologue called "The Mud Shark," a sordid road tale featuring the antics of the band members of the Vanilla Fudge, a band with whom the Mothers had toured.[53] Zappa, it seems, had a bit of a grudge against the Fudge, writing many years later in the liner notes to *You Can't Do That on Stage Anymore, Vol. 1* that many audience members during the Mother's last tour in 1969 "seemed to prefer the dynamic musical stylings of the Vanilla Fudge." The story that he tells on *Fillmore East* is one of utter sexual degradation. It is the first of the songs on the album that take Zappa's revolutionary arguments about sex and sexuality to another level altogether.

In his retelling of the story, Zappa likens the debauchery to a dance that, according to a number of sources, involved the following: "open your legs, clasp your hands together & squat! To do it in 4 / 4 time, step left, step right, squat, rest. All the time you should have your hands together down by the knees."[54] Zappa's glee in this incident is evident: it is an odd story involving fish and groupies and bands he did not admire. In a way, Zappa is able to revel in the strange sexual antics of bands while removing himself from the narrative (in other words, no matter how depraved Zappa's music and band were, the Vanilla Fudge were far worse); it is a great bit of amateur anthropology.

The song is followed by a story that was a bit closer to home. "What Kind of a Girl Do You Think We Are?" is the first part of a multipart story featuring Mark Volman playing a groupie and Howard Kaylan playing a horny pop star. "What Kind of Girl" is interesting, in part, because of the gendered nature of the playlet being performed. This song, as in "Bwana Dik," "Latex Solar Beef," and "Do You Like My New Car?" is about what depths a pop star will sink to in order to score with a groupie. Watson cites these songs as the beginning of "the ambivalent crowd-pleasing which has allowed him to survive twenty years of audience miscomprehension," and certainly these songs are defiantly different from what folks had come to expect.[55] In one sense, after several years of paying attention to music, these songs are filled to the brim with words, many of them dirty.

"What Kind of Girl" is the story of a girl / groupie who will not have sex with a member of the band unless he plays his big hit record. This story line, which is continued in several other songs on the album, says a lot about Zappa's reluctance to give crowds what they wanted or expected. Zappa's primary indictment is about falsity. Both the band members and the groupies are liars, going through an elaborate ritual with a preordained outcome: the girls will have sex with the band members, the band will play its big hit record, and all will be right with the universe. What is false are the lies the various characters tell in the song—to themselves and to each other—about the situation. In the song, which is done with a nice blues vamp, the groupies inform the audience that "Me and my girlfriend, we came here / Lookin' to ball." In other words, they are ready for action, yet by the end of the song they are incensed that anyone would think they are easy, arguing with the band, "what kind of girl do you think we are?" And that "we wouldn't ball you just because you're a star." This kind of duplicity is what Zappa has been fighting since his very first album. He is not, as it might appear, casting a cruel eye on the groupies. Indeed, the argument is easy: Sex is great. Have sex. Feel free to want to have sex. Just admit it! Indeed, perhaps the most honest part of the song is where the female groupie describes the particular sexual fetishes that turn her on. In this Zappa argues that women, just like men, enjoy all sorts of unusual sexual ideas. When the groupies describe what they like, the response from the fake pop star is simply "you two chicks sound really far out and groovy"—hardly a condemnation.

The condemnation comes from the Victorian ideas of sexuality that Zappa is fighting. In his book *The History of Sexuality,* French philosopher of history Michel Foucault argues that before the Victorians, most people "had a tolerant familiarity with the illicit," and that "It was a time of direct gestures, shameless discourse, and open transgressions."[56] Foucault argues that sexual repression is a tool used by those in power to assure the people's silence (thus the church and the government become the biggest censors because they have the most to loose with an enlightened and educated citizenry; if sex is only for procreation then there is a lot more time to work and go to church). Foucault, like Zappa, argues that the only way to free ourselves from the silence of repression will involve "nothing less than a transgression of laws, a lifting of prohibitions, an irruption of speech, a reinstating of pleasure within reality."[57] This refusal to go along is Zappa's vision on the Flo & Eddie albums. The worst thing you can do to sex, Zappa argues, is to not talk about it and to pretend it does not happen.[58]

The idea that sex is not morally bad is one that Zappa would make consistently throughout his career. In the eighties (as will be discussed more fully later), Zappa found himself suddenly thrust into the media spotlight after testifying before Congress about supposedly dirty lyrics. In a letter written to President Ronald Reagan and reprinted in *The Real Frank Zappa Book,* Zappa argued that "If you [Reagan] support the PRMC [the antiporn lyrics group headed, in part, by Tipper Gore] in their efforts to perpetuate the myth that SEX EQUALS SIN, you will help to institutionalize the neurotic misconception that keeps pornographers in business."[59] The real clue to Zappa's critique of morality is contained in a line from his testimony to Congress in September 1985: "Bad facts make bad law, and people who write bad laws are, in my opinion, more dangerous than songwriters who celebrate sexuality."[60] Zappa's is a classic case of the individual fighting against the system. It is about freedom and responsibility against fanaticism and infantilization. Zappa is attempting, even with the silliest and raunchiest of his lyrics on *Fillmore East, June 1971,* to tell people to make up their own minds. If you do not like it, fine. The beauty of capitalism is that you do not have to buy it, do it, or think it.

In the song "Bwana Dik," which follows (and continues) the narrative started on "What Kind of Girl Do You Think We Are," we discover that the name of one of the groupies is Madge. This name, of course, has already appeared in the song "Harry, You're a Beast" and is representative of repressed middle-class sexuality. When the fictitious band member propositions Madge with the enticing come-on "I am endowed beyond your wildest Clearasil-spattered fantasies," Zappa is mocking not only the band member (the shameless bragging about penis size) but the notion, explored countless times before, of how the media helps young people create a fantasy world of idealized relationships. Despite the surface-level supposed filth of the song, it is really a fairly hilarious critique of the way men boast about their sexual accomplishments. We find our succulent pop star bragging to Madge (and, in an indirect way, to the other boys in the band as well as the audience members and listeners) that people "Flock to write my name on the toilet walls of the Whisky A-Go-Go." The title of the song conflates clichéd fifties movie terms and smutty adolescent sexuality (*bwana* is the kind of racist crap that shows up in old Tarzan films), which is just the kind of complex wordplay that interests Zappa. Another interesting idea is the use of the word *monster* to represent unrepressed sexuality. In "Bwana Dik" (and again in the song "Do You Like My New Car?") we learn that one of the band members' "dick is a monster."[61] We find the same terminology being used on "Would You Go All the Way" from *Chunga's Revenge* ("the monster from the U.S.O.").

"Bwana Dik" leads into the song "Latex Solar Beef," which continues the theme of repressed sexuality in a heavy metal setting. The song is a veiled ode to anal sex that quickly devolves into an extended slow instrumental jam based on the musical theme to "Willie the Pimp." Given the theme of the rest of the songs on the album, "Willie the Pimp" seems particularly appropriate.[62]

"Do You Like My New Car?" is the final act of the narrative that started on "What Kind of Girl." In this song, the groupies start by denying that they are going to have sex with the members of the band, claiming that they have told a number of other famous rock stars, including Robert Plant and Roger Daltrey, no and that "we only like musicians for friends." Finally they get down to negotiating the inevitable groupie–rock star sex act. They run through a number of illicit acts (Zappa again exposes the fact that talking about sex never hurt anyone) and finally discover that the groupies will have sex with them if they play their big number-one hit record. The musicians decide to play it. In a moment of delicious irony, the band then breaks into an energetic and faithful version of "Happy Together," a huge number-one hit for Flo & Eddie's previous band, the Turtles.

The album ends with three interesting selections from other parts of the Fillmore East concert, including an excerpted synthesizer solo by Don Preston ("Lonesome Electric Turkey"), a killer version of the *Hot Rats* song "Peaches en Regalia," and a wonderfully upbeat traditional love song sung by Flo & Eddie, "Tears Began to Fall."[63]

In *The Dangerous Kitchen*, Kevin Courrier does a nice job of summarizing the various arguments about *Fillmore East, June 1971,* arguing that it "became a favorite party album among adolescent males who never gave Zappa's other music a moment's notice" while at the same time serving to alienate long time critics.[64]

Despite a lack of appreciation by the critics, the album hit No. 38 on the *Billboard* charts, and no doubt sales were driven by the very adolescent boys that Zappa is critiquing. Contemporary critical reaction is a bit more ambivalent on this album than others. Steve Huey writes that "The humor is often glib and juvenile, marking the beginnings of Frank Zappa's tactic of making complex music more accessible with half-sardonic arena–front-man antics and crowd-pleasing dirty jokes. Whether one considers the results funny and parodic or crass and pandering, the band is undeniably good."[65] *Musichound Rock* ignores it completely and *The New Rolling Stone Album Guide* simply calls it "either lame or silly." In a gushing, yet astute, review on Amazon.com, Bill Holdship argues,

> Zappa was still obsessed with the ridiculous phenomenon of pop stars, and now he had two genuine articles in his band. Thus, in between live renditions of some of his soon-to-be instrumental classics, Zappa, Volman, and Kaylan delighted the Manhattan audience with rude and crude skits about pop stars and groupies. The whole shebang is then climaxed with Flo & Eddie doing a letter-perfect rendition of the Turtles' "Happy Together."[66]

While Zappa and the band were out playing these songs, United Artists was preparing to release Zappa's film *200 Motels,* an extended treatise on the theme the band was already exploring on stage.[67]

The sound track recording to *200 Motels* is as glorious a mess as *Lumpy Gravy* or *Uncle Meat*. It sheds new light on those two albums because it becomes clear after only one listening that Zappa always thought in theatrical terms. *200 Motels* has orchestral music, snippets of dialogue, and songs that move the story forward.

The film, which has been in and out of print over the past several years,[68] was released to mixed critical acclaim. The film was shot in seven days on videotape (with every intention to eventually transfer it to 35 millimeter film) with a half-million dollar budget, and it is a pretty insane piece of film. Starring the Flo & Eddie version of Mothers of Invention, the London Philharmonic Orchestra (looking very out of place and uncomfortable), Keith Moon, Ringo Starr, and Theodore Bikel (a folk singer, activist, and, since 1967, one of the stars of *Fiddler on the Roof*), it is the filmed story of the early years of the Mothers and the insanity of life on the road. (Zappa has commented that 200 was the number of motels the Mothers stayed in while they were touring in 1966–69).

Because this is a book about Zappa's audio recordings, it will not deal directly with the film's narrative. For an interesting argument about the film's importance, see Watson's *The Negative Dialectics of Poodle Play* and Peter Evans's article "Frank Zappa's *200 Motels* and the Theater of the Absurd." Both of these pieces give in-depth analysis of the film's plot.

The sound track album, which was released on the same day as the film, is as interesting a piece of music as Zappa had released up to this point. Shamefully out of print for years, it was finally released by Ryko in the late nineties and immediately went back out of print (it is out of print as of the writing of this book). The first thing the listener notices about the album is that Zappa the orchestral composer has wrested control away, at least for the moment, from Zappa the rock composer. From "Semi-Fraudulent / Direct-from-Hollywood Overture" (which begins the album) to "Strictly Genteel" (which ends it), Zappa's compositional abilities have become much more sophisticated. He seems much more assured of himself. Instead of slipping his compositions in, as he has done on previous albums, he puts his orchestral work front and center. And it is well worth it. The music is creative and challenging. Stravinsky seems to be the biggest influence, making the music recognizable but not boring. In many ways, it can be considered atonal music. It is atonal in the sense that it does not make sense to the person looking for a classical resolution (i.e., it does not come back to where it started, which is the hallmark of tonal sonata form).

The album, more than most, needs to be heard as a series of musical movements. Many of the themes are developed from movement to movement. For instance, "This Town Is a Sealed Tuna Sandwich" contains a prologue, a promenade, a dance, a reprise, and a bolero. Like everything Zappa was doing at the time, he is paying homage to the music he loves, making fun of it, and calling attention to the artificial division between rock and classical (the themes that are developed also move, at times, between rock songs and rock instruments to orchestral instruments and music). Peter Evens argues that Zappa is creating a musical theater of the absurd, writing, "Musical absurdity arises from the juxtaposition of these three opposed musics: classical, modern and rock and their corresponding cinematic images."[69]

Kevin Courrier astutely compares much of the music on the record to that of Kurt Weill and Bertolt Brecht.[70] Weill is especially important in understanding Zappa's musical project. Weill is a significant influence on "art composers interested in pursuing stylistic pluralism, whether this is taken to mean the adoption of popular idioms, the 'crossover' from art to commercial music, or stylistic contrast as a compositional element in its own right."[71] Zappa's musical project on this album, and on several of his albums from the preceding few years, is a specific and serious crossing of genres and a pushing of the boundaries of art and commercial music.

Lyrically, the album continues the themes that Zappa started on *Chunga's Revenge* and *Fillmore East, June 1971:* the desperation of men and their pathetic attempts to get with the ladies while on the road. Unlike other albums, however, Zappa adds a female point of view on a number of songs, including "She Painted up Her Face," "Half a Dozen Provocative Squats," and "Shove It Right In." Like many of his earlier songs, Zappa is arguing for personal responsibility for one's actions; the women in these songs are responsible for their own actions and are, in most of the situations, in control.

In "She Painted up Her Face," we find a woman preparing to go out on the town (perhaps to look for a band member to seduce). As she sits before her mirror she is practicing "The 'secret stare' she would use / If a worthy-looking victim should appear." This puts the power of the sexual situation squarely in the hands of the female. Zappa continues the narrative by describing the particular sexual frustrations of this woman, brought about because the last person she had sex with "got in and got soft." This is not a powerless woman. When the woman finally comes face to face with her so-called victim, in the next song, "Shove It Right In," we see the desperation of both sides of this equation: "Twenty or thirty at times there have been— / Somewhat desirable boys there / Waiting for girls they can shove it right in." As Flo & Eddie sing these words, the music goes from Rock to a much more show-tune-like setting. This is an interesting antipop move (having the pop stars singing about the life of a pop star while singing in a decidedly antipop idiom).

At the same time that we are discovering what the girls want, in "Lonesome Cowboy Burt" and "This Town Is a Sealed Tuna Sandwich," we find out what the boys in the band want, which is, to be blunt, "some hot local action." In the face of the criticism that he has endured, Zappa's argument about sexuality on this album is rather surprising: men are simple and women are complex. The motives of the men on the album are simple: sex, as much as possible, as soon as possible. For the women it is a much more complex relationship.

"This Town Is a Sealed Tuna Sandwich" presents us with the pitfalls of life on the road (much the same as "Road Ladies" from *Chunga's Revenge*): bad food, small towns. There is a snobbish part of Zappa that seemed to think that only New York or L.A. was sophisticated enough. Zappa writes of the folks who live in the small town, "What if part of it's crumbling down? / Most of them prob'ly won't be 'round," which makes the longing to get back home even more poignant. This represents a sort of innocence in which the boys in the band and the girls they meet have a sort of mutual need: the girls are frustrated with their crummy small town and the boys in the band are lonely in the crummy small town. This theme, which would be explored to an even more hilarious end on *Joe's Garage*, is contrasted with the one group who gets left out of the mutual need equation—the local boys, who in "Lonesome Cowboy Burt" see their local girls wander off with whatever pop group happens to come through town at the time.

In many ways, "Lonesome Cowboy Burt" is the story of the loser local boys (it is also Zappa's attack on the various local white boys he had to endure as a youth in Baltimore and as an adolescent in Southern California). Musically, the song is a farcical parody of country and western music, something Zappa had not done much of but would do with increasing frequency in the future. Lyrically, the song attacks many of Zappa's favorite targets: the white male who feels girls are just dying to be with him, the lazy union member, and the smelly person.

Critics pick on the song because of its fake country musical setting. Kevin Courrier, for instance, is somewhat critical of the song, arguing that "Zappa didn't have many blind spots, but when it came to country music (or as he called it 'cowboy music')...Zappa failed to recognize that not all country singers, or country fans, were rednecks out to kill hippies," but I am not sure where in a reading of the song Courrier gets this.[72] The song is an indictment, like many of Zappa's songs, of a certain kind of person. The character of Burt is proud of his redneck past, singing, "My name is Burtram / I am a redneck" and that he and his family "Make their livin' diggin' dirt." What Zappa is critiquing is the pride that Burtram evidently feels in being a redneck, the idea that a person would refuse to better himself or herself is something that Zappa could never understand. If Zappa is intolerant of anything, it is an intolerance born of being a self-made and self-employed person. Burtram is anything but. We find out in the next verse that he has come to California simply to meet pretty girls and wants to be with the girls so badly that he will even pay or buy them things, including furs. He gets the money to buy these women because he is a "Roofer by trade" and that instead of doing a great job at work, he belongs to a union that protects him, thus giving him all the more time to work on picking up girls. The connection between the corrupt system of the union and the laziness of Burtram (instead of earning a woman, he simply buys them with his ill-gotten gains) is the real indictment the song makes.

The second act of the sound track becomes much more self-referential, dealing in part with bass player Jeff Simmons's desire to leave the band because he did not want to play Zappa's so-called comedy music, and in part because of the contradictions and conflicts that Zappa seemed to feel about his own career. Zappa seems to be playing out, in public, his own internal conflict between writing and playing serious music and being an entertainer. In an insightful bit of self-reflexivity, Zappa presents himself as a wildly controlling figure, something that someone with less self-confidence might deny. There are several places in the film script and on the album where Zappa is simply referred to as "He" or "Him." Ben Watson finds this to be a significant part of the project, arguing that *200 Motels* is an exploration of "the artist as all powerful mediator, shaping reality like God."[73] It is a theme that Zappa would return to in *Joe's Garage* and *Thing Fish*, but I think too much can be made out of the control freak argument. In many ways Zappa is satirizing his own public image as a hard person to work for (the recordings of his band members complaining about how little they were being paid by Zappa on *Uncle Meat* seem to be working this same vein). The character of the Central Scrutinizer in *Joe's Garage,* which is Zappa's most obvious controlling entity, is much more indicative of Zappa's growing feeling of unease at the government's regulation of art and artists than it is a comment on his own public image, which is a very different critique from the one being posed in *200 Motels*.[74] The sound track ends with Howard Kaylan telling the audience, "He's making me do this, ladies and gentlemen. I wouldn't do it if it weren't for him...HE is over there. HE is over on the left. HE is the guy that is making me do all this shit." In some ways Zappa seems to be presenting himself as the mad scientist (à la the science fiction films of his youth) or the puppeteer pulling all of the strings. There is some irony to this, of course, because of the powerlessness Zappa felt in the face of the record companies, film studios, orchestras, and unions that he had been fighting. Zappa was a control freak who had, outside of his band and band members, very little control.

200 Motels made it to No. 59 on the *Billboard* chart and provided a number of songs that many of Zappa's bands would play, as well as several pieces that Zappa would refine for orchestral compositions.[75] The fact that it went in and out of print so quickly has made it a more marginal album than many in Zappa's catalog. Contemporary critics have been overwhelmingly unkind. This is due, in part, to the album being a sound track, which makes the narrative a bit less linear than some might like. Songs seem to be included to advance a narrative that, without access to the film, the listener can not understand. There is also a significantly larger amount of orchestral music that may well drive off some rock fans. Neither *Musichound Rock* nor *The New Rolling Stone Album Guide* even bother to mention the album. The All

Music Guide calls it "peripheral entry in his discography."[76] Amazon.com has some interesting thoughts about the record, writing that the record is:

> Essentially a filmed dadaist opera…*200 Motels* incorporates sporadic patches of Mothers of Inventions rock into the atonal, largely European, musical framework that Zappa was clearly more interested in. He shrewdly used contemporary pop merely as a marketing shill for the complex, often difficult, music that drove him.[77]

None of these reviews attempts to understand how the album fits into Zappa's larger critical project. There is, in many of the reviews, talk of the decline of Zappa's humor or the overall wackiness of the lyrics.

200 Motels, both the film and the sound track, were released on October 29, 1971. In many ways it sums up 1971, a huge year in terms of musical output but an incredibly difficult year in terms of career. Things got off to a bad start in February when, to coincide with the ending of filming of *200 Motels,* Zappa had booked the Royal Albert Hall in London to perform selections from *200 Motels* with the Mothers and the Royal Philharmonic. At the last minute, and at a huge cost, the manager of Albert Hall canceled the show, costing Zappa thousands of dollars.[78] In November and December, in support of the release of *200 Motels,* the Mothers toured throughout Europe. On December 4 the Mothers were playing in Geneva when, toward the end of the concert, the concert hall caught fire and burned down.[79] Although Zappa was in favor of ending the tour right there and returning to the United States for the holidays, the rest of the band voted to go on (in order to make some final cash). At the next concert, at the Rainbow theater in London, Zappa was pushed off the stage into the orchestra pit by an audience member. It took him the better part of the next year and half to recover.[80]

As a stopgap move to buy some time for new music, Zappa released *Just Another Band from L.A.* in March 1972. It is a recording of the same band from the *Fillmore East, June 1971* lineup recorded two months later.[81] The album only contains three new songs: "Billy the Mountain," "Eddie, Are You Kidding?" and "Magdalena." It also contains a couple of early Mothers of Invention songs: "Call Any Vegetable" and "Dog Breath." The album is nonetheless important for a number of reasons. It shows that the Flo & Eddie version of the Mothers was able to pull off the early Mothers music with a great deal of passion and fun; it also shows that Zappa, along with Howard Kaylan and Mark Volman, were perhaps more interested in commenting upon the current political scene than they have been given credit for.

"Billy the Mountain" is an incredible song—a huge, rambling piece of progressive rock theater filled with inside jokes, improvisations, musical quotations, and all-around hilarity.

The main narrative of the song is a nonsensical story about a mountain named Billy who is given a huge royalty check for all of the postcards that have his picture on it. Upon receiving his check, Billy and his girlfriend Ethel head off on vacation, which seems to be going well until Billy receives his induction notice and Ethel is outed as a Communist and practitioner of witchcraft. Billy and Ethel are confronted by the newest superhero in the United States, Studebaker Hoch.

The interesting part of the song is what happens when you look behind the narrative. The song attacks the draft, right-wing media commentators, religion, the establishment, the royalty system, and the cheesiness of the previous generation (signified by the repeated quotation of the "Theme from the *Tonight Show,*" which was one of the more recognizable pieces of swing / jazz music in the United States at the time). Other musical quotes include "Suite: Judy Blue Eyes" by Crosby, Stills, and Nash, "Pomp and Circumstance" (the music most often played at high school and college graduations), "The Star-Spangled Banner," "Somewhere over the Rainbow," "Off We Go into the Wild Blue Yonder," and "Oh, Mein Papa." Each of these musical cues sends the listener off into his or her own particular set of connections. What makes the musical allusions in "Billy the Mountain" so interesting is that every person who hears the different musical quotations and cues is going to have a different, unique, and individual set of experiences to relate to these allusions. Take, for instance, the way in which the "Theme from the *Tonight Show*" is fraught with meaning; different audiences will relate differently to it, depending upon age, location, agreement as to the relative hipness of the show, and so forth. There are two extant recordings of "Billy the Mountain," one from Los Angeles (on *Just Another Band from L.A.*) and one from New York (on *Playground Psychotics*). It is interesting to hear to which musical cues each audience reacts. "Theme from the *Tonight Show*" is greeted with applause in the New York version and with ambivalence from the L.A. crowd. In 1972, the *Tonight Show* was still produced in New York and was identified closely with that city.

The song also features numerous references to local Los Angeles stores, streets, and suburbs within the Inland Empire (i.e., the cities not on the beach). These, as you might imagine, are met with silence by the New York crowd and with applause by the Los Angeles crowd.

The song has become, in many ways, a Rorschach test for critics. Barry Miles claims that the song is about "the great cultural wasteland of the Californian suburbs,"[82] whereas Watson claims that it is about "the importance of trivia."[83] Kevin Courrier calls it "filled with the kind of in-jokes a person from Southern California would understand."[84] Although it is indeed filled with references to towns in Southern California, it is also a pop cultural mélange, with references to Howard Johnson's restaurants (including a hilarious clam reference, which refers to the all-you-can-eat clam special at most HoJo's); references to Las Vegas, New York, and Columbus, Ohio; the draft; old movie clichés; *The Wizard of Oz;* and Aunt Jemima syrup, to name just a few. It is a quick survey of the cultural detritus of the early seventies.

The rest of the album continues in this vein, with "Eddie, Are You Kidding" and "Magdalena" also referencing a number of current cultural events. "Magdalena" is a rare coauthored piece credited to Kaylan/Zappa. It is a supposedly true story of a father who molests his daughter. It seems to be a Kaylan attempt at Zappa journalism. Halfway through the song, it takes a savage and sad turn as Kaylan discusses all of the things that he would like to do to Magdalena. Although Zappa is once again blaming bad parenting for the way that some women act (this same theme would be explored again in "Wet T-Shirt Contest" on *Joe's Garage*), the long spoken section from Kaylan is far more vulgar and far less metaphorical than some of his other work with the band.

"Eddie, Are You Kidding" is a hilarious takeoff on a local Los Angeles menswear advertisement. The main theme of the song is the lies that this advertisement was spreading about Eddie's ability to fit anyone into a suit that looks great. Like the other songs on the album, it pales in comparison to "Billy the Mountain."

The album has an odd place in the Zappa canon. Francois Couture sums up much of the contemporary response, writing, "Fans of the Flo & Eddie period will love the improvised storyline developments. Others should approach with caution, even though this one has much better sound quality than *Fillmore East, June 1971*."[85] *The New Rolling Stone Album Guide* calls the album "either lame or silly," whereas Amazon.com ignores it completely. In many ways it is a completist's album. *Fillmore East* is the hilarious album with all the sex and groupie jokes; *Chunga's Revenge* is the studio album; *200 Motels* is the opera. *Just Another Band from L.A.* has "Billy the Mountain," better recording and producing, and a tighter band. That is it.

These four albums, which represent an incredibly fertile and active period for Zappa, also make for a clean break with the old/original Mothers. With Zappa's accident and forced recovery, the Flo & Eddie years would come to an end as well (and although they would talk about getting back together occasionally, even going so far as rehearsing together for the 1988 tour, they would not tour or record together again).

WAKA/JAWAKA AND *THE GRAND WAZOO*

Healing and the Retreat into Jazz/Rock. *Waka/Jawaka* (originally released on the Bizarre/Reprise label in July 1972; currently available as Rykodisc RCD 10516). Highest *Billboard* chart position: No. 152.

The Grand Wazoo (originally released on the Bizarre/Reprise label in November 1972; currently available as Rykodisc RCD 10517).[86] Highest Billboard chart position: unavailable/did not chart. "It was time to take stock of the situation."[87]

After the excesses of the Flo & Eddie years, where does one go? In a strange way, it is the same dilemma that classical music faced at the turn of the century.

Classical music had become more and more extravagant, reaching its excessive peak with Gustav Mahler's *Symphony Number Eight,* better known as the "Symphony of a Thousand" (the number of people it took to perform it properly). After Mahler, there was really no place to go but away from the excesses of late romanticism. What came next, of course, was the move toward minimalism, atonality, serial music, and the avant-garde.

For Zappa, the enforced vacation brought about by the attack on stage in London and subsequent hospitalization in England forced him to examine where his music had been and where it might go. Although he would continue to have fun on stage and continue to write biting and satirical social criticism, his whole act toned down a bit. He would place a much higher premium, both on his records and in his stage shows, upon musicianship and ability. There would be fewer and fewer sacrifices in his compositions toward comedy.

The two albums recorded while he was still in a cast and a wheelchair, *Waka/Jawaka* and *The Grand Wazoo,* are wonderful curveballs in light of what audiences had come to expect from Zappa. Both albums are essentially big band/jazz fusion albums, and both show an increasing amount of technical, musical, and compositional sophistication.

Waka/Jawaka (often referred to as *Hot Rats II*) is an interesting studio construction. Unlike *The Grand Wazoo,* it was recorded with a small band that was then overdubbed and edited until it sounded like a band far bigger than it actually was. Sal Marquez is the only trumpet player on the album and yet the album is recorded so that it sounds like there are many different players. Marquez played an important role on both records, working with Zappa as an arranger of the intricate horn charts and filling, in many ways, the role that Ian Underwood had been playing for Zappa as ace wind instrument player (that said, there were other wind players on the albums, including trombones, saxes, etc.).

Most critics cite Miles Davis as the main inspiration for both albums. Barry Miles claims that while Zappa was in the hospital he "had clearly been listening to a lot of jazz fusion."[88] Watson compares both albums, somewhat unfavorably, to Miles Davis's *Bitches' Brew,* whereas Courrier writes that "Big Swifty," the song that opens *Waka/Jawaka* is "a flurry of electronic jazz that resembles some of Miles Davis' early-'70s experiments."[89] There is defiantly a more sophisticated sound on these albums; if *Hot Rats* errs on the side of rock, then *Waka/Jawaka* and *The Grand Wazoo* err on the side of jazz.

"Big Swifty," the song that kicks off the album, is a fine piece of fusion that would not sound out of place on a Phish or Dave Matthews Band album. It is a relaxed, groove-oriented piece with an intricate horn chart that ends up being a rocking guitar duel between Zappa and slide guitarist Tony Duran. For an indication of how Zappa was thinking about the song later in his life, listen to the version on *Make a Jazz Noise Here,* which strips most of the rock out of the song and replaces it with a number of clichéd jazz moves, including lounge piano and a muted trumpet solo and quotations from a number of recognizable classical pieces, including *1812 Overture* and *Carmen*.

The next song on the album, "Your Mouth," is an interesting piece of faux blues that plays on a number of the standard blues clichés, especially the "woman done me wrong" kind. The song starts in an interesting enough manner, arguing that "Your mouth is your religion / You put your faith in a hole like that?" This premise, however, mutates into a more standard (and, for a Zappa song, surprisingly violent) blues lyric.[90] This song segues into "It Just Might Be a One-Shot Deal," a fairly legitimate piece of country-swing / jazz. Courrier remarks that it is one of Zappa's few country-type songs that does not involve a put-down of people who listen to country music. It is an interesting song with an excellent pedal steel guitar solo. The lyrics are nonsensical, having to do with a frog and a forest.

The final song on the album is the title piece, "Waka / Jawaka," another big band fusion blowout, featuring excellent solos by Don Preston (synthesizer) and Aynsley Dunbar (drums).

The album marks a new seriousness for Zappa; on his previous albums, even his most experimental works, *Lumpy Gravy* and *Uncle Meat*, Zappa leavened the seriousness with humorous pieces, sometimes in song form and sometimes as dialogue. On *Waka / Jawaka* it is as if Zappa had taken stock of himself and realized that the part of his life that the original Mothers and the Flo & Eddie Mothers represented was over and that it was time to get into something new. Although Zappa would return to often side-splittingly funny songwriting in the future, the high hilarity and anything-goes abandon of the first several years was over.

The trend toward serious musicianship continues on *The Grand Wazoo*. This album is a much more accomplished piece of jazz / art-rock fusion than was *Waka / Jawaka* and really reflects Zappa's growth as a composer and arranger. Where *Waka / Jawaka* had a lot of *Hot Rats* in it, *The Grand Wazoo* is a much more fully realized and original piece of work. There is, for the first time in a while, a real sense of musical adventurousness (something that seemed to be largely missing in the Flo & Eddie years).

The Grand Wazoo is an album that both fans and critics tend to agree on as well. French critic Dominique Chevalier calls it "one of the most essential LPs in the whole Zappa catalogue,"[91] whereas Watson, Miles, and Courrier all seem to agree that its craftsmanship is far superior to *Waka / Jawaka*'s.

One unusual feature of this album is the complex story that Zappa included in the liner notes (something Zappa had not done since *Uncle Meat*). The story, titled "The Legend of Cletus Awreetus-Awrightus & the Grand Wazoo" describes the trials and tribulations of Cletus and his "army of unemployed musicians." In the story, Zappa is having some not-so-gentle fun with the state of the music business, claiming that Cletus's arch enemy was Mediocrates of Pedestrium and that the battles between Cletus and Mediocrates were held every Monday, with results being posted in "stone tablets called the charts."

uch. His quest for commercial success seems to be made
s unwillingness to write more commercial music. "Blessed
Zappa could, if he wanted to, write completely accessible
s a lovely piece of jazz that seems to be informed as much
i and Burt Bacharach than it does by Zappa's avant-garde
eroes (I will admit that the first time I heard it I thought it
d track to the film *The Odd Couple,* a very late-sixties piece).
eat through melody that resolves itself and a very laid back
on a clear, effects-free guitar.

ne make of these two albums? They were, compared with
albums, different. They showed, at least in the case of *The*
me real compositional development. But sandwiched as they
Flo & Eddie years and the "Yellow Snow" years, they seem
for fair-weather fans, somewhat forgotten.

ral, tend to be kinder to these albums than they are to the
Rolling Stone calls *Waka/Jawaka* and *The Grand Wazoo* "an
of Mothers-less albums,"[93] whereas Francois Couture calls
hostly "filler," and *The Grand Wazoo* "essential for anyone
pa's instrumental works."[94] Andrew Boscardan calls *Waka/*
the most eclectic releases of Frank Zappa's hyper-eclectic
h damns it with faint praise: "this stew of diverse musical ele-
the diehard fan and anyone with a taste for the unusual."[95]
rand Wazoo alone.

ne these albums will climb to their deserved place in the
. It is tough for a satirist to play it straight, as Zappa was
lbums, and make serious, complicated music. In many ways,
h these albums to have a career that is much more in com-
of Leonard Bernstein than one might think. Bernstein, who
self as a composer first, musician second, and conductor last,
ould only really make money conducting and spent much of
il because he was thought of as a conductor and composer
nstead of a serious composer of orchestral music. Especially
in his career onward, Zappa, too, seems caught in this bind;
ate more serious music, whereas his fans are screaming for
ies.[96]

The Grand Wazoo is, in the
to the people, although it
sort of funny-hat-wearing p
(close in some ways to a libr
the songs. In fact, the first s
of the libretto, in which Zap
their turf by marching to a r

The album begins with th
mentioned blues / jazz shuffl
soon becomes a stinging ele
It is a 13-minute excuse for e
what-out-of-place synthesizer
most fully realized soloing a
Dunbar.

"For Calvin (and His Next
semitrue story told to Zappa
about two hippie hitchhikers
and who would not leave eve
with vocals on the album, incl
when did they come from," alt
featuring an extended woodwi
orchestral music than jazz.

"Cleetus Awreetus Awrightu
romp that Courrier aptly calls "
composer for many of the classic
Bunny" and "Road Runner"] ar
some interesting piano work, a ti
the end, "par rump pa pa pum
ing "The Little Drummer Boy,'
Christmas special made by the sa
Rudolph the Red-Nosed Reindee
time). Zappa, who has quoted fr
to be mocking the optimistic and

"Cleetus" is followed by "Eat T
nally titled "Eat That Christian," i
electric piano playing, Zappa's gu
driven solo), and one of Zappa's b
in the outro in which the horns are
music that is at the same time mart

The album ends with another on
"Blessed Relief." It is a mystery as t
of melody and such an ability to w
Umbrellas," "Twenty Small Cigar
melon in Easter Hay," or "Sexual H

kind of music so
much harder by h
Relief" shows tha
music. The song i
by Henry Mancin
jazz and classical l
was part of a soun
The song has a g
solo from Zappa

So what does
the previous four
Grand Wazoo, so
are between the
to be slight and,

Critics, in gen
three previous—
impressive clutch
Waka / Jawaka
interested in Za
Jawaka "one o
career," and ther
ments is best fo
He leaves *The G*

Perhaps in ti
Zappa pantheon
doing on these
Zappa begins o
mon with that
thought of him
found that he
his life in turm
of show tunes
from this point
he wants to cr
stories of grou

The Duke-Brock/Progressive Rock Bands, *Läther,* and the Terry Bozzio Albums

OVER-NITE SENSATION AND APOSTROPHE (')

Zappa at the Crossroads. *Over-Nite Sensation* (originally released in September 1973 on the DiscReet label; currently available as Rykodisc RCD 10518). Highest *Billboard* Chart position: No. 32. Personnel: Ralph Humphrey, Sal Marquez, George Duke, Tom Fowler, Bruce Fowler, Ian Underwood, Ruth Underwood, and Jean-Luc Ponty.

Apostrophe (') (originally released in March 1974 on the DiscReet label; currently available as Rykodisc RCD 10501).[1] Highest *Billboard* chart position: No. 10. Personnel: Same as on *Over-Nite* plus Jim Gordon, John Guerin, Aynsley Dunbar, Jack Bruce, Sugar Cane Harris, Napoleon Murphy Brock, Tony Duran, and many backup singers, including an uncredited Tina Turner. "Despite the mumblings of the hippies-who-refuse-to-die, Zappa's 'alternative rock' phase finished because that possibility died in the real world."[2]

There are two albums that stand at the center (literally, if not figuratively) of Zappa's career: *Over-Nite Sensation* and *Apostrophe (')*. *Over-Nite*, originally released in September 1973, was Zappa's definitive move away from any relationship with the Mothers of Invention. The argument the album makes is that Zappa could do the kind of satirical rock he had been doing with both early versions of the Mothers with far better musicians. Coming quickly on *Over-Nite*'s heels, in April 1974, *Apostrophe (')* was responsible for moving Zappa out of cult status and into the bedrooms and living rooms of middle America. In some measure, these are both, difficult albums to essay, in large part because of their popularity. Zappa's countercultural credentials are seriously called into question by records rife with melody, relatively short songs, and lyrics that wander from silly to, in the case of "Don't Eat the Yellow

Snow," novelty. Watson, for one, agrees, arguing that "*Overnite Sensation,* in all its neon-lit brashness, was an atrocity committed on a counter-culture now revealed as hypocritical and collusive."[3] It was Zappa, of course, who revealed this. Both of these albums have proved to be troubling to fans and critics alike, yet they are, at the same time, responsible for bringing a large number of new fans into the Zappa camp.[4]

The two albums set the tone for a number of albums to come (especially the next two, *Roxy & Elsewhere* and *One Size Fits All*): a wide variety of styles (rock, reggae, jazz, and a sort of "American Popular Song format")[5] and an expanded cast of musicians, including former Mother Ray Collins, new Mother Napoleon Murphy Brock, and one bona fide superstar (Jack Bruce, late of the supergroup Cream), working on songs that were from a number of eras (some dating back as far as *Hot Rats*). The music (individual songs will be discussed later) is, in general, far more accessible than fans had come to expect. Both albums are certainly informed by jazz ideas, but they are much closer to contemporary pop / rock albums than Zappa's several previous albums. The two albums previous to *Over-Nite, Waka / Jawaka* and *The Grand Wazoo,* were both largely instrumental jazz / rock fusion albums featuring large ensembles (20 members in the case of *The Grand Wazoo*), and because of an injury Zappa had sustained during the 1971 tour (Zappa was pushed off the stage at the Rainbow Theater in London and suffered broken ribs as well as wrist and ankle injures that took more than six months to heal),[6] "the focus was more on Zappa's skills as a composer and arranger" than on his skills as a singer and guitarist.[7] *Over-Nite* and *Apostrophe (')* are important, therefore, as a return to Mothers of Invention form and as close to traditional pop albums as Zappa would ever come.

Critical reception at the time was, in general, mixed. *Rolling Stone* disliked *Over-Nite* quite a bit, taking the stance, shared with a number of fans, that Zappa had done his best work with the Mothers and was now a "spent force."[8] *New Music Express* called *Over-Nite* "Not one of Frank's most outstanding efforts."[9] Both seemed to like *Apostrophe (')*; many, including *Melody Maker* and *Crawdaddy,* found both albums too commercial.[10] Contemporary reevaluation has not been so kind. *The New Rolling Stone Album Guide* lumps them together in a 1992 review and declares that both records are "squawking, predictable, and only desperately 'hilarious',"[11] whereas *Musichound Rock* ignores *Over-Nite* and "evaluates" *Apostrophe (')* by mentioning that it was Zappa's best-selling album. Steve Huey, writing for the *All Music Guide* Web site argues, "Love it or hate it, *Over-Nite Sensation* was a watershed album for Frank Zappa, the point where his post-'60s aesthetic was truly established"[12] and that on *Apostrophe (')* the "dirty jokes are generally more subtle and veiled."[13] Out of 43 reviews posted to Amazon.com, only two are negative, and several cite the *Over-Nite* as Zappa's best work ever.

For all of its other merits (many of which are discussed later), *Over-Nite Sensation* and *Apostrophe (')* will be forever known as the sex albums. *Over-Nite* contains a number of songs that would be performed by nearly all of Zappa's bands: "Dinah-Moe-Hum," "Cosmik Debris," "Camarillo Brillo," "Dirty Love," and "I'm the Slime." All became concert favorites. *Apostrophe (')* became even better known, largely on the back of "Don't Eat the Yellow Snow," "Cosmik Debris," and "Stink Foot. Two of the songs on the album, "Dinah-Moe-Hum" and "Dirty Love," certainly became two of Zappa's more controversial songs.

Musically, "Dinah-Moe-Hum" is a very interesting attempt at writing a pop song by someone apparently uninterested in the form. The song is filled with a number of musical clichés, including what Zappa called *artificial cowboy* style; there are also elements of gospel and rock in the song. The music is written in order to not get in the way of the words.[14] (The background of this and many of Zappa's more overtly funny songs features a stock electric piano sound that apes the kind of ubiquitous Nashville studio sound prevalent in many early seventies middle-of-the-road country tunes; this is carried farthest in the song "Truck Driver Divorce" from the album *Them or Us*). In *The Real Frank Zappa Book,* Zappa argues that this kind of background (unobtrusive or full of obvious musical jokes) is a sign that he thinks the characters or subjects of the song are doing something stupid.

The song begins with a burbling guitar riff (similar, in some respects, to the sound Heart would make famous in "Barracuda") and becomes more complex, featuring rapid and unexpected tone and tempo changes and some challenging keyboard and percussion work. The center section of the song, which features a spoken-word narrative by Zappa, sees the music transform into the kind of background music one might hear underneath the action sequence in a cheesy seventies television show or porn movie.

There are a number of ways to view this song: as a cheap shot (one of many Zappa would take) at ideological posturing (in this case the sort of privileged, white, middle-class feminism that he would attack again and again); as a song about the arrogance and ineptitude of men; as a mean and defensive attack on women's liberation; or as, simply, a product of its time.

The narrative is fairly straightforward: a woman offers the narrator $40 if he can make Dinah-Moe hum. The narrator accepts and proceeds to apply all manner of erotic techniques to Dinah-Moe and is not successful, even after three hours of work. Taken this way (as a linear narrative), the song is somewhat juvenile (and there are a lot of lame, potty-mouthed sex jokes in the song), but a close analysis of some of the lyrics shows us that even in this silliest of songs, Zappa is offering a strong and potentially misunderstood critique of U.S. sexual mores.

The lines "I got a spot that gets me hot/but you ain't been to it" seem clearly to be a reference to the burgeoning feminist movement; 1973, the year the song "Dinah-Moe-Hum" was written, also marks the first publication of *Our Bodies, Ourselves.* Although these lines are silly, they also seem to represent the challenge that women's sexuality was presenting to men. The strongest challenge to a patriarchal society, as many feminist theorists have argued, is a strong female sexuality, one that demands of men the same thing that men had been demanding of women since the beginning of time. This argument is made more complex by what immediately follows: "Just get me wasted...then my body don't care." There are two fairly obvious readings of this. The first is of the frat-boy just-get-her-drunk" variety. The second, however, is a more difficult leap to make: that Zappa, through the construction of this character, is making a statement about drugs and sexuality (in other words, by making the female character rather foolish, he can make her argument about needing to be chemically altered to enjoy sex a bad thing). This verse is also consistent with Zappa's strong antidrug stance. Another, more interesting (and more traditionally second-generation feminist) reading of these lines, of course, is that the song argues that men are so crude and ill-equipped sexually (and / or were so sexually unenlightened at the time) that a woman had no real choice but to divorce her mind from her body in order to gain even a small amount of pleasure.

The song goes on and degenerates into a fairly odd tale of voyeurism, masturbation, dominance and submission, and, finally, sexual satisfaction for Dinah-Moe. The point in all of this, I feel, is that Zappa is making an argument, one he made before and one he would make until the end of his life, that Americans carry with them, because of their Puritan heritage, an odd tendency to both like and hate sex at the same time and that white, middle-class men are prone to stupidity and selfishness when it comes to sexual gratification (the narrator, it must be said, does work very hard to make sure that Dinah-Moe reaches orgasm).

I am not willing, completely, to buy Zappa's argument that he is just telling the truth or just trying to entertain; however, I do think that it is unfair to view a song like "Dinah-Moe-Hum" through the lens of early-twenty-first-century morality; things were different in 1973, and that, in many ways, is what Zappa is arguing.

The other song on the album that is overtly about sex is "Dirty Love," one in a long line of Zappa songs that supposedly exposes the hypocrisy of love songs. Musically, this song is as straightforward as Zappa's writing gets: no rapid shifts in meter, tone, or style, just straight-ahead blues / jazz riffing with a short and tonal guitar solo during the break. In his autobiography, Zappa discusses this idea that lead him to write a song like this, arguing that traditional love songs are fundamentally dishonest (see previous discussion).

In many ways, "Dirty Love" embodies this philosophy.[15] Lyrics such as "I don't need your sweet devotion / I don't want your cheep emotion" are direct and to the point. Much like "Dinah-Moe-Hum," however, "Dirty Love" strays in the end, in this case into a sordid tale of bestiality, for no other reason than it fascinated Zappa.[16]

There are a number of interesting interpretations of this song by Zappa's critics. David Walley calls it "your basic ditty about road mania and lust with some Dada poodle business thrown in."[17] Barry Miles writes:

> In "Dirty Love" the narrator encounters a groupie whom he treats entirely as a
> sex object.... For Zappa, that was all there was to sex: as long as everyone had
> an orgasm, everything was all right. "Dirty Love" concludes with [a] young
> woman having sex with her poodle. It probably never occurred to Zappa that
> this description of bestiality might offend people.[18]

Continuing on the poodle theme, Neil Slaven writes, "Dirty Love was less
graphic [than 'Dinah-Moe-Hum'] but how explicit do you need to be when
you write a song about a woman receiving oral gratification from a poodle?"
Slaven then quotes Zappa as defending himself by arguing "Poodles serve as
a convenient mechanism for conveying certain philosophical ideas that might
otherwise be more difficult."[19] Although Zappa never describes what these
certain philosophical ideas might be, one can make an educated guess that it
was sexual repression.

I would like to argue that the song is not an endorsement of bestiality but
an example of what James Wood calls "the comedy of correctness." In his
argument, Woods argues that this oldest form of comedy was "written to
prove how repetitively stupid we all are, by a writer whose comedy is often
cruel [and] who was obsessed with the folly and vices of bourgeois idiocy."[20]
This is Zappa in a nutshell. If one looks, the characters of whom Zappa is
most critical—politicians, televangelists, priests, Jewish American Princesses,
groupies, the members of his own band—one finds that there is a definite
target that Zappa continually hits: the overinflated sense of ownership of the
white, middle-class American. Looked at in this way, in the context of the
time and through the framework of Zappa's ongoing project of social critique, "Dinah-Moe-Hum" and "Dirty Love" can be seen, perhaps, as simply
parts of a larger, lifelong project of social critique.

The two songs on the album that are most overtly political are "Camarillo
Brillo" and "I'm the Slime." Both of these songs seem to target what Zappa
thought were the excesses of the early seventies. In "I'm the Slime," Zappa
makes the argument that television is "gross and perverted," yet at the same
time is "the tool of the government / and industry too." In many ways, this
is Zappa's double critique of both the entertainment industry and the people
who support the television industry. Zappa is on the record in a number of
places about thinking that making an industry out of entertainment is the
worst kind of capitalist impulse. This is a simplistic and problematic argument, of course, because at times Zappa comes off looking as if he is merely
jealous that his art is not making the kind of money the Beatles or Beach
Boys were making. Perhaps this is the tension between being self-conscious
and uncompromising. The only thing worse than creating art that only a few
people enjoy, of course, is knowing it.[21]

Musically, "I'm the Slime" has a lot going on. The introduction makes the
listener believe that he or is hearing a true jazz / rock workout. Starting with
a solo guitar, drums, and keyboards, the song quickly segues into a keyboard

and brass theme (much like something Chicago, Three Dog Night, or Earth, Wind & Fire might have been doing at the same time) that builds to a climax in less than a minute. The song then radically shifts; the music becomes background music for Zappa's spoken-word discussion (much as it does in "Dirty Love" and "Dinah-Moe-Hum"), returning to the big jazz / rock theme for the chorus (featuring an uncredited appearance by Tina Turner and the Ikettes) and a blazing and bluesy out-solo that runs until the end-of-song fade.

Lyrically, "I'm the Slime" retreads much of the ground first covered with "Trouble Every Day" (which would be rerecorded in 1974 as "More Trouble Every Day"). Zappa sings, "I am gross and perverted / . . . I am destined to rule / And regulate you." His increasing anger at what he saw as the collusion of the government and the entertainment industry (an argument to warm the hearts of Marxists and postmodernists everywhere) would show up more and more on future albums.

Both musically and thematically, the most interesting song on the album is "Camarillo Brillo," one of the few pop songs in the Zappa catalog written in an understandable idiom (all major-chord changes and grand piano flourishes). Musically, the song avoids some of the excesses that mar even the best of Zappa's work. There are very few odd time signatures or shifts in tone, meter, or style, and the musicians play together instead of against each other (as they seem to be doing in many of Zappa's other songs).[22] Production-wise, it is reminiscent of early-seventies Allman Brothers or Black Oak Arkansas. If not for the questionable subject matter, the song would have been right at home on the radio; it is catchy and memorable.

Thematically, it is a cold shot at the sort of hippie mysticism that Zappa had been attacking since "Who Needs the Peace Corps?" The narrator of the story meets up with a woman who has a "Camarillo Brillo," which, I am apt to believe, is a sort of white Afro, the kind of hairstyle that a middle-class woman who was attempting to be "down with the struggle" might have worn. The narrator informs us that this woman thinks of herself as a "magic mama" and is someone who could "throw a mean tarot"; her room has an "incense stencher" where she "hung her castanets." All of these are signs that the woman in the song is putting on her street credentials as affectation. Perhaps the most damning accusation against her (one that would return on the next album in the song "Cosmik Debris") is the narrator's question: "is that a real poncho or a sears poncho," which returns to one of Zappa's favorite themes: the fakeness of the counterculture. Although the woman in "Camarillo Brillo" would go ahead and have sex with the narrator, her reasons for doing so are questionable.

The remaining songs on the album include concert favorites "Zomby Woof" and "Montana" as well as the interesting blues workout "Fifty-Fifty." "Zomby Woof" is an incredibly difficult piece of music that shows off the vastly increased technical proficiency of this edition of the Mothers. Courrier calls it a "heavy metal hybrid of Louis Jordan and Fats Waller,"[23] as good a description as exists. Lyrically, it continues Zappa's obsession with cheesy fifties horror film references, this time neatly juxtaposing them with a story of morning-after regret.

"Fifty-Fifty" is the forgotten cut on the album. Sung by Ricky Lancelotti, who would be dropped from the band almost immediately after performing on this song, it is a vaguely blues-based workout that returns to the theme of the uselessness of love songs: "Ain't gonna sing you no love song / How my heart is all sore . . . 'Cause you heard it before." The song features, among other things, some wild soloing by George Duke, Jean Luc Ponty, and Zappa on guitar.

The album closes with the song "Montana,"[24] more of an exercise in pure parody and silliness (with a great guitar solo) than a political statement. Zappa's ode to dental floss is hilarious and memorable.

Coming quickly on the heels of *Over-Nite Sensation*, *Apostrophe (')* brought Zappa the kind of fame he had been nearly missing for the previous 10 years. In part, the fame was an accident, the result of a DJ in Pittsburgh putting together an edited version of "Don't Eat the Yellow Snow" and making it, essentially, into a novelty song. Despite that, the album features some interesting and excellent playing and a continuation of Zappa's explorations of U.S. culture.

Ben Watson, in an apt bit of hyperbole, calls *Apostrophe (')* "Frank Zappa's *King Lear*."[25] It is an album that is worth both the praise and damnation it has received through the years. Listen, for instance, to the intricate and complex music in "Father O'Blivion" (the incredible stop-time drumming and lightening-fast percussion work) or the sick blues workout in "Cosmik Debris" and you will see what many critics and fans feel is Zappa's best band working at the height of their power. These are jazz players and conservatory-trained musicians playing for a composer and arranger who knew how to take advantage of their abilities but who also knew how to get them to relax and work in a recognizable rock idiom.

The song starts with the now-famous four-part art song "Don't Eat the Yellow Snow," "Nanook Rubs It," "St. Alphonzo's Pancake Breakfast," and "Father O'Blivion." Lyrically, the songs are fairly silly examples of Zappa's dumb-lyrics theory. The story of an Eskimo named Nanook, who, among other things, runs afoul of a fur trapper who is attempting to capture and kill Nanook's "favorite baby seal" and is forced to attack the fur trapper with a handful of "deadly yellow snow" is fairly absurd, although both Watson and Courrier attempt to attach very significant meaning to the song, going so far as to compare Zappa with Shakespeare, James Joyce, and Prokofiev. Both critics make fairly significant logical leaps, arguing, for instance, that the pancake batter that Father O'Blivion is mixing up is really made of semen and is used to control the flock.[26] Read in a certain way, this makes sense. Although Zappa's delight in mocking the mundane habits of white, middle-class Americans makes the idea of a pancake breakfast even funnier and more ironic. Zappa's argument, that he did not want lyrics to get in the way of his more challenging music, seems to make especial sense with this album. Critics have read any number of things into the lyrics, but it is the music of which one needs to take note.[27] The precision of this band would remain unrivaled, and one needs only listen to "Nanook Rubs It" or "Father O'Blivion" to see that Zappa realized that he had something special with this band and wanted it to stretch out (as it would on subsequent albums).

"Cosmik Debris" is, like "Camarillo Brillo" before it, an attack on the dying counterculture, featuring a debunking of a number of great sixties-like clichés, including a "mystery robe," "oil of Aphrodite and the dust of The Grand Wazoo," natural cures, the concept of a guru, crystal balls, and so forth. The United States, at this time, was starting to struggle with the excesses of the sixties (another lost generation), and the next two years would see the country crawl out of Vietnam and a sitting president resign. Many of the post-sixties seekers would turn to any number of potential cures. Zappa hits the nail right on the head with the idea of debris. The sixties are over, the counterculture in tatters, and all that is left is the scattered remnants of a once-great idea. As if to confirm this, the narrator asks the guru in the song if his poncho "is a real poncho or a Sears poncho," thus replicating the authenticity test given to the sixties leftover in "Camarillo Brillo." The narrator then ends up turning the tables on the guru, robbing him and giving him some apt career advice: "Don't you know, / You could make more money as a butcher / So don't you waste your time on me."

Another political statement on the album, albeit somewhat more radical, is found in the song "Uncle Remus," cowritten with George Duke. Uncle Remus is the name of a terrifically racist character in a series of books by Joel Chandler Harris but, more significantly, is the main character in the Walt Disney film *Song of the South,* a film that, although unavailable today, was readily available in 1973. Uncle Remus, much like Uncle Tom, is a stereotype of the shuffling house Negro. In the film, it is Uncle Remus who takes care of the lonely white boy (much like Bill Robinson's character always took care of lonely Shirley Temple or Uncle Tom took care of little Eva St. Clare). The song asks the same kinds of questions that Zappa had been asking about the counterculture. This time, however, Zappa is asking if the civil rights movement is really having the effect it was supposed to have. Zappa sings, "We look pretty sharp in these clothes / Unless we get sprayed with a hose." This, like the contradictions in the counterculture and the feminist movement that Zappa has exploited, is Zappa pointing out that the civil rights movement still has some work to do, that African Americans were caught in a bind, and wanting to accept the gains of the civil rights movement but necessarily acknowledging that there was still a lot of work yet to be done.

Even more political than the lyrics is Zappa's band at the time. Although Zappa had always seemed to have a racially mixed band, as he began to tour in support of *Apostrophe (')*, Zappa had a band that was about as racially mixed as you were apt to find then or now: African Americans, women, Hispanics, and Caucasians, all led by a second-generation Italian immigrant from Baltimore. That kind of political statement was right up Zappa's alley. Any overt political statement that "Uncle Remus" makes is strengthened immeasurably by the fact that Zappa and his band were a living representation of the kind of integration that the United States was struggling with, and continues to struggle with.

The album ends with the comedy piece "Stink Foot," a popular concert piece for years to come (in part because it is an excellent vehicle for solo work; it was played by almost all of the bands except the 1982 version). The lyrics are somewhat inscrutable. Watson and Courrier both make the argument that there is a Platonic search for meaning contained within, whereas Neil Slaven argues that the song simply provides some poodle continuity between "Dirty Love" and "Evelyn, a Modified Dog." Although it does tease the audience with the statement, "The crux of the biscuit / Is the Apostrophe (')," it does not, I feel, go much beyond that.

The success of *Apostrophe (')* creates a unique situation for Zappa, and for a while he falls into a very routine schedule: album, tour, album, tour, and so on. Although there would be interruptions (in 1975, for instance, he had to go to England to be part of the lawsuit he and manager Herb Cohen had brought against Royal Albert Hall; Zappa lost, but the transcripts are hilarious and indicate the intellectual quickness that Zappa possessed), Zappa would also, in 1974, celebrate the 10th anniversary of the original Mothers of Invention. Sadly, only Don Preston was interested in taking part.

With *Over-Nite Sensation* and *Apostrophe (')* in the can, Zappa entered what biographers would probably call, were it the seventeenth century, his mature period. His music seems, from this point on, much less desperate and much more focused. The albums would show an increasing ability and maturity. It would take a real disruption to move him back to pure humor. Lucky for listeners and fans, there were plenty of those to come.

ROXY & ELSEWHERE, ONE SIZE FITS ALL, AND BONGO FURY

The Professionals. *Roxy & Elsewhere* (originally released in September 1974 on the DiscReet label; currently available as Rykodisc RCD 10520). Highest *Billboard* chart position: No. 27. Personnel: George Duke, Tom Fowler, Ruth Underwood, Jeff Simmons, Don Preston, Bruce Fowler, Walt Fowler, Napoleon Murphy Brock, Ralph Humphrey, and Chester Thompson.

One Size Fits All (originally released in June 1975 on the DiscReet label; currently available as Rykodisc RCD 10521). Highest *Billboard* chart position: No. 26. Personnel: George Duke, Napoleon Murphy Brock, Chester Thompson, Tom Fowler, Ruth Underwood, James "Bird-Legs" Youman, Johnny "Guitar" Watson, and Bloodshot Rollin' Red (Captain Beefheart).

Bongo Fury (originally released in October 1975 on the DiscReet label; currently available as Rykodisc RCD 10522). Highest *Billboard* chart position:

No. 66. Personnel: Captain Beefheart, George Duke, Napoleon Murphy Brock, Bruce Fowler, Tom Fowler, Denny Walley, Terry Bozzio, and Chester Thompson. Also of interest: *You Can't Do That on Stage Anymore, Vol. 2: The Helsinki Concert* (originally released in October 1988 as Rykodisc RCD 10083/84). Personnel: George Duke, Napoleon Murphy Brock, Ruth Underwood, Tom Fowler, and Chester Thompson. "The universe is one size—it fits all."[28]

This period of Zappa's career tends to give fans, yet again, some pause. After the craziness of the first 10 years of the Mothers, Zappa moved toward a much more technically precise, progressive rock/jazz form of music made by musicians with a jazz and conservatory background. All of these albums were recorded with roughly the same band members over a very short period of time and mark a real turn for Zappa.

Roxy & Elsewhere was largely recorded in December 1973 at the Roxy in Los Angeles with some music taken from two concerts in early 1974. Much of it is live, which adds to the excitement. Without Flo & Eddie, the band's onstage antics had been toned down. It is on these albums that one finds Zappa beginning to adopt more of a master-of-ceremonies roll, as is evident in his narration of certain concert events on "Dummy Up" and "Cheepnis." Like Flo & Eddie before them, he leaves a lot of the craziness to George Duke, Napoleon Murphy Brock, and, on *Roxy,* Jeff Simmons.

The album is an audacious piece of work: a live album containing all new material (few, if any, bands play concerts made up primarily of unreleased material, and it is a testament to Zappa's belief in his fans that he would trust them to go along with his musical experimentations). The only songs on the album that were all familiar to fans are "Son of Orange County," a sloweddown version of "The Orange County Lumber Truck" (from *Lumpy Gravy*), and "More Trouble Every Day," a modernized version of "Trouble Every Day" (from *Freak Out!*), which deemphasizes the particulars of the Watts riots and seems to focus more on the failure of the media to do their job.

Interestingly, *Roxy & Elsewhere* is kind of a forgotten album, sandwiched, as it is, between two of Zappa's best: *Apostrophe (')* and *One Size Fits All.* Except for Watson, none of Zappa's biographers and critics does much more than mention the album. The songs are surprisingly funky (a genre of music Zappa had not really explored), undoubtedly courtesy of George Duke.

Musically, the songs emphasize the excellence of the bands. They are all in multiple time signatures and move from key to key with tremendous force. Although many of the songs have lyrics, the emphasis on nearly all of them is the technical prowess of the bands. There are some incredible instrumental workouts, including "Echidna's Arf" and "Be-Bop Tango," and all of the songs feature extended soloing, something Zappa seemed to really be devoting himself to at this point in his career.

Thematically, Zappa is working in familiar territory: sex ("Penguin in Bondage") and crummy fifties movies ("Cheepnis"). Although both of these songs have narrative structure, they are both very much organized around the abilities of the musicians.

"Penguin in Bondage" kicks off the album in fine style. Actually, before the song begins, we get an explanation of just what exactly Zappa is trying to do. The monologue is an interesting example of Zappa's sense of satire and irony. The song is a humorous attempt at writing about sex in a socially acceptable manner. Zappa tells the audience that the song "suggests to the suggestible listener that the ordinary procedure, uh, that I'm circumlocuting at this present time in order to get this text on television." This seems to be yet another piece of Zappa's commentary on his art, much like his comments about *Lumpy Gravy* and *Cruising with Ruben & the Jets*. The introduction to the song is another indication of Zappa's liberation project. His gleeful tone in describing what consenting adults can do to each other if the spirit moves them is hilarious. Watson devotes several pages in his book to discussing the song, arguing that, among other things, "Penguin in Bondage" is "a literal enactment of bourgeois property relations to shore up fear of losing everything."[29] Although it could be that, it could also be another attempt from Zappa to comment on how society is still repressing sexuality as well as the selling of a commodity called sexual liberation. Watson seems to be making this same argument when he writes that "Zappa insists on the aspects of sexuality that tie it into the current relations of property,"[30] but it is hard to tell. It is one of the few places in *Negative Dialects* were Watson gets carried away by Marxist jargon.

The lyrics refer to sexual practices and are somewhat frank (although certainly far more socially acceptable than the Flo & Eddie lyrics), including "Way over on the wet side of the bed" and "Tremblin' like a Penguin / When the battery fail," two obvious references to a burgeoning female sexuality. Bondage, the ostensible subject of the lyrics, is representative of a liberated sexuality. In many ways it is the complete opposite of sexual repression; the freedom, confidence, and trust that a bondage situation requires is not a repressive notion at all. The fact that women, as Zappa seems to imply, are freely indulging in these acts (acts that include, as Zappa mentions in his presong rap, devices) is a far cry from Madge's unwilling participation in sex in the song "Harry, You're a Beast." Musically, the song is fairly simple (certainly one of the less complex songs on the album, although that is saying a lot, it is still much more difficult than many rock songs). There is an extended guitar solo in the middle, a return to the lyrics, and then a quick segue into "Pygmy Twylyte," a tremendous jazz / rock workout featuring absurdist lyrics along the line of "Green hocker croakin' . . . Crankin' an' a-coke'n / In the Winchell's do-nut Midnight." But the lyrics, as inscrutable as they are, are not the reason for the song. What really is happening here is Zappa showing off the incredible tightness of his band; the ability of this band to play this kind of music night after night just boggles the mind. The song, which segues seamlessly into "Dummy Up," also becomes a platform for the vocal stylings of Napoleon Murphy Brock, who definitely brings a touch of street credibility to Zappa's band. In fact, if one listens to the interplay between Brock, George Duke, Zappa, and Jeff Simmons on both *Roxy & Elsewhere* and *You Can't Do That on Stage Anymore, Vol. 2,* which is a recording of roughly the same band (with the exception of Jeff Simmons) in 1974, one can see that black sexuality and white sexuality are coming from very different places.

"Dummy Up" is largely a spoken-word piece (with the band burning underneath Zappa, Brock, Duke, and Simmons) that spins an absurdist narrative with a number of hilarious comments on the educational system (as well as some ridiculousness about Desenex foot powder). Zappa's anti-intellectualism raises its ugly head when he comments that, "No no, the college-degree is stuffed with absolutely nothing at all . . . you get nothing with your college-degree." After this climax, "the results," says Zappa, "of a college education," the song fades out.

"Village of the Sun" is another one of Zappa's beautiful songs. Most commentators are surprised by this song because of its complete lack of irony; it is a heartfelt homage to the place, Palmdale, California, where Zappa went to high school. Musically, it gets dangerously close to the sort of easy-listening music that Zappa would parody so effectively in the late seventies. Lest one think that Zappa is getting sentimental, the song segues directly into "Echidna's Arf (Of You)," an intense instrumental featuring some incredible stop-time drumming, rapid tone and tempo changes, and some propulsive percussion work. This is, to be frank, some of the finest progressive rock ever recorded. It is far more musically coherent than much of the progressive rock being performed and released at the time (think *Tales from Topographic Oceans,* the only truly unlistenable Yes album, which was released in 1973) and much more capable of surprising. It is a song that can really stand up to repeated listenings; one finds new things each time one hears it. After hearing it the first time, one must listen for the horns (a bit buried in the mix) and the great percussion work from Ruth Underwood.

The song segues into another instrumental workout, this one much closer to jazz than rock, "Don't You Ever Wash That Thing?," which features solos from Bruce Fowler (in one of the great rock trombone solos on record), Ruth Underwood, George Duke, a drum duet between Chester Thompson and Ralph Humphrey, and a blazing wah-wah guitar solo at the end. It is no wonder that Thompson would go on to join Weather Report soon after. It is some of the finest, most exciting fusion music ever made.

"Cheepnis" is one of the great fan favorites of Zappa's career (certainly up there with "King Kong," "Inca Roads," "Peaches en Regalia," and "Sofa"). It really indulges Zappa's love of cheesy old fifties monster movies. (Zappa tried, at various times, to write and film science fiction films and would take on the subject at various times in various songs, including the semicontroversial "The Torture Never Stops.") Before the song begins, Zappa delivers another humorous monologue that explains the meaning of the song, arguing that "I simply adore monster movies, and the cheaper they are, the better they are." Zappa also takes the opportunity to recognize that the clichéd genre of the monster movie had done a lot to create contemporary ideas about gender, telling the audience that typical films of this genre might feature "a little revolver that they're gonna shoot the monster with, and there is always a girl who falls down and twists her ankle." Most people can recognize this as a standard trope of horror films (a trope satirized so well in *Scream* and the *Scary Movie* films); the fact that Zappa feels the need to point it out is indicative of his more-progressive-than-one-might-think politics. The song, which is only about four minutes long, strings together a number of great verbal clichés and sets them to a great progressive rock piece (played at a blazingly fast speed), one that starts with a heavy blues / rock riff and segues into a much more up-tempo chorus. The song then features another Zappa narration, this time about a giant poodle named Frunobulax that is endangering the people of earth to the point that they feel they might have to use nuclear weapons in order to destroy it. Suddenly, the clichés of the monster movies verge on and merge into a cold reality: the country's loosing effort in Vietnam had brought, every so often, discussions of the use of nuclear weapons, so the idea was not that far-fetched. Zappa's argument with this song seems to be, in some way, the ultimate satire, that we are living in our own monster movie.

Following "Cheepnis" are revisions of two of Zappa's older songs, "Son of Orange County" and "More Trouble Every Day." "Son" has been radically slowed down and made into a blues jam. In part, this version of the song seems to be the result of Zappa's 10th anniversary shows; Zappa tried to reconvene the Mothers for a series of shows celebrating their early work, but only Don Preston accepted (he plays on this song). It is an incredible taste of how Zappa is able to reimagine his work. The song bears little resemblance to the original song until, at the very end, the band restates the theme from the *Lumpy Gravy* classic. The song seamlessly segues into "More Trouble Every Day," which has also been slowed down (although, unlike "Son," it is closely related to the original). Lyrically, only the first part of the lyrics from the *Freak Out!* version is used. Despite this, as Courrier argues, the song is clearly to be seen as "an indictment of the Nixon administration."[31] The song ends with a great blues guitar solo that is absolutely locked into the groove that the musicians have created. The three songs that make up the original side three of the vinyl release—"Cheepnis," "Son of Orange County," and "More Trouble Every Day"—are a terrific indictment of the politics of the day: Late 1973 and early 1974 saw the presidential administration of Richard Nixon under daily attack (Nixon would ultimately resign in August 1974). Zappa was not the only person who thought that the Nixon administration was populated by cheap thugs and wannabe fascists (Hunter Thompson made a career out of savaging this administration), and thus the idea that we is living in our own horror movie is not so far-fetched. The segue into "Son of Orange County" (which features Zappa repeating Nixon's famous phrase "I am not a crook"), and then into "More Trouble Every Day," is important to keep in mind. At the time, with the possible exception of the Kent State shootings, nothing had so violently shaken the United States than the Watts riots. The fact that Zappa seems to be comparing or damning the Nixon administration by associating it with the Watts riots is significant. A number of biographers relate that as part of this suite of songs, the band would play the song "Dickie's Such an Asshole" (originally written for the Flo & Eddie bands and available on *You Can't Do That on Stage Anymore, Vol. 3*), thus completing the song sequence critiquing the Nixon administration.[32]

The album ends with the incredibly odd and wonderful "Be-Bop Tango." This 16-minute piece of controlled chaos includes a trombone solo, scat singing by George Duke, audience participation, and a blues guitar jam by Zappa. It is another in a long line of songs that leaves the listener wondering how this band could perform this kind of music night after night with such precision.

Although the biographers seem to ignore this album, contemporary critics and reviewers seem to love it. Francois Couture argues that it creates "a bridge between his comedy rock stylings and Canterbury-style progressive rock" and that "The sequence 'Echidna's Arf (Of You)' / 'Don't You Ever Wash That Thing?' stands as Zappa's most difficult rock music."[33] Andrew Boscardan writes that "[George] Duke steals the show on several tracks, and Zappa's guitar work and 'master of ceremonies' showmanship is in top form."[34] Neither *The New Rolling Stone Album Guide* nor *Musichound Rock* mentions the album at all. It is too bad that it is kind of a lost album. It is an album that must be heard to be believed and one that really can stand repeated listening. The album that would come next, although much more popular with fans and critics alike, is somehow less satisfying in the long term.

If one listens to *You Can't Do That on Stage Anymore, Vol. 2,* a complete recording of the Duke-Brock band playing live in Helsinki, Finland, in September 1974, it is apparent that Zappa was at a creative nadir. Two of the songs on this album would be released on subsequent albums ("Inca Roads" on the *One Size Fits All* and "RDNZL" on *Studio Tan,* part of the ill-fated *Läther* album), and several songs from *Roxy* got the kinds of revisions that playing the same songs for a year with the same band members might provoke. Significantly different versions of "Village of the Sun," "Echidna's Arf," "Pygmy Twylyte," "Don't You Ever Wash That Thing," and "Cheepnis" are necessary listening to capture the full spirit and excellence of the 1973–75 band.

In between touring and attempting to film a concert (entitled *A Token of His Extreme*), Zappa also went into the studio to record a number of songs, some of which would appear on his next release, *One Size Fits All,* some of which were for his huge project *Läther* (which would be released as three different albums: *Sleep Dirt, Studio Tan,* and *Orchestral Favorites*), and some of which would end up on much later albums ("Little Green Rosetta" finds its way onto *Joe's Garage*). It is a fertile period, one that, given the trauma of the past several years (the fire in Geneva, the injury in London, the breakup of the Flo & Eddie band, the huge success of *Apostrophe (')*), indicated Zappa was ready to resume his manic pace. Courrier quotes Zappa as saying of this period, "I was in the studio for four months, ten to twelve hours a day, and by God I want people to hear the thing."[35] The album is a reflection of this relentless pursuit. It is, quite frankly, one of the best-sounding albums of the period. The production is sterling, each instrument is clear, and the channel separation is phenomenal. It is surprising to the contemporary listener to find out that it was recorded in 1974.

The album contains several songs that would go on to become concert staples for years (and, in the case of "Sofa," had been performed since 1972). It is a marvelous balance of rock, satire, funk, jazz, blues jamming, technical prowess, and adventurousness. It is a bit of a surprise that the album did not do all that well at the time. Watson argues that although it is a current fan favorite, it was a disappointment to Zappa.

All criticism aside, it is probably one of the easier albums in Zappa's catalog; even the longer progressive-rock type songs ("Inca Roads," "Florentine Pogen," and "Andy,") avoid some of the difficulties of Zappa's previous work. Indeed, from this point on, Zappa's albums would become, with a few exceptions (see *Shut Up 'N Play Yer Guitar* and *Thing-Fish*) much more accessible.

The album kicks off with "Inca Roads," a grand piece of art rock with a driving bass / drum / marimba beat and spacey George Duke vocals that can be considered a parody of the kinds of lyrics one might hear on a Moody Blues, Yes, or ELP album of the time. In fact, the sort of pseudocosmological ramblings that were familiar to fans of progressive rock seem to be embedded within the entire album. Ben Watson devotes more than four pages of *The Negative Dialectics of Poodle Play* to an attempt to decode the star map that is found on the back of the album cover. There is also an incredible Web site, *One Size Fits All* Star Map, at http://members.shaw.ca / fz-pomd / stars.html, that does a point-by-point dissection of the star map. The point of the map, in brief, is to mock the kind of New Age cosmology that was working its way through the United States at the time. The post-Watergate / post-Vietnam era had left many in the United States searching for something. This was the beginning of the age of the Jesus freak, Linda Goodman's *Sun Signs*, and the rise of the televangelist. Zappa's mocking cosmology is perfectly placed to poke fun at both the turn toward spirituality and the grand excesses of progressive rock.

The lyrics to "Inca Roads" are absurdist in the extreme. They veer wildly from spacey—"Did a vehicle / Come from somewhere out there / Just to land in the Andes?," which both Watson and Courrier claim is Zappa's satire on the popular-at-the-time book *Chariots of the Gods*—to the inevitable road stories, including a number of inside jokes about band members and their misadventures, including one with the "Guacamole Queen" in Texas.

The music, however, is the reason for the song. The guitar solo is lifted intact from the same 1974 concert in Helsinki that shows up as *You Can't Do That on Stage Anymore, Vol. 2,* and it is a beauty, an extended blues / jazz-based jam that radically alters the mood of the song from its absurdist and highly charged beginning to a smoky, slow-burning middle. No one but Zappa seems capable of capturing so many different moods and emotions in one song.

Ironically (or fittingly, depending upon your sense), "Can't Afford New Shoes" is a straight-ahead blues / rock rave-up about the mid-seventies recession.[36] In the song, Zappa takes swipes at both the Third World (developing nations) and the Krishna movement (which was sweeping California at the time). The song, like "Inca Roads," is really an excuse for a gritty solo. It is fun to hear Zappa writing simple tunes and it works well as a contrasting piece of music between the various art-rock pieces on the album. As the song comes crashing to an end, with Zappa playing a rocking blues scale solo, the mood shifts completely once again into "Sofa," another in the long line of great "themes" from Zappa. "Sofa #1" (the version without words) and "Sofa #2" (the version with words) were played by many of the bands and have a long and storied history. Originally, it was part of a longer piece of Flo & Eddie madness (partially captured on *You Can't Do That on Stage Anymore, Vol. 1*) that involved Mark Volman pretending to be a giant double-knit sofa ("I am portly, and I am maroon"); by *One Size Fits All* it is stripped down to its core theme ("Sofa #1") and a set of hysterically funny German lyrics that presage the German lyrics in the song "Stick It Out" from *Joe's Garage.*[37] A sample of the lyrics (which many critics spend many pages trying to decode) include "Ich bin der Dreck unter deinen Walzen / Ich bin dein geheimer Schmutz" ("I am the dirt beneath your rollers / I am your secret smut"). This is not groundbreaking philosophy; it is more than likely the result of years of touring Europe and a fascination with the Germans (which Zappa had commented upon as early as "Holiday in Berlin") and German culture and society.

The album's other fantastic piece of art rock is "Andy" which is, depending upon whom you believe, either about early Hollywood star Andy Devine, rock star Todd Rundgren, or an old road manager of Captain Beefheart's. The song starts with a piece of written guitar, keyboards, and drum music that builds to a climax and then leads into the first verse, a neat mix of spoken-word lyrics and blues (sung, in part, by Zappa's early hero, Johnny "Guitar" Watson) that ends up back where it started with the introductory theme. The chorus then comes out of nowhere: a straight-ahead piece of pop / rock that leads, yet again, back to the introductory theme, which is extended in a series of variations in odd time signatures (musically it is very similar to the music toward the end of the "Wet-T-Shirt Night / Todo-Line" sequence in

Joe's Garage). The song then resolves itself first with a rave-up chorus sung by Watson ("Andy Devine / had a thong rind") and an extended piece of blues jamming to the fade. It is an incredible song, one that was performed live to great acclaim by the 1974, 1979, 1980, 1984, and 1988 bands. It is a difficult piece to pull off live, and what is most amazing about the piece is how loose it sounds, but, when one listens closely, it becomes clear that it is a very difficult song.

"Florentine Pogen," another longtime concert favorite, sits at the center of the album. Sung by Napoleon Murphy Brock, it is a nice mash-up of Zappa's obsessions (cars, the spoiled rich) and extreme progressive-rock clichés. Lyrically it is a celebration of the liberated rich woman who goes slumming with a member of the band and the band's road manager. This is the kind of liberation that Zappa has been arguing for: that a rich woman (one who might have a reputation to consider) could consent, freely, to have sex not only with the drummer but with someone not even in the band. Throughout the song, it is the woman who is in control of the action: "She was the daughter of a wealthy Florentine Pogen / Read 'em 'n weep / Was her adjustable slogan." It is interesting that this woman, for whom sex is a happy, liberating function (indeed, she is frustrated when she can not get any), is European (many claim that the Florentine Pogen is a Swedish cookie). Zappa is still subtly critiquing American women and their sexual hang-ups.

The music in the song is interesting. It verges from art rock to heavy metal (if one listens, one can even hear echoes of the great Cheech & Chong theme "Earache My Eye" in the middle). In many ways, the song is the perfect blend of what Zappa has been trying to accomplish: silly / funny lyrics in a complex musical setting.

"Po-Jama People" is a more conventional blues workout along the lines of "Road Ladies" from *Chunga's Revenge*. It starts out with a nice bit a blues guitar that leads into the song, a standard pop setting with lyrics that make fun of some of Zappa's band members whom he found to be boring. It is one of Zappa's many contradictions; he wanted to surround himself with increasingly technically proficient musicians but found them to be boring. This reached its height with many of the members who toured in the *Grand Wazoo* band who were, according to Zappa, more interested in playing chess and reading books than they were in getting laid. It is for them that "Po-Jama People" is dedicated. Despite the song being a paean to the boring members of the band, it ends with one of the greasier blues solos on the album, another instance in which the music works to consciously contradict the lyrics.

Much like "Po-Jama People" is "San Ber'dino," another bluesy celebration of the ordinary average life of middle-class Americans. San Bernardino, California, is, in many ways, the opposite of Los Angeles, in both the good and the bad. Zappa's song, which has autobiographical elements (the Zappas lived, for a time, in many of California's Inland Empire cities, of which San Bernardino is one), seems to defend the average folks, many of whom were, undoubtedly, fans. Zappa argues that it is too simple to claim that they are "Dumb an' lonely / But you're wrong / 'Cause their love is strong." This is a striking and somewhat unusual bit of populism coming from Zappa, but it seems in line with his more libertarian instincts. The folks in the song do not bother anyone, so why should people look down upon them? The fact that the song is in a classic blues setting only seals the argument; blues has always been the populist music of choice for the downtrodden.

One Size Fits All is ignored, as many of the Duke-Brock albums are, by both *The New Rolling Stone Album Guide* and *Musichound Rock* (although both give the album 3.5 stars). Francois Couture calls it "An essential third-period Zappa album."[38] Andrew Boscardan argues, "The pinnacle of his jazz-rock work of the early '70s, *One Size Fits All* boasts some of the most memorable songs of Frank Zappa's career performed by one of the most beloved Mothers of Invention lineups ever assembled."[39]

Of course, as has come to be expected, this album and the subsequent tour saw the end of much of this lineup of the Mothers (which was the last lineup to be called the Mothers). Although many would record songs that would end up on other albums (both *Bongo Fury* and some of the *Läther* project), it was nearly over for the George Duke–Napoleon Murphy Brock incarnation of the band.

The Brock-Duke band would have one last swan song, although it would be muted by two things: the addition of Captain Beefheart on vocals and the loss of Chester Thompson on drums (and the subsequent addition of Terry Bozzio as his replacement). The band went into the studio in late 1974 and recorded a number of songs that would end up on the next Zappa album, *Bongo Fury:* "200 Years Old," "Cucamonga," and part of the song "Muffin Man." Then the band, minus Chester Thompson, ended up on tour and recorded a number of shows at the Armadillo World Headquarters in Austin, Texas, with Terry Bozzio, new guitarist Denny Walley, and new vocalist Captain Beefheart, who had temporarily made up with childhood friend Zappa (it would be a brief partnership).

The album is an odd duck in Zappa's catalog. In many places it is as much a Beefheart album as it is a Zappa album (one indication of this is that Zappa includes two original Beefheart compositions on the album: "Sam with the Showing Scalp Flat Top" and "Man with the Woman Head"). Watson argues of *Bongo Fury* that "After the majestic clarity of *One Size Fits All*, the sound is guitar heavy, clotted and ugly."[40] In general it is a great move for Zappa, as far from the progressive rock he had been playing as he could get and back to the roots blues that he became attached to as a kid in Southern California. "Advance Romance," for instance, finds Zappa trading guitar licks with slide player Denny Walley and Beefheart on harmonica. It is old-school blues.

Many of the songs on the album are the result of what Miles calls "some very esoteric collaboration."[41] None more so than the first song on the album, "Debra Kadabra." The song starts with a great classic / high-energy bluesy riff that finds Beefheart singing "Say she's a witch / *Shit-ass Charlotte!* / Ain't that a bitch?" It is clear to the listener that Beefheart is a very different kind of singer and lyricist than Zappa; his lyrics are deeply influenced by Beat poetry and the writing of William Burroughs. There is little irony of self-reflexivity in his writing. Zappa's lyrics, on the other hand, are full of references to pop culture, past events, or current history. There is a wealth of self-referential material in the later lyrics (both Watson and Courrier devote several pages to explaining them), including information about Beefheart's mom and a favorite monster movie of both Zappa's and Beefheart's.

The song leads into the blues workhorse "Carolina Hard Core Ecstasy." What begins as a song about a typical encounter with a woman becomes a song about the deepest and oddest depravity. Indeed, it is a tough song to look at closely, in part because it lacks any sort of awareness of the one-sided nature of groupie sex (the first verse begins with "I coulda swore her hair was made of rayon / She wore a Milton Bradley Crayon / But she was something I could lay on"). Although Zappa has written many songs about sex, about groupies, about desperate men, and so forth, he has not really written anything as blatantly sexist as "she was something I could lay on." It is a low point, lyrically, but it becomes a setup point. As the song develops, it turns out that the woman wants the man to stomp on her with a pair of "14 triple D" shoes. It is also, to be frank, not all that funny, despite the cutting references to the Doobie Brothers and Roger Daltrey. As if to confirm the rather sick seriousness of the song, Zappa finishes it with a ripping blues jam that takes up the last third of the song.

Two other live tunes of Zappa's take up the majority of the album: "Advance Romance" and "Muffin Man." "Romance" was played by nearly all of the subsequent bands and became a rather standard piece of blues, an excuse for Zappa to really engage in some guitar pyrotechnics (on *Bongo Fury* one gets a taste of Denny Wally's abilities as well; before you hear Zappa's solo you get a long slide guitar workout from Wally that is pretty intense). The lyrics are a hilarious send-up of the heartbroke genre of the blues: "No more credit from the liquor store / Suit is all dirty, my shoes is all wore / Tired an lonely, my heart is all sore," but the lyrics, as was becoming common, were largely filler to get to the increasingly excellent music.

"Muffin Man" is an oddity. It contains some clues to other Zappa albums, including many of the ideas that would show up in "Little Green Rosetta" on *Joe's Garage* (it is also the first mention of the Utility Muffin Research Kitchen, the name Zappa would give to his home studio). After the rather silly introduction (which features Zappa as both singer and narrator), the song becomes a great three-chord blues workout for Zappa to solo over. The Web site *We're Only in It for the Touring,* which features detailed analysis and comparisons of various touring versions of Zappa's bands and the songs those bands played, writes

> Wow! This premieres as an "in-yer-face" instrumental, following hot-on-the-heels of an as wicked "Camarillo Brillo." No lyrical nonsense, just the blistering

riff followed by Frank's most biting guitar work. Lyrics eventually surfaced by the time Austin [*Bongo Fury*] rolled around.[42]

It is not hard to agree. The song, which would become a grand concert-ending workout (as it is on *Bongo Fury*), is really Zappa at his raunchiest and blusiest best.

The center piece of the album is three short songs: "Poofter's Froth Wyoming Plans Ahead," "200 Years Old," and "Cucamonga." "Poofter," which got Zappa into a spot of trouble with him claiming not to know that *poofter* is English slang for "homosexual," is a fine piece of fake country music featuring a great use of what Zappa would come to call stock modules. In this case, the band plays a standard country piece, complete with slide guitar and basic A-B bass lines (and, for added effect, some nice squonking harmonica). The lyrics take direct aim at the selling of the U.S. bicentennial, which, as anyone who went through it can attest, was the United States at both its best and worst. It was a year when one could buy red, white, and blue anything and every town, big and small, had huge vaguely jingoistic celebrations. Zappa's take on the whole thing is fairly straightforward: "T-shirt racks, rubber snacks, / Poster rolls with matching tacks, / Yes, a special beer for sports." Zappa's argument, that Americans need to buy stuff and be drunk in order to properly celebrate U.S. independence is in line with his critique of the country's desire to fake political commitment; in other words, the celebration of the bicentennial is just an excuse to drink and buy stuff.

"200 Years," which, when placed after "Poofter Froth," might indicate another swipe at the bicentennial, is a more metaphorical piece of work, fashioning the United States as a woman who is "so mean she couldn't grow no lips" and who is dancing along in front of a jukebox "poppin' up / Like she had true religion." This is Zappa's way of saying that the United States is a young thing (a girl dancing in front of a jukebox is both exciting and melancholy; who is her partner, and why is she dancing alone?) and is kind of fake (is her religion rock and roll?). Longtime fans of Zappa could not be surprised at his accusation that the religion of the United States is largely a put-on. The fact that the song is done in a basic blues setting reveals the underlying authenticity of the argument: Zappa's the one with true religion—the blues, the truest U.S. art form.

"Cucamonga" is, like "Village of the Sun," another trip down memory lane, this time to the places that both Zappa and Beefheart know well: the Inland Empire town of Cucamonga, California. In some ways the song presages "Joe's Garage" as a genesis story of Zappa's bands. Zappa simply tells the story of some guys in Cucamonga who meet "Near a Holy Roller Church" in order to play music. We will find out what happens to this band later in *Joe's Garage*.

Bongo Fury is a hard album to love, especially if one likes the precision and excellent production of the several previous albums (certainly going back as far as *Waka/Jawaka*). It is a sloppy, dirty, bluesy album, one that marks another turning point in Zappa's career. With his next album, Zappa would turn toward rock and make a great, classic parody of seventies heavy metal (or what, at the time, was graciously called blues-based rock).

Critical reaction to *Bongo Fury* is decidedly mixed. Most critics both love and hate the record. A good example is when Lindsay Planer writes:

> Most Zappa enthusiasts either love or hate *Bongo Fury*. Much of the disparity has to do with the lack of the extended fusion-based instrumentals that had graced their predecessors *One Size Fits All* and *Roxy & Elsewhere* as much as it does with the inclusion of Captain Beefheart. Conversely, those consumers whose passions tend toward both Zappa and Captain Beefheart consider this disc as a mutual zenith.[43]

Andrew Boscardan seems to agree, writing, "Best when showcasing his evolving guitar skills and Terry Bozzio's thundering drums, *Bongo Fury* contains some of Zappa's more enduring songs."[44] *The New Rolling Stone Album Guide* calls it "a stronger Beefheart performance than a Zappa one," whereas *Musichound Rock* ignores it completely.[45]

In many ways, it is a good-faith album. Zappa was trying to keep the Duke-Brock band together and to help the career of his old friend Captain Beefheart. The coming years would find Zappa more and more taking center stage, to great effect. To indicate this, it is the last album that has the word *Mothers* anywhere in the title. From this point on, it is all Frank, all the time.

ZOOT ALLURES

> The night of the Iron Sausage. *Zoot Allures* (originally released in October 1976 on the Warner Bros. label; currently available as Rykodisc RCD 10523). Highest *Billboard* chart position: No. 61. Personnel: Varies by song but includes Terry Bozzio, Davey Moire, Roy Estrada, Andre Lewis, Napoleon Murphy Brock, Ruth Underwood, Captain Beefheart, and Dave Parlato. "A stripped-down-for-action rock 'n' roll album."[46]

The mid-seventies were an odd time, especially for music. It was the time of the singer-songwriter, disco, and corporate rock; punk, although finding its legs in England, was a ways off. It was the era of the Captain & Tennille, the Eagles, Fleetwood Mac, Paul McCartney & Wings, England Dan & John Ford Coley, Kiss, and the Bee Gees. It was, in other words, time for the marimbas and horn sections to go and time to get down to it, to make a down and dirty record full of rock tunes.

Of course, it is Zappa, and although he seems to have correctly read the spirit of the times, he is still incapable of following the straight path. What he does in *Zoot Allures* is give the world his version of a heavy-metal record, one that both mocks the clichés of hard rock and creates some exquisitely beautiful

be thought of as dumb, and certainly no one wants to be thought of as the other, so the challenge that Zappa issues in the first verse sets up the audience to go along with the argument in the rest of the song; that is, if you continue with your public education, the best you will be able to hope for is to "wind up workin' in a gas station."[48]

In many ways, *Zoot Allures* seems to be a celebration of down-to-earthness. Two of the other songs on the album, "Ms. Pinky" and "Find Her Finer," also seem to deal with a celebration of the less than sophisticated. Zappa seems at home exploring the sort of stuff that goes on with the everyday folks. In "Miss Pinky," for instance, Zappa is celebrating, in a nice sort of heavy-metal/industrial groove, the love of a $69.95 rubber doll. The message is very simple: the singer has a rubber girl that he loves because "She never talk back like a lady might do/An' she looks like she loves it every time I get through." There are a couple of meanings one could find in these lyrics. The idea of "never talk back like a lady might do" is consistent with Zappa's argument that white, middle-class women had many more sexual hang-ups than others. It can also be read, of course, with the idea that talking back is somehow offensive to men, an unfortunate argument that seems to be made occasionally in songs as far back as "Harry, You're a Beast."

Related, in some ways, to "Ms. Pinky" is "Find Her Finer," another song about horny men and the women who will not love them. In this song, Zappa seems to be arguing that women do not want smart men, singing, "Don't never let her know you are smart...You gotta play it straight from the heart." This is an interesting twist on the standard sentiment that men like dumb women. Musically, the song is interesting, a very slow blues (with some nice harmonica by Captain Beefheart) with acoustic guitar instead of electric and vocals recorded very close to the microphone (creating an intimacy that is missing on some of Zappa's earlier works).

"Wonderful Wino" is a Zappa critique of alcoholics, and not a particularly nice one at that. The song has an interesting history: It is based on a guitar riff by Jeff Simmons and was an instrumental on his album *Lucille Has Messed My Mind Up*. Zappa later put words to it, and the 1970 and 1971 bands performed it nightly and, according to the *Turtles All the Way Down* Web site (http://ourworld.compuserve.com/homepages/turtlestew/70sf.htm):

> Another tune that simply rocks. With Simmons on vocals, Dunbar frantically thrashing away in the background, Flo 'n' Eddie relegated to background vocals, and Frank playing the role of rock 'n' roll guitar player, this song infuses a high dose of energy into the nightly proceedings.

By the time the song makes it to *Zoot Allures,* it is a pretty standard piece of heavy metal that would not sound out of place on a Led Zeppelin or Black Sabbath album from the same era (except, perhaps, for the horn section that occasionally peeks out from the background). Lyrically, it is a pretty straightforward attack on public drunkenness; each verse shows the main character attempting to do something, only to be defeated by his drinking habit. It is both a nasty song and a moralizing song, as if Zappa was becoming less tolerant of what he perceived as being the bad habits of others.

"Disco Boy" is, like many of the other songs on the album, a pretty straightforward argument: the type of guy who goes to discos is leaving himself pretty open to ridicule. It is also one of Zappa's first songs to use scatological references as an argument against middle-class pretension, which is something he was thinking of at the time. In the spoken-word introduction to the concert version of "Black Napkins," Zappa is quoted as saying, "this is an instrumental song, it's a tender, slow-moving ballad sort of a song, that carries with it the implied message that the complete woman must also have an asshole."[49] Zappa would return to this argument in the song "Broken Hearts Are for Assholes" and would apply it to men in the song "Disco Boy." The song returns to a favorite theme: the boy who thinks he is irresistible to women. Unlike many of Zappa's earlier songs, however, which seem to end in heartbreak, this song ends with a third-person commentary from Zappa (i.e., instead of telling a story that the audience is supposed to understand, this song is sung directly to the disco boy by a godlike narrator). After a series of disco actions, the narrator/Zappa tells the disco boy, "A disco drink / A disco wink / 'You never go doody!' / (That's what you think)." Zappa has always argued that there are a few things we all do, from princes to paupers: eat, sleep, shit, and fuck. The argument that the disco boy might assume that he "doesn't go doody" or that the beautiful maiden does not have an asshole (the place, in other words, wherein the shit comes out) is part of this larger populism: we're all the same. Deal with it. What makes the song even more interesting is that it sounds closer to a pop radio song than almost all of Zappa's work. The guitar sound is modified to sound very close to the sound that the band Boston achieved. This is, I feel, Zappa's way of taking a dig at the corporate nature of rock. Disco was, in the opinion of many, a manufactured fad (much of the music was machine made, with robotic backbeats); Boston, a corporate rock band of the highest order, fits in with Zappa's arguments about the record companies' increasing unwillingness to take musical chances. So the fact that the guitar sounds like a Boston record and that there is a drum machine keeping the beat make this song a fine piece of musical satire.

The centerpiece of the record is the song "The Torture Never Stops." This is one of those songs that have as many readings as there are critics. The song had its origins as a Beefheart-Zappa tune (you can find the original version on *You Can't Do That on Stage Anymore, Vol. 4*), a blues/boogie workout that would not be out of place on a ZZ Top album. By the time it gets to *Zoot Allures,* it is all Zappa; he plays guitar, bass, and keyboards, leaving the drums to Terry Bozzio. Although the original was sung by Beefheart, Zappa takes the vocals on the studio version. The song is slowed way down and made much more sinister. It goes from blues to horror. Sort of.

In a juxtaposition that both Courrier and Watson discuss in some detail, throughout the song, with its descriptions of torture—"Flies all green 'n buzzin' in his dungeon of despair / Prisoners grumble and piss their clothes and scratch their matted hair"—Zappa has, in the background, two women (his wife Gail and a friend) moaning in fake / mock sexual ecstasy. It is a nice irony. As both Courrier and Watson point out, Donna Summer's song "Love to Love You Baby," which featured her moaning in fake ecstasy over a disco beat, was a huge hit in 1975. One certainly needs to consider for a moment that Zappa, who loved a good musical joke, was making fun of Summer's hit. Another possible explanation of the song is to tie it to Zappa's love of fifties science fiction and horror movies and literature. In "Who Needs the Peace Corps," Zappa had mocked the so-called psychedelic dungeons in San Francisco. Dungeon was one of Zappa's favorite comedy concepts—it is a place so removed from reality—and the evil doctor in his dungeon of despair was high comedy.[50]

The song, musically, is very interesting. It is an excruciatingly slow piece of blues music filled with great mid-seventies electric piano and hilarious sound effects. Both on the record and in concert it became an excuse for some of Zappa's best soloing. The versions on *You Can't Do That on Stage Anymore, Vol. 1* (from the 1977 tour) and *The Best Band You've Never Heard in Your Life* (from the 1988 tour) are both excellent and interesting because they give the listener a sense of Zappa's creativity as an arranger. They are both great versions of the song, but, taking into account the various strengths of the members of the band, are radically different.

Although the album only made it to No. 61 on the *Billboard* Charts, it is one of the albums that has been most popular over the long run. Francois Couture calls it "masterpiece of dark, slow, sleazy rock."[51] Kevin Courier comments, "With its emphasis on recession, impersonal sex, and disco glamour, *Zoot Allures* vividly seized on the decade's nascent narcissism."[52] "Disco Boy" became a minor hit single, and "Zoot Allures," "Black Napkins," and "The Torture Never Stops" all became concert favorites. It was also boding well for Zappa at the time that he had surrounded himself with undeniably creative musicians. His musical relationship with Terry Bozzio and bassist Patrick O'Hearn (who was featured on the album cover but not on the album and would play with the band for several years to come and would quit, with Bozzio, to form the new wave band Missing Persons) would be fertile.

Unfortunately, as seemed to always be the case, just as this band was finding its pace, Zappa became embroiled in much offstage controversy: not one but two lawsuits, one against his longtime manager, Herb Cohen, and one against his record company, Warner Bros. These would keep Zappa from releasing records for quite a while.

ZAPPA IN NEW YORK, STUDIO TAN, AND SLEEP DIRT

Läther, lawsuits, and record company madness. *Zappa in New York* (originally released in March 1978 on the DiscReet label; currently available as Rykodisc RCD 10524/25). Highest *Billboard* chart position: No. 57. Personnel: Ray White, Eddie Jobson, Patrick O'Hearn, Terry Bozzio, Ruth Underwood, Dave Samuels, Randy Brecker, Michael Brecker, Lou Marini, Ronni Cuber, Tom Malone, and Don Pardo (also includes percussion overdubbing by Ed Mann and John Bergamo and harp overdubbing by Louanne Neil).

Studio Tan (originally released in September 1978 on the DiscReet label; currently available as Rykodisc RCD 10526). Highest *Billboard* chart position: No. 147. Personnel: Because the music was recorded at different times with different bands, the personnel varies, but it includes George Duke, the Folwers, Chester Thompson, Davey Moire, Eddie Jobson, Max Bennett, Paul Humphrey, Don Brewer, James Youman, and Ruth Underwood.

Sleep Dirt (originally released in January 1979 on the DiscReet label; currently available as Rykodisc RCD 10527). Highest *Billboard* chart position: No. 175. Personnel: Terry Bozzio, George Duke, Patrick O'Hearn, Ruth Underwood, Thana Harris, James Youman, and Chester Thompson (also includes drum overdubbing by Chad Wackerman). "Most fans knew of Zappa's problems with Warner's and were merely waiting for him to join a new label."[53]

All of these albums are the result of Zappa's long-running argument with Warner Bros. Records. The story is fairly simple: After the release of *Zoot Allures,* Zappa owed Warner Bros. four albums (most recording contracts are written so the artist owes a record company a certain number of albums; most record companies do not want all of those albums to come at the same time). After the *Zoot Allures* tour ended, Zappa turned in four albums to Warner Bros. Zappa claims that the company refused to pay him for the albums. He then turned in a four-album boxed set to Mercury/PolyGram, who wanted to sign Zappa and who did a test pressing but ultimately refused to release the album. Therein lies the disagreement. At this point, Zappa felt he had more than lived up to his legal and contractual obligations to Warner Bros. To make a long story short, Zappa is unable to release much music at all for a number of years, although he wrote and recorded an extraordinary amount of music during this period. The four-album boxed set, named *Läther,* did undergo a test pressing by Mercury of about 100 units, one of which Zappa took and broadcast on KROQ radio in Pasadena, California. The album was ultimately not released until 1996, using much of the material that was released on several different records by Warner Bros. as well as Zappa's blueprint for the record. The album as a whole will not be discussed here; Watson does an astoundingly complete job of discussing it in *The Negative Dialectics of Poodle Play* (312–45).

The first album that Warner Bros. did release, under protest by Zappa, was *Zappa in New York*, a live album recorded during a series of shows at the

Palladium in late December 1996. The band is one of Zappa's better collections of musicians, with Terry Bozzio on drums being the lone holdover from the *Zoot Allures* days. There is also a horn section, led by crack New York session men Michael and Randy Brecker, as well as several folks who would go on to play in the Blues Brothers Band (Zappa had just filmed an episode of *Saturday Night Live* and was able to get the *SNL* announcer, Don Pardo, to do a couple of hilarious introductions on *Zappa in New York*).

When Zappa remixed and rereleased the album in 1991, he included the songs that Warner Bros. left off the album as well as several songs from the concerts, including new versions of "I'm the Slime," "The Torture Never Stops," "Pound for a Brown," and "Crusin' for Burgers" (done in a fantastic nine-minute instrumental version).

It is an interesting album. The expert musicianship is mated with some of Zappa's least-clever humor. The album is an interesting mix of intense instrumentals, including "The Black Page, Parts 1 & 2," and humorous songs, including "Titties and Beer," "Punky's Whips," "Honey, Don't You Want a Man Like Me?," and "The Illinois Enema Bandit."

"Titties and Beer" and "Punky's Whips" have probably garnered the most attention over the years: "Beer," because of the relative crudeness of the song (Zappa gets accused, from this album onward, of becoming broader and cruder in his humor), and "Punky's Whips," because Warner Bros. would not release it on the original album for fear of a lawsuit from the subject of the song, Punky Medows, of the rock band Angel (the kind of "style over substance" band that Zappa loved to parody). In the song, drummer Terry Bozzio professes his onanistic tendencies when confronted by a picture of Punky Medows in all of his blow-dried fabulousness. The song is more of a skit with a long guitar solo than a song. Bozzio, who would often play the foil in Zappa's dramatic works, including the lead in *Thing-Fish*, is hilarious, singing lines such as "I can't stand the way he pouts / ('Cause he might not be pouting for me!)." After the middle solo break, the song offers a critique of the increasing androgyny of rock stars, name-checking Steven Tyler, lead singer of Aerosmith and one of the folks who seemed to be blurring the line between boy and girl. The song ends with an extended debate that Bozzio has with himself over whether or not he is gay for being in love with Punky. It is an interesting argument, coming, as it does, at the height of the glam movement in rock. Disco, KISS, and bands like Angel had changed the way bands presented themselves, and the blurring of the line between masculinity and femininity was something that challenged rock. What made these gender-bending rock stars such complex political figures was the fact that their audiences were mainly male. The idea that male heavy-metal fans, a very masculine segment of society, were worshipping men who dressed in a manner that made them look as if they were women is what the song really seems to be dealing with.

In fact, if one looks at the album as dealing with issues and themes of masculinity, it is easy to come to the conclusion that Zappa was highly amused by the increasingly sad attempts of men to cling to outmoded ideas of masculinity. The main narrative in the four humorous songs on the album is, in each song, about a man and his foolish (and at times illegal) quest for sex and the outlandish lengths he will go to in order to satisfy his urges.

For instance, the song that follows "Punky's Whips" on the album, "Honey, Don't You Want a Man Like Me," is a classic Zappa tale of the arrogant buffoon who thinks more highly of himself than anyone else does: "He was the Playboy Type (he smoked a pipe) his favorite phrase was 'OUTA-SITE!'" This kind of mid-seventies hipster is a great target for Zappa (the same kind of man he seems to be writing about in "Dancing Fool" and "Disco Boy"). Zappa also uses the song to continue his argument that women have free will and with that free will comes the opportunity to do stupid things. The woman whom the main character meets is described by Zappa: "her favorite group was HELEN REDDY." There is no excuse for ignorance (Helen Reddy is not a group, and she is not very good), and both of these characters are ignorant. The girl should have more than likely been able to see through the suave moves of the pseudohipster who has taken her out for the night, and even if she can not see through him, there is no way, after the way she is treated when she will not put out on the first date—"He called her a slut a pig and a whore"—that she should have sex with this man. Yet she does. Why? It is clear that this man does not have anything going on, and even if she is taken in by his appearance, after he yells at her and leaves in a huff, she should let him go; yet, when he returns to her house after his car will not work she proceeds to sexually satisfy him anyway. Again, in perhaps a slightly cruder manner than he had been doing since the sixties, Zappa is essaying freedom: this woman should have turned this man down yet she did not. That is freedom (the same kind of freedom that the HBO show *Sex in the City* would dwell upon for a number of seasons).

Freedom is not the issue in "The Illinois Enema Bandit," a disturbing piece of blues-based sociology that is a frequent topic of discussion for critics and biographers alike. Barry Miles claims that it is "genuinely offensive."[54] Biffyshrew@aol.com argues, on the *ARF* Web site (http://www.arf.ru / Notes / Ziny / enema.html), that "One of the shittier things FZ ever did (at least in public) was to compound the humiliation [real-life enema bandit Michael] Kenyon's real-life victims experienced by performing this song making a joke out of their sexual assault." Although I am not sure that is what he was doing, the argument is undeniable that Zappa is closer to the edge of pure offence with this song than he has been before.

Of all of Zappa's songs, "The Illinois Enema Bandit" might be the toughest to defend. Zappa's own defense of the song is pretty simple: Apparently he was driving between shows in central Illinois and heard about the enema bandit on the radio and found the whole concept hard to believe and set about writing a folk song about the character (similar, as one Web fan argues, to Bob Dylan's song celebrating the life and times of boxer Hurricane Carter).

There is no reason to doubt this explanation, but it is not entirely satisfactory. There is, as Biffyshrew mentions, a certain cruelty in celebrating this character. Although the cruelty is likely unintentional, it is a bit thoughtless. This is, however, more than likely the explanation: Not all jokes are as funny as one thinks they are, and this may be one of them. Of course, the scenario of the enema bandit was more than likely hard to resist. Zappa's fascination with things that go in and out of a person's behind had already shown up on a number of albums and would show up on a few to come. The argument could be made, although I will not really make it here, is that Zappa found the enema bandit to be administering the kind of reality check that he [Zappa] had been singing about in his songs.

A final argument about the song is a bit more complicated. At one point in the song, Ray White sings "Well, one girl shout: 'Let the Bandit be!',", which is an interesting comment on the strange social phenomenon of women falling in love with criminals. Whether one calls it the Stockholm syndrome or something else, it is undeniable that people as disparate as Charles Manson and Ted Bundy have had, at their trials and court appearances, young women who professed to love them. To many, including me and perhaps Zappa, this is very difficult to believe (and kind of funny). It certainly is not what would be called normal in any society.

What upsets people about the song, perhaps, is that it is taken so seriously by the band. There is an impassioned vocal performance by Ray White and a blistering guitar solo from Zappa. Perhaps Flo & Eddie could have carried off this kind of humor, but the seriousness with which the song is performed by this particular band (and subsequent bands) makes the argument that it is a comedy song a tough sell.

The final humorous song on the album, and the one that certainly qualifies as one of the dumbest ever written by Zappa (even for a man who argues that his own lyrics are stupid), is "Titties and Beer," a narrative that is, ostensibly, about the Devil's theft of the narrator's girlfriend and the narrator's attempts to win her back. Miles calls the song "stupid rather than offensive," which is more than likely true but also sells the song a bit short.[55]

One very interesting way to look at this song is, as many critics have argued, as Zappa's modern retelling of Stravinsky's *L'Histoire du Soldat*. Zappa cites Stravinsky as an influence in a number of places and had played the character of the Devil in an orchestral performance of the piece in the early seventies. If it is a direct retelling, it is a twisted piece of work indeed!

Musically it is a great piece of art rock, using the horn section to great advantage. It starts with a typically fifties piece of rock but quickly moves into the skit portion of the song that has Zappa and Bozzio trading dialogue (Zappa as the narrator, Bozzio as the Devil). What makes the lyrics interesting are the insight they give into a number of subjects that seemed to be on Zappa's mind at the time: politics, contracts, and white male buffoonery. For instance, Bozzio, as the Devil, brags, "I mean you shoulda' seen some of the souls that I've had" and then cites "Why there was Milhous Nixon 'n Agnew, too." Later we find out that the narrator compares himself to the members of the audience and then claims that he has only two interests: the aforementioned titties and beer. This seems to be another piece of Zappa's long-running argument with the sort of middle-class white men: titties and beer seems to be a sort of lowest common denominator argument; that is, at their most basic, men can be reduced to a bunch of drunken fraternity boys, interested only in sex and alcohol. This argument at this time makes a lot of sense. Many biographers claim that one of the unintended consequences of the Flo & Eddie years and the increasingly direct humor on the subsequent albums was that the audiences at Zappa's concerts were made up, more and more, of adolescent and college-age men who wanted to hear songs with dirty words in them. In many ways, "Titties and Beer" seems to be a very sly comment on this sort of attitude.

A final way of looking at this song is in the way it discusses, even briefly, contracts. At one point, the Devil hands the narrator a contract for the narrator's soul, and the narrator replies "Gimme that paper...bet yer ass I will sign." This must have seemed terrifically ironic to Zappa at the time, because he was mired in a number of contractual and legal disputes (and had seen Captain Beefheart become entangled in what seems to be one of the most complicated contractual disputes in music history). There is little doubt that Zappa felt that having to sign recording contracts was akin to working with the Devil, that the kind of soul-selling involved in trying to get one's music heard was demeaning in the extreme. Indeed, in a version of "Titties and Beer" recorded the next year and released in 1983 on the album *Baby Snakes,* Zappa adds the argument that going to hell would not be a problem because he already knew what hell was like, having been "signed with Warner Brothers for eight fucking years."

The new instrumentals on the album (all contained on the second disc), including "The Black Page," "Manx Needs Women," and "The Purple Lagoon / Approximate," are all interesting and show a lot of musical development.

"The Black Page," named after a band member's comment that the sheet music for the song had so many notes that it was a black page, is really two songs. "The Black Page #1" is an intense and complicated drum solo that iterates into a wonderfully complex piece of avant-garde composition that is percussion driven but features keyboards and horns. According to Zappa's comments at the beginning of "Black Page #2," "The Black Page #1" was originally written for Terry Bozzio. Zappa then added a melody that was still too complex for some people. "The Black Page #2," which Zappa calls "The Easy Teen-Age New York Version," is, in all honesty, still a pretty challenging piece of music. It seems, in many ways, to be influenced by the works of U.S. composer Conlon Nancarrow, whose ideas about rhythmic complexity were unequaled in the twentieth century. Nancarrow's work is praised as having an "unparalleled fusion of visceral excitement and structural elegance,"[56] which also seems to be speaking about Zappa's later compositions. If one looks ahead in anticipation, "The Black Page #1 & #2" are an indication of where Zappa will be going with his compositions.

"Manx Needs Women" is interesting in the sense that it is purely an intellectual exercise. According to the liner notes on *Zappa in New York,* the song was originally written and published in *Guitar Player* magazine. It is very similar to the music that Zappa would use as segue pieces on *Sheik Yerbouti* and in the film *Baby Snakes.* It is a short, 1:50, piece that is atonal in nature and ends without classical resolution.

The final song on the album, "The Purple Lagoon / Approximate," is a tremendous band workout that borrows freely from the hard bop jazz of Ornette Coleman. According to the liner notes on the album, the song is really two songs and musical themes played against each other. Zappa says that "Approximate" "dates from the days of *The Grand Wazoo*" (and can be found in its entirety on *You Can't Do That on Stage Anymore, Vol. 2*), and "The Purple Lagoon" is a song written and performed on an early episode of *Saturday Night Live.* Standout moments of the song include a fantastic sax solo by Mike Brecker (one of the better saxophonists with whom Zappa would ever work), a nifty bass solo by Patrick O'Hearn, and a crazy, effects-modified trumpet solo by Randy Brecker.

Despite the excellence of the band and the complexity of the music, the album would be forever tarred with the brush of comedy music. The controversy over "Punky's Whips" and "Titties and Beer" would forever cloud the musical excellence of disc two. Most contemporary reviews agree. Biographers and critics, including Watson, Miles, and Courrier, devote pages and pages to the comedy music and make the instrumental music largely an afterthought. Reviews of the album at The *All Music Guide* and Amazon.com both ignore the instrumental music in favor of recounting the legal headaches Zappa was undergoing at the time.

It is an album that really holds up over time, especially the second disc. "The Black Page" became a standard showcase for soloing, especially Zappa's increasingly excellent guitar work (for a full description of different touring versions, see the *Information Is Not Knowledge* Web site at http://globalia. net / donlope / fz / songs / Black_Page.html). Versions of the song would appear on *You Can't Do That on Stage Anymore, Vols. 4 & 5* as well as *Make a Jazz Noise Here.*

Unfortunately for both Zappa and his fans, the next several years would see piecemeal releases and a number of albums put out by record companies without the input or acquiescence of Frank Zappa. *Sleep Dirt, Studio Tan,* and *Orchestral Favorites* are all part of the *Läther* project (although, according to at least two sources, they were delivered first to Warner Bros. as *Studio Tan, Hot Rats III,* and *Orchestral Favorites* and reedited later as *Läther*).

It is important to hear both *Sleep Dirt* and *Studio Tan* as albums that were never supposed to be released as they were. Although both of them are good albums and contain many songs that Zappa would play for years as part of his live shows, they were released under the control of Warner Bros. and were approved and released by Zappa much later.

Studio Tan kicks off with the song "The Adventures of Greggery Peccary," which is, depending upon which critic you want to believe, about actor Gregory Peck or Pope Gregory XIII. It is an extended piece of musical theater on par with "Billy the Mountain" although done in a slightly more sophisticated manner (for instance, "Greggery" is a purely studio creation, thus Zappa is able to indulge in various studio manipulations that he was unable to use on "Billy"). The song, much like "Billy," is a long narrative about a "nocturnal, gregarious, wild swine" who stands in for the white, middle-class, conservative businessperson, the same type of person we have already met in "Brown Shoes Don't Make It." Greggery works for a company that invents trends "like 'the twist' or 'flower power'." It is at this point that the song becomes a fairly savage critique of U.S. consumerism. Greggery is surrounded by all of the latest hep devices, including a water pipe and a copy of the *Whole Earth Catalogue,* and spends his days trying to dream up ways of getting Americans to spend their hard-earned cash on new, and largely inconsequential, things.

Then the song takes an odd and wonderful left turn toward the near cosmological. Greggery, in search of his newest trend, invents the calendar. From this point on, Zappa moves from a critique of U.S. consumerism to a critique of time itself. Greggery claims that people did not like his invention of the calendar because it made them aware of how old they were. Time seems to be something that Zappa thought a lot about. As a professional musician, Zappa was surrounded by folks who were, in large part, ambivalent about time. Rock musicians are not known for their clock-based lifestyles (and, in fact, in "Brown Shoes Don't Make It," Zappa seems critical of the rather structured life of the middle manager), yet, at the same time, Zappa was known to be intolerant of musicians in his employ who abused the time that was so precious. Zappa's extraordinary artistic output shows an individual obsessed with the short amount of time allotted to him to make an artistic or cultural mark. Although Watson claims that Zappa's critique in the song is of the sort of boredom or exhaustion that late capitalism was breeding in America, I feel that it is more personal.[57] Zappa, like a freelance writer, has not held a regular job since the early sixties; time, for a successful artist, takes on a wildly different meaning than it does for someone who has to punch a clock for a living. Having been a successful musician for a number of years, time, has become a rather abstract concept.

Musically, the song seems to blend the art-rock ideas of "Billy the Mountain" with the avant-cartoon music of "Manx Needs Women." There are two extended instrumental breaks within the song (which is more than 20 minutes long) that are much more traditional in nature. It is an interesting piece of music, one that gets better the more times one listens to it.

"Revised Music for Guitar and Low-Budget Orchestra" is a piece that Zappa originally wrote for the Jean Luc Ponty album *Plays the Music of Frank Zappa*. It is a wonderfully complex suite of songs and themes that begins with a slow piano-and-acoustic-guitar figure, becomes more abstract in a midsection that owes a bit to Eric Satie and Charles Ives, segues into a big-band theme, returns to the avant-garde, and then segues without pause into the very upbeat pop song "Let Me Take You to the Beach." Miles writes that "Revised Music for Guitar" is "an extraordinary tour de force and a good example of the complexity of Zappa's music."[58]

"Let Me Take You to the Beach" is a return to pop parody. It is a dead-on satire of the kind of Top 40 / AM radio stuff that was popular in the mid-seventies: the spacey keyboards seem indicative of the disco-era music that was nearly ubiquitous. When one hears the song for the first time, inevitable comparisons to Wings (Paul McCartney's post-Beatles hit-making machine) or the Bee Gees pre-*Saturday Night Fever* music can be made. Lyrically, the song sends one back even farther: to the early sixties clichés of beaches, cookouts, and innocent hand-holding fun. By the end of the song, Zappa is even quoting himself, writing, "Have a freak out ... you're on restriction / So you'll probably sneak out!" The music, which is merrily upbeat, stands in nice contrast to this particular sentiment.

The album ends in fine form with "RDNZL," an extended instrumental that features some excellent band playing and another in a long line of blistering guitar solos; this one is notable because, unlike many of the solos and experiments that Zappa was doing at the time, this one is played fully within the confines of the song's melody. No one, except perhaps Zappa, knows what the title of the song means (and he never really felt the need to explain). There are several interesting theories on the *ARF* Web site (http://www.arf.ru / Notes / Stan / rdnzl.html), none of which seems to be any more definitive than another.

Studio Tan is an overlooked work. Contemporary reviews are sparse, with most commenting on the legal entanglements and ignoring the music. It is a worthwhile album in the sense that, like the *Burnt Weeny Sandwich / Weasels Ripped My Flesh / Chunga's Revenge* era records, it collects some old and some new and represents a demarcation point in Zappa's career.

Sleep Dirt is part of the same story. Originally titled *Hot Rats III* (as mad as Zappa was at Warner Bros. for putting the two albums out without his input, he was furious that *Sleep Dirt* was put out under another name). It is another interesting and overlooked record in Zappa's catalog, although not one for beginners (or for purists; like *Cruising with Ruben & the Jets,* Zappa made some modifications to the album when he got the masters back from Warner Bros.).

Sleep Dirt collects songs from three different projects: *Zoot Allures, Hunchentoot,* a musical Zappa had written while in a wheelchair recovering from his injuries sustained in the infamous incident in London, and the larger

Läther project (although it is important to remember that *Läther* comes after Zappa turned in *Hot Rats III* to Warner Bros., so it is possible that the album really takes things from *Zoot Allures* and *Hunchentoot* as well as the original *Hot Rats III* cuts).

The album begins with the excellent, slow, dirty ,and grinding instrumental "Filthy Habits," which sounds as if it were taken right off of *Zoot Allures*. It has the same excellent blues / metal interplay between a guitar / bass / drums trio (with additional keyboards by Zappa). Recorded about the same time that *Zoot* was recorded (in Los Angeles in 1976), it is a fantastic piece of work. Different versions of the song can be found on *FZ:OZ* (with a very interesting keyboard solo) and *You Can't Do That on Stage Anymore, Vol. 4* (which features the always interesting big-band arrangement of the 1988 group).

"Flambay," which was originally an instrumental on the vinyl / Warner Bros. release was restored to Zappa's specifications in the early eighties. As it stands on the CD, it is part of the *Hunchentoot* musical. Sung by Thana Harris, the song is an interesting piece of cabaret music with a strong narrative about the evil Queen Drakma's love of the giant spider Hunchentoot. Of course, it is a musical with typical Zappa obsessions; for instance, the way love is discussed in "Flambay" is very different than it is usually discussed in musical theater (this would become one of the controlling themes of *Thing-Fish*): "A SPIDER'S FOOL! / (When it's ME he needs / To fondle his tool!)." The narrative continues in the next song, "Spider of Destiny," in which Drakma urges Hunchentoot to eat the people of the Earth. Taken together, it is a hilarious peek into Zappa's love of cheesy fifties horror films (indeed, at least one Web site has Zappa's ultimate ode to fifties horror films, "Cheepnis," listed as part of the larger *Hunchentoot* score).[59]

"Spider of Destiny" segues into the great instrumental "Regyptian Strut," a fully orchestrated piece with all of the brass dubbed by Bruce Fowler and a great percussion section led by Ruth Underwood. It is much more cinematic or theatrical than much of Zappa's instrumental writing of the time (and lacking in a guitar solo) and seems to have naturally progressed from the *Hot Rats / Hunchentoot* writing. It has a very strong melody that is repeated a number of times, much in the way an overture or instrumental segue might function in a theatrical piece.

This leads to the last *Hunchentoot* piece, "Time Is Money," which features Queen Drakma sitting upon the cosmic sofa (the same sofa, evidently, that is featured in the song of the same name and on the album cover to *One Size Fits All*).

The *Hunchentoot* pieces, although interesting, do not seem to do much to advance Zappa's ideological obsessions (they are more akin to cultural homage than they are to critique). The fact that the musical had been hanging around since at least 1972 is an indication that, much like the period between the breakup of the original Mothers and the Flo & Eddie Mothers, Zappa is going back through his catalog and straightening up.

"Sleep Dirt" is another oddity, a complete acoustic duet for two guitars. It features a fairly simple rhythm pattern and some lovely acoustic soloing by Zappa. Although it slightly foreshadows the Zappa instrumental "A Watermelon in Easter Hay," it is really one of a kind. It shows a real Spanish / classical guitar influence along with the kind of acoustic blues work that Zappa did not really do very often (Zappa was a master of the electric blues but rarely seems to venture into acoustic territory).

After "Sleep Dirt" suddenly ends (with James Youmans stopping because, as he tells Zappa, his hands got stuck in the strings), the album segues directly into "The Ocean Is the Ultimate Solution," a song originally intended for the two-disc set *Night of the Iron Sausage* (cut to one disc and renamed *Zoot Allures*). It is a 13-minute tour de force of drum / bass / guitar interplay (the drum / bass work by Terry Bozzio and Patrick O'Hearn is some of the best on the record). Especially notable is the stand-up bass solo work by O'Hearn that starts at about 5:00 into the song and continues intermittently throughout; listen especially closely for the stuff starting at 6:30, with O'Hearn messing up and muttering "damn it" under his breath!

Contemporary critical reaction to the album is mixed, with many making the argument that Zappa should have left the album alone after reacquiring the masters or that the album is simply for purists and not for beginners. A good example is Francois Couture, writing for *All Music Guide,*

> A strange mixture of the gloomy atmosphere of *Zoot Allures* and more theatrical (even cabaret-like in the case of "Flambay") writing, *Sleep Dirt* is somewhat sweet and sour. There are strong guitar solos, but the whole thing lacks panache (and the cover artwork is truly awful). This item remains more for the completist than the newcomer.[60]

Despite the lawsuits and the ever-changing band lineups, Zappa ended the seventies on a high note, with two of his better albums: the very popular *Sheik Yerbouti* and the bona fide masterpiece *Joe's Garage*. It took a while (Zappa, his managers, and Warner Bros. tangled for almost three years in total; the toll on Zappa was both financial—he was unable to make money from his recordings—and physical—because he could only make money from touring, he had to tour constantly). He would, however, find himself finishing the decade stronger than ever.

SHEIK YERBOUTI

The Peter Frampton years, *Sheik Yerbouti*, (originally released in March 1979 on Zappa Records; currently available as Rykodisc RCD 10528). Highest *Billboard* chart position: No. 21. Personnel: Adrian Belew, Tommy Mars. Peter Wolf, Patrick O'Hearn, Terry Bozzio, Ed Man, David Ocker, Napoleon Murphy Brock, Andre Lewis, Randy Thornton, and Davey Moire. "We've got to get into something real."[61]

Sheik Yerbouti is the first in a string of albums (including *Joe's Garage, Tinsel Town Rebellion, You Are What You Is,* and *Ship Arriving Too Late to Save a Drowning Witch*) that feature Zappa the songwriter. A reduced emphasis on instrumentals (with some stunning exceptions), an attention to songwriting, and a return to the bawdy, sexually explicit work that had been missing from the albums since *Apostrophe (')* gave Zappa a string of albums that were closer to hit records than he had been in a while.

Sheik Yerbouti is named, depending upon whom you believe, after a famous Saudi Arabian sheik much in the news at the time or after the K.C. & the Sunshine Band's hit "(Shake Shake Shake) Shake Your Booty" (I would guess it is probably named after both: 1979 being a year of both long gas lines and the Iranian hostage crises). The song sets the pattern for the albums to come with lots of humorous songs featuring crack bands playing with tremendous precision interspersed with a few instrumentals that seem sort of snuck in on an unsuspecting audience. (For those who were looking for Zappa's more adventurous instrumental work, he would release, around the same time, the *Shut Up 'N Play Yer Guitar* series of albums. More on those later.)

The album, in general, seems to be commenting on both where music has been and where it is going. It also seems to have, in and around the parody and irony, some profoundly disturbing things to say about life at the turn of the decade.

The album has an interesting sound, in large part because it is made up of basic tracks that were recorded in concert and then reworked in various studios, often with different or additional musicians. There is a lot of echo in many of the songs, the result of late-seventies live recording techniques. It is also, soundwise, the last album to really sound indicative of a certain age. Zappa would complete work on his home studio, the Utility Muffin Research Kitchen, late in 1979 and would do a lot of his recording there in the state-of-the-art confines he had constructed for himself.

Songwise, Zappa has several pieces of cultural critique that he was returning to after a long layoff: Americans' odd ideas about sex, the duplicity and corruption of unions, and the constructedness of musical fads, especially disco, punk, and good old pop.

The first song on the album is "I Have Been in You," discussed at length in Chapter 2, which sets the tone for the rest of the album: savage critique. It is as if Zappa had been saving up and storing his bile for several years. This song segues into "Flakes," which takes on the state of folks who "don't do no good / They never be workin' / When they oughta should." Although Watson is critical of Zappa's supposed antilabor stance in this song (and again in "Baby Snakes"), it is important to look closely: Zappa is not, and has never been, against the working man; he is against the folks who take money for a service and then do not provide said service. It is the typical lament of the small businessman; again and again Zappa is making the complaint that he works hard and tries to deliver a service commensurate with the fee he is charging, so why cannot others? Although he seems in this song to be pretty hard on the working stiff in late-seventies California (especially his hilarious reference to the Betty Crocker cake icing commercial in which a woman spreads frosting-in-a-can on a cake with a paper knife in order to demonstrate the moistness of the frosting—very seventies!), it can be seen as directed at the various flakes Zappa has been dealing with for most of his artistic life: musicians who accept his money but do not perform, record companies who distribute his product but do not pay him what they have agreed to pay him, mangers who use the money he has generated to sign and record other acts, the list goes on. The song, which is pretty straightforward rock, ends with a repeated chorus of "we're coming to get ya," a sure sign that Zappa saw his career in perpetual danger from the outside forces he was constantly being forced to deal with.

"Broken Hearts Are for Assholes" is an update of his earliest work; in fact, it can be seen in much the same vein as "I Ain't Got No Heart," a song that decries standard ideas about love. The argument that the song makes is simple: it is stupid to be so emotional about something, and if that something is going to break your heart, it is not worth it (another way of putting this: is it really love if it causes you so much pain?). Zappa does two things in the song that have caused some controversy. The first is that Zappa lampoons the growing gay scene in the United States, writing in the song that "Maybe you think you're a lonely guy / 'N maybe you think you're too tough to cry / so you went to *The Grape* just to give it a try." This argument takes Zappa's absurdist antilove song idea to its fullest form: that love will break your heart so much that it will turn you gay. This should be seen as hilarious. One reason that people have a more difficult time with this song now than they did in 1979 is that the ensuing years have not been all that great for the gay community. Between AIDS and the fire and damnation of evangelical preachers, homosexuality is viewed in a very different light than it was in 1979. At the time that Zappa is writing this song (as well as "Bobby Brown" from the same album and "Sy Borg" from the next), homosexuality is undergoing a renaissance unparalleled in U.S. culture. Gay culture, in other words, is in. Zappa's gay references in "Broken Hearts" are not, as some would claim, malicious, but humorous. There is no independence, Zappa seems to be claiming, until one can laugh at oneself. The gay rights movement has always had a lot of high-camp humor in it, and looked at in this way, "Broken Hearts Are for Assholes" can be seen as another example of Zappa reveling and enjoying the oddness of the country's uncertain relationship with sex, especially any sex that is not straight, heterosexual, missionary-position-type sex.

What makes the song doubly controversial is that, as he has done throughout his career, Zappa holds women as accountable as men for this silly dance. The final verse of the song returns to Zappa's ass fetish, picking right up where "Illinois Enema Bandit" left off, singing, "You say you can't live with what you've been through / Well, ladies you can be an asshole too / You might pretend you ain't got one on the bottom of you." This insistence upon freedom and responsibility repeatedly gets Zappa into trouble. But his argument is simple: just like the disco boy, the women in "Broken Hearts Are for Assholes" are reminded that the worst sin one can have is that of pride; acting like you do not have an asshole is simply against human nature. We all, as has been mentioned, shit, eat, sleep, and fuck.

Related to this song in both tenor and tone (and in fall-out-of-your-chair-funny) is "Bobby Brown," the surprise Scandinavian hit single about Zappa's favorite character, the arrogant upper-middle-class white boy who thinks he is entitled to an easy time of it. He is not.

"Bobby Brown" is perhaps the most misunderstood song in Zappa's canon (and that is saying a lot). Watson, for instance, who is normally a great defender of all things Zappa, seems to tow the party line on the song, arguing that Zappa uses the song to attack feminism.[62] I disagree. The song, if read as a character study and not as a monologue (and Zappa, who never had a fear of his own opinions, would not have made the distinction if he had not wanted to), is about Bobby Brown, a stock character (related, undoubtedly, to the typically corrupt American family unit in "Brown Shoes Don't Make It"). Bobby is the worst kind of overprivileged white male: the date rapist / fraternity boy / drunk who feels that he is God's gift to women and who feels he can take anything he wants. In the first verse of the song, we find that Bobby has no qualms about his own place in the universe, admitting "I got a cheerleader here wants to help with my paper / Let her do all the work 'n maybe later I'll rape her." In the next verse, Bobby decides to blame women's liberation for turning him gay, claiming that his unhappiness is due to "When I fucked this dyke by the name of Freddie." One can see the continuing themes of the sex act as rape (only someone with the ego of Bobby would find sex with a lesbian as something she wanted) and the absurdity of blaming others (women's liberation) for one's own choices. Bobby's subsequent humiliation at the hands of Freddie is payback for Bobby's actions, not, as many would have it, Zappa's hatred of feminism. Indeed, if there is a critique of feminism going on in the song, it is Zappa's lampooning of the white, middle-class male fear of feminism (along with gay rights, the other big sexual revolution movement occurring during the late seventies is the attempt to, yet again, pass an equal rights amendment; fear of feminism was everywhere!). The third verse of the song continues along in this vein, with Bobby now happily embracing the gay lifestyle. Another subtle cultural critique of Zappa's is the fear that straight men have that they can be turned gay by some cataclysmic social or sexual event. The narrative of "Bobby Brown" just seems too far-fetched to be seen as an outright attack on feminism. Combine this with Zappa's career-long critique of the arrogance of the white, male bourgeoisie and one can see "Bobby" (along with a number of songs on the album) as critical of the hegemony, not the minority.

The third in the trio of truly ribald songs on the album, and the song that is the most difficult to defend, is Zappa's paean to the Jewish American Princess. This is where Zappa's just-keepin'-it-real attitude seems to suffer. It is true, as Zappa repeated ad nauseam as he defended himself against the protests of the Anti-Defamation League, that the Jewish American Princess exists, and it is also true that the things Zappa says about her in his song may well be accurate to a certain extent. But the fact that Zappa reveled in the telling of this tale (and, to be honest, seemed to enjoy defending himself against the accusations of anti-Semitism the song encouraged) makes little sense. Zappa's music has always been about forcing people to realize the relationship between freedom and responsibility and the relationship between systems and the individual; the song "Jewish Princess" makes little sense in either of these lights. The only real way the song makes much sense is in the purely folkloric manner of some of Zappa's road songs. In other words, Zappa undoubtedly knew women like this and felt they needed coverage in his sociological project. Lyrics like "I want a nasty little Jewish Princess ... / With long phony nails and a hairdo that rinses" are a double-edged sword. Are there women like this? Certainly (the actress Fran Drescher has made a career out of playing this woman; see her as publicist Bobbi Fleckman in the film *Spinal Tap*); but the worry of the Anti-Defamation League is that it gives people who might have an intent more harmful than Zappa's (and I honestly believe that he was simply amused by these characters as he was by the gay rights movement) the right to their own anti-Semitism.[63] Zappa would revisit this theme on his next album, writing a song for "Catholic Girls," a subject that, due to his upbringing, Zappa knew a bit about.

What Zappa seems to be trying to expose in all of these songs ("Flakes," "Bobby Brown," "Jewish Princess," "I Have Been in You," and "Broken Hearts Are for Assholes") is the gross hypocrisy of the late twentieth century. Whether you are a union member, a pop star, a white male date rapist, or a Jewish princess, Zappa is making the claim that you do not deserve any sort of emotional protection, especially, in the case of many of these groups, you keep acting as if "you ain't got one on the bottom of you."

There is another set of songs on the album that is not nearly as direct as the previously mentioned songs. "Baby Snakes," "Trying to Grow a Chin," "I'm So Cute," "Jones Crusher," "City of Tiny Lights," "Wild Love," and "Yo Mama" are far more innocuous, although many of them are getting after the same topics.

"Trying to Grow a Chin" and "I'm So Cute" seem to be referencing both punk music (which Zappa thought of as a manufactured fad akin to disco) and the various terrors of the adolescent male. "Trying to Grow a Chin" features a nice, propulsive beat and a hilarious vocal by Terry Bozzio, who recites the travails of a young man desperately trying to grow a chin, which, in this case, is a beard, a sign of manhood. The song ends with the character wishing he were dead ("I wanna be dead in bed, please kill me"), a reference that seems to carry one all the way back to "Stuff up the Cracks" from *Cruising with Ruben & the Jets,* another Zappa reference to the silliness of adolescence. "I'm So Cute" seems to fit the same mold. Although it rocks much harder (with a much more pseudopunk beat), the lyrics are just as silly, this time celebrating the utter narcissism of the white American male. At one point Terry Bozzio, the song's vocalist, tells everyone else to "get some cyanide / and die" and that being ugly is so bad that it is the same as being in hell. This is a perfect comment on both punk and disco. Punk, which made a great show of ignoring the beauty culture and proudly flaunted convention was, in the late seventies, coexistent with disco, the ultimate triumph of the beauty culture; in other words, one way to see "I'm So Cute" is as a punk song celebrating disco culture—not a bad piece of juxtaposition. "I'm So Cute" is followed immediately by "Jones Crusher," a semifunny piece of music with a great vocal by Adrian Belew and some great guitar work by both Zappa and Belew. The song is about a woman who can crush a man's manhood. It is one of Zappa's lamer double entendres but it does serve as proof of the argument that Zappa was far harder on men than he was on women.

One interesting note about both "I'm So Cute" and "Jones Crusher," as obsessively chronicled on the "We're Only in It for the Touring" home page (found at the *Turtles All the Way Down* Web site at http://ourworld. compuserve.com / homepages / turtlestew / wereonly.htm): Both of these songs began as slow Rolling Stones–influenced blue pieces (with Ray White working the vocals on both). When Belew joined the band, both were sped up, either in response to Belew's abilities (Zappa often argues that songs are written and rearranged to suit a particular group) or to up the fake-punk aspects of the songs.

"Baby Snakes," which is one of the catchier tunes that Zappa ever wrote, is lyrically on the sillier side, although it does have the classic line "They live by a...code / That is usually SMPTE / Which stands for / *Society of Motion Picture & Television Engineers.*" The rest of the song, interestingly enough, seems to be more about male genitalia (the baby snakes of the title) than about tape coding.

"Wild Love" and "Yo Mama" end the album with a nice one-two punch. "Wild Love" is a much more constructed piece of music than the other songs on the albums (it is one song that does not seem to have the live recording sound). It is a great piece of music that harkens back to the work Zappa had been doing with the Brock-Duke bands: lots of art / jazz rock changes and stop-on-a-dime tempo shifts.[64] "Yo Mama" is a 12-minute song that has lyrics, it seems, to justify the solos. There is an unfortunate bit of mean-spiritedness about the lyrics, related by keyboard player Tommy Mars, who said in an interview in *Keyboard* magazine,

> Frank wrote that song at the very beginning of the '77 European tour, and it has a personal relevance to me. We were doing this rehearsal in London and

> Frank was getting very tense. He expected certain things to be there when
> we got to rehearsal, and certain things were not there. We were gonna do
> the song "Zoot Allures," and he started playing this 11th chord and got very
> angry at everybody because nothing was happening right. I got fined because
> I hadn't memorized this little piece called "Little House I Used to Live In."
> I hadn't realized he wanted it totally memorized. So this rehearsal ended in a
> total fiasco. The next day, he came in with these lyrics: "Maybe you should stay
> with yo' mama."

Despite the mean in-joke of the lyrics (and Mars would stay with Zappa for
a number of subsequent albums and tours), the song is really an excuse for
12 minutes of down and dirty soloing. According to the liner notes, the solo
in "Yo Mama" was recorded at a different time as part of a different song, a
technique Zappa would turn to more and more as he constructed his songs.
It is an interesting solo and one worth listening to several times; after the
jazz/fusion solos of the past several albums, this is a very slow rock-based
solo that grinds along at a pace that is unusual in its measured tempo.

"Dancin' Fool," which became the hit single off the album (and that is a
fairly subjective consideration; certainly a hit single in comparison to other
Zappa singles), is one of the songs people seem to remember when they
are thinking about Zappa (it is also one of the songs he played on a return
appearance on *Saturday Night Live*, which introduced him to a bigger audience than he might reach in a year of touring). It is certainly a more realized attack on the disco lifestyle than "Disco Boy" had been (although the
metal guitar/drum machine music of "Disco Boy" is a better musical joke).
One of the best parts of the song is Zappa's self-reflexivity—in many ways
the song is at least in part autobiographical—the protagonist of the song,
we find, is suffering from the same physical malady that Zappa is: "One of
my legs is shorter than the other/'N both my feet's too long." (As a result
of being pushed off the stage in London in 1972, one of Zappa's legs was
indeed longer than the other.) Other than celebrating the desire to dance,
even when one has no real talent (an admittedly subjective term) for dancing
(about this time Zappa had started to invite the audience onstage to dance to
"The Black Page," an almost impossible song to dance to), the song is really
a fairly critical indictment of the lifestyle that had sprung up around disco.[65]
When Zappa sings, later in the song, about "disco people," including those
who would not go out without "a spoon for up my nose," he is describing,
perfectly, the Studio 54 lifestyle that was being so aggressively celebrated in
all of the hep, and not so hep, places in the United States.[66] Zappa ends the
song with a hilarious name check of the film *Looking for Mr. Goodbar,* an
antifeminist film about the dangers of women wanting to be single and sexually active. The song then descends into a series of clichés that men might
use to pick up women. It is clear that Zappa found great humor in the disco
lifestyle, as well he should have. It seems, in reading this song, that Zappa

found the lifestyles of the late seventies as manufactured as he found the hippie lifestyle of the sixties.

Even with all of these songs, there is still room for a number of interesting
instrumentals, including another, more advanced incidence of xenochrony
called "Rubber Shirt." According to Zappa, the song was constructed from
parts of a 1974 performance with Patrick O'Hearn overdubbing selected
parts onto a master tape with drums from a third performance added later. In
the liner notes, Zappa writes that "All of the sensitive, interesting interplay
between the bass and drums never actually happened."

Two final instrumentals, "Rat Tomago" and "The Sheik Yerbouti Tango,"
are live recordings of solo sections of longer songs (most of the *Shut Up 'N
Play Yer Guitar* and *Guitar* albums would be excerpted guitar solos from
longer pieces). In the case of "Rat Tomago," it is clear that the piece is a solo
taken from a performance of "The Torture Never Stops" (if you listen carefully you can hear the groans and screams in the background). "The Sheik
Yerbouti Tango" is an excerpted guitar solo from the song "The Little House
I Used to Live In" recorded in Germany in 1978.

In general, *Sheik Yerbouti* is a tremendous return to form: humorous songs,
intense instrumentals, and a great band all well recorded. It is no wonder that
it was one of Zappa's biggest hits, selling well over one million copies. It is a
nice debut for the new label.

Contemporary critical reaction to the album is more mixed than one might
guess. The *All Music Guide* writes: "Even if it sometimes drifts a bit, fans
of Zappa's '70s work will find *Sheik Yerbouti* on nearly an equal level with
Apostrophe and *Over-Nite Sensation,* both in terms of humor and musical
quality."[67] Andrew Boscardan writes, "One of his most popular and infamous
albums, *Sheik Yerbouti* finds Frank Zappa unleashing his unique brand of
sociological documentation on the disco-injected culture of the late '70s."[68]
Both *The New Rolling Stone Album Guide* and *Musichound Rock* ignore it
completely, as do many critics and biographers. After the hell of the Warner
Bros. / *Läther* fiasco and coming, as it did, right before *Joe's Garage,* it tends
to be forgotten by critics. The fans have not forgotten it. Many of the songs
on the album were performed for years afterward, and a couple of them—
"Bobby Brown," "Dancin Fool," and "City of Tiny Lights"—were to stay
around for a good long time.

Politics: 1979–88

JOE'S GARAGE, ACTS I, II & III

The Masterpiece. *Joe's Garage, Acts I, II & III* (originally released as two records: *Joe's Garage, Act I*, on Zappa Records in September 1979 and *Joe's Garage, Acts II & III*, on Zappa Records in November 1979; currently available as Rykodisc RCD 10530 / 31). Personnel: Warren Cucurullo, Denny Walley, Ike Willis, Peter Wolf, Tommy Mars, Arthur Barrrow, Ed Man, Vinne Colaiuta, Jeff, Marginal Chagrin, Stumuk, Dale Bozzio, Al Malkin, Craig Steward, and Patrick O'Hearn, with a special appearance by Terry Bozzio as Bald Headed John. "A stupid story about how the government is going to try to do away with music."[1]

Although many fans feel that Zappa did his best work in the sixties (on *Absolutely Free* and *We're Only in It for the Money*), with Flo & Eddie, or with the Duke-Brock Bands (especially on *One Size Fits All*), there is no argument that for sheer musical expertise, technical brilliance and ability, and highly charged political lyrics that were able to look clearly into the all-to-near-future, *Joe's Garage* is a masterpiece. It is an incredible achievement, excellent from start to finish. It encompasses all of the musical styles Zappa had been working with since his start: blues, jazz, doo-wop, lounge, orchestral, rock, pop, and, as a new addition, reggae. It takes on all of the lyrical themes that Zappa had been essaying since he started in music: the danger of systems, the foolishness of white males, the responsibility of individual freedom, and the strange relationship Americans have with sex and sexual frankness.

The album, despite its coherence and interesting through-narrative, did not start out that way. Zappa, according to Barry Miles, was working on a bunch of songs for a follow-up to *Sheik Yerbouti* when he discovered that they had some internal coherence, "So I [Zappa] went home one night midway through recording, wrote the story and changed it into an opera."[2]

Nearly all of the critics and biographers offer fairly complete narrative synopses of *Joe's Garage* (Courrier's is the most complete, whereas Watson's is the most interesting, offering up a myriad of political analyses). The narrative, should one listen to the album as if it were a Broadway show recording, is actually fairly straightforward: The Central Scrutinizer, a sort of controlling intelligence character that Zappa has played around with before (especially in some of his early tape experiments), tells a cautionary tale about Joe, a typical American male of indeterminate age (although clearly an adolescent of some sort) who decides to start a band. Unfortunately for Joe, the government has decided that music is bad (which, as the liner notes mention, the government of Iran had recently done and, as Zappa would find out in the mid-eighties, the government of the United States would try to do). In order to prove that music leads to bad things, the Central Scrutinizer shows us the slippery slope that Joe goes down: girls, drugs, disease, religion, strange sexual practices, prison, and, ultimately, insanity. There is, of course, a lot more; along the way, Zappa takes shots at the Catholic Church, rock journalists, U.S. pop culture, new-age theology, and his own band.

What makes the album truly great is the music. It is unbelievable. From start to finish, *Joe's Garage* is a collection of some of Zappa's most perfectly realized pop songs. It is as if Zappa was proving to people, especially critics, that he was capable of writing fairly serious pop music. This is pop music unlike any other, however. The more one listens, the more one realizes that Zappa, even when writing short pop songs with catchy melodies, is unable to stick to formula. In some senses, if one listens carefully enough, *Joe's Garage* is a tour of U.S. popular music from the forties to the present.

After a short speech from the Central Scrutinizer who explains what we are all doing here (listening to his presentation), we get the song "Joe's Garage," a beautiful fifties-inflected piece about an idealized garage-band experience that seems somewhat autobiographical, especially in the argument that true musicians should be able to get off on the music and not need substances: "We didn't have no dope or LSD / But a coupla' quartsa' beer." As the band practices a bit more, girls start coming around and the band realizes that they will be able to reap a certain reward for all of their practicing.

Another interesting, autobiographical feature of the song: Zappa sings at one point that the band had to play the same song repeatedly simply "cause it sounded good to me." Zappa has often said, as a defense of his music, that he is the only real audience, that he writes and plays music for himself, and this line seems to let one peek into this subconscious.

After some more practice and some local fame, including some work in a local go-go bar, the band gets a record deal (the perils of which Zappa was intimately familiar) that turns out to be, unsurprisingly, not everything it is cracked up to be. So the band breaks up and Joe imagines a number of musical fads, including new wave, heavy metal, disco, and glitter rock. Then Joe decides to revive his song and is promptly arrested by the police and sent, because it is a first offence, to church.

The song "Joe's Garage" is, like many of the pieces on the album, deeply political. For much of his career, Zappa bemusedly watched the state of the music industry. Coming, as he did, from a world in which musicians could be self-made and could literally go from the garage to the Whisky-A-Go-Go to a recording contract (as a gloss of the early Mothers of Invention might have it) and existing in a world in 1979 in which bands were packaged and processed and in which music was called product and sold in units, "Joe's Garage" becomes a specific and cutting critique of the state of the music industry.

The critique continues as Joe gets in trouble and is sent to church as punishment. Many critics argue that "Catholic Girls" was written to get Zappa off the hook for the criticism he had been receiving for the song "Jewish Princess," and there is a bit of truth to that: the entire album *Joe's Garage* began, according to a number of sources, with Zappa recording the songs "Joe's Garage" and "Catholic Girls" to be released as a single, and in the fade-out of the song a sitar plays the "Jewish Princess" theme. It fits well into the extended narrative, however, and is especially valid today, living as we do in a country in which the current presidential administration has made religious organizations eligible for government funds to relieve the federal government of some of its rehabilitative functions (i.e., you could get sentenced to church as punishment).

The song, despite its hilarious lounge-singer vocals (which secure, at least in this author's opinion, the complete genius of Ike Willis as Zappa's best vocalist and foil) and the various juvenile sexual innuendos, is a biting criticism of the hypocrisy of the church. One of the worst-kept secrets of my childhood was that of the sexually charged nature of church-related social activities— especially those such as confirmation classes and church camps, coming, as these activities did, in the middle of adolescence—and the hypocrisy of the myth of the good Catholic girl. One of the things that Zappa seems to be saying in this song is that some Catholic girls are not as pure and innocent as the church, and the media, would have you think and that, indeed, they are, like many adolescent girls, just as horny and irresponsible as boys are. Zappa and company sing, "In a little white dress...They never confess." This great ironic juxtaposition of the white dress, representing this myth of innocence, and the lack of confession is really a pretty damning argument. Another argument that Zappa makes in the song, one that at the time was based on rumor, is about the homosexuality of Catholic priests. Although Zappa would not live to see the huge scandal within the Catholic Church caused by a number of priests molesting children and the church's subsequent cover-up of the facts, it is eerily prescient when Zappa sings, "Father Riley's a fairy/But it don't bother Mary." Zappa's Catholic upbringing has never been more apparent than it is in this song.

Musically, the song is hilarious. It features a rocking sitar melody and, in the breaks, a great mock-lounge beat reminiscent of both Zappa's and Tommy Mars's experiences playing in lounge bands, with Ike Willis doing a sick lounge-singer pseudoscat vocal (which owes at least a small debt to Bill Murray's wildly popular lounge-singer character from *Saturday Night Live*).

After Joe discovers that his friend Mary is not quite as innocent as she might appear (she is, after all, a Catholic girl), he also discovers the power of music that he had forgotten. After making a date with Mary to meet at the social club, Joe is stranded as Mary leaves him to go with some girlfriends to see a band at the local armory. Mary, in an attempt to get a ticket to see the show, and perhaps meet the pop star of her choice, performs an act of oral gratification upon a member of the road crew of the band and becomes the subject of the next song, "Crew Slut."

In many ways this is the only problematic song on the album. The degradation that the terms *crew slut* implies is vastly different from the rather ambivalent term *groupie*. The humor of the song seems to develop out of the idea that some girls are so desperate to meet the band that they will have sex with the nasty members of the crew (i.e., they are so low class that they will not hold out for a band member). The larger argument, however, is one that Zappa has made time and time again: Women are just as free as men to do stupid stuff, and if this is what you are willing to put yourself through to see a show or meet a famous pop star, than so be it (these girls, it should be said, could have waited in line and bought tickets like everyone else).

As Zappa sings in the beginning of the song, one of the possible explanations for this kind of behavior is boredom: "Hey Hey Hey all you girls in these industrial towns/I know you're prob'ly gettin' tired/Of all the local clowns." This is an age-old argument (see, for instance, the very popular film *An Officer and a Gentleman* for a representation of the same sort of behavior); the attraction that women feel to the traveling salesman (something that is played for laughs in the Broadway musical *Oklahoma*) is the same that they might feel to a band coming through town (indeed, there is both a certain illicitness and anonymity in being with a band member for one night and then watching him move on to the next town). This is of course still true today, although in some ways the rock star groupie has been replaced by the professional athlete groupie, in part because the rock star groupie has become part of the charming cultural past of the United States (see, for instance, the way groupies are represented in the film *Almost Famous* or the book *I'm with the Band*).[3]

"Crew Slut" becomes a great blues jam, with some excellent Denny Wally slide guitar and a neat little harmonica break. It is a great contemporary updating of the blues that is more Rolling Stones or Aerosmith than it is Gatemouth Brown or Guitar Watson.

The narrative continues with Mary deciding to travel along with the band (named Toad-O in a not-so-subtle swipe at the band Toto). Zappa's narrative, that Mary had been lured into this life because of music, is of course reminiscent of the kinds of slippery-slope arguments that have always been made about music; from Frank Sinatra to Elvis to the Beatles, young girls and their fascination with pop stars have always been the subject of parental disapproval. As the Central Scrutinizer helpfully shows us, Mary's life is the direct result of a young girl's fetish for popular music. The connection between Mary's Catholicism and her willingness to give up her life to follow the band around is not explored, although psychologists tell us that women who are raised to follow the orders and suggestions of strong male authority figures (a priest, for instance) are often predisposed to follow the suggestions of other male authority figures.[4] Mary is abandoned by the band in Miami and in order to raise money to return home takes part in a wet T-shirt contest.

In what is one of Zappa's finest pieces of sociology, "Fembot in a Wet-T-Shirt" (originally titled "Wet-T-Shirt Contest") presents a great piece of theater / journalism about the stupid things people will do for entertainment. Courrier comments that "Wet-T-Shirt Night" came from an experience that Zappa had at the Brasserie, a strip club in Miami, that "was so sickening that I didn't even stay to see the T-shirts get wet."[5]

The song is an excellent contempo-jazz workout featuring a percussion chart that shows why the tandem of Vinne Colaiuta and Ed Mann may well be the most accomplished percussion duo Zappa ever worked with.[6] It is hard to describe the swirling up-tempo music of this piece that segues into a spoken-word section in the middle in which Zappa, as Buddy Jones, the wet T-shirt night MC (who is in reality a defrocked Father Riley), and Dale Bozzio, as Mary, engage in some hilarious banter about the formalities of the wet T-shirt contest. The line that seems to indicate what Zappa is critiquing is when Buddy Jones describes the T-shirts that all the girls are wearing: "a thoroughly soaked, stupid-looking white sort of male person's conservative kind of middle-of-the road cotton undergarment." This is, perhaps, the same kind of T-shirt one might wear if he is also wearing brown shoes and running the world from city hall.

Mary, as we also find out in this song, is "the kind of red-blooded American girl who'll do anything for fifty bucks," which may have been slightly shocking in 1979, but in the age of *Girls Gone Wild,* this seems comparatively tame. There is one final idea that comes up, very briefly, in the song that remains unexplored. At one point Mary tells Buddy that she needs the prize money to get home. Buddy makes the statement that Mary's father is waiting for her "in the tool shed." This idea, often explored on the Howard Stern radio show of all places, that strippers and porn stars and other sexually active women are products of abusive homes remains unexplored on the rest of the album but seems worth mentioning here. As current political events have indicated, Mary's upbringing by an abusive father and a Catholic Church desperate to hide the sexual proclivities of its clergy have led her down the path to the wet T-shirt contest.

The song quickly fades into the first of several interesting instrumental workouts on the album. Originally called "On the Bus" and retitled "Toad-O-Line" for the CD release (perhaps because, as a number of fans argue, the first several notes of Zappa's solo are taken from the big Toto hit of the time "Hold the Line"). The musical track is new, but the solo comes from a performance of "Inca Roads" recorded in Germany in March 1979. This is the case for most of the instrumentals on the album (except for "A Watermelon in Easter Hay"). Zappa has told the story often of how he had recorded most of his guitar solos from the 1979 tour and had many of them on tape and, for the instrumentals on *Joe's Garage,* fit them into the backing tracks that had been recorded in the sessions for the album.

Joe, meanwhile, lamenting the loss of Mary, has hooked up with Lucille, a woman who works at Jack in the Box, a fast-food restaurant ubiquitous in California and the Southwest. An unfortunate result of Joe's adventures with Lucille is that he catches a communicable disease. This is presented in the two-song minisuite "Why Does It Hurt When I Pee?" and "Lucille Has Messed My Mind Up."

According to Zappa's onstage comments during the premier of the song (in September 1978), "Why Does It Hurt When I Pee?" was the comment shouted by a roadie in the bathroom of the tour bus that, unfortunately, was overheard by the rest of the band. On *Joe's Garage* the song is a pretty hilarious list of common myths and misperceptions about VD from the late seventies, including the all-time favorite, "I got it from a toilet seat / it jumped right up / and grabbed my meat." Musically the song is a fine piece of fake heavy metal, with cascading distorted guitars and a funny metal-like guitar break (which has the guitarists doubling their solos along with Ed Mann on percussion). If the listener can get past the words, there are some hilarious musical moments that mock the sort of pompous seventies heavy metal that bands like Boston were making. The instrumental break in the middle of the song involves very dramatic use of tympanis and chorus that ups the pomp-factor by 10.

The song segues directly into the lament (and Ike Willis showcase) "Lucille Has Messed My Mind Up." The music for this song comes from an old Jeff Simmons album (which Zappa had played on). For *Joe's Garage* it is reworked into a reggae-based soul song that emphasizes the power of Ike Willis as a vocalist. This is the first of many reggae-based songs that Zappa would do. For some reason, Zappa would increasingly turn toward reggae (and away from blues) as the basis for his soloing, although there is no solo in either this song or "Sy Borg," the other reggae-based song on the album. At the end of the song (which ended the original *Act I* set), the Central Scrutinizer returns to sum everything up (and review the slippery-slope thesis of Zappa's): "girls, music, disease, heartbreak...they all go together."

At this point in the libretto, Zappa takes time out to discuss his theory of "Total Criminalization," which, in short, dictates that all people are inherently criminals and that it is the government's job to invent laws and crimes that will give them (the government) the legal grounds to arrest folks. This, Zappa argues, "is one of the reasons why Music was eventually made illegal."

Acts II & III pick right up where we left off, with Joe, trying to recover from his heartbreak, turning toward the new-age religion of L. Ron Hoover and the First Church of Appliantology.[7] Using as its musical basis the same song with which he had opened his 1974 concerts (called "Tush Tush Tush (A Token of My Extreme)" on *You Can't Do That on Stage Anymore, Vol. 2*), Zappa's lyrics lay out the story of a modern megachurch that seems as much a media hustle as a theological sanctuary. Perhaps as an indication of how Zappa saw this kind of new-age mysticism, he has L. Ron Hoover sing to Joe, "Don't you be *tarot-fied*," which, in all likelihood, refers back to the main character in "Camarillo Brillo," who can "throw a mean tarot." The idea of the tarot card was emblematic of the kind of new-age silliness that was still pervasive in the late seventies and of Zappa's continuing amusement at the ways in which people would seek spiritual fulfillment.

The character of Hoover can have a number of meanings. The most obvious is that the character is a direct reference to L. Ron Hubbard, the founder of the Church of Scientology, a California-based quasi-religious organization that is based largely on individual notions of spiritual happiness. Hubbard was a prolific author, lecturer, and wearer of cravats who was famous for his pithy pronouncements, such as "All the happiness you ever find lies in you."[8] Hubbard's belief is in the person, as opposed to the Christian belief in the spiritual. When L. Ron Hoover tells Joe that he (Joe) is a "Latent Appliance Fetishist," this is satire working on a couple of different levels: the first is a satire of the pseudo religiousspeak of the real-life L. Ron Hubbard, and the second is a reference to Zappa's delight at the oddities of human sexual behavior.

From this point, Zappa spins the tale into absurdity, having Joe find redemption through appliances, although not specifically sexual appliances (at one point Joe remarks that he's "never craved a toaster or a color t.v."). Hoover (the name for a famous vacuum cleaner company, get it?) sends Joe to the closet, which is a bar where Joe can find a nice appliance. It is a nice domestic joke (most middle-class U.S. homes have a closet full of appliances) and a metaphor for those who are hiding their homosexuality. Hoover/Zappa reverse the joke, however, telling Joe that he must "go into the closet" not "come out." The relationship between religion and sexual freedom is key in this song. As Zappa has already critiqued the classical religious hypocrisy in "Catholic Girls," he is using "A Token of My Extreme" to critique the new-age babble and the backsliding on the sexual revolution. Imagine a church leader who would tell someone to go and have sex with a "magical pig with marital aids stuck all over it." Indeed, however, if all happiness lies within, and within lies a latent appliance fetishist, then all one can do is follow the bliss.

"A Token of My Extreme" leads into two of the sickest, silliest, and downright funniest songs in the Zappa canon. "Stick It Out," which was originally part of the Flo & Eddie "Sofa" routine, becomes a hilarious funk/disco song sung first in German and then in English about the mating habits of single, white Americans in the late seventies. Imagine the sheer absurdity of a robot, a "pan-sexual-roto-plooker," using a number of clichéd pickup lines on Joe, including "do you come here often?/... You must be a Libra...your place or mine." Several of the lines at the end are not only clichés but are lines from other Zappa songs—"What's a girl like you" is from Flo & Eddie; "I've got it, you're an Italian" comes from the end of "Dancin' Fool." The combination of the faux-disco beat and the hilarious disco-era pickup lines makes for extreme comedy. It also reverses a lot of the normal sexual politics; the man, who would normally be saying these cheesy pickup lines, is now put on the other side of the power dynamic, having to fend off or accept the advances of the chrome pig.

After Joe accepts the pig's offer to go back to his place, we get the song "Sy Borg," another great piece of ironic juxtaposition. The music is a soft, thoughtful funk-reggae-R&B, whereas the lyrics are as filthy as anything Flo & Eddie ever did. Over this great R&B beat, we find Joe and Sy (the pig) engaging in a conversation about various sexual activities (many of them government sponsored) that they have done or are going to do, both with each other and with Sy's roommate, a "modified gay Bob doll (he goes all the way)."

Finally, after Joe has satisfied himself by abusing both of the devices, he is arrested for accidentally killing Sy ("the golden shower must have shorted out his master circuit") and sent to prison.

The song "Sy Borg" is fascinating in a number of ways. Certainly Zappa's glee in the weird sexual practices of others (this is the second album in a row that has featured the golden shower) and in the various devices, especially the devices he would see while touring in Europe (which is, perhaps, why Sy is German), gives the song its surface humor. The song is also notable, however, for the extraordinary way it references other Zappa songs. The emphasis upon chrome goes back to "The Chrome Plated Megaphone of Destiny" (which was also referring to a doll); Joe, at one point, tells Sy, "Oh no, I can't believe it," a reference to the song "Oh No." The gay Bob doll is a reference not only to "Ms. Pinky" (the doll is described as a "miniature rubberized homo-replica") but, perhaps, to potato-headed Bobby (from "San Ber'dino") and/or Bobby Brown. It is exhausting just trying to keep up!

The song that follows, "Dong Work for Yuda," is either an exquisite or an excruciating inside joke. Based, the story goes, on the fractured grammar of Zappa bodyguard John Smothers (as voiced by former drummer Terry Bozzio), the song does not really fit in the narrative of *Joe's Garage,* although it could be an indication of Joe's slipping sanity (as we start to see in the next few songs, his sanity is becoming tenuous). The libretto's discussion of the song describes Bald Headed John as a former record company promotions manager who is now the king of the plookers, Zappa's term for gay prison sex. "Dong Work for Yuda" leads to "Keep It Greasy," a song that Zappa had been performing since 1975 (there is an interesting bluesy version on the *FZ:OZ* album with a different band). The song is Zappa's straightforward ode to anal sex. Although he had worked around the edges of this subject in the past, he had never really come out and written a song about the technical details of the act. "Keep It Greasy" rectifies this situation. Musically, the song starts as a nice straight-ahead rock song. The lyrics simply tell a person to "keep it greasy so it'll go down easy." Philosophically, the song is another in a long line of songs that has argued that women need sex as much as men do.

Just as the album has entered the realm of the completely absurd, Zappa pulls it back and really changes direction. Starting with the solo section of "Keep It Greasy," Zappa turns introspective. Around the 3:15 mark of "Keep It Greasy," Zappa launches into a fantastic solo (the music is a twisted Latin-influenced drum, bass, and percussion breakdown, and the guitar solo comes from a performance of "City of Tiny Lights" from March 1979). The solo winds around the percussion (which is fascinating because the solo and the percussion have little to do with each other in a compositional sense) until the song builds to a climax and slides into "Outside Now," a huge soul ballad that features both the vocals of Ike Willis and another long solo by Zappa.

"Outside Now" seems like the ultimate bit of nightmare fortune-telling. Joe, who has been repeatedly gang raped in prison, is a broken man (all, one must remember, because of music). He lies in his prison cell and imagines the notes he would play on his guitar if only the government would let him. This, of course, seems to clearly parallel Zappa's own career: Record companies and managers and deranged fans who push him offstage have all conspired to keep Zappa from making music at one time or another, and he is sick and depressed about it. Zappa has Ike Willis relate the various troubles that Joe has been having and then ends the discussion with the short, emotional, and soul-baring line, "all I ever really wanted to do was play the guitar and bend the string." The naked emotion in Willis's voice leads one to believe that he is the singer through whom Zappa was best able to communicate his own emotional state. Zappa has repeatedly said in his autobiography and in interviews that all he wants to do is make music—write it, perform it, talk about it, and so forth. And yet, throughout his life, he has been prevented from doing so by outside forces. "Outside Now" (along with the two songs that follow) directly addresses the rage and sorrow Zappa seemed to be feeling. As Joe / Ike sings "I would dream of guitar notes that would irritate an executive kind of guy," Zappa launches into a discordant solo that was the antithesis of rock / pop soloing; indeed, one gets the sense that Zappa was intentionally creating music that record companies would not support. The song ends with a two-minute guitar solo (also taken from a "City of Tiny Lights" solo from March 1979) that plumbs the depths of the emotional state of Joe / Zappa.[9]

The slow blues continues with "He Used to Cut the Grass," a much longer (nearly eight minutes) solo (no information is available on where the solo may have come from) that is much more lyrical than the "Outside Now" solo. The libretto to the album describes what is happening when the solo occurs: "Joe wanders through the world which by then has been totally epoxied over, carefully organized, with everyone reporting daily to his or her appointed place in a line somewhere." Heard with the idea that Zappa is creating a musical equivalent of a dystopian future, the song takes on a much more visual dimension.

After the return of the Central Scrutinizer, who tells us that Joe is living entirely inside his head and has gone so far as to start dreaming up imaginary interviews and reviews about his music, Zappa gives us "Packard Goose," a nasty shot at his somewhat antagonistic relationship with the press and a nearly seven-minute guitar solo, much of which is taken from the "Easy Meat" solo from March 1979.[10]

The song starts off with the challenge: "Maybe you thought I was the Packard Goose / Or the Ronald MacDonald of the nouveau-abstruse / Well fuck all them people, I don't need no excuse." If there ever was a Zappa credo, this is it. If one looks at Zappa's press coverage from the days of the early Mothers until the end of his career, it is easy to see where Zappa's complaints were coming from. Once the darling of the press, Zappa has, since the early seventies, been the subject of an increasingly hostile press who seem to be engaging in the original-Mothers-were-the-only-band-worth-listening-to sort of myth making that must have driven Frank up the wall. "Packard Goose" gives vent to the rage that Zappa felt at a press that did not seem to be interested in doing much more than "seeking a method by which they can reinforce conclusions they've already arrived at."[11] This is, on the one hand, a fairly cynical attitude, but it is one born of 20 years of interactions with the press. It is a common lament among artists and entertainers and gets down to the fundamental dissonances between artists, journalists, and critics. The critic's role in society is to discuss the possible meaning(s) of a text or texts. This, as might be expected, tends to drive the artist nuts. Zappa, and only Zappa, the argument goes, should be able to determine what kind of meaning(s) people might get out of his art. In the final verse of the song, Zappa returns to the argument that if you are on his side, he is on yours. This is Zappa setting up the terms of the artistic relationship with the audience: *like* is the important word here (like is a subjective determination). What Zappa seems to be saying is that if you enjoy or agree with what he is doing artistically, then you are OK. If you do not like what he is doing (if you do not agree with it or enjoy it), then the problem is yours, you do not understand the art, and you are either too dumb or too much the tool of the media to get it. This is a deeply problematic argument, what rhetoricians call the fallacy of the false dilemma, although it is an argument that nearly all artists fall prey to at one point or another in their careers: the they-just-do-not-get-it / me argument.

Sandwiched between the two verses about journalism is a nifty piece of philosophy that Zappa has Mary, who has been absent from the text since she was trying to get back home to see her father who was waiting for her in the tool shed at the end of "Wet-T-Shirt Contest," present, which is essentially an anti-Platonic theory of knowledge. For Zappa, truth is, for the most part, contingent upon what we know and upon how we use and approach it. He takes great pains to delineate the differences between information, knowledge, wisdom, and truth and how each one of them informs the others (i.e., information to Zappa is just data; any sort of knowledge or meaning that one gets out of information depends upon who the speaker is and who the listener is). Had he not been a musician, Zappa would have been a worthy rhetorician or philosopher.

"Packard Goose" segues in to the crowing achievement of the album, "A Watermelon in Easter Hay," which is simply one of the most gorgeous pieces of music ever produced. A slow blues along the lines of "Black Napkins," "Watermelon" is the aural representation of Joe's last imaginary guitar solo. It is a deeply emotional piece of music, one that can not really be described.[12]

There is really nowhere to go from here, so the album ends with a coda of sorts, "A Little Green Rosetta," a song that was originally written for the *Läther* album, which seems to be Zappa's last attempt to have some sport at the expense of the music industry. After "Watermelon" ends, the Central Scrutinizer returns to tell the listener that "music can get you pretty fucked up" and that what a good citizen ought to do is "hock your imaginary guitar and get a good job." Of course, for anyone who has followed Zappa's work from at least "Brown Shoes Don't Make It" knows that the worst thing one can do is conform and get a good job, especially one as dull and mind-numbing as the one Joe settles for, which involves putting the little frosting rosettes on top of the muffins that come down the assembly line. Indeed, Zappa's comments during the song seem to indicate that there is more than a little drudgery in the making of most pop records and that to be an original, as Zappa is, means to demean yourself. As the song winds down, the chorus becomes "They're pretty good musicians / But it don't make no difference … Because anybody who would buy this record / Doesn't give a fuck if there's good musicians on it."

This final, bitter comment seems to be indicative of a larger anger, and, in many ways, this anger is justified. Zappa, at the end of the seventies, is at the top of his game. Yet he has been screwed by record companies, managers, former band members, and even fans (the constant clamoring that nothing is as good as the original Mothers, despite the increased levels of technical expertise of various bands) as well as the critics.

Even contemporary critics can not discuss *Joe's Garage* without bringing up the Mothers. Steve Huey writes:

> In spite of its flaws, *Joe's Garage* has enough substance to make it one of Zappa's most important '70s works and overall political statements, even if it's not focused enough to rank with his earliest Mothers of Invention master-pieces.[13]

The Amazon.com review simply retells the narrative, although it does add that "Zappa's aim is true and his scope wide."[14] *The New Rolling Stone Album Guide* barely mentions the albums, citing it only for its "sophomoric smutti-ness."[15] The question that all of these reviews raise, however, is whether they are mad at the music or the man. Zappa, like all truth tellers, made a lot of enemies. As he headed into the eighties, and another 12 years of Republican presidents, the torture for Zappa the artist would indeed never stop.

TINSEL TOWN REBELLION

Roaring into the Eighties. *Tinsel Town Rebellion* (originally released in May 1981 on Barking Pumpkin Records; currently available as Rykodisc RCD 10532). Highest *Billboard* chart position: No. 66. Personnel: Ike Willis, Ray White, Steve Vai, Warren Cucurullo, Denny Walley, Tommy Mars, Peter Wolf, Bob Harris, Ed Mann, Arthur Barrow, Patrick O'Hearn, Vinnie Colaiuta, and David Logeman. "We cannot return to a past in which Americans harmoniously shared one set of moral values."[16]

The eighties find Zappa in an interesting quandary. His records, especially *Zoot Allures, Sheik Yerbouti,* and *Joe's Garage, Acts I, II & III,* are selling well, his concerts are increasingly sold out, he has built his own studio, and he is even beginning to be seen by many in the classical music world as a legitimate composer (both the conductor Kent Nagano and the composer and conduc-tor Pierre Boulez will work with Zappa in the early eighties). Zappa's film *Baby Snakes* comes out to moderate acclaim (a soundtrack will be released in 1983), and the mail-order-only records *Shut Up 'N Play Yer Guitar, Shut Up 'N Play Yer Guitar Some More,* and *The Return of the Son of Shut Up 'N Play Yer Guitar* do surprisingly well considering the limited audience (the records, which this book will not discuss, consist entirely of excerpted guitar solos).

So how does one top all of this? Zappa, in what has become typical fash-ion, decides to do a number of things at once. He begins writing a theater piece (which will eventually become *Thing-Fish*); he completes work on the

Utility Muffin Research Kitchen, his technologically advanced home record-ing studio; and he even records a single, "I Don't Want to Get Drafted," in response to the Reagan administration's decision to make men register for the draft.[17] In what was becoming an unfortunately regular occurrence, Zappa also switched record companies, starting his own Barking Pumpkin label to be distributed by CBS records.

After *Joe's Garage,* Zappa had planned to release an album called *Warts and All,* which would cull a number of concert performances from the 1978 and 1979 bands. As the album began progressing toward completion, it became apparent that it was going to be unwieldy (Courrier has it as a three-album set). After putting out double albums with *Sheik Yerbouti* and *Joe's Garage, Acts I, II & III,* Zappa was trying even the most sympathetic record company's patience by putting out another huge set. Zappa demurred and shelved the project, sort of.

Some of the music recorded in 1979 ended up on the double live album *Tinsel Town Rebellion,* an interesting mix of old, new, improvisations, spoken-word segues and bits, and some of the best playing by one of the most accomplished bands with whom Zappa ever worked. Three key players make this album worth hearing: Steve Vai, a young, wunderkind guitarist (who would go on to have a wildly successful career as a guitarist with David Lee Roth and Whitesnake and as a writer and producer of his own instrumental guitar albums); drummer Vinnie Colaiuta, who had played on *Joe's Garage* but really shines on *Tinsel Town;* and keyboard, trumpet, and vocalist Bob Harris, who added a falsetto of the likes not heard since the Ray Collins and Roy Estrada days.

It is an interesting album, full of songs that challenge the status quo and radical rearrangements of beloved Mothers of Invention songs that seem cal-culated to either please or upset most everyone. The album begins with two songs about women that have inspired much critical debate. The first, "Fine Girl," is a pop-reggae song that shows a great deal of professional craft and polish. According to Zappa's comments in the liner notes, it was recorded and released as a potential single (it is only 3:29, has no guitar solo, and fea-tures a nice, chanting chorus). It is well produced and catchy as hell. So what is wrong with it?

Lyrically, the song marked a new trend in Zappa's music, one that would find its full realization in *Thing-Fish.* On "Fine Girl," Zappa and Ike Willis sing together in a sort of African American dialect that can only be described as cartoonish and based, at least in part, on the dialect developed by the white actors in *Amos 'n Andy,* a caricature of black speech. The song seems to cel-ebrate the kind of subservient woman that contemporary U.S. men might, after a number of years of feminism, imagine themselves longing for. By giv-ing the song its additional racial dimension, it changes the scope and focus and creates some interesting dynamics. On the one hand, women in the song are considered fine girls if they can perform a number of domestic tasks (do the laundry or change a tire), none of which is terrifically demeaning. In fact, a woman's abilities to change a tire and chop wood for the fire are decidedly unfeminine activities, a sure sign of a particular kind of feminist progress. Indeed, one of the messages of the song seems to be that a woman is a fine girl if she can do it all, which was a common advertising notion at the time. Virginia Slims cigarettes was making the same sort of argument, as was Enjoli perfume, which used as its advertising jingle "I can bring home the bacon, fry it up in a pan, and never let you forget you're my man." The idea behind this jingle was that women could enter the so-called male sphere (bring home the bacon) and yet remain both sexy and desirable. It is problematic but vastly different from the fifties.

"Fine Girl," makes a not-so-subtle shift, however; in the final verse, we find out that a fine girl is also someone "With a bucket on her head / Fulla water from de well / She could run a mile." These rather obvious *National Geographic* stereotypes of an African woman makes the song much more politically challenging. Courrier calls it "a mock celebration of strong and noble servant woman,"[18] whereas Barry Miles calls it "an unconscious expression of Zappa's violent dislike of the women's liberation movement."[19] I think that Courrier is probably mostly on track; the song, like the songs on *Thing-Fish,* is so exaggerated it would take someone with a real ideological axe to grind to make the claim that Zappa "really meant it" (whatever that might mean). The argument that the song seems to make is that the characters singing are longing for these old days or these kinds of women (this is different than Zappa longing for these days). At around the same time singer-songwriter Randy Newman wrote a song with lyrics like, "This English girl from the North somewhere...Talkin' about the poor niggers all the time...I tell her, Darling, don't talk about things you don't understand,"[20] yet no one assumed that he was a racist or even sympathetic toward his character. The argument that "Fine Girl" is somehow a racist fantasy is further complicated by the fact that Zappa had two African American band members at the time (and had featured African Americans in nearly all of his bands). For someone who was a stone racist, Zappa seemed to go out of his way to surround himself with black folks.

As if "Fine Girl" were not enough of a problem, it then segues into an older (albeit unrecorded) song "Easy Meat." "Meat" had been performed by the Flo & Eddie band and had been used as a vehicle for extended soloing for a number of years. The version on *Tinsel Town Rebellion* is expanded to include an orchestral interlude that comes from the 1975 UCLA concert. The first part of the song comes from a concert in Philadelphia, and the solo and outro come from a concert in Santa Monica. Musically, it is one of Zappa's catchiest songs. It has a dramatic guitar-based opening and, with different lyrics, would have been a big hit.

Ah, but the lyrics. Miles claims that this song is indicative of a Zappa double standard, imagining that, in Zappa's ideology, "if women asserted their sexuality they were 'sluts' or 'easy meat.' "[21] It is not quite that easy for two reasons. (1) There was a growing sense in the eighties of women taking more control and more responsibility for their own sexuality. The Victorian idea that a woman needed to be protected from men (often by men) was shifting. AIDS, the Reagan backlash, and MTV were all parts of what would become (by the nineties) a fairly complete and radical change in the way both men and women thought about gender roles. (2) The song is another in a long line of Zappa songs about individual responsibility. Take, for instance, the first lines of the first two verses: "This girl is easy meat, I seen her on the street," and "She wanna take me home, Make me sweat and moan." The girl may be so-called easy meat, but she is in control of her sexuality. Although the male character singing the song may well be guilty of objectifying the woman, it is apparent in the second verse that she has a part to play in all of this. In her mind, the boy that she takes home is easy meat as well.

It is a tough sell. The song tends to be a sort of Rosetta stone for Zappa critics. Courrier writes that the song is "not so much a sign of misogyny as Zappa's insistent love of '50's R & B slang."[22] Watson claims that the song is "a combination of sleaze and pomp" and that the real "joke is the concerto in the middle" of the song.[23] (The middle of the song contains a long instrumental break that references a number of ideas from classical music, including a blistering solo.) In other words, one can read into the song just about anything one wants to. It is important, however, to see the song as both part of a larger, career-long project of critique and as endemic to the time (written in the seventies, finally released to the public in the early eighties).

The song that follows, "For the Young Sophisticate," is a nice breather. Critics tend to ignore this song, but it is important to see it as another of Zappa's critiques of the shallowness of the culture and the shallowness of love, especially as it is influenced by the media. In the middle of the song, Zappa sings about a "young sophisticator" who falls in love with a woman who is "an aggressive agitator," and falls out of love with her because, in large part, she "doesn't shave her underarms."

Although this song has some similarities to the Barbara Streisand–Robert Redford movie *The Way We Were,* it is also Zappa's critique of the shallowness of both the characters, that their so-called love is based largely on surface issues. The punch line of the song is when Zappa argues, in the final verse, that the boy would still love the girl no matter that she looked like. Musically, the song features an interesting percussion track featuring some excellent work by Ed Mann and some fine drumming by Vinnie Colaiuta.

Two of the songs on the album, "Panty Rap" and "Dance Contest," are interesting for fans, perhaps, because they give one a taste of what made a

Zappa concert a unique event. Although bands have always had vocalists screaming at the audience to try to get them to sing along, Zappa becomes an old-fashioned lounge-band master of ceremonies, talking to the audience, telling them stories, goading them into all sorts of weirdness. In "Panty Rap," Zappa is asking the women in the audience to throw their panties up on stage, not for the gratification of the band but for a quilt being prepared by a woman named Emily James.[24] Although Miles finds this to be more evidence of Zappa's growing sexism (throwing panties was, according to Miles, "something Elvis and Tom Jones didn't have to *ask* their audiences to do"[25]), I find it to be fine evidence of Zappa's absurdist project: (1) Zappa was, musically and artistically, the complete opposite of Elvis and Tom Jones; and (2) the fact that these panties were being used as an art project must have struck a chord in Zappa. The rap is played over the music from "Black Napkins," which also shows off the ability of the band to capture a particular mood. The band members are clearly following Zappa closely, and one can hear small musical cues within the background that force one to pay attention.

The same thing occurs during "Dance Contest." Zappa had been holding dance contests for a while, usually getting everything set up and then launching the band into "The Black Page," a song that is virtually impossible to dance to (that is the joke, get it?). On *Tinsel Town*, Zappa allows the listener to hear the kind of controlled chaos that he loved to create through enforced audience participation (for an incredible example of this, listen to the version of "Don't Eat the Yellow Snow" recorded with the same band that is on *You Can't Do That on Stage Anymore, Vol. 1.*). In "Dance Contest," Zappa makes the statement:

> I have an important message to deliver to all the cute people all over the world. If you're out there and you're cute, maybe you're beautiful, I just want to tell you somethin'—there's more of us ugly mother-fuckers than you are, hey-y, so watch out.

In many ways this is Zappa's philosophy: From his earliest recordings Zappa has been mocking and critiquing the unearned privilege of the beautiful people. This flat-out statement of contempt for the beautiful, and the realization that the ugly have an unacknowledged power, is important in understanding both Zappa and his fans.

After "Dance Contest" come two fairly interesting pieces: "Blue Light" and "Tinsel Town Rebellion." "Blue Light" is a marvelous postmodern collage of various pieces of sixties pop culture detritus: Winchell's donuts, Shakey's Pizza, Brut cologne, Donovan (and his song "Atlantis," always a favorite target of Zappa's). The song is more than a list, however; it is a discussion of how Americans are drowning in consumerism as the country turns more toward the right (the Reagan-era economic theory labeled trickle-down economics dictated that if tax breaks were given to people—especially people already making a lot of money—then people would have more money to buy stuff, and that, in turn, would stimulate the economy). It is a hilarious critique of the willingness of the American people to believe anything. Speaking of believing anything, at one point Zappa warns of "*Death Valley Days* straight ahead." This is clearly a reference to newly elected president Ronald Reagan, who had been a host on the television show *Death Valley Days* early in his career and, according to some, had never really understood that his role as president was fundamentally different from his role as cowboy. Zappa, of course, as a long-term Californian, had experienced Reagan before—he was governor during much of the unrest in the sixties—and was, to Zappa at least, a known quantity. The title of the song is a bit of a mystery, although I have always liked to think that it was related to the Kmart (a U.S. discount chain that, until the rise of Wal-Mart, had set the standard for inexpensive shopping experiences) advertising gimmick called blue light specials, for which Kmart would discount already discounted goods.

The music in "The Blue Light" (as it is in "Tinsel Town Rebellion") is superb. It starts with a fantastic rock groove that segues into a tight backing track for Zappa's spoken-word thesis.

"Tinsel Town Rebellion" is not only the title song but the thesis. A savage critique of the state of the U.S. music scene, Zappa argues (in a simple and straightforward manner, which should indicate the seriousness) that punk and new wave are merely fads. Zappa was clear about his disdain for punk, arguing in *Telos* magazine, "I am glad that someone sneaks in there and makes a mockery of the business. But how much of a mockery is it if they wind up being sold and distributed by the same business they intend to mock."[26] Of course, the fact that Zappa had once been able to get away with this kind of thing (certainly *Freak Out!* and *We're Only in It for the Money* were attempts to subvert the system by using the system) makes his critique of punk fairly acid. Musically, it is a pretty fantastic song, one that was the antithesis of punk (and inevitably part of the joke). It features manically fast changes, quotations from other songs (on *Tinsel Town* the band quotes Cream's "Sunshine of Your Love," the "Theme from the *Tonight Show*," and the theme from *I Love Lucy*. Later bands would quote "Light My Fire" (the Doors), "Whip It" (Devo), "I Write the Songs," (Barry Manilow), theme from *The Twilight Zone*, "Rock You Like a Hurricane" (Scorpions), and "I'll Tumble 4 Ya" (Culture Club).[27] The band's ability gives lie to the truth of punk. Zappa's dislike of punk seems to have as much to do with the punk aesthetic (that bad/sloppy is somehow virtuous) as it does with the relationship between punk and commercialism. His disdain for new wave seems to come from a different place; the fact that bands were being signed largely based upon a look was anathema to Zappa. It would be a thesis he would explore in years to come.

The final two original songs on the album both return to the theme of women. "Pick Me, I'm Clean" comes from something Zappa overheard a

French fan tell one of the band members (in an attempt to get him to take her back to the hotel). This is just the kind of absurdity Zappa seemed to love. The song becomes a list of the different arguments this woman might make in order to meet the band. The song, set to a catchy, major-chord romp, is an interesting piece. The pure journalism / sociology of the song makes it interesting as a snapshot of life on the road. It certainly should lead one to ask the question "why do these women do these things," but that is a question Zappa is never interested in asking. The fact that they do, and that they should not be judged for doing so, is what interests and concerns Zappa. The song then, starting at around 2:08, becomes another vehicle for extended soloing that, because the solo was actually part of the recorded song (and not a xenochronos mash up), is very interesting and expressive.

The final original song on the albums is "Bamboozled by Love," a standard blues song that features the old my-woman-done-me-wrong trope. In the song, Ike Willis sings "I came home the other day and she was / Suckin' off some other man" and, as a price for this, "I'm gonna make her bleed." Although Zappa has received some criticism for these lyrics, they are definitely in the old blues genre. The subject of death comes up quite a bit in music—from Johnny Cash to "Stagger Lee"—so the song's subject can not be too shocking, despite Barry Miles's comments that "the level of hatred in the song is really quite extraordinary."[28] The music on *Tinsel Town* is down and dirty blues with a kicking solo. Later versions of the song (such as the version captured on *You Can't Do That on Stage Anymore, Vol. 3*) feature a much more new-wave arrangement, complete with a subtle shift in the middle to the melody of the Yes hit "Owner of a Lonely Heart." It complicates the reading of the song.

The rest of the album is made up of interesting versions of old Zappa songs: "Love of My Life," "I Ain't Got No Heart," "Tell Me You Love Me," "Brown Shoes Don't Make It" (which really shows off the ability of the band), and "Peaches III," a sick version of "Peaches en Regalia." It also contains the instrumental "Now You See It—Now You Don't," which is an excerpted solo from a performance of "King Kong."

Critical reaction to the album has been underwhelming. Steve Huey likes the new versions of the old songs but decries what he calls the "violent sexual juvenilia" of many of the new songs.[29] Amazon.com, *The New Rolling Stone Album Guide,* and *Musichound Rock* all ignore it. Dominique Chevalier writes that "Zappa constructs his own world which delights some and exasperates others."[30]

It is a better album than critics give it credit for, being if, for no other reason, that this may well have been Zappa's best band. The work that Ed Mann and Vinnie Colaiuta do throughout is unreal. It is an album for musicians, despite the silly lyrics, and if listened to with attention has a lot to teach those who are looking to expand their ideas of composition and the rules of rock.

You Are What You Is

Fighting the Reagan Revolution. *You Are What You Is* (originally released in September 1981 on Barking Pumpkin records; currently available as Rykodisc RCD 10536.[31] Highest *Billboard* chart position: No. 93. Personnel: Ike Willis, Ray White, Bob Harris, Steve Vai, Tommy Mars, Arthur Barrow, Ed Mann, David Ocker, Motorhead Sherwood, Denny Walley, David Logeman, Craig Stewart, and featuring background vocals by Jimmy Carl Black and Ahmet and Moon Zappa. "Modern Americans behave as if intelligence were some sort of hideous deformity."[32]

After several years of beating around the bush (or chipping around the edges) of direct political critique, Zappa, in 1981, unleashed *You Are What You Is,* his most overt and sustained piece of political writing since at least *Absolutely Free* or *We're Only in It for the Money.* The album, which consists of four minisuites, each attacking a different, worthy, target, is an incredible piece of songwriting and studio craft. It is a carefully constructed polemic that goes right to the heart of the swinging eighties.

Despite the excellence of the album, it has been sort of forgotten. Several of Zappa's biographers, including Michael Gray and Barry Miles, completely ignore the album (they seem to be in a rush to deal with *Shut Up 'N Play Yer Guitar* and "Valley Girl"), and although Neil Slaven devotes several pages to the album, most of them are a discussion of the technical aspects of recording.

It is an amazing album, both musically and lyrically, and, looked at as part of Zappa's vast catalog, an amazingly accomplished record. It is the first record to be entirely recorded in the Utility Muffin Research Kitchen, and it shows; hundreds of overdubs and impossible musical pieces combine to make this an album of technical achievement and artistic brilliance.

The suites in the album deal with subjects that had become old hat to many of Zappa's fans: the silliness of adolescence, the stupidity of the privileged, the corruption of the government, and the doubled-edged sword of aggressive female sexuality. It also, for the first time, overtly tackles the erosion of the church-state boundary and the takeover of the government by the religious right. The album is also unusual in that it features only one instrumental, "Theme from the 3rd Movement of Sinister Footwear," which is part of a larger, unrealized ballet called *Sinister Footwear.* According to Zappa fan A. J. Wilkes, "*Sinister Footwear* is very typical of Frank Zappa's musical world—both musically complex and almost cartoon-like at the same time, it has been recorded by an orchestra and performed in a rock arrangement by a number of his touring bands."[33] The part that is excerpted on *You Are What You Is* has an interesting history. Parts of the same solo/backing show up as the guitar solo from "Packard Goose," "Wild Love," and "Now You See It—Now You Don't." Another interesting aspect of the song is that, after taking the live recording of the solo, Zappa had Steve Vai and Ed Mann double some of the solo and backing parts on guitar and percussion. The effect is astounding. It is one of the more interesting of Zappa's solo instrumentals.

The album starts with a suite based around the stupidity of men. The first two songs, "Teen-Age Wind" and "Harder than Your Husband," are fine examples of Zappa's twin irritations: the gross stupidity of adolescent males and the ridiculousness of country music laments.

"Teen-Age Wind" begins with the typical teenage boy whining that he can not get any tickets to see the Grateful Dead or find any glue to sniff. This is a shot across the bow of the eighties adolescents and their rediscovery of the sixties (an argument Zappa would make again with "We're Turning Again" on *Meets the Mothers of Prevention*). Following the Dead became a huge teenage enterprise in the eighties. The idea that Zappa seems to be trying to get across in this song is that teenagers in the eighties, much like teenagers in the fifties, had no idea how good they had it. The song goes through a litany of teenage complaints—parents who do not love and teachers who do not teach as well as a number of teenage remedies, including glue sniffing and Grateful Dead concerts—until it reaches its real argument. Zappa and company sing over and over again that "Free is when you don't have to pay for nothing or do nothing / we want to be free / free as the wind." This attack on what Zappa saw as spoiled children is an effective way to kick off the album. In many ways it deals in large part with the thesis that Americans in the early eighties, especially as a supposed result of the Reagan revolution, had become spoiled. Historian C. Vann Woodward, writing in 1981, tells us that "President Reagan and the opinion polls assure us that Americans have made a sudden recovery from their malaise, restored their self-esteem and self-confidence, and face the future and a skeptical world with old-time assurance."[34] Zappa is indeed calling Americans a bunch of spoiled teenagers.

The hilarious double entendre of "Harder than Your Husband" comes next. Original Mother Jimmy Carl Black sings, in his best cowboy voice (last heard on "Lonesome Cowboy Burt"), that "I'll be harder than your husband to get along with / Harder than your husband every night." In many ways this song is identical to "Lonesome Cowboy Burt." One can almost imagine that Burt has scored with the waitress he was trying to pick up in the first song and has had an affair that he now wants to end. The song is a mix of country music clichés (harmonica, pedal steel guitar, thudding and plodding major-chord bass line) and lyrics about our cowboy trying to end his affair. Zappa never had a lot of patience with country music's clichés (as his Congressional testimony in 1986 would prove), and in the early eighties, the sudden rise of so-called country-politan music (led by Kenny Rogers, Crystal Gayle, Dolly Parton, and the surprising success of the film *Urban Cowboy*) made country music an irresistible target.

The two songs that follow, "Doreen" and "Goblin Girl," are more typical Zappa fare. "Doreen," described ably by Ben Watson as "an extravagant wide-screen symphony of multi-tracked singing and guitars," features an incredible soul / R&B vocal from Ray White.[35] (For an interesting contrast, listen to the live version of the song on *You Can't Do That on Stage Anymore, Vol. 5;* it was obviously a song that the band enjoyed playing and that Ray White loved to sing—it is a standout vocal.) The song makes an interesting transition to "Goblin Girl," a far less interesting double entendre than "Harder than Your Husband." "Goblin Girl," according to Courrier, "is a coarse tribute to the ladies in the audience who appear in costume during the band's Halloween concerts."[36] It is also a song that features Ike Willis and Zappa experimenting with the kind of black dialect that they would use to an absurd extent on *Thing-Fish.* Much like "Fine Girl" and "Easy Meat," "Goblin Girl" takes a beautiful, radio-ready melody (the song would get some airplay, and it is one of the few Zappa songs one might hear on the radio, usually around Halloween) and then sullies it with lyrics that would cause parents to stop the car and explain what the song might mean. Although the lyrics "When they're a goblin I start a-wobblin'" are vaguely suggestive, it is toward the end when Zappa has the band playing both "Goblin Girl" and "Doreen" at the same time (a great bit of musical mayhem that owes more than a little debt to U.S. composer Charles Ives, famous for often having an orchestra play a variety of recognizable pieces on top of one another; see his *Second Symphony* for a good example of this) and one set of lyrics tells us "My snout is burning with love / And it wants you tonight." This is, to say the least, a far more obvious lyric.

This first suite of songs is the least cohesive of the bunch. In many ways it is four separate songs separated from the rest by "Sinister Footwear," and although "Doreen" and "Goblin Girl" seem to hold together, it does not appear as if Zappa meant for these four to be heard as parts of a whole. This is not true of the songs that follow.

Immediately following "Sinister Footwear" is Zappa's trenchant and hysterical attack on the social-climbing yuppies (for those of you who do not remember, yuppie was short for "young urban professionals"; it was the era of successful, college-educated women and men putting off having children and concentrating entirely on making—and spending—money) who were overrunning the United States in the eighties.

It is tough to remember, if one did not go through them, what the early eighties were like: the bright clothes, the fast cars, the cocaine. It was an age of extraordinary and conspicuous consumption. It was a moment, one of a few, when the rich started to get significantly richer while the poor were being left behind in ever-increasing numbers. Zappa, who was always aware of his upbringing as part of the lower middle class, saw the Reaganite trickle-down policy as destructive. The songs that Zappa writes that directly touch on these changing economic times, "Society Pages," "I'm a Beautiful Guy," "Beauty Knows No Pain," as well as "Charlie's Enormous Mouth," "Any

Downers?" and "Conehead," which personalize the story Zappa has started, tell the story of the obscene pursuit of wealth and happiness that makes his attacks on the sacred cows of the sixties look tame in comparison.

"Society Pages," which begins with a nice Grateful Dead-like groove (with some tasty slide work by Denny Wally) and works itself into a sort of protorock frenzy in the middle (with neat rock-and-roll piano), tells the story of the small-town matron who is all too familiar to anyone who has had the fortune (or misfortune) to live in a town where there are a few families who have always been in power. In many ways this song harkens back to a day when old money was really old money (the way things happened before the go-go eighties, when anyone could make it rich in the stock market). Zappa writes about the old folks who seem to run all small towns, looking backward and finding that people were just as callous and cruel with money then as they are now; it is an interesting way to open the argument. Toward the end of the song, Zappa argues that what is wrong with folks like this is that they "pass out jobs to yer relatives 'n such / So you all keeps a lot, 'cept but nobody else." This argument, that small-town society is against individual excellence (i.e., in Zappa's world, it did not matter who your parents were, just whether you could do the job or not) is continued in the next song, "I'm a Beautiful Guy."

Sung by Ike Willis in his best lounge singer voice, "I'm a Beautiful Guy" is a direct attack on the sort of brainless coke-headed rich kid Zappa was increasingly encountering at his concerts. The song contains elements of the kind of buffoonish white guy we have already seen in many Zappa songs (certainly "Bobby Brown" comes to mind), the kind of guy whose sense of self is so inflated that he simply can not understand why the girls do not all love him. In the case of "Beautiful Guy," we find that, in order to get the girls to love him, the protagonist takes a new-wave eighties approach to wooing her: "Your athletic approach has a lot of appeal / The girl is responding to your little deal." Compare this to the antics of the boys in Zappa's earlier songs, who worried about having pressed khakis or the right car. Zappa's genius is to point out that these kinds of men have the same sorts of problems, but the eighties have given them a different set of solutions. Another argument that comes and goes pretty quickly in "Beautiful Guy" is about the whole health fad of the early eighties (this is the time, remember, when the number-one song for 10 weeks in 1981 was Olivia Newton-John's "Let's Get Physical," the video of which featured John working out in a skimpy leotard). The various cultural icons and fads that Zappa invokes—including jogging, bottled water, and tennis clubs—place the song in a very specific context. The key to the argument is when Zappa, at the end of his list of (stupid) things people are doing, remarks, "What could be *whiter*?" Giving the health, beauty, and money craze a racial dimension raises some interesting and important issues that Zappa would come back to in the song "You Are What You Is." The fact is, Zappa only had to take one look at what was happening to the country to see that not only were the rich getting richer but, when investigated, it turned out that the rich were white and that the economic boom had a deep racial divide. As someone who had always believed in hard work, the idea that someone's skin color would make them automatically qualified to do better than someone of a darker hue must have been an irritant.

The short song segues into "Beauty Knows No Pain," which is Zappa's argument that women, too, were stupid to abuse themselves in order to project some sort of (false) public image. Again, this argument is not new. Zappa has been making it for years. By the time Zappa has written this song we have seen a tremendous rise in elective plastic surgery and are entering a beauty culture that will transform our ideas of American womanhood.

Musically, the song harkens back to the fake heavy-metal stylings of *Zoot Allures:* huge guitar chords and keyboards and vocals with lots of echo to create a real sense of enclosed space. Lyrically, it is a straightforward attack: "Beauty is a bikini wax 'n waitin' for yer nails to dry / Beauty is a colored pencil, scribbled all around yer eye / Beauty is a pair of shoes that makes you wanna die," although we find out in the very next verse that the beauty culture forced women to become something they were not in order to succeed at the U.S. rituals of love and marriage and success. Zappa, despite his unpopular writing about sexuality, should certainly be credited with the argument that it is far more important how you are on the inside than how you look on the outside.

The next song, "Charlie's Enormous Mouth," gives us a specific example of someone for whom beauty was not enough. In one of the most depressing songs on the album, Zappa describes Charlie's enormous features as a metaphor for consumption of all kinds: "The girl got a very large nose, but it's all white / She got stuff all around the hole / Where she puts her spoon in." The obvious allusion to cocaine and its relationship to the beauty and consumptive culture of the eighties brings Zappa full circle; where he was once arguing against the use of LSD, he is now arguing against the use of cocaine. Where he was once arguing against a hippie culture that seemed to encourage people to pretend to drop out, he is now arguing against a yuppie culture that encourages people to spend their money on coke and nose jobs.

The song cycle takes an odd turn after we find out that Charlie has died from all of her excess. At the funeral, the mourners all stand around her grave and ask one another if anyone has any downers. Downers are a drug far more associated with the seventies than the coke and speed of the eighties. When the characters/mourners find out that no one has any downers (or coke), they turn to television to block out reality. In returning to the themes first argued in "Trouble Every Day," Zappa is again coming full circle. In a nice bit of intertextuality, Zappa argues that, when the folks turn on the television, they watch the Coneheads, recurring characters from the first five years of *Saturday Night Live,* a show of which Zappa was a big fan (when he was on the show in 1978 he was in a Conehead sketch and can be seen laughing on the set at the sheer absurdity of it). The Coneheads sketch on *SNL* seems to have delighted Zappa both because of his love of cheesy fifties movies and because of his ideas that people were easily fooled. The song's lyrics seem to touch on both of these themes. (As well, they are a fairly literal description of the action of a typical coneheads sketch). It is an odd song that seems sort of crammed into the ongoing narrative. A possible explanation is that we find out that television is a drug and the Coneheads, despite Zappa's own enjoyment of the sketch, was really a pretty dumb skit.

On the vinyl release, "Conehead" ends the first record. The second album picks up with a series of songs that should be placed among the most political pieces of songwriting in the eighties.

The side starts with the title song, "You Are What You Is." This is a particularly poignant critique of contemporary racial politics done in a typically Zappa-esque manner. Perhaps no song of Zappa's makes a better argument for the relationship between freedom and responsibility than this one does. Zappa's main argument is about people and their refusal to accept themselves or others at face value (indeed, the argument that Zappa seems to make in many of his songs about women is, ultimately, this same argument: if a woman wants to have sex, or dress a certain way, or act a certain way, fine, let her) and who borrow or steal from other cultures to find some sort of self-worth.

Zappa makes a second, more subtle, and more political argument in the song about race and the racist appropriation of culture. The first verse of the song finds Zappa arguing that white appropriation of black culture is both silly and racist, informing the listener that it is a slippery slope from "singing the blues" to talking like the "kingfish from *Amos & Andy*" (in other words, it is one thing to appropriate black musical styles—something Zappa himself was guilty of at times—it is another thing to appropriate racist stereotypes). The more dangerous slippery slope, as Zappa seems to see it, is when the African American turns his back on his own culture. Zappa has Ike Willis sing, "He learned to play golf / An' he got a good score / Now he says to himself '*I ain't no nigger no more*'." This obviously false piece of racial wishful thinking (as just about any African American will tell you, the United States will not let a black person, no matter how wealthy or powerful, forget they are black) is Zappa's indication that he understands the complexities of racial politics. While he does not really have an answer, he does seem to indicate, as one might imagine, that sex is one way out of our painful national crisis about race. By the end of the song "You Are What You Is," Zappa has Ray White singing a marvelous call and response vocal (which is, in a great piece of musical argument, a form of music that comes directly from the black church; in other words, Ray White is staying true to his own African American musical roots) that segues into the song "Mudd Club," a piece of reporting on the desperate attempts of consciously hip New Yorkers to score with each other. An entry about the Mudd Club in the online Wikipedia encyclopedia describes it as thus: "The club featured a bar, gender-neutral bathrooms, and a rotating gallery on the fourth floor. Live performances showcased punk rock, new wave, and experimental music." It goes on to describe the club as very self-consciously cool and as a breeding ground for the (often self-proclaimed) leading lights of the art and cultural world of the eighties.[37] Zappa's mockery of this world is right in line with his general critique of U.S. culture that has been going on throughout the album. In "Mudd Club," Zappa provides a long list of antics and attitudes of the self-consciously hip: "In a black sack dress with nine inch heels/And then a guy with a blue mohawk comes in." The fact that Zappa dwells upon what these people are wearing indicates that his critique of the fashion and beauty culture begun in "I'm a Beautiful Guy" has continued. The fact that the album offers an indictment of both the rich, straight, and normal person as well as the downtown, Village, Lower East Side person indicates Zappa's individualist and libertarian politics. The final lyrics, which mention the "ruins of Studio 54," make a damning argument: the more things change, the more they stay the same. Zappa is arguing that the club culture created by Studio 54 has simply created a mockery of itself at the Mudd Club. The cool people— the people who set the trends (artists, avant-garde musicians, self-proclaimed philosophers) who were at the Mudd Club at this period of time—are no more important than the bond traders and wealthy relatives that they (the hip New York artists) spend so much time mocking.

"Mudd Club" fades into the final suite, which is Zappa's attack on systems, in this case both organized religion and organized government. "The Meek Shall Inherit Nothing" does what it says it is going to do: critique the false hope that many religions seem to hold out to the poor. Zappa sees, clearly, the hypocrisy of churches spending millions of dollars on houses, cars, and airplanes for the leadership and more millions on fancy buildings when they should be spending that money helping the poor. The argument that Zappa makes in "The Meek Shall Inherit Nothing," and refines in "Heavenly Bank Account," is that religion is a scam and that, under the Reagan administration, this scam is being protected by a government filled with members of this religion.

The song that glues these two critiques of religion together is "Dumb All Over," which is perhaps the most direct political song of Zappa's entire career. This song is a direct attack on the hypocrisy and falsity of religions that claim to be based on philosophies of peace and harmony and brotherhood and yet always seem to find themselves at the center of bloody conflict. Throughout the song, Zappa repeatedly comes back to the idea that, throughout history, war and conflict seem to be based on differing interpretations of what their book says and argues that bad things will happen "If the geeks over there/Don't believe in the book/We got over here."[38] There was no one else saying these things at the time and no one saying them after. It is dangerous stuff to look into the abyss, and Zappa found that the sudden lurch to the right was not where he wanted the United States to go.

"Dumb All Over," which gets its name from the syllogism that Zappa constructs, points out one of the great fallacies of Christianity, that if God made us all in his image, then "If we're dumb .../Then God is dumb .../(An' maybe even a little ugly on the side)." It is deeply blasphemous, yet terrifically challenging because it points to some of the extraordinary gaps in logic in biblical faith.

"Dumb All Over" is followed by "Heavenly Bank Account," Zappa's first attack on what he called video Christians.[39] The song is a direct attack on the influence that televangelists Jerry Falwell and Pat Robertson seemed to have on the Reagan administration and its policies. One of the strangest philosophical shifts in U.S. culture has been the century-long shift in the relationship between capitalism and Christianity. If one reads much Benjamin Franklin, one will quickly realize that the relationship between money and religion and the American dream is firmly rooted in the Calvinist ideas of thrift, hard work, and moral purity. By the 1980s this has changed. Fundamentalist, evangelical Christianity had, with the election of Ronald Reagan, aligned itself with the core tenets of capitalism: greed, power, competition, and consumption. The fact that U.S. Christianity has found a way to embrace capitalism (looked at philosophically, the two are pretty far apart in what they believe and how they operate) strikes Zappa as not only absurd but as dangerous. In his autobiography, Zappa spells out this idea in no uncertain terms, arguing that what is wrong with contemporary U.S. Christianity is the idea that "Americanism equals Christianity equals good fiscal policy equals fifteen minutes from Armageddon—but Armageddon is okay because WE'RE all going to Heaven and THEY'RE NOT."

His argument in "Heavenly Bank Account," that television preachers are treating religion as a money-making scheme would be shown to be correct only a few years later. Zappa begins the song by warning listeners, "And if these words you do not heed/Your pocketbook just kinda might recede." It is as if, after almost 20 years of searching, Zappa has found the people who truly are only in it for the money.

The other point that Zappa makes in the song is that religion can, and often does (see Father Coughlin in the thirties for a good example), misdirect people's attention away from the bad stuff the government is doing. A government closely aligned with the predominant religion in the culture has it made, mainly by making regular folks scared. By putting the fear of God in the common man, the religious majority can, in concert, direct people's attention away from how miserable their own lives are and keep these people from trying to understand how miserable their lives are (and, as a consequence of this understanding, revolt). It is a philosophy not unheard of; both the Romans (bread and circuses) and Karl Marx understood what a powerful diversion can do to keep the common people from noticing how they are being screwed. Although not Marxist by any means, side three of *You Are What You Is* presents a powerful Marxist critique of religion. An additional layer is added to this argument when one hears the live version of "Heavenly

Bank Account" on *You Can't Do That on Stage Anymore, Vol. 1*. During the final verse, in which Zappa and company sing "you ain't got nothing people," Zappa then says directly to the audience, "tax the churches" and "tax the businesses owned by the churches."

Zappa's increasingly vocal arguments that people would not use their own native intelligence seem to find their proof in the increasing turn toward fundamentalism in the early eighties. The only choice one is left with, if one is not willing to join the religious hegemony, is, according to Zappa, suicide. Of course for Zappa, suicide is a pretty stupid answer as well.

"Suicide Chump" is performed in a rollicking blues-based manner with excellent slide guitar and fine keyboard work (one critic compares the music to the Doors "Roadhouse Blues"). The lyrics refer back to one of Zappa's oldest themes: the stupidity of killing yourself because you're sad or depressed over how your life has worked out, a theme that goes all the way back to "How Could I Be Such a Fool" off of *Freak Out!* Zappa's argument with this song is interesting. He seems to be particularly scornful of those who try suicide but do not succeed: "Just make sure you do it right the first time /'Cause nothin's worse than a Suicide Chump." This is part of Zappa's larger, individualist philosophy: You are responsible for your own self, which includes your own happiness, and blaming society for your problems, and taking your own life as a result of these problems is not only unnecessary but selfish as well.

The song that follows, "Jumbo Go Away," is perhaps the oddest and saddest song in all of Zappa's catalog. The song is ostensibly about a groupie whom a band member had known (one of the lines is "No, Denny, don't hit me!" so it can be assumed that Zappa is talking about Denny Walley) and who had formed an attachment to said band member and would not go away. It is an extraordinarily sad song, in large part because it reveals a fundamental part of the way Zappa viewed attachments. Zappa had often claimed that he did not really have any friends, just employees and family members, and one gets the impression from "Jumbo Go Away" that Zappa felt that because he did not really have any attachments that attachments were unnecessary or stupid. The girl, Jumbo, is made to appear stupid for wanting to have more than a one-night stand with the band member, and although there is some truth to the idea that groupies are not coerced into being groupies and should know, going in, about the fairly defined, transactional nature of the groupie-band member relationship, the fact that a groupie did occasionally delude herself into thinking that her time with the band member was special is more tragic than deserving of the kind of scorn that is heaped upon Jumbo.

What makes the song even more difficult to listen to is the wonderfully melancholy music that is backing the track. Lots of keyboards and acoustic guitar make the music compelling and force one to listen to the lyrics. It is one of the songs that most critics agree is really on the edge of good taste, and Zappa's repeated response that he is just reporting on something that really happened does not answer the question of why this needed to be reported.[40]

For someone as interested as Zappa was in the relationship between freedom and responsibility, it is one instance in which, perhaps, he needed to see that although he was certainly free to write this song, he had a responsibility to understand the effect this song might have on the subject and the listener.

The final two songs on the album, "If Only She Woulda" and "Drafted Again," are a nice ending to the album. "Woulda" tries to end the story of the album and create a segue into "Drafted Again," a song that had been recorded several months earlier. "Woulda" features some tasty sixties music, including a pretty hilarious keyboard solo that is obviously calling up Ray Manzarek's work with the Doors (at one point it sounds identical to the keyboard solo in "Light My Fire"), which leads into a scorching guitar solo that then leads into a rerecorded version of "I Don't Want to Get Drafted," called on the this album "Drafted Again." The song, a slight protest of the Reagan administration's reinstatement of the draft registration, is a hilarious statement both against the possibility of a draft and against the stupid and intellectually immature arguments that kids make against things (in this case, war). In one verse, Zappa has his daughter, Moon, sing, "I don't want nobody / To shoot me in the fox hole." The lyrics are sung in a wonderfully bratty tone that goes well with the overall emotional feel of the piece (the rest of the members of the band were way beyond draft age, although some— Zappa, Jimmy Carl Black, and Motorhead Sherwood, for instance—could certainly remember the Vietnam War draft and its consequences).

It is unfortunate that the album did not do well, although not surprising. There was little room for protest in the early Reagan years (although that would change with his second administration and the uncovering of Oliver North's misadventures in Central America and the Middle East), and in 1981 Reagan could do no wrong. For Zappa to point out the fact that Reagan was doing a lot of wrong was not appreciated.

Zappa, for one, always felt that this album was unappreciated. Zappa told a reporter for the Canadian Broadcasting Company, "I still think it stands as one of the best albums that I've made, yet at the time it was released no one would touch it."[41] Watson remarks that "It remains one of the most ambitious public stands against Reaganism in the 80s."[42]

Contemporary reviews have been kinder. The *All Music Guide* writes,

> *You Are What You Is* is quite ambitious in scope and in general one of Zappa's most accessible later-period efforts; it's a showcase for his songwriting skills and his often acute satirical perspective, with less of the smutty humor that some listeners find off-putting.[43]

The Amazon.com review argues that the album "trades in much of Zappa's usual musical acrobatics for more polished and understated fare and increasingly political satire."[44] *The New Rolling Stone Album Guide* even finds something nice to say, writing that the musical parodies were varied enough to carry the day. Mock versions of reggae, ska, Journey-style power ballads, and country music, plus a hilarious Doors takeoff, produced the most inventive comedy he's attempted in years.[45]

It is an album that is in desperate need of reappraisal. What is most fascinating about the album is that the things Zappa saw happening in the country in 1981 would go on to get not better but worse. The religious right, which had made itself known as a political force during the Regan administration would, by the middle of the first decade of the twenty-first century, be able to declare victory in most matters cultural and political. If only we woulda' listened.

SHIP ARRIVING TOO LATE TO SAVE A DROWNING WITCH

The Unexpected Hit. *Ship Arriving Too Late to Save a Drowning Witch* (originally released in May 1982 on Barking Pumpkin Records; currently available as Rykodisc RCD 10537). Highest *Billboard* chart position: No. 23. Personnel: Steve Vai, Ray White, Tommy Mars, Bobby Martin, Ed Mann, Scott Thunes, Arthur Barrow, Patrick O'Hearn, Chad Wackerman, Roy Estrada, Ike Willis, Bob Harris, Lisa Popiel, and Moon Zappa. "It didn't sell a lot…but sociologically it was the most important record of 1982 in the United States."[46]

You never know. Zappa certainly did not. After years of killing himself to get his records made, released, and played on the radio, Zappa records a song with his daughter and it goes through the roof. The cultural phenomenon that was "Valley Girl" can not be ignored. It is yet another one of those moments in Zappa's career that he did not look for and, to hear him tell it, did not want, and yet the net result was an intense increase in interest in Zappa's works. Weird.

There are lots of good stories and histories about the making of "Valley Girl." Most of the stories have Moon, then 13, slipping a note under her father's door asking if she could be on his record. Around the same time, Zappa had been playing around with a bass-heavy theme and, after some fits and starts, woke Moon up in the middle of the night, brought her down to the studio, and had her re-create the conversations she was hearing at her friend's houses. At the end of the recording and mixing of the album, Zappa gave his daughter an acetate of the single (a test pressing to see how it would sound of vinyl) as a keepsake. Later, Moon took the acetate with her to an interview at a Los Angeles radio station. They played the single. The rest, as the cliché goes, is history.

Zappa's problem with the song was not necessarily musical—it is a great pop song—the bass is so low and guttural that it simply blows apart the lower register. It is an incredibly well-produced song that lit up the radio whenever it came on.[47] Zappa's problem was that the song was helping to paint him into an artistic corner: Except for a small, hard core group of fans, Zappa was becoming known to millions of Americans as a writer and singer of novelty songs. His three most famous hits were "Don't Eat the Yellow Snow," "Dancin' Fool," and "Valley Girl." He was also known as that guy who got his song about Jewish Princesses protested. This is not a position in which a serious composer wants to find himself, and Zappa chafed at the whole thing (there is no record of him every playing the song live, a sure clue as to Zappa's mindset).

What makes the album great is that there is a chance that Zappa really pulled some folks into his world. The rest of the album, outside of "Valley Girl," is full of well-produced, well-played, and highly challenging music.

The album starts off with one of Zappa's catchiest songs, "No Not Now," which, among other things, features the return of old Mother Roy Estrada (and old Zappa character Opal the waitress). The song is a wicked little pop ditty that could have been a neat country song (along the lines of "Harder than Your Husband" or, on the next album, "Truck Driver Divorce"). Thematically it is old Zappa territory; it is a metacommentary on the media-influenced idea of the country-and-Western lifestyle. The song features a truck driver who is trying to juggle the intense pressure of delivering "string beans to Utah" in his "transcontinental hobby horse" while trying to juggle "a wife and a waitress too." There are even cheap shots at Utah's most famous citizens, Donny and Marie Osmond, the television show *Hawaii Five-O*, and the idiotic U.S. cultural phenomenon of mechanical bull riding, popularized in *Urban Cowboy*. It is a perfect Zappa song, combining serious pop music with lyrics that offer both a cultural critique and a few nasty asides at the same time. In many ways, the repeated chorus of "No Not Now" seems to be Zappa's rallying cry: We have just gone too far; the culture is a wreck; slow down and enjoy those things we have worked so hard to get.

In many ways, then, the song is a perfect lead-in to "Valley Girl." The song, despite its silly, Valley-girl lyrics, is a pretty savage critique of the gross consumerism of the early eighties. The characters that Moon is playing throughout the song are obsessed with shopping and beauty and status. The choruses, sung by Zappa and band, then offer a metacommentary on Moon's narrative. For instance, in the first verse, Moon sings, "I love going into like clothing stores and stuff / I like buy the neatest mini-skirts and stuff." The band then sings, "Tosses her head 'n flips her hair / She got a whole bunch of nothin' in there." This relationship, between buying for the sake of buying (the root of conspicuous consumption; you do not buy things when you need them, you buy things because you want them, because the act of buying becomes fulfilling in and of itself instead of filling some greater need) and stupidity is classic Zappa. Although many probably did not see or understand a relationship between "Valley Girl" and the Marxist theory of commodity fetishism, it is there, buried under four minutes of pure pop confection. It is one of the more subversive acts of art in the eighties.

"I Come from Nowhere" is another fantastic pop song. The music seems to ape the kind of pop-rock that is extremely popular at the time. (The year 1982 is the beginning of the age of MTV. Artists like Marshall Crenshaw, Tommy Tutone, and the Producers were all over MTV. Light, poppy rock was the order of the day.) As soon as the vocals start, however, the song takes a decided left turn into weirdness.

Rejoining Zappa after a long layoff is Roy Estrada, who manages to sing, Terry Bozzio-like, completely against the melody and the beat, creating a manic piece of contemporary psychedelia.[48] The lyrics are a paean to escapism: "I come from nowhere…The people from nowhere / Always smile." The idea that coming from nowhere and knowing nothing makes one happy is a new, more nihilistic theory; it is the first creeping indication that Zappa has started to give up on any sort of hope that people will listen to him and what he has to say. Despite the lyrics, the song is really an excuse for an extended (more than three minutes) guitar solo. Although the song's melody is constructed to sound like a mid-eighties super hit, the solo is pure acid rock/blues. The contrast of the heavy guitar over the poppy bass and drums is devastating.

"Drowning Witch" is another song that, although featuring an interesting melody and some incisive lyrics, is really an excuse to blow it all out musically. Clocking in at more than 12 minutes, it is the musical centerpiece of the album. Pieced together from at least three different recordings from 1980 to 1981, with, according to Zappa, bits and pieces from more than 15 different performances, it is an old-school piece of Zappa music with a new twist. Owning his own studio had given Zappa license to spend countless hours (hours that he would have had to pay for at a commercial studio) trying to get the song just right, and although some feel that this is borderline obsessive, it makes for an interesting aural experience. The song is seamless; it sounds as if one band at one time is playing the song, but it is not. At just less than two minutes, Zappa abandons the lyrics, and the song becomes a complete instrumental. And what an instrumental! Zappa seems to delight in writing music that is too difficult even for the most accomplished of musicians. In the liner notes to *You Can't Do That on Stage Anymore, Vol. 3,* Zappa writes of "Drowning Witch": "The 1984 band *never* played it correctly during its 6-month tour, and the 1982 band only managed to get close on *one* occasion." There is more than a little sadism in this statement; in some ways, however, it is Zappa the untrained musician taking great pleasure in the fact that he has surrounded himself with wonderful, conservatory- and university-trained musicians who can not play his stuff. Ah, sweet revenge.

"Envelopes," an instrumental that would go on to have a nice life as a classical piece (a version can be heard on *London Symphony Orchestra, Vol. 1*), is a bit of a letdown after "Drowning Witch," if only because after the 12-minute madness of "Witch," almost anything is a downer. Featuring Steve Vai playing impossible guitar parts, it heavily foreshadows the Synclavier music that Zappa would be recording in a few years.

The album ends with "Teenage Prostitute," sung by Lisa Popeil, daughter of the world-famous Ron Popeil, inventor of the pocket fisherman, among other things, and ubiquitous star of late-night infomercials. It is a strange little song. With "The Blue Light" on the *Tinsel Town Rebellion* album, Zappa had developed a style of talk-singing that he used on both "Drowning Witch" and "Teenage Prostitute." Musically it is another one of the songs that seems very influenced by the eighties music popular at the time (although it does feature some interesting instrumental breaks). Lyrically, it is another Zappa song that claims that female sexuality, even that of a 17-year-old prostitute, is a woman's responsibility. It is a bit more difficult than that, however, and Zappa does seem to indicate that there are reasons why a woman might end up a prostitute, arguing, for instance, that "Her mom was destitute / Her daddy doesn't care / She's a teen-age prostitute." Later in the same song her pimp keeps her drugged in order to force her to work. It is hardly a song celebrating prostitution, as some have claimed. Few agreed, and the reception of the song was a counterpoint to the mania that greeted "Valley Girl."

Because of the sleight nature of the album (it was very short compared to the barrage of double albums Zappa had released since 1979), it sort of came and went, and although it got to a pretty lofty chart position, it also left just as quickly. It is an album about which most contemporary critics have little to say except for the obligatory "it is the 'Valley Girl' album." Amazon.com, *The New Rolling Stone Album Guide,* and *Musichound Rock* all ignore it, and the best *All Music Guide* can do is argue, "This album clearly lacks ambition and tends to get lost among the man's humongous discography."[49]

Despite the popularity of "Valley Girl," the album quickly disappeared. It is indicative, however, of the direction Zappa's music was going. The next two albums, recorded at the end of the 1982 tour and released a year apart, would continue the short, pop-song-based work that Zappa had been doing since the beginning of the eighties. The problem would be, would anyone care to listen?

THE MAN FROM UTOPIA AND THEM OR US

Making good music for people who do not listen. *The Man from Utopia* (originally released in March 1983 on the Barking Pumpkin Label; currently available as Rykodisc RCD 10538). Highest *Billboard* Chart position: No. 153. Personnel: Steve Vai, Ray White, Roy Estrada, Bob Harris, Ike Willis, Bobby Martin, Tommy Mars, Arthur Barrow, Ed Mann, Scott Thunes, Chad Wackerman, Vinnie Colaiuta, Craig Steward, Dick Fegy, and Marty Krystall.

Them or Us (originally released in October 1984 on the Barking Pumpkin label; currently available as Rykodisc RCD 10543). Highest *Billboard* chart position: Unavailable/did not chart. Personnel: Ray White, Ike Willis, Bobby Martin, Tommy Mars, Arthur Barrow, Chad Wackerman, Johnny "Guitar" Watson, Napoleon Murphy Brock, George Duke, Moon Zappa, Steve Vai, Dweezil

Zappa, Scott Thunes, Ed Mann, Roy Estrada, Thana Harris, Bob Harris, Patrick O'Hearn, and Brad Cole. "Hey! It's the twentieth century...whatever you can do to have a good time, let's get on with it so long as it doesn't cause a murder."[50]

The Man from Utopia is perhaps the most underrated of all of Zappa's pop and rock records. It is a well-recorded, insightful, playful, and funny record that features some great songs, some interesting experiments, and some of the tightest, catchiest instrumentals ever committed to vinyl.

Of course, it was a bomb. By 1983, no one seemed much interested in hearing an album that was for sex (remember AIDS?), against unions, against cocaine, and filled with weird talked-sung songs done in a style Zappa would label *meltdown* that featured Zappa talking over wild free-jazz improvisations that would then be taken back to the studio and subjected to typical Zappa overdubbing. There were also covers of old fifties songs and a bunch of instrumentals.[51]

The album kicks off with the straightforward political statement "Cocaine Decisions," an all-out assault on the coke-fueled go-go eighties culture. It is a pretty dead-on argument, one that is open to a number of interpretations. For instance, when Zappa is writing about cocaine decisions, is he talking about decisions made while on cocaine or decisions about cocaine? It could be either one. For instance, in the first verse he sings, "the cocaine decision that you make today / Will mean that millions somewhere else / Will do it your way." Is this person making a coke deal that affects the people in the coke-producing countries in Central and South America, or is this person a coked-out Wall Street person who is making bad decisions about investments because he is too whacked out to know any better? They are both valid arguments, the kind of which were played out every day in the eighties. Musically, the song is a nice grinding blues (with a cool harmonica breakdown throughout), with the music mixed down low so the audience can hear what Zappa has to say.

"Cocaine Decisions" fades right into "SEX," which can be considered a manifesto. A lot of what Zappa has been arguing for throughout his life he lays bare here, arguing, for instance, "Ladies they need it just like the guys / ... Maybe you could use a protein surprise." Despite its relative crudeness, it is pretty standard fare for Zappa. He is simply making the life-long argument that sex is just about the best thing two people can engage in, and the fact that the culture has dictated a system wherein only men are allowed to enjoy it is ridiculous. The song also features a nice bit of political argument (that is again hidden in the vaguely crude lyrics) in which Zappa sings about the virtues of big women (doing so, of course, in a negative way, arguing that sex with flat or skinny women is no fun). Although this could be considered as somehow crude, the argument Zappa is making is that women do not have to look like the coked-out supermodels to get laid, that a regular-looking woman is more preferable than a skinny model wannabe.

One of the things that Zappa manages to avoid in his professional career is reinforcing the culturally constructed ideas of beauty. Although Zappa wrote many songs about the way men and women behave, he never worked to enforce ideas of beauty; in Zappa's world, as long as people are having sex, it should not matter what they look like.

The first instrumental on the album, "Tink Walks Amok," is a really cool bass-based piece featuring the fretwork of Arthur Barrow (whose nickname was Tink.). It is a great mixture of syncopated automation, funk bass, jazz drumming, and strong central melody. Barrow has discussed the origin of this song a number of times and makes some pretty interesting comments about it on the *ARF* Web site (http://www.arf.ru/Notes/Utopia/tinka.html).

"The Radio Is Broken" is the first of the so-called meltdown songs on the album. This song, sung by both Zappa and Roy Estrada, is an ode to old fifties movie clichés (see "Cheepnis" for more of this kind of madness). The song is interesting in that it features the spoken-word sections separated by some wicked instrumental breaks featuring some great drum-percussion-guitar interplay. The lyrics are fairly absurdist stuff, along the lines of "The germs from space! / The negative virus knitwear / The blobulent suit." There are points in the song that you can hear Zappa and Estrada trying hard not to laugh at the silliness of the proceedings.

"We Are Not Alone," one of Zappa's most interesting melodies, follows. The best way to describe it is as perfect music to play over the end titles of a surfer film. It is a passionate, upbeat release of musical energy that reminds one of the kinds of music that Zappa would have known growing up in California in the late fifties and early sixties. There is a great melodic sax theme that is followed by some interesting percussion parts by Ed Mann that lead back into another sax section.

"The Dangerous Kitchen" is a catalog of items, sung in meltdown form, about what might happen if you do not keep your kitchen very clean. Musically, it is kind of funny, if only because it sounds like a parody of the cool jazz of the beatnik era. It is a song that a lot of critics and fans like, but it seems kind of slight (Zappa has gone from journalist trying to determine what something means to photographer just telling what there is).

"The Man from Utopia Meets Mary Lou" is a medley of fifties songs done in a very reverent form. Once again, Zappa is telling us how much he really likes this kind of music.

"Stick Together" is Zappa's last blast at unions. Ben Watson takes great pains to discuss this song at length,[52] so I will not bother, but it is important to consider at least a couple of ideas: Zappa had been arguing, since at least as far back as the song "Rudy Wants to Buy Yez a Drink," that unions, for all the good they had done, had become bloated and corrupt and that they needed to look at themselves in a more critical light. Several times during the years that Zappa was attempting to get his classical music recorded (from the mid-seventies until the end of his life), Zappa had come in contact with musicians unions that he felt were gouging him. A close second to the musicians unions were the stagehands and electricians unions. One famous story has Zappa doing a show in New York in the early eighties that was to be broadcast by the Westwood One radio network, MTV, and recorded by Zappa. According to Zappa, the electricians and stagehands unions charged each of these entities the full price of the show even though, according to Zappa, his road crew did all of the setup, takedown, and recording. It is this kind of treatment that has made Zappa furious at the unions, which had gone, in his opinion, from protecting the little guy to protecting the interests of union management.

The song that follows, "The Jazz Discharge Party Hats," is hard to describe; it is incredibly filthy and incredibly funny at the same time (this, more than likely, depends upon one's sense of humor). Another in a long line of road stories, "Jazz" is talk-sung over a beat that originally came in the center of a long version of "The Torture Never Stops," in this case in 1980 at a performance at Southern Illinois University. There is simply no way to describe it within existing copyright restrictions and do it justice. To put it mildly, it is the story of what happens to some band members when they are bored and trying to find a way to pass the time with some girls in Albuquerque, New Mexico. Zappa is, as always, far more critical of the guys in the band than he is of the girls, writing, "A couple of the guys in the band / Who were desperate for THAT KIND OF ACTION / Kept workin' on 'em for two days / (Which is a waste of fuckin' time anyway)." It is here that Zappa points out one of the central hypocrisies of the groupie scene: Many men get a tremendous amount of power by using, abusing, and putting down groupies, yet, as Zappa repeatedly points out, men will go to desperate and hilarious lengths to be with these girls. It is a very odd form of power indeed.

The album ends with another interesting instrumental, "Moggio," a wickedly paced instrumental that the band often played live. According to Neal Slaven, the title of the song comes from Zappa's daughter Diva:

> One day, when Diva was real young, she crawled into bed with us, and I was going to bed, like, seven o'clock in the morning, and she had been sleeping in bed with Gail during the night. As I got into bed, she was just waking up, and she was telling me about this dream that she had, that she had a tiny, little father named 'Moggio' who lived under the pillow...and gave me this complete scenario about this character that she was familiar with.[53]

It is not the last song Diva would name. "Chana in De Bushwop," found on *You Can't Do That on Stage Anymore, Vol. 3*, is another Diva creation.

The album has been somewhat forgotten as Zappa's reputation has been sorted out. Amazon.com ignores it (they sell it, of course, but offer no criticism of the album), whereas the *All Music Guide* offers up only that it is "more varied and engaging than "Them or Us."[54] Both *Rolling Stone* and *Musichound* ignore it completely.

It is another album well worth investigating, especially for new fans trying to cope with Zappa's more experimental works. It is short, with very tightly focused pop songs and instrumentals that are not musically challenging that feature bright, resolved melodies and easy-to-follow narrative lines.

Zappa's next album, his last full studio rock album, was a fine way to go out. (Zappa would do a number of other original albums after this, including *Thing-Fish*, which is much more a play than a rock record, *Meets the Mothers of Prevention*, which has a few studio songs but is largely made up of Synclavier pieces, live albums of original material, and countless albums of classical / orchestral music.) It looked both backward, to classic fifties music and old Mothers tunes as well as a hilarious Allman Brothers song that was the result of an inside joke, and forward, taking a good hard look at what MTV had done to the culture, making fun of the French, and, for good measure, Steve Vai's sex life.

Them or Us is a fine record for the middle of the eight years of the Reagan administration (and if one needs proof of the fact that Zappa is taking aim at the Reagans, the cover of the album, with its portrait of a dog in a dress sandwiched between a Heinz ketchup bottle and a bottle of baby's milk, is squarely representative of the era's increasingly mean-spirited conservative ethos; Reagan, or the members of his administration, is remembered by many for declaring in a debate about school lunch funding and proper diet that catsup should be considered a vegetable). It is a startling album in the sense that, much like the mid-eighties nostalgia wave encouraged by Reagan (the Reagan administration was all about looking backward; his use of "city on a hill" and "morning in America" are indicative of this Puritan nostalgia), Zappa starts the album by going all the way back to his youth. "The Closer You Are," an intimate, slow, doo-wop number starts the album. It is a lovely piece originally recorded by New York doo-wop band the Channels in 1956.

"In France," sung by Zappa's guitar hero from his youth, Johnny "Guitar" Watson, is a hilarious, albeit cheap, shot at the conditions Zappa had endured while he toured Europe in the late seventies and early eighties. Although the song did not make the French particularly happy, it is a pretty funny piece of reporting on what France is like, especially to someone who is used to things a certain way (and Zappa, despite the fact that he had toured around the world for close to 20 years, comes off as somewhat narrow in his cultural interests—see his chapter on food in *The Real Frank Zappa Book* for more on this). In what is perhaps a great artistic irony, it would be the French composer and conductor Pierre Boulez who would give Zappa an aura of legitimacy in the classical world. "In France" is a nice, greasy piece of blues, with Johnny Watson growling his Beefheart-like vocals, although the lyrics take a sort of jingoistic view of France, making fun of the way people dress and the fact that the public restrooms in Paris are right on the street.

"Ya Honza," is a backward version of "Sofa," the effect is unsettling and slightly unmusical, although it is a pretty funny comment on what was, at the time, a significant national debate over backward-masking in records (a number of groups and artists, including Led Zeppelin and Black Sabbath, were accused by parents of putting satanic messages on their records that were accessible if one listened to the records backward; I tried and tried to find these messages as a kid and failed miserably every time).

"Sharleena" is a reworked version of the Flo & Eddie classic featuring Zappa's son Dweezil on some burning, Eddie Van Halen- and Frank Zappa-influenced guitar. The vocals are interesting because, for the money, Zappa probably never had a better set of vocalists than Ike Willis and Bobby Martin. The technical brilliance is astounding. (For an interesting take on the song, the version on *You Can't Do That on Stage Anymore, Vol. 3* has Dweezil and Frank Zappa exchanging solos in a nice moment of father-son bonding.)

"Sinister Footwear II" is an instrumental that features two different guitar solos by Zappa and some interesting written guitar lines (the technically difficult melodies) played by Steve Vai and doubled by Ed Mann on marimba. Melodically, the song sounds akin to the *Joe's Garage* instrumentals, especially "Packard Goose" and "Watermelon in Easter Hay," although toward the end it becomes much more free-jazz oriented, with melodic lines that do not manage to resolve themselves.

"Truck Driver Divorce" picks up right were "No Not Now" left off, even including the delivery of a load of "string beans to Utah." Most information indicates this song has its origins in the kind of talk-singing that Zappa featured on *The Man from Utopia*. The unique feature of this song is that it devolves in the middle into a long solo by Zappa that, musically, has nothing to do with the melodic themes developed in the beginning of the song. It is almost as if Zappa is trying to take not only solos from different times and wed them to songs but also parts of different songs with different solos and different melodies and mash them together and see what the fans think. It is a somewhat jarring shift, happing as it does without any sort of transition, but upon repeated listening, it becomes clear that Zappa is trying to do something so startlingly new that it takes some time to get used to. Information on the *Information Is Not Knowledge* fan Web site (http://globalia.net/donlope/fz/lyrics/Them_Or_Us.html#Divorce) indicates that the music for the song was recorded in mid-1982 and the solo was taken from a performance of "Zoot Allures" from November 1981. The song, which only has a minute and a half of melody and lyrics, has around seven minutes of solo. An interesting version of the song on *You Can't Do That on Stage Anymore, Vol. 4* cuts the majority of the solo (reducing the song from the nine-minute workout on *Them or Us* to around four minutes); it also blends performances from the 1982 and 1984 touring bands (the band is 1984, whereas the solo is 1982). It is an interesting comment on how even live music for Zappa is really a studio construction.

"Stevie's Spanking" is Zappa's ode to Steve Vai's introduction to the road. It is an interesting song in the sense that the main characters, both Steve

Vai and groupie/fan Laurel Fishman, agreed to have their names used in the song, giving some credence to Zappa's repeated claims that he is just reporting from the road.[55] The song then enters into a nice three-chord heavy-metal vamp and features solos from Steve Vai (really the first time he had been allowed to cut loose on record) and Dweezil (in a moment of wonderful generosity Zappa takes the rhythm guitar parts throughout).

"Baby Take Your Teeth Out" is a great piece of Ike Willis sleezery about the process of getting orally gratified by a woman with no teeth. It is thankfully short, albeit wonderfully bright and happy. It is one of the tossed-off pieces of hilarity that never cease to amaze. The middle of the song features Ike Willis doing one of his stage voices (pretending he has no teeth) and finishing the song with more of his *Thing-Fish* dialect: "The little girl must be praketin' richcraft!" It is a slight piece of music that is made contextually all the more funny when one realizes that it was the album's single (not a bad joke in and of itself).

"Marqueson's Chicken," is an old-school instrumental that features some interesting introductory melody work by Vai and Mann followed by an extended solo set largely to a deeply rooted repetitive bass line courtesy of Scott Thunes, drums that both follow and lead, and some tasty reggae-influenced backing by the rest of the band.

"Planet of My Dreams" is another in the *Hunchentoot* songs (the rest of which are found on *Sleep Dirt*). It is an interesting anticapitalist and anticonsumerist song, a damning indictment of the highly acquisitive eighties. The first verse ends with the lines "The glory of our sciences / And militant alliances...along the mounds of dead appliances!" Zappa's increasing criticism of the disposable nature of the world presents an interesting argument. In the one sense, Zappa was an artist who was trying to achieve the kind of permanence that only composition can. His scores and recordings are permanent in some way; he treated technology and, to some extent, band members as only semipermanent at best. At the same time that Zappa was recording *Them or Us,* he was busily replacing the bass and drums from the first couple of Mothers of Invention albums, thus showing the rather disposable nature of recording itself. Zappa was also well known as a fiend for technology and would quickly abandon old recording techniques for new in his life-long quest for perfection. The advances that he had seen in his lifetime—from 2-track analog to 48-track portable digital—are pretty amazing.

"Be in My Video" is the best song on the album. Period. A cold shot at how, even by the early eighties, MTV was ruining music, it was the kind of incisive political commentary in which only Zappa seemed to be willing to regularly engage. The song repeats what were, by then, the standard MTV video clichés, many of which seem tied to David Bowie, who in 1982 had a huge comeback with the *Let's Dance* album that featured a number of videos that made Bowie, who had, admittedly, no problem in selling an image that went along with his songs, the center of the story (and not the music, a cardinal sin in Zappa's eyes). Zappa and band sing, "Pretend to sing the words / I'll rent a gleaming limousine / Release a flock of birds." The song instantly conjures videos by Prince, Mötley Crüe, and Duran Duran—all of the folks for whom MTV was the fast track to the Top 40.[56]

"Them or Us" is a recorded guitar solo (excerpted from a performance of "The Black Page") that shows off the versatility of the Wackerman-Thunes rhythm section.

"Frogs with Dirty Little Lips" comes from Zappa's son Ahmet, who evidently would wander around the house singing a song that always seemed to have at its core the phrase "frogs with dirty little lips." Musically, the song is quite interesting in that it foreshadows the kind of stuff Zappa would do on *Thing-Fish*. It is very sterile and claustrophobic; the vocals, for instance, are recorded very close to the microphone and are mixed to the front, meaning the vocals are right in the listeners' faces. It is a great children's song, capturing as it does the predilections of children: "Dirty 'n green / Tiny 'n mean / Floppin' around by the edge of the stream." It is a nice song in the sense that it challenges the increasing accusations by critics and biographers of Zappa's supposed misanthropy toward the end of his career. This song, along with the song "Chana in de Bushwop," a 1984 composition credited to Zappa and daughter Diva and found on *You Can't Do That on Stage Anymore, Vol. 3,* shows that Zappa delighted in the innocence and absurdity of children.

The album ends with another cover, this time of the Allman Brothers classic jam "Whipping Post," which is also a hilarious in-joke. During the last song on *You Can't Do That on Stage Anymore, Vol. 2: The Helsinki Concert,* an audience member is heard to shout "Play 'Whipping Post'" right before the band begins the song "Montana." No one in the band knew how to play "Whipping Post." The version on *Them or Us* (and the live version found on *Does Humor Belong in Music,* a nice, albeit too short, souvenir of the 1984 band) shows that Zappa was able to work with standard source material in his own unique manner.

For some reason, perhaps because there had been a glut of Zappa releases within the same short period (*Them or Us* was released less than a month before *Thing-Fish* and *Francesco Zappa* and within three months of *Boulez Conducts Zappa: The Perfect Stranger*), perhaps because the United States was not at all ready for any sort of protest of the Reagan administration, perhaps because Zappa was unable to fit into a music scene that was increasingly dominated by MTV. Contemporary critical evaluations of the album are almost entirely nonexistent beyond the typical discussions of how the album got put together (critics, it seems, become increasingly fascinated with Zappa's technical abilities, forgetting that he is always using them in the service of making music). The *All Music Guide* writes, "It contains a little of everything for everyone, but most of all it has that cold and dry early-'80s feel that made this and other albums like *The Man From Utopia* and *Frank Zappa Meets the Mothers of Prevention* sound dated pretty quickly."[57] It is not, to be perfectly honest, the greatest album of Zappa's career. It is, like many of his albums, a sort of assemblage, with all of the good and bad that comes with that. (Zappa, with his home studio and ability to record live, no longer needed to collect a set of songs before he recorded an album; so unlike many composers, Zappa's albums often lack the kind of cohesiveness or coherence that comes from having a group of songs all written and recorded within a specific time frame.) At the same time that Zappa was putting the finishing touches on *Them or Us,* he was, however, getting ready to unleash a monster on an unsuspecting public.

THING-FISH

"Is THIS entertainment?"[58] *Thing-Fish* (Originally released in November 1984 on the Barking Pumpkin label; currently available as Rykodisc RCD 10544 / 45). Highest *Billboard* chart position: Unavailable/did not chart. Personnel: Steve Vai, Ray White, Tommy Mars, Chuck Wild, Arthur Barrow, Scott Thunes, Jay Anderson, Ed Mann, Chad Wackerman, Steve De Furia, and David Ocker. Features the vocal / narrative talents of Ike Willis, Terry Bozzio, Dale Bozzio, Napoleon Murphy Brock, Bob Harris, and Johnny "Guitar" Watson. "Is this the theater? I thought it would be ablaze with light and finery."[59]

When I teach writing I always use a baseball metaphor: For a writer it is far better to swing for the fences and strike out than it is to play it safe and hit for average. Throughout his career, Frank Zappa was always thinking big. From the beginning, Zappa was always trying to get record companies to release double and triple albums and boxed sets. When he set out to make a point or create something new, Zappa always took a big cut.

Thing-Fish is perhaps the biggest cut of his career. A massive (three LPs when it was originally released, now available on two CDs) piece of political theater that works on a number of different levels, it is a scream of rage at the state of art, politics, religion, race, class, and science during the eighties.

As good as the album is now, it is important to remember the context in which it was recorded. During the early eighties, Broadway underwent a pretty significant overhaul. Writing about the Broadway season of 1981–82, Frank Rich, theater critic for *The New York Times,* argues that "This has been a season in which playwrights seem to have forgotten even the basic grammar of their craft"[60]; and writing about the show *Pump Boys and Dinettes* (a very popular country-rock play / show / revue), "We may have reached the point where we're so grateful to enter a theater where we're greeted as guests at a family party, where we're not assaulted by pretensions and rude noise, that we're willing to accept less as more."[61] As if to put a cherry on the top of this theory, the musical *Cats,* which many believe is more than responsible for changing Broadway for the worse, opens on Broadway on October 8, 1982.

Zappa's characters seem to be reacting to exactly the issues Rich identifies. Toward the very beginning of the show, Rhonda (voiced by Dale Bozzio as a

"Is your face paying the prices of success?" worried a 1988 Nivea skin cream ad, in which a business-suited woman with a briefcase rushes a child to day care—and catches a glimpse of her career-pitted skin in a store window. If only she were less successful, her visage would be more radiant....Most at risk [claimed *Mademoiselle* magazine] are "high achieving women," whose comely appearance can be ravaged by "executive stress."[65]

The conservative reaction to the feminist movement, first hinted at in "Bobby Brown" and fully exposed in *Thing-Fish*, is indicative of the complex ways in which Zappa's work of the late seventies and early eighties can be read.

Along with the various bits of what would come to be called identity politics, *Thing-Fish* also takes on some of the larger issues that Zappa had been considering for much of his career. The biggest, and most prevalent on the album, is the idea that the government actively works to oppress certain groups of people or to keep certain unpopular ideas from its citizens. The conservative revolution started by Ronald Reagan was not shy about trying to remake the world in its image (or return it to a fantasy image conservatives had constructed).

Although the jury is still out on whether AIDS was, as Zappa seems to be arguing in *Thing-Fish*, the result of a government conspiracy to keep black people and gay people from gaining any sort of hegemony, there is plenty of evidence that the Reagan administration was working pretty actively to keep any sort of progressive ideas out of the heads of Americans. It is well documented in Randy Shilts's devastating history of AIDS, *And the Band Played On*, that although the Reagan administration knew of the AIDS epidemic for quite some time (the first *New York Times* article about it is in July 1981), Ronald Reagan was unable or unwilling to discuss it publicly for several years (the first official statement by Reagan is purported to have been in October 1987), and he and his administration repeatedly cut, reduced, or denied funding to the agencies working to try to discover the origins of the disease. Reagan's unwillingness was more than likely due to the influence of conservative Christians both inside and outside the administration; this is an era, for instance, when religious leader Jerry Falwell said "AIDS is the wrath of God upon homosexuals," and Ronald Reagan's communications director, Pat Buchanan, argued that AIDS is "nature's revenge on gay men."[66]

Instead of making the AIDS epidemic the direct story of the show, Zappa creates a very complex narrative that mixes up aspects of the government's poor reaction to the AIDS epidemic with the government's use of African Americans as unwitting test subjects for syphilis studies: "From 1932 to 1972, 399 poor black sharecroppers in Macon County, Alabama were denied treatment for syphilis and deceived by physicians of the United States Public Health Service."[67] The syphilis study, of course, reinforces the kind of conspiracy that Zappa saw as potentially at the heart of the AIDS epidemic.

grown up, fleshed out, feminized Mary, her memorable character from *Joe's Garage*) tells her husband Harry (played by Dale's real-life husband, former Zappa drummer extraordinaire Terry Bozzio) that "this is not *Dreamgirls*!" (a favorite of Rich's) and, in the most damning statement about Broadway this side of Frank Rich, "What's happened to Broadway, HARRY? Used to be you could come to one of these things and the wind would be RUSHING DOWN THE PLAIN or a fairy on a string would go over the audience... but NOW! Harry, I ask you: is *THIS* entertainment?"

Since the beginning of his career, Zappa has been arguing against the dumbing down of the culture. Broadway, for Zappa, is the most visible symbol of this. (Of course, to be honest, there are more than a few mouthfuls of sour grapes involved in this particular complaint. Zappa tried throughout his career to have a number of shows—most famously *Hunchentoot* and *Thing-Fish* as well as a musical version of William Burroughs's *Naked Lunch*—mounted on Broadway and found the stage closed to him.) It is a perfect time for Zappa to write a Broadway show about how bad Broadway shows had become.

Of course if *Thing-Fish* were just about Broadway it would not be a Zappa project. The show takes on so many themes that were hotly debated in the early eighties that it is astounding to consider: AIDS, feminism, gay chic, government conspiracy, race, greed, and class, all done up in a framework of Broadway show tunes and some of the most glorious filth ever committed to record.

There is no real way to do a song-by-song analysis of this particular album (it would take up that much space). What I would like to do is offer some comments about some of the more important themes that the album develops, especially in light of Zappa's increasing political activism (indeed, after the release of this album, Zappa would find himself spending an increasing amount of time doing nonmusical, political work).

Thing-Fish is a difficult album to approach, especially after 20 years of discussion of political correctness. The main character in the piece, the Thing-Fish, is played by Ike Willis, who speaks throughout in a dialect taken straight from *Amos 'N Andy*. Without having seen or heard *Amos 'N Andy*, it is hard for many to understand that for a time it was the most popular show on television. A hit for CBS from 1951 to 1953 (and a much bigger radio hit in the years prior to the TV show), it is certainly a show that both Zappa and Ike Willis would have seen. In many ways, the show is the prototype for the media's intentional misrepresentation of race. The show regularly presented African Americans as unable to deal with even the simplest of problems and soon led to protests by the NAACP, which may or may not have driven the show off the air. The dialect spoken by the characters, especially by Amos, Andy, and the Kingfish, a family friend, was a mangled version of Standard American English that made a very clear argument: black people are too dumb to speak English.

By choosing to have Ike Willis speak in this kind of dialect throughout the album, Zappa is throwing up a direct challenge to white Americans (this is the same person who, in the song "The Blue Light" on *Tinsel Town Rebel-lion,* sings "you can't even speak your own fucking language"). One of the surest, if not most controversial, signs of African American progress had been the use by African-Americans of racist language for their own political purposes, starting in many ways with Richard Pryor's appropriation of the word *nigger* in his stand-up performances (something that directly descends from Lenny Bruce's work in the early sixties). Willis's black dialect is the sound of a man having great sport at the expense of white racists. Willis's character, the Thing-Fish, is part of a chorus of characters who all display outsize African American characteristics. Called the Mammy Nuns, the char-acters call up a number of racist stereotypes; they are all round, dressed like Aunt Jemima (perhaps Zappa is finally atoning for "Electric Aunt Jemima"), and, in being given the name "Mammy," cemented to a stereotypical past of black servitude. The mammy is considered one of the most offensive of all black stereotypes, in part because it is largely made up (there were, until long after the Civil War, almost no so-called mammies; it is a character based in part on Mammy in *Gone with the Wind* and the mammy character in *Uncle Tom's Cabin,* both, incidentally, written by white folks) and in part because it represents the worst of all white wish fulfillments about blacks. Mammies, according to one historian, "convey the notion that genuine fulfillment for black women comes not from raising their own children or feeding their own man ... but from serving in a white family's kitchen."[62] By creating the characters of the Mammy Nuns and Thing-Fish, Zappa and Willis have put together an interesting argument against racism: both of the characters that are named (mammies and the Kingfish) were made up by white people. In a show that is about, in one extent, white racism, these characters, by their very existence, are a tremendous statement.

What makes the character of the Thing-Fish doubly political is that Zappa has the other two main characters stand in for the worst excesses of white people in the early eighties. Harry and Rhonda are introduced by Zappa as the prototypes of normality: "Harry, in a tux, and his wife Rhonda, in a stylish suit with a fox collar." As we find out during the course of the show, Harry and Rhonda are the very prototypes of the upwardly mobile young urban professionals who seemed to rule the eighties. The narrative arc that we follow with Harry and Rhonda is a bit more difficult than that of the Thing-Fish. In brief, we follow Harry and Rhonda through a number of eighties political movements that are presented by Zappa as a set of ideologi-cal fads. Harry, for instance, is soon confronted as the character Harry-as-a-Boy, who discusses the "serious bidniss o' growin' up in ermaerica": "Well, I plan on making a few mistakes, having my heart broken and so forth, using all kinds of drugs, and turning gay as soon as possible in order to accelerate my rise to the top of the heap." A quick review of Zappa's songs from the first Mothers record onward will show these themes as being some of the oldest in his ideological catalog. We also find out, in a reference to "Bobby Brown,"

that Harry-as-a-Boy becomes gay because he "lost all desire for ir with females when they started carrying those briefcases and wearii ties." Harry, who is Zappa's stand-in for the spoiled middle-class w is once again reinforcing the argument that it is not necessarily Zap who fears feminism (Zappa's wife at this time had almost comple over the business aspect of Zappa's career, leading them to unpr profits; so much for men being better than women at business Zappa is lampooning the deeply entrenched antifeminism of co white men.

In many ways *Thing-Fish* can be seen as a lampooning of many co sacred cows. As Ben Watson argues, many of the ideas that Harr expresses about his own latent homosexuality seem to be the kind phobic arguments presented by conservatives. Indeed, the idea pr Harry-as-a-Boy that homosexuality is selfish because it prevents procreating is one of the arguments currently being used against th tion of gay marriage (i.e., that because gay people can not have ch should not be allowed to marry).

The character of Rhonda is also a pretty vicious satire on conse reotypes. As Zappa presents her in the second half of the sho becomes the monstrous, man-hating feminist that had been cons the Right to make women ashamed of feminism (and thus unwilli for their equality); this is the character that Susan Faludi so co deconstructs in *Backlash: The Undeclared War against Americ* writing that "the central argument of the backlash [is] that womer is responsibility for women's unhappiness."[63] As anyone who ha Zappa's career would understand, the idea that the movement is r unhappy is ridiculous.

Rhonda, although several years before the fact, is the mythol inazi so carefully constructed by right-wing radio personality baugh. Toward the end of the show, Zappa exposes this stereotyp Rhonda choose her career over her husband (one of the great fea the antifeminist movement); in an even more incisive bit of politi Rhonda then decides that she does not need Harry: "I have m Harry! I'm going to fuck my briefcase...it's big Harry! It's full papers...from my career!" One of the great threats that conserv feminists have used for years to try to dissuade women from havi is that it will get in the way of their so-called natural roles as wife (and, not coincidentally, as support person for the male head of ho Related to this threat of a career is the idea, again reinforced by co that feminists are somehow antibeauty and/or ugly. Rhonda, w seem to get Harry's attention by fucking her briefcase, then tells going to put my glasses on, Harry! I'm going to put my hair up Writing in 1991, feminist author Susan Faludi exposed this myth was, a crass attempt by conservatives to convince women to stop

The three evils of the conservative movement—black people, gay people, and feminists—were all effectively eliminated by AIDS.

Musically, the album brings back a number of old favorites, including "The Blue Light," "The Torture Never Stops," "You Are What You Is," "Mudd Club," "The Meek Shall Inherit Nothing," and "No Not Now." There are also several new songs as well as some experiments with the Synclavier, a pro-grammable digital music machine that would increasingly become Zappa's favorite compositional and musical tool. (Much of the Synclavier music is used as underscoring for the dialogue.)

There are several new songs on the album as well. One of Zappa's finest pop songs, "He's So Gay," is the final song on the first CD (it stands as a sort of show-stopping act-closing song). A light pop/faux new-wave beat drives the song and makes the lyrical argument that homosexuality was somehow a power move. When Zappa sings "He's so gay / He's almost everyone today," he is making a definite comment on the feminization of the culture. Zappa also continues his delight in the odd sexual practices of others by listing a litany of things that people might do with their newfound sexual free-dom (including the mention, for the third time—"Bobby Brown" and "Sy Borg" are the others—of the golden shower, obviously something that either intrigued or disturbed Zappa quite a bit). At the end of the song, Zappa has the band play a bit from the Culture Club hit "Do You Really Want to Hurt Me?," which works on a number of levels. Culture Club is just the kind of band that Zappa has been arguing against (an MTV pretty band), and their proud allegiance to homosexuality affirms Zappa's argument that being gay was a quick way to corporate success.

The second CD, which contains most of the new music, continues with some of Zappa's favorite themes, including, in a return to 1964, a great song about a young, white male's obsession with his automobile. In "The White Boy Troubles," Zappa lists a number of things that are considered problems for young white men: "his car's fucked up," "she ripped up de 'polstry." For fans who had been following Zappa since the earliest days of the Mothers of Invention, this has to sound familiar. On their first album, when Zappa and Ray Collins sing, "I had my car re-upholstered," he is starting a 30-year his-tory of associating car issues with white boys. It is a nice piece of conceptual continuity.

"Brown Moses," which is interesting in the sense that it is done in a style of music that Zappa had not really explored that much—the African American spiritual—is the climax of the second act. Closely sung harmonies by Zappa, Ray White, and Ike Willis show once again Zappa's complete absorption of U.S. musical genres.

The musical ends in a wild flight of degeneracy, with an orgy, anal rape, and enemas all featured into the narrative. It is almost unspeakable. Ben Watson reminds us, however, that almost all of Zappa's works have ended in a chaotic mess like this: "Strictly Genteel" at the end of *200 Motels* and "Little Green

Rosetta" at the end of *Joe's Garage* both feature the same sort of psycho-sexual madness.[68]

Despite everything I have just written, there are a number of themes and narratives that have been left out (many because of my legal inability to quote lyrics from the songs); in fact, one of the things that makes *Thing-Fish* so interesting is its massive complexity. One can listen to it again and again and get different meanings each time. Other themes to pay attention to when listening to the record include the minstrel show (pay attention to all of the discussions of the napkin); fifties science-fiction films; sadomasochistic fetishes; aggressive female sexuality; the predominance in U.S. entertainment, especially on Broadway, of African Americans, televangelism, and/or the classism of the U.S. ruling class.

Contemporary criticism of the album has improved. Ignored upon release (it was a huge and hugely expensive album to buy), it has undergone a minor critical reappraisal over the past several years. Andrew Boscardan writes that "Those who get past its prickly skin will be pleased to discover an ambitious, hilarious, and catchy look at life and love in the 1980's—with an outlook not so good" and "Maybe not one of Zappa's best albums, but certainly one of his most daring."[69] Francois Couture calls it "his most controversial, misunderstood, overlooked album" and "It's crazy, offensive, barely holding together, but it sure is entertaining."[70] *The New Rolling Stone Album Guide* ignores it and *Musichound Rock* writes that it is "one to avoid."

It is a huge album with huge problems. It is one of the records that, I hope, will take on greater significance as the United States moves farther and farther to the right (Zappa would, undoubtedly, be unsurprised at the swift turn to the right in post 9/11 United States). Undoubtedly, it is a record that deserves a scholarly monograph all its own.

FRANK ZAPPA MEETS THE MOTHERS OF PREVENTION

When music and polemic meet. *Frank Zappa Meets the Mothers of Prevention* (Originally released in November 1985 on Barking Pumpkin Records; currently available as Rykodisc RCD 10547). Highest *Billboard* chart position: No. 153. Personnel: Steve Vai, Ray White, Ike Willis, Tommy Mars, Bobby Martin, Scott Thunes, Chad Wackerman, and Ed Mann. Featuring the voices of Moon Zappa, Dweezil Zappa, Senator John Danforth, Senator E. "Fritz" Hollings, Senator Slade Gorton, Senator Paula Hawkins, Senator Jim Exon, Senator Trible, Senator Albert Gore, Tipper Gore, Reverend Jeff Ling, Spider Barbour, All Nite John, and the Unknown Girl in the Piano. "If you support the PMRC...in their efforts to perpetuate the myth that SEX EQUALS SIN, you will help to institutionalize the neurotic misconception that keeps pornographers in business."[71]

Sometime in 1985, the story goes, Tipper Gore, wife of Senator (and later Vice President) Al Gore, bought her eight-year-old daughter a copy of the soundtrack to the Prince film *Purple Rain*. As the Gores listened to the album, they came to the song "Darling Nikki," the first two lines of which inform us: "I knew a girl named Nikki, I guess U could say she was a sex fiend / I met her in a hotel lobby masturbating with a magazine." This was too much for Mrs. Gore, who, in a fit of morally induced rage, formed a supersecret quasi-lobbying group who called themselves the Parents Music Resource Center (PMRC). There are other stories about this, and one would do well to read the chapter entitled "Porn Wars" in *The Real Frank Zappa Book* for a hysterical narrative of Zappa's battles with the PMRC. To make a long story short, Zappa, along with Twisted Sister's Dee Snyder and folk musician John Denver, testified in front of the Senate Commerce, Technology and Transportation Committee on September 19, 1985 (Zappa reprints his opening statement in his autobiography).

Out of these hearings comes the small but interesting album *Frank Zappa Meets the Mothers of Prevention*. Rushed out a few months after the hearings (it came out in November of the same year), it is interesting for several reasons: it features Zappa's first use of the Synclavier on a rock album (he had used it to underscore *Thing-Fish* and had used it on some quasi-classical experimentations, including *The Perfect Stranger* and *Francesco Zappa*); it features a return to *Lumpy Gravy*-like experimentation on the track "Porn Wars," which mixes Synclavier scoring with edited pieces of conversations from the Senate hearings; and it features two of Zappa's finest pieces of satire. All this and a couple of excellent live instrumentals and you have a vastly underappreciated album.

The CD that is available now (and approved by Frank Zappa in 1993) is significantly different from the original album. What happened, in short, is that Zappa created about an album-and-a-half worth of material and decided that the European release did not need a 12-minute composition about a U.S. Senate hearing, so that song was left out and others included. The current CD features all of the songs from both the European and U.S. vinyl releases.

It starts with "I Don't Even Care," a 1981–82 tour sound-check jam with lyrics and vocals (by Johnny "Guitar" Watson) added later. It is a great piece of pop-blues songwriting with a surprising guitar solo by Watson. Lyrically, it is closer to the blues than many of Zappa's blues-based songs; Watson lists a number of things that he does not even care about, including "the blue, the red and the white," and the fact that they want to "send me up to fix the satellite," a perhaps oblique reference to the disintegration of Skylab (a monster space station that had failed and crashed to Earth in summer 1979).

"One Man One Vote," "Little Beige Sambo," and "Aerobics in Bondage" are all Synclavier compositions. It is hard to describe these human-composed–machine-realized compositions. For long-time fans of Zappa's, they come as kind of a surprise. For Zappa, the Synclavier represents the best of several possible worlds. Throughout his career, he has been frustrated by the inabilities of his band members to play his music (that is, the music as Zappa was hearing it in his head as he composed it); throughout his autobiography,

Zappa argues that all he really wanted out of life was to be able to hear what all the little dots on the page sounded like when played well. With the Synclavier, he was able to get this. There was no music too complicated for the Synclavier to play or realize. As Zappa remarks, the machine is great because it allows him to make the kind of music that he had always wanted to make—extraordinarily complex and difficult music that was, occasionally, simply too difficult for humans to play and record. The problem, as Zappa (and his fans) soon discovered, is that the Synclavier is a machine, and its realized compositions are sterile and cold. There is little feeling (an admittedly tenuous and subjective term) in many of these songs.[72]

The two songs on the album, "We're Turning Again" and "Yo Cats," are both hilarious stabs at two of Zappa's favorite targets: the sixties revival and musicians unions.

"Turning Again" is an acrid blast at the attempts in the mid-eighties by the former hippies (those stuck in the past) and by the current generation of kids (a subject he had first introduced in "Teen Age Wind") to revive the sixties. The music, which features nice percussion work by Ed Mann and some great written guitar work by Steve Vai, is in a nice piece of satire, a very un-rock-type song, moving along at a fast pace and having an almost Vaudeville or Tin Pan Alley feel. Lyrically it is a song that has caused some consternation. Many fans and critics have accused Zappa of being mean-spirited in his attacks, including Barry Miles, who writes, "This nasty, vicious song exposed Zappa as a cold nihilist with no emotions and no feelings for anybody else,"[73] and Neal Slaven, who calls the song "an almost petulant attack on 60s revivalism."[74] Both Tommy Mars and Steve Vai have tried to distance themselves from the song. Listening to "Turning Again," however, it is not entirely apparent where the mean-spiritedness is. Zappa seems to be attacking not the sixties but the people who were attempting to bring back the hippie ethos without any real idea about what the counterculture actually stood for. Zappa, who had been against what he perceived as fake hippies in the sixties, is doubly enraged at the fake-fake hippies in the eighties. Zappa does this by heaping scorn upon those who served as bad examples for the kids in the eighties (these are the kids, remember, of the folks who were the original hippies). Zappa writes about the kids who would come in from Long Island on the weekend to hang around Greenwich Village (something he had seen up close during the Mothers residency at the Garrick Theater in 1967). To Zappa, the poseur hippies have spawned poseur children. (Notice, if you will, the "tightenin' up their headbands" line and its direct reference to the same lines found in "Teen Age Wind," from the *You Are What You Is* album. It was an interesting time for poseurs.)

"Yo Cats" may be one of the funniest songs in the Zappa catalog. A sleazy bit of cheesy lounge organ leads off the song, which has Ike Willis listing the various reasons why unionized studio and session musicians were worthless, including the ultimate insult, "You have made it, you are cool / You have been to the Berklee School," which was a breeding ground for session musicians, including, among others, Vince Colaiuta (class of '75) and Steve Vai (class of '79).[75] Zappa's fights with the musical establishment had become legend in the time between *Them or Us* and *Meets the Mothers of Prevention;* during this time Zappa had been working with orchestras, trying to get his music performed, and was running into problem after problem, especially with the absurd union agreements that many orchestras have with their musicians.

Where the album really excels, however, is on the instrumentals "Alien Orifice" and "What's New in Baltimore." Both songs have their origins as live pieces on the 1981–82 tour, and both seem to be making a counterargument to Zappa's increased use of the Synclavier. Ed Mann and Steve Vai, in particular, seem to shine on both songs.

"Alien Orifice" features some of Mann's best percussion work, following a wandering bass line in an intensely dramatic fashion. The song then moves to a reggae beat to a colossal Zappa solo that comes straight out of the Spinal Tap school of heavy metal soloing. It is an extremely good-natured solo that makes for enjoyable repeated listening.

"What's New in Baltimore" is a darker song that starts with a nice guitar-percussion motif that really moves the song forward; it has a melody that is dramatic, intense, and straightforward and makes for enjoyable listening. About halfway through the song enters an extended solo workout for Zappa that is one of his more melodic offerings. Played fairly high in the register, it is a classic heavy-metal guitar solo (unlike much of Zappa's work) that shows off a good band working at peak ability.

It is a good album, albeit one that critics have sort of written off as polemical. Some say it was rushed, others say it was dated (and indeed, the hearings are now going on 20 years). The *All Music Guide,* for instance, remarks that "Apart from the political issues of 'Porn Wars,' which quickly became dated, the album lacks memorable moments."[76]

It is a very interesting album because it shows that Zappa, musically, is at a tremendous crossroads. The Synclavier music was an indication of where he was going, the instrumentals show that he has become a master of that art form, and the pop songs show that his critical focus is as sharp as ever. With all of these tools in his toolbox, Zappa seems confused about what direction he wants to go. As the next few years would indicate, Zappa would go in several directions all at once, including into the political arena. Sadly, it is one Zappa's last original studio rock album. Although there would be other albums (a tremendous number of live releases as well as classical and jazz/Synclavier releases), this is Zappa's rock swan song. Sort of.

BROADWAY THE HARD WAY

Reagan and Swaggart and Bakker, oh my! *Broadway the Hard Way* (originally released in October 1988 on Barking Pumpkin records; currently available as

Rykodisc RCD 10552). Highest *Billboard* chart position: Not available/did not chart. Personnel: Ike Willis, Mike Keneally, Bobby Martin, Ed Mann, Walt Fowler, Bruce Fowler, Paul Carman, Albert Wing, Kurt McGettrick, Scott Thunes, Chad Wackerman, and featuring guest vocalists Eric Buxton and Sting. "Although it gets stale very quickly in the short term, in the long term it may be an interesting historical document."[77]

What a way to go out. Although no one, least of all Frank Zappa, knew that this would be his last album of original rock songs, it is a fantastic testament to all that was great about Frank Zappa as an U.S. singer and songwriter. Although it features no long instrumentals and only three real guitar solos ("Any Kind of Pain," "Outside Now," and "Hot Plate Heaven at the Green Hotel"), it does have 12 original songs (along with interesting covers, including "Bacon Fat," "Stolen Moments," and "Murder by Numbers") and four versions of older songs (the rewritten versions of "Why Don't You Like Me," which takes the central melody of "Tell Me You Love Me" and recasts it as a critique of the very public weirdness of Michael Jackson; a version of "What Kind of Girl Do You Think We Are," which is redone as a critique of televangelist Jimmy Swaggart's hypocritical adventures with a prostitute; a lovely version of "Outside Now," which stays fairly true to the original; and a version of the unreleased 1973–74 song "Dickie's Such an Asshole"). The rest of the songs on the album are very focused on a specific time: 1988. After eight years of the Reagan administration, which included a spectacular rise of religious conservatism, a pseudowar in Grenada, the financing of a secret war in Central America, and the Ed Meese commission on pornography, Zappa had a few things to say.

For the most part, this album serves as a precise snapshot of what life was like for Americans in 1988. It also, however, serves as a snapshot or keepsake of the best band Zappa ever worked with. It is an incredible group of musicians that play Zappa's songs in new and interesting ways. As the subsequent albums of older material, including *The Best Band You Never Heard in Your Life* and *Make a Jazz Noise Here,* indicate, Zappa's orchestral and Synclavier work, as well as his past work with big bands on *Waka/Jawaka* and *The Grand Wazoo,* had made him a gifted and careful arranger of rock music. Compare, for a moment, the work that the Who was doing around the same time; on a trip through the United States, the Who brought an augmented band with them, including a second guitarist, keyboard players, percussionists, and a horn section (this is captured in the live CD *Join Together*). Although the band is tight and the songs are played with great intensity, they sound just like the original versions. When the horns are used, they are used to double melodies. When Zappa uses the horns on the 1988 tour, he uses them to create additional melodies, to create harmonies that cut across the existing melodies, to double second keyboard parts, or to play entirely new parts. It is really quite thrilling, in a musical sense, to listen to these albums.[78]

Broadway the Hard Way starts off in a fairly tame manner with the song "Elvis Has Just Left the Building," a response to the repeated sightings of Elvis that graced the covers of tabloid weeklies during the eighties. The song, done in a sort of mock-country tone, features new guitarist Mike Keneally singing in his best pompous-country-singer vocals about the various Elvis-related myths, especially the bloated, seventies Vegas-Elvis. It is a sneaky song because it also critiques the growing sense that certain music was beginning to be associated with certain ideological positions. Conservatives, especially George H. W. Bush, who was then running for president, had identified themselves squarely with country music. Elvis, who famously asked Richard Nixon if he could be sworn in as a secret deputy of the Drug Enforcement Agency, was part of this neoconservative movement to associate certain kinds of music with certain kinds of belief. Elvis also represents one of the great crimes in musical history: the white appropriate of African American music, especially blues and gospel. Zappa, who had always taken great pains throughout his career to point out and sight the great blues guitarists and singers who had influenced him, was not an Elvis fan. Zappa repeatedly mentions in the song that Elvis and Jesus were together in Heaven; this is a certain critique of the deification of Elvis and of the Christianization of country/rock.

"Planet of the Baritone Women" and "Any Kind of Pain" pick up where the adventures of Rhonda in *Thing-Fish* had left off. "Baritone Women" is another play on the theme that women, in their quest for feminist power, have become just like men (and that, in the process, men have become feminized). It is a song that leaves a lot open to question. Zappa never judges the women in the song, but he does question the idea (the same idea that many feminists were questioning at the time) that to be successful in a male world one had to act like a male. It is a classic Zappa dilemma: In a perfect world you should be free to be yourself; you should not have to act like a man to get ahead in a male world (and although some have accused the song of being antifeminist, there is no question about whether the women should be in the workplace; the question is how they have to act in order to get there and/or how they act after they are there). The one place in the song where Zappa questions the entrance of women in to management is when he writes, "They roll their eyes upward . . . and slam their legs closed / When they sing about men!" But this can be read in an interesting way as well: men, as we were finding out in the eighties, had always brought sex into the workplace. A heightened sense of what sexual harassment was and how it had always operated in U.S. business was a common topic of discussion in the late eighties. Zappa seems to be making the argument that women no longer had to play the game of sleeping their way to the top. Is it true that some women had to act like men in order to get ahead? Undoubtedly. Is it sad? Yes.

A neat counterpoint to "Baritone Women" is "Any Kind of Pain," a song that had been hanging around in one form or another since 1976. As performed with the 1988 band, it is as close to an overtly profeminist statement as Zappa ever gets. In a nutshell, the song is about how our media-obsessed culture destroys women by forcing them into very narrowly defined ideals of beauty. In the case of "Any Kind of Pain," we find that the main character is a model of some sort: "You're All-American, / And, darling, they said so." The idea that Madison Avenue is perpetuating the ideal woman as blonde, dumb, and promiscuous (we find out later in the song that this woman is able to "bring the bus ride to a thrilling conclusion," a little reference to Mary's adventures on disc one of *Joe's Garage*). The statement that Zappa seems to be making is that it is not these girls' fault that the media has saturated the culture so thoroughly that there is nothing women can do but try like hell to fit into this fairly obscene ideal of beauty. As if to seal the argument, Zappa returns to the "Bobby Brown" idea of male privilege, writing, "And all the yuppie boys, they dream they will rape her." This is a fairly clear statement from Zappa on the idea of white, male sexual privilege, and it makes the song particularly interesting. Musically it is pretty out of character; Zappa puts the lyrics in a sort of soft rock/light jazz setting (and has a wonderful, distortion-free guitar solo in the middle) that is intensely melodic and, dare it be said, hummable?

Then we get to the political stuff. "Dickie's Such an Asshole," a song about Richard Nixon, gets revived (hey, political corruption is political corruption); this leads to "When the Lie's So Big" ("let's bring," Zappa says as a segue, "the Republican party up to date"); "Rhymin' Man," a critique of Jesse Jackson's racially polarizing run for the presidency in 1988; and "Promiscuous," a rap song (no really, it is, check it out!) about C. Everett Koop, the surgeon general of the United States, who had been speaking out about AIDS. It is a pretty intense set of songs and ones that certainly serve as historical documentation of a particular time and particular place. The songs, when looked at as a suite (and they only really exist as a suite on the album; they were not often performed in this order in concert), offer up a critique of government trickery that puts the conspiracy theories of *Thing-Fish* to shame. By starting the section with "Dickie's Such an Asshole," Zappa reminds us that presidential administrations, especially Republican presidential administrations, have a fine history of trying to pull fast ones on the American people. The thesis is clear from the first verse: "Won't somebody kindly tell me, / What the government's tryin' t' do?" Done in an old 12-bar blues format, the song gives the suite a nice feeling of history, which makes the next song, "When the Lie's So Big," a tremendous counterpoint.

Starting with the music, which sounds like a sort of new-wave/new-age radio/MTV-friendly hit single, "When's the Lie's So Big" takes on the idea of the big lie, the idea, originally theorized by those looking at how Hitler had been able to hoodwink so many Germans, that a lie, repeated often enough, simply becomes the truth. The song, like the other political songs on the album, is straightforward in its politics: "a flag and a pie...a mom and a bible / ... buy any line / Any place, any time." For Zappa, the fact that Reagan seemed to wrap most of his oppressive policies in the flag or the past or a vague and gentle Christianity was what enabled him to slip past the watchful eyes of the media. Reagan, who carried with him the deeply optimistic style of Franklin Roosevelt, was revered for bringing hope back to the United States. It was just this kind of mindless stuff that had Zappa worried the most.

"Rhymin' Man" takes a long and hard look at the supposed hypocrisy of presidential candidate and African American preacher Jesse Jackson. Jackson had risen to power on the belief that he had been with Martin Luther King Jr. the day he died. Zappa claims in an interview to have read an essay or article that caused him to doubt this. In the eighties, when Jackson was running for president, he was caught calling New York City "Hymie-Town," an anti-Semitic slur that was, more than likely, the cause for his loosing the democratic primary. Zappa gets right to the point: "Rhymin' man made a run for Prez / Farrakhan made him a clown, / Over there near *Hymie-Town*." Zappa goes to show, once again, that no matter who you are, if you screw up, he will call you on it.

Musically, the song is done in the fake cowboy style that would be used throughout the songs on the tour (there would be, for instance, huge versions of "Lonesome Cowboy Burt" played most evenings), more than likely to signify the fact that much evangelical Christianity had its roots in the South, a place Zappa did not have a lot of use for. (A quick glance at http://home. swipnet.se/fzshows/88.html, a list of all shows played by Zappa, shows that the closest the band got to the South was Washington, D.C.) The song is also amazing for the huge number of musical quotes that Zappa includes. After nearly every line, Zappa has the band playing something that directly or indirectly provides another layer of context or meaning. Some of the quotes included "The *Twilight Zone* Theme," "Theme from *Mission: Impossible*," "Theme from *The Untouchables*," "Happy Days Are Here Again," "Halvah Nagilah," "Hail to the Chief," "La Cucaracha," and "My Sharona." Ben Watson sites a second-by-second analysis of the various musical quotes in "Rhymin' Man" done by Den Simms. It is a pretty interesting document. Watson goes on to savage Zappa for failing to understand Jackson's liberal agenda. It is an interesting argument, although one that seems to misunderstand what Zappa was up to (there was, and is, a tendency, especially on the left, to consider any criticism of an African American political candidate as racist; Zappa was having none of that). Zappa seems to be angry at Jackson's duplicity. If Zappa can be accused of anything it is feeling, much like Hunter Thompson felt about political candidates, that wanting to be president was proof enough that person should not get to be president and that the system is so corrupt it can not help but ruin those who make it through. It is a fairly cynical thought but one that did not seem out of place in 1988.

"Promiscuous" is simply hilarious. Zappa, who wanted little to do with rap (he had been outspoken about people who used samples of music without crediting the authors), here has written a rap song about surgeon general C. Everett Koop, whose theory that men got AIDS from monkeys caused quite a national furor. According to a number of sources, the song was performed only once, in February in Detroit (there is no information as to why it was not performed again). The song is really a critique of the Reagan-era emphasis upon chastity (another backward-looking idea); from Nancy Reagan's antidrug slogan "Just say no" to attempts to have sex education removed from schools, Zappa seemed to feel that the anti-intellectualism of the Reagan administration was actually dangerous. Zappa writes, "It's the work of the Devil, so / Girls, don't blow!" The kind of medical and sexual misinformation that was going around during the early advent of AIDS is exactly what Zappa is arguing against. Later in the song, Zappa writes, "Did you ask the C.I.A.?...Or have THEY been promiscuous?" This idea, that someone's bad professional behavior can be directly tied to (or blamed upon) their morality (something that would get pinned squarely on Bill Clinton's actions as president), is what Zappa argues against.

It is an interesting group of songs that are varied in musical tone and structure and lyrically direct in ways that Zappa has never been before (in the past, he has always worked through characters or metaphors or stories). Listening to the album now, almost 20 years removed, it is sadly prophetic: the way Bill Clinton was crucified by the conservative sex police, the way the religious right has become the dominant force in U.S. political and cultural life, the way the presidential administration will lie with a completely straight face to the American people (anyone seen those weapons of mass destruction around lately?). All of these were issues that Zappa saw, argued against, and, seemingly, failed to convince anyone to look out for.

The second half of the CD is a far more mixed bag. There are only a few original pieces: "Jezebel Boy," which is musically interesting, with its sound effects and ripping electric guitar, is another number, like "Promiscuous," that was played only a few times on the tour. In general it is not his best work and is mainly the story of a male whore who avoids the roundup done by the sheriff's office. Although it has promise (Mike Keneally remarks that it was occasionally rehearsed using the phrase "Jessica Hahn" instead of "Jezebel Boy"),[79] it ultimately does not seem to do much more than stand between the Sting appearance (he comes on stage to sing the Police song "Murder by Numbers") and the great version of "Outside Now."

"Hot Plate Heaven at the Green Hotel," which had been written and performed extensively during the 1984 tour (a version of which can be found on the album *Does Humor Belong in Music?*), is a rousing big-band blowout (it is a defiantly old-fashioned swing/jump blues–based number) that features a wicked guitar solo in the middle. It is also a fine statement about Zappa's own politics: He does not like either party (his distrust of systems would prevent him from joining a party, which is, ultimately, a system). Zappa writes that neither political party is any good because "neither of 'em CARE / 'Bout that

Hot-Plate Heaven, / 'Cause they ain't been there." Zappa's argument could not be simpler: Both parties, both Republicans and Democrats, have turned their backs on the poor because, in larger part, the working members of these parties (in Congress and in the White House) have never known real poverty; even the Democrats in recent memory who have come from humble beginnings (Michael Dukakis and Bill Clinton come to mind) had net worths far beyond those of most Americans). It is a rousing song that forces one to look at the system of government we have. It ain't pretty.

The final song on the final album of original material, "Jesus Thinks You're a Jerk," is about as fitting a way to end one segment of a career as there is. A nine-minute opus that savagely goes after the relationship between Christianity, money, and Republican politics, it is ruthless. The song targets Jim and Tammy Faye Bakker, who were among the sleaziest of the televangelists in the eighties; Pat Robertson, the founder of the *700 Club*, a television show that unabashedly mixes prayer and politics;[80] the Republican Party; the Ku Klux Klan; the NRA; Oliver North; and Ronald Reagan. Zappa's argument, again, is simple and direct: If you can not see what these folks are trying to do—in this case, completely erode the wall separating church and state—then you are stupid. It is the same argument that informs "Dumb All Over," among other things. Although it is not rhetorically sound to call someone who does not agree with your argument stupid for not agreeing, Zappa presents such an incredible argument that his assertion at the end of the song, "And if you don't know by now, / The truth of what I'm tellin' you, / Then, surely I have failed somehow" is compelling.

The song ends. Zappa tells the audience that it is intermission and that he will see them in half an hour. The cheering fades, and the album comes to a close.

Of course Zappa was not done yet. In the time between the release of *Broadway the Hard Way* and his death from cancer in 1993, Zappa would release an incredible amount of music: nine more albums while he was still alive and more than 21 albums and compilations after his death.

In general, the album was lost a bit in the barrage of releases going on around the same time (1988 would see the release of five different albums; 1991 would see released four more CDs of material from the same band). Most of the critics tend to agree, citing the album as worth a listen. Steve Huey, for instance, writes that "many of Zappa's political observations hit the mark, as do some of the jokes, easily making *Broadway the Hard Way* one of his best and most intellectually stimulating post-'60s political efforts."[81]

Conclusion

Hard though it may be to believe, despite the length of the last section, there are many Zappa albums left undiscussed. These include his orchestral works (*Orchestral Favorites, London Symphony Orchestra 1 & 2, The Perfect Stranger, The Yellow Shark,* and parts of *Civilization, Phase III*), his Grammy Award winning Synclavier-jazz album *Jazz from Hell,* a multitude of live albums (*Ahead of Their Time,* which chronicles the famous 1968 Royal Albert Hall performance of the Mothers of Invention), *Baby Snakes* (documents the Bozzio / O'Hearn band of 1977–78), *Does Humor Belong in Music?* (documents the 1982 band), *The Best Band You Never Heard in Your Life* and *Make a Jazz Noise Here* (both of these document the 1988 big band), *FZ:OZ* (documents the 1976–77 band), *Halloween* (documents the 1978–79 band), and *You Can't Do That on Stage Anymore, Volumes 1–6* (which spans a 30-year touring history). There are also a number of releases that are uncategorizable, including *Lost Episodes,* which collects material from throughout Zappa's career in rare, debut, or archival fashion; *Playground Psychotics,* which consists mainly of recordings of the antics of the Flo & Eddie band; two CDs of excerpted guitar solos *(Shut Up And Play 'Yer Guitar* and *Guitar); Joe's Corsage* and *Joe's Domage,* which present historical and archival music from specific periods in Zappa's career; and *QuAUDIOPHILIAc,* which presents quadraphonic mixes of existing material, much of which was originally recorded in quadraphonic stereo, a sort of proto-surround sound technique.

These albums are left undiscussed for a variety of reasons. The primary reason being that this is a book on *The Words and Music of Frank Zappa* in a series on American singers and songwriters, and although Zappa was a singer and a songwriter, he was much more.

I started this project for two simple reasons: the first is that I wanted to present a reading Zappa's works that grounded his music and lyrics as both products and artifacts of a certain time and place. The second is that Zappa's songs, at least many of them, make me laugh, and I felt it would be fun to spend a year or so listening to them. The fact of the matter is, for all of the commentary and argument, Zappa's songs and the performances by his various band members can be wildly funny. I will never forget the first time I heard Ike Willis's pseudo-lounge singer take in "Catholic Girls," the hilarious commentary on the male reaction to feminism in "Bobby Brown," the disgusting road stories from the Flo & Eddie years, or the glee that Zappa and his band members found in attempting to crack each other up on stage in the various *You Can't Do That on Stage Anymore* collections.

What doing this project has forced me to do, however, was to appreciate a number of things about Zappa and his work that I did not really consider as a fan:

1. The complexity of his so-called serious music. In his autobiography, Zappa writes a lot about the fact that his music (and the music of his that he seemed to like the best) was very difficult. This is the music that I did not appreciate before I began this project. His work as a composer of serious, avant-garde symphonic and ensemble music is vastly underrated and will be, I feel, increasingly studied, despite Zappa's disgust with academics.

2. The importance and originality of his early cut-and-paste albums, especially *Lumpy Gravy* and *Uncle Meat*. These two albums, perhaps more than any others, necessitate repeated, attentive listening. It was only after listening to them over and over again in an attempt to find something to say about them that their power and originality shone through. These are fantastic, complex, and important creations that seem to anticipate what Fredric Jameson will eventually come to call the Postmodern Turn.

3. Zappa the cultural critic. Although I often would defend the word of Zappa in conversation with others, until I sat down and carefully listened to his records over and over (and over) again, I had failed to see the kind of life-long pattern / project in which Zappa seems to be engaging. As well, Zappa's many comments about his simple desire to make music often make murky the cultural and political project in which his lyrics and music seem to be engaging. This project has given me a great opportunity to engage in the most enjoyable thing I have ever done professionally: spend a year listening to Zappa's records and looking for the critical connections between his lyrics, his music, and the time in which he lived and worked.

4. Zappa the bandleader. As a fan of Zappa's later music, when I started this project I did not have the appreciation for the work of Zappa's earlier bands, especially the George Duke / Napoleon Murphy Brock band. The most consistent argument that I have heard about Zappa for the last 20 years has been that he did his best work with the Mothers of Invention. This, as I

have discovered, is debatable. Each band that Zappa created or constructed brought its own unique collection of abilities to both the historical work and the new stuff. Although the Mothers were original in a number of senses (certainly, if the stories are true, their stage shows were legendary), each band that Zappa put together forced Zappa to reconsider his music. It is also said that being in Zappa's band was akin to graduate school for musicians, and although Zappa and his former band members occasionally had bad things to say about each other, the list of folks who had been in his band reads like a who's who of contemporary rock and jazz players. From Don Preston to Mike Keneally, Zappa always tried to surround himself with folks who were the best.

5. Zappa the arranger. As I listened to all of Zappa's music, especially the music featuring horns and woodwinds, I started to notice that one of Zappa's greatest untold abilities was as an arranger. His ability to size up the members of his band and create music that was especially suited to them is remarkable. One of the great joys in listening to a lot of Zappa's works is to listen to how certain songs evolved over the years; from "Son of Mr. Green Genes" to "Eat That Question," Zappa's constant revisions of arrangements show an active mind in constant motion.

There are certain aspects of this book that I wish, given another year or so, I had the time and wherewithal, to revise. Two of Zappa's more interesting philosophies, those of the Project / Object and conceptual continuity, are worth a book of their own. Although there are many Web sites devoted to the idea of Zappa's conceptual continuities, a long, scholarly work devoted to trying to piece them all together and find some greater meaning would be an invaluable addition to Zappa scholarship. Zappa describes Project / Object as the idea that all of his works, including music, film, interviews, and political statements, are part of a larger project and should be the subject of serious scholars; it takes up elements of intertextuality, discourse community, and postmodern critical theory and would result in a tremendously interesting book. In other words, there is a lot left to say about Zappa.

When my wife heard that I was thinking about writing a book on the work of Frank Zappa, she was, to say the least, taken aback. Zappa's reputation among many people—from feminists to members of the Anti-Defamation League—is shaky. Zappa's argument, made a number of times, that he is an equal opportunity offender does not seem to fly any farther than it does when Lenny Bruce or Howard Stern are the topic of conversation. Yet it is just about the best one can do.

Frank Zappa, for one, never seemed to be bothered that people were offended by his work. There is no record of him ever evincing doubt that he was not doing the right thing or maintaining his own artistic integrity. In a 1993 interview in *Playboy* magazine, Zappa still maintained his position that he did not invent the Jewish American Princess, sex in the rectory basement, or the Dinah-Moe-Hum.

That said, when looking at Zappa's work as a critic of contemporary U.S. culture, it is important that his songs about the sexual mores of the American teen, aging hipster, Catholic priest, groupie, and radio promotions man be dealt with first. Indeed, it is a subject many cannot seem to get past. But it is one they should. Zappa is an infinitely interesting, complex, and contradictory man. Which makes him just like everyone else.

Discography of Available Zappa Recordings

Upon Zappa's death there were rumored to be hundreds of hours of tapes of concerts and unreleased recordings. The official Zappa discography, currently located at http://www.zappa.com/spifnificent.html, has the most up-to-date information on new and pending Zappa albums. Unfortunately, as of the writing of this book (October 2005), the zappa.com store (Barfko-Swill) is closed, making several of the most recent releases unavailable (or, at best, very difficult to get). There are several very good Web sites that track releases and availability, including the Zappa discography at www.allmusic.com and the fan Web site http://globalia.net/donlope/fz/lyrics/index.html. Listed here is a discography of Zappa's works based on the list at Zappa.com, including all available information on the Rykodisc releases (please note that the Zappa Family Trust and Ryko are currently arguing about these releases, and any information here may well be out of date by the time you read this). Check the zappa.com Web site, the Ryko Web site (http://www.rykodisc.com/Catalog/CatalogArtist_01.asp?Action=Get&Artist_ID=195) or your local record store for availability, especially for the more recent releases. As well, as this book was going to press, most of the Zappa albums, in whole or part, became available on iTunes and other music download Web sites. I have not listed unofficial releases, bootlegs, concert tapes, and so forth, although they are out there. I have listed several of the compilations that Rykodisc has put together. These were done, to the best of my knowledge, without contribution by the Zappa family. The following list is, to the best of my ability, chronological. I have listed the original release dates. Because most of the albums have been released on CD at lest twice (and many three times), I have not attempted to list current release dates. For an excellent, and exhaustive, review of all vinyl albums and CDs (and their differences), one must see *A Completist's Guide to Regular Frank Zappa Records,* at http://www.lukpac.org/~handmade/patio/vinylvscds/complete.html.

As this book was going to press, the Zappa Family Trust reached an agreement with online music distributor Musictoday.com to release both older titles and a slew of new records. Several of Zappa's out-of-print albums, including *Everything Is Healing Nicely, Frank Zappa Plays the Music of Frank Zappa, Civilization Phase III, Joe's Domage, Joe's Corsage,* and *FZ: OZ* as well as two brand new albums, *Joe's Xmasage* and *Imaginary Diseases* can now be found at http://stores.musictoday. com/store/dept.asp?band_id=1039&sfid=2&dept_id=8494.

Freak Out! Frank Zappa & The Mothers of Invention. Originally released in February 1966. Currently available as Rykodisc RCD 10501.

Absolutely Free. Frank Zappa & The Mothers of Invention. Originally released in April 1967. Currently available as Rykodisc RCD 10502.

Lumpy Gravy. Frank Zappa. Originally released in December 1967. Currently available as Rykodisc RCD 10504.

We're Only in It for the Money. Frank Zappa & The Mothers of Invention. Originally released in September 1968. Currently available as Rykodisc RCD 10503.

Cruising with Ruben & the Jets. Frank Zappa & The Mothers of Invention. Originally released in November 1968. Currently available as Rykodisc RCD 10505.

Uncle Meat. Frank Zappa & The Mothers of Invention. Originally released in March 1969. Currently available as Rykodisc RCD 10506/07.

Mothermania. Frank Zappa & The Mothers of Invention. Originally released in April 1969. Currently unavailable.

Hot Rats. Frank Zappa. Originally released in October 1969. Currently available as Rykodisc RCD 10508.

Burnt Weeny Sandwich. Frank Zappa & The Mothers of Invention. Originally released in February 1970. Currently available as Rykodisc RCD 10509.

Weasels Ripped My Flesh. Frank Zappa & The Mothers of Invention. Originally released in August 1970. Currently available as Rykodisc RCD 10510.

Chunga's Revenge. Frank Zappa. Originally released in October 1970. Currently available as Rykodisc RCD 10511.

Fillmore East, June 1971. Frank Zappa & The Mothers of Invention. Originally released in August 1971. Currently available as Rykodisc RCD 10512.

Soundtrack to the Film 200 Motels. Frank Zappa. Originally released in October 1971. Often available used (Rykodisc RCD 10513). Not listed as currently available on the Rykodisc Web site.

Just Another Band from L.A. Frank Zappa & The Mothers of Invention. Originally released in March 1972. Currently available as Rykodisc RCD 10515.

Waka/Jawaka. Frank Zappa. Originally released in July 1972. Currently available as Rykodisc RCD 10516.

The Grand Wazoo. Frank Zappa. Originally released in November 1972. Currently available as Rykodisc RCD 10517.

Over-Nite Sensation. Frank Zappa. Originally released in September 1973. Currently available as Rykodisc RCD 10518.

Apostrophe ('). Frank Zappa. Originally released in March 1974. Currently available as Rykodisc RCD 10519.

Roxy & Elsewhere. Frank Zappa. Originally released in July 1974. Currently available as Rykodisc RCD 10520.

One Size Fits All. Frank Zappa & The Mothers of Invention. Originally released in June 1975. Currently available as Rykodisc RCD 10521.

Bongo Fury. Frank Zappa / Captain Beefheart. Originally released in October 1975. Currently available as Rykodisc RCD 10522.

Zoot Allures. Frank Zappa. Originally released in October 1976. Currently available as Rykodisc RCD 10523.

Zappa in New York. Frank Zappa. Originally released in March 1978. Currently available as Rykodisc RCD 10524 / 25.

Studio Tan. Frank Zappa. Originally released in September 1978. Currently available as Rykodisc RCD 10526.

Sleep Dirt. Frank Zappa. Originally released in January 1979. Currently available as Rykodisc RCD 10527.

Sheik Yerbouti. Frank Zappa. Originally released in March 1979. Currently available as Rykodisc RCD 10528.

Orchestral Favorites. Frank Zappa. Originally released in May 1979. Currently available as Rykodisc RCD 10529.

Joe's Garage Acts I, II & III. Frank Zappa. Originally released in September 1979 *(Act I)* and November 1979 *(Acts II & III)*. Currently available as Rykodisc RCD 10530 / 31.

Tinsel Town Rebellion. Frank Zappa. Originally released in May 1981. Currently available as Rykodisc RCD 10532.

Shut Up 'N Play Yer Guitar. Frank Zappa. Originally released in May 1981. Currently available as Rykodisc RCD 10533 / 34 / 35.[1]

You Are What You Is. Frank Zappa. Originally released in September 1981. Currently available as Rykodisc RCD 10536.

Ship Arriving Too Late to Save a Drowning Witch. Frank Zappa. Originally released in May 1982. Currently available as Rykodisc RCD 10537.

The Man from Utopia. Frank Zappa. Originally released in March 1983. Currently available as Rykodisc RCD 10538.

Baby Snakes. Frank Zappa. Originally released in March 1983. Currently available as Rykodisc RCD 10539.

Boulez Conducts Zappa: The Perfect Stranger. Frank Zappa. Originally released in August 1984. Currently available as Rykodisc RCD 10542.

Them or Us. Frank Zappa. Originally released in October 1984. Currently available as Rykodisc RCD 10543.

Thing-Fish. Frank Zappa. Originally released in November 1984. Currently available as Rykodisc RCD 10544 / 45.

Francesco Zappa. Frank Zappa. Originally released in November 1984. Currently available as Rykodisc RCD 10546.

The Old Masters Box I. Frank Zappa. Originally released in April 1985. Currently unavailable.

Frank Zappa Meets the Mothers of Prevention. Frank Zappa. Originally released in November 1985. Currently available as Rykodisc RCD 10547.

Does Humor Belong in Music? Frank Zappa. Originally released in January 1986. Currently available as Rykodisc RCD 10548.

The Old Masters Box II. Frank Zappa. Originally released in November 1986. Currently unavailable.

Jazz from Hell. Frank Zappa. Originally released in November 1986. Currently available as Rykodisc RCD 10549.

London Symphony Orchestra, Vols. I & II. Frank Zappa. Originally released in June 1983 *(Vol. 1)* and September 1987 *(Vol. 2).* Currently available as Rykodisc RCD 10540/41.[2]

The Old Masters Box III. Frank Zappa. Originally released in December 1987. Currently unavailable.

Guitar. Frank Zappa. Originally released in April 1988. Currently available as Rykodisc RCD 10550/51.

You Can't Do That on Stage Anymore, Vol. 1. Frank Zappa. Originally released in May 1988. Currently available as Rykodisc RCD 10561/62.

You Can't Do That on Stage Anymore, Vol. 2: The Helsinki Concert. Frank Zappa. Originally released in October 1988. Currently available as Rykodisc RCD 10563/64.

Broadway the Hard Way. Frank Zappa. Originally released in October 1988. Currently available as Rykodisc RCD 10552.

You Can't Do That on Stage Anymore, Vol. 3. Frank Zappa. Originally released in November 1989. Currently available as Rykodisc RCD 10565/66.

The Best Band You Never Heard in Your Life. Frank Zappa. Originally released in April 1991. Currently available as Rykodisc RCD 10553/54.

You Can't Do That on Stage Anymore, Vol. 4. Frank Zappa. Originally released in June 1991. Currently available as Rykodisc RCD 10567/68.

Make a Jazz Noise Here. Frank Zappa. Originally released in June 1991. Currently available as Rykodisc RCD 10555/56.

You Can't Do That on Stage Anymore, Vol. 5. Frank Zappa. Originally released in July 1992. Currently available as Rykodisc RCD 10569/70.

You Can't Do That on Stage Anymore, Vol. 6. Frank Zappa. Originally released in July 1992. Currently available as Rykodisc RCD 10571/72.

Playground Psychotics. Frank Zappa & The Mothers of Invention. Originally released in November 1992. Currently available as Rykodisc RCD 10557/58.

Ahead of Their Time. Frank Zappa & The Mothers of Invention. Originally released in March 1993. Currently available as Rykodisc RCD 10559.

The Yellow Shark. Frank Zappa & Ensemble Modern. Originally released in October 1993. Currently available as Rykodisc RCD 40560.

Civilization Phase III. Frank Zappa. Originally released in December 1994. Currently unavailable.

The Lost Episodes. Frank Zappa. Originally released in February 1996. Currently available as Rykodisc RCD 40573.

Läther. Frank Zappa. Originally released in September 1996. Currently available as Rykodisc RCD 10574/76 (three disc set).

Frank Zappa Plays the Music of Frank Zappa: A Memorial Tribute. Frank Zappa. Originally released in November 1996. Currently available from musictoday.com.

Have I Offended Someone. Frank Zappa. Originally released in May 1997. Currently available as Rykodisc RCD 10577.

Mystery Disc. Frank Zappa. Originally released in September 1998. Currently available as Rykodisc RCD 10580.

EIHN (Everything Is Healing Nicely). Frank Zappa. Originally released in December 1999. Currently available from musictoday.com.

9. Barry Brummett, *Rhetoric in Popular Culture* (New York: St. Martin's Press, 1994), 70.

CHAPTER 1

1. John Covach and Walter Everett, "Preface," in "Rock and Classical Music," special issue, *Contemporary Music Review* 18, no. 4 (2000): 1.

2. F. Volpacchio, "The Mother of All Interviews: Frank Zappa," *Telos* 87 (spring 1991): 124.

3. Christopher Smith, "'Broadway the Hard Way': Techniques of Allusion in the Music of Frank Zappa," *College Music Symposium* 35 (1995): 39.

4. Trey Anastasio, "Frank Zappa," *Rolling Stone,* 21 April 2005, 78.

5. Covach and Everett, "Preface," 2.

6. Jonathan Bernard, "Listening to Zappa," *Contemporary Music Review* 18, no. 4 (2000): 68.

7. Kevin Holm-Hudson, "Introduction," in *Progressive Rock Reconsidered,* ed. Kevin Holm-Hudson (New York: Routledge, 2002), 3. Much of this, according to Holm-Hudson, comes from Jerry Lucky's *The Progressive Rock Files* (Burlington, ON: Collector's Guide Publishing, 1998).

8. These comments and others are in an e-mail published in Holm-Hudson, *Progressive Rock Reconsidered,* 60 n.43.

9. Frank Zappa with Peter Occhiogrosso, *The Real Frank Zappa Book* (New York: Poseidon Press, 1989), 139.

10. Barry Miles, *Zappa: A Biography* (New York: Grove Press, 2004), 295.

11. Dirk Von der Horst, "Precarious Pleasures: Situating 'Close to the Edge' in Conflicting Male Desires," in *Progressive Rock Reconsidered,* ed. Kevin Holm-Hudson (New York: Routledge, 2002), 169.

12. Volpacchio, "The Mother of All Interviews," 2.

13. Ibid., 125.

CHAPTER 2

1. Stuart Hall and Paddy Whannel, "The Young Audience," in *On the Record: Rock. Pop & the Written Word,* ed. Simon Firth and Andrew Goodwin (New York: Pantheon, 1990), 27–37.

2. Emily Gowers, "Satire," in *The Oxford Companion to Classical Civilization,* ed. Simon Hornblower and Antony Spawforth, *Oxford Reference Online* (Oxford University Press, 2005), http://oxfordreference.com.

3. David Simon and Edward Burns, *The Corner: A Year in the Life of an Inner-City Neighborhood* (New York: Broadway Books, 1977), 89.

4. During his youth, Zappa also spent some time in Florida. The time there seems as inconsequential as it was short.

5. This is a touchy subject. Although this book is not a forum for the airing (or reairing as it were) of old, unsettled grievances, many folks, especially those in the early incarnations of the Mothers of Invention, accuse Zappa of intellectual ungenerosity (to the point of multiple lawsuits), but this seems to be belied by at least three arguments. The first is the oft-told story of the Zappa family's giving away all of their

FZ:OZ. Frank Zappa. Originally released in August 2002. Currently available from musictoday.com.

Halloween. Frank Zappa. Originally released in February 2003. Currently unavailable.

Joe's Corsage. Frank Zappa. Originally released in May 2004. Currently available from musictoday.com.

Joe's Domage. Frank Zappa. Originally released in October 2004. Currently available from musictoday.com.

QuAUDIOPHILIAc. Frank Zappa. Originally released in September 2004. Currently unavailable.

Joe's XMASage. Frank Zappa. Originally released in December 2005. Currently available from musictoday.com.

Imaginary Diseases. Frank Zappa. Originally released in January 2006. Currently available from musictoday.com.

The following compilations have been assembled by Rykodisc without the aid of the Zappa Family Trust.

Cheap Thrills. Frank Zappa. Originally released in May 1998. Currently available as Rykodisc RCD 10579. Contains no new material.

Son of Cheap Thrills. Frank Zappa. Originally released in April 1991. Currently available as Rykodisc RCD 10581. Contains no new material.

Strictly Commercial. Frank Zappa. Originally released in August 1995. Currently available as Rykodisc RCD 40500. Contains no new material.

Strictly Genteel. Frank Zappa. Originally released in May 1997. Currently available as Rykodisc RCD 10578.

Threesome No. 1. Frank Zappa & The Mothers of Invention. (The first three Mothers of Invention albums in one package.) Originally released in April 2002. Currently available as Rykodisc RCD 40582.

Threesome No. 2. Frank Zappa. (Contains the three so-called jazz albums in one package: *Hot Rats, Waka/Jawaka,* and *The Grand Wazoo*). Originally released in April 2002. Currently available as Rykodisc RCD 40583.

Notes

INTRODUCTION

1. Steve Vai, "Frank Zappa: Musical Pioneer," *Pro Sound Nev* 2004, 98.

2. Charles Scribner Jr., "Ernest Hemingway: A Publisher's Assessi *Only Thing That Counts: The Ernest Hemingway-Maxwell Perkins C* ed. Matthew J. Bruccoli (New York: Scribner, 1996), 13–14.

3. One of the things that Rykodisc has done, apparently against the Zappa family, is attempted to make it easier to get into Zappa's wor collections *Strictly Commercial* and *Have I Offended Someone?*, as well a tions *Cheap Thrills* and *Son of Cheap Thrills*, make it much easier to find accessible music.

4. In fact, if you ask most serious music fans about Zappa, the best up with is "didn't he give his kids weird names," or "didn't he take a and eat it?" And although it is true the names of his children are, to sa the beaten path, Zappa's contention that it is the last name that will ge ble (Frank Zappa with Peter Occhiogrosso, *The Real Frank Zappa Bi* Poseidon Press, 1989], 247) is more than likely true. As to the crap on never happened.

5. Ben Watson, *Frank Zappa: The Negative Dialectics of Poodle P* St. Martin's, 1995), 534.

6. Indeed, in *The Negative Dialectics,* Watson makes a much larg his chapter "Epilogue: Going to Meet the Man" that Zappa, when th him, had a great sense of playfulness about his songs and lyrics and argues that one is not supposed to take his lyrics, for the most part, se

7. Zappa, *Real Frank Zappa Book*, 185.

8. Watson, *Negative Dialectics,* 549.

winter clothing to an African American family they had met while traveling from Baltimore to California (Zappa, in other words, saw a kind of generosity exhibited by his parents). The second is that all of Zappa's critics and biographers indicate that Zappa would let anyone try out for his band, let almost anyone sit in with the band, and try, especially during the time at the Garrick Theater in 1967–68, to involve the audience creatively with the show. All of these show a man who was generous with his time and his art. The third argument, and the one that Zappa made most often, is that he was simply a generous employer, paying his bands while they were rehearsing and touring and often paying them a retainer to be ready to perform. Zappa's response, when criticized for incorporating the ideas of band members into his own work, was that they (the band members) were paid employees and that he was entitled to use their improvisations and other work as his own, especially because he provided the framework (financial and artistic) for this work to flower in the first place. It is a significant philosophical argument, but perhaps one best left for those who were there to make.

6. F. Volpacchio, "The Mother of All Interviews: Frank Zappa," *Telos* 87 (1991): 124–37.

7. Frank Zappa with Peter Occhiogrosso, *The Real Frank Zappa Book* (New York: Poseidon Press, 1989), 24.

8. Neil Slaven, *Electric Don Quixote: The Definitive Story of Frank Zappa* (London: Omnibus Press, 1997), 20.

9. Zappa, *Real Frank Zappa Book,* 31.

10. Ibid.

11. Ibid., 34.

12. Billy James, *Necessity Is: The Early Years of Frank Zappa and the Mothers of Invention* (London: SAF, 2005), 91.

13. Zappa, *Real Frank Zappa Book,* 298. Emphasis in original.

14. His most overt political statements are on his later albums: *Joe's Garage, Thing-Fish, You Are What You Is, Them or Us, Frank Zappa Meets the Mothers of Prevention,* and *Broadway the Hard Way.* For a good idea of where Zappa was politically toward the end of his life, see the last two chapters of Zappa, *Real Frank Zappa Book.*

15. James Woods, *The Irresponsible Self: On Laughter and the Novel* (New York: Farrar Straus and Giroux, 2004), 6.

16. Ibid., 7.

17. "Do You Like My New Car?" from the album *Fillmore East, June 1971.*

18. "Crew Slut," from the album *Joe's Garage Acts I, II & III.*

19. John Bullitt, *Jonathan Swift and the Art of Satire: A Study of Satiric Technique* (Cambridge: Harvard University Press, 1953), 3.

20. Donald Horton, "The Dialogue of Courtship in Popular Song," in *On the Record: Rock, Pop & the Written Word,* ed. Simon Firth and Andrew Goodwin (New York: Pantheon, 1990), 15.

21. Lenny Bruce, *How to Talk Dirty and Influence People* (New York: Quality Paperback Books, 1996), 150–51.

22. Zappa, *Real Frank Zappa Book,* 90. Emphasis in original.

23. Ibid., 89.

24. "I'm in You" needs to be heard to be believed. Frampton himself has said that he was really rushed by his record company trying to follow up *Frampton Comes Alive* and is not really excited by this song. It is hard to believe, almost 30 years later, how

popular *Comes Alive* was; it was the largest selling album in CBS Records history until Michael Jackson's *Thriller* came along. Three of its songs—"Show Me the Way," "Do You Feel Like We Do," and "Baby I Love Your Way"—were huge hits. Frampton had started in rock as a guitarist for the British blues band Humble Pie (who had a huge hit with the rocker "I Don't Need No Doctor"), so he had some bona fide rock credentials. "I'm in You" is about as far as one can get from Humble Pie.

25. Hall and Whannel, "The Young Audience," 29.

26. Kevin Courrier, *The Dangerous Kitchen: The Subversive World of Frank Zappa* (Toronto: ECW Press, 2002), 327.

27. Barry Miles, *Zappa: A Biography* (New York: Grove Press, 2004), 263.

28. Edward Rosenheim, *Swift and the Satirist's Art* (Chicago: University of Chicago Press, 1963), 17.

29. Ibid., 27.

CHAPTER 3

1. Zappa attempted to collect many of these and released them under the general name of *Beat the Boots* Volumes I & II. In general, these albums are typical bootleg recordings: although they are good in terms of representing a certain band at a certain period of time (and are refreshing because Zappa did not often release extant concert recordings), the recording quality, at least on the discs I have heard, is terrible.

2. Especially because, with the release of *Mystery Disc* and the *Joe's Corsage/Domage* series, a lot of early and unreleased music is seeing the light of day.

3. Barry Brummett, *Rhetoric in Popular Culture* (New York: St. Martin's, 1994), 73; emphasis in the original.

4. For more, see Brummett, *Rhetoric in Popular Culture,* especially chapter 3, "Rhetorical Methods in Critical Studies."

5. Loraine Alterman, review of *Freak Out!* in the *Detroit Free Press,* reprinted in Frank Zappa with Peter Occhiogrosso, *The Real Frank Zappa Book* (New York: Poseidon Press, 1989), 222.

6. Liner Notes, *Freak Out!*

7. Zappa, *Real Frank Zappa Book,* 68–69.

8. Todd Gitlin, *Sixties: Years of Hope, Days of Rage,* rev. ed. (New York: Bantam, 1993), 205.

9. Zappa, *Real Frank Zappa Book,* 89; emphasis in the original.

10. For a more detailed description, see Chapter 2 of this book.

11. Todd Gitlin calls "'plastic' the most damning word possible" in the counter-culture movement. See Gitlin, *Sixties,* 215–16, for more.

12. He would return to this theme again and again, finally returning to it in the scathing antihippie song "We're Turing Again," on *Frank Zappa Meets the Mothers of Prevention* in 1985.

13. This contextual referencing would come to play a big part with *Thing-Fish.*

14. Lester Bangs, *Psychotic Reactions and Carburetor Dung,* ed. Greil Marcus (New York: Vintage, 1988), 374.

15. David Walley, *No Commercial Potential: The Saga of Frank Zappa,* rev. ed. (Cambridge, MA: Da Capo, 1996), 65.

16. For more on this, see Barry Miles, *Zappa: A Biography* (New York: Grove Press, 2004), 100–103.

17. In this light, Don Henley's song "Dirty Laundry" can be read as an homage to "Trouble Every Day."

18. Gitlin, *Sixties*, 4. The revisions of this chapter happened during the 40th anniversary of the Watts Riots. CNN ran a 10-second piece on them.

19. Miles, *Zappa: A Biography*, 107.

20. By the time he founded the Mothers of Invention, Zappa had scored two films: *The World's Greatest Sinner* (1963) and *Run Home Slow* (1965).

21. Simon Emerson and Denis Smalley, "Electro-Acoustic Music," in *Grove Music Online*, ed. L. Macy, http://www.grovemusic.com.

22. Gary Graff, ed., *Musichound Rock: The Essential Album Guide* (Detroit: Visible Ink Press, 1996), 757.

23. Nathan Brackett with Christian Hoard, eds. *The New Rolling Stone Album Guide: Completely Revised and Updated Fourth Edition* (New York: Simon & Schuster, 2004), 903.

24. Steve Huey, "Review: *Freak Out!*" *All Music Guide*, http://www.allmusic.com.

25. Andrew Boscardan, "Review: *Freak Out!*" http://www.amazon.com.

26. Barry Miles, *Frank Zappa: In His Own Words* (London: Omnibus Press, 1993), 34.

27. Kevin Courrier, *The Dangerous Kitchen: The Subversive World of Frank Zappa* (Toronto: ECW Press, 2002), 111.

28. Billy James, *Necessity Is: The Early Years of Frank Zappa and the Mothers of Invention* (London: SAF, 2005), 50.

29. Neil Slaven, *Electric Don Quixote: The Definitive Story of Frank Zappa* (London: Omnibus Press, 1997), 60–61.

30. For a much more thorough treatment of Zappa as postmodernist, see Paul Suton, "'Bogus Pomp' and Bourdieu's Paradox: Zappa & Resentment," International Conference of Esemplastic Zappology (London, 16 January 2004), http://www.militantesthetix.co.uk/ice-z/paul.htm.

31. The performance of these on stage presents an interesting challenge, and, as I will discuss in the later parts of this chapter, Zappa's greatest gift may be as an arranger; the fact that each band performs these songs in vastly different ways is a testament to the fact that, because they were such studio creations, Zappa was under little obligation to re-create them note for note on stage, because to do so would have been nearly impossible.

32. See Slaven, *Electric Don Quixote*, 68–69. This is the same riot that led Stephen Stills to write "For What It's Worth" for the Buffalo Springfield.

33. Miles, *Zappa: A Biography*, 134–35.

34. Zappa seems to be setting the tone for experimental rock records that many of his contemporaries would follow, perhaps most famously the Beatles *(Sgt. Pepper's Lonely Hearts Club Band)*, The Who *(The Who Sell Out* and *Tommy)*, and Brian Wilson and the Beach Boys *(Pet Sounds* and *Smile)*.

35. Quoted in Slaven, *Electric Don Quixote*, 71.

36. James, *Necessity Is*, 51.

37. Zappa, *Real Frank Zappa Book*, 185.

38. Ibid.

39. James, *Necessity Is*, 51.

40. He would do it again on *Absolutely Free*, quoting Stravinsky toward the end of the song "Status Back Baby."

41. The CD features two additional songs, "Big Leg Emma" and "Why Don'tcha Do Me Right," both of which were recorded later in New York and released as singles. These are more standard songs in the mock doo-wop / blues vein that Zappa was not really using on the *Absolutely Free* album.

42. Miles, *Frank Zappa: In His Own Words,* 24.

43. It is exactly the kind of song that was parodied so effectively by Spinal Tap with their song "Cups and Cakes."

44. Although this work is probably not the proper forum for this discussion, Zappa seems to support French philosopher Louis Althussar's idea / theory that the U.S. public school system is part of a vast ideological state apparatus that is set up to reinforce the dominant hegemony while at the same time keeping any sort of change or difference at bay. Also of note is the tremendous rise in the last few years in literature addressing this same subject. Educators are, finally, dealing with the issues of conformity and status in high school.

45. Ben Watson, *Frank Zappa: The Negative Dialectics of Poodle Play* (New York: St. Martin's, 1995), 83.

46. Slaven, *Electric Don Quixote,* 66–67.

47. For a more detailed account, see Miles, *Zappa: A Biography,* 98–99.

48. Zappa's writing about groupies will be discussed more fully in the section on the Flo & Eddie years.

49. Interestingly enough, the year *Absolutely Free* came out is the same year the film *The Graduate* was released. In many ways, the song and the film deal with the same subject, albeit in vastly different ways.

50. Watson, *Negative Dialectics,* 84.

51. For many years, Zappa's works have all been copyrighted and administered through the aptly named Intercontinental Absurdities.

52. Zappa is not the only one to feel this way. Joan Didion, in *The White Album* (New York: Noonday, 1990), and Hunter Thompson, in *Fear and Loathing in Las Vegas* (New York, Vintage Books, 1989), both of whom were keen observers of the sixties, have argued that the disappointment many felt with the sixties is that it held out some sort of promise for a different way of looking at the world but somehow missed or escaped. Thompson put it best when he wrote in *Fear and Loathing in Las Vegas,* "We were riding the crest of a high and beautiful wave.... You can almost see the high-water mark—the place where the wave finally broke and rolled back."

53. James, *Necessity Is,* 52.

54. Brackett and Hoard, eds. *The New Rolling Stone Album Guide,* 903.

55. Steve Huey, "Review: *Absolutely Free.*" *All Music Guide,* http://www.allmusic.com.

56. *Absolutely Free,* http://www.amazon.com.

57. In a controversial move that alienated many fans, Zappa overdubbed many of the drum and base parts from a few early albums, including *We're Only in It for the Money* and *Cruising with Ruben & the Jets.* RCD 40024 is one of those albums. As a bonus, however, the entire *Lumpy Gravy* album is also included. In 1995, Zappa released the original *We're Only in It for the Money* as a single CD.

58. Although listed as part of the band, Ray Collins was feuding with Zappa and does not perform on the album.

59. Although I still think that *Joe's Garage* is Zappa's ultimate triumph, *We're Only in It for the Money* is, especially in context, an incredible achievement.

60. James, *Necessity Is,* 71.

61. Ibid. Emphasis is Zappa's.

62. Gitlin, *Sixties,* 213.

63. William Manchester, *The Glory and the Dream: A Narrative History of America: 1932–1972* (New York: Bantam, 1975), 1113.

64. In ibid., 1115, Manchester writes that "sometimes a hippy would run alongside the bus, holding up a mirror."

65. It is at the San Francisco event that Timothy Leary is supposed to have given his "turn on, tune in, and drop out" speech.

66. James, *Necessity Is,* 82.

67. Zappa, *Real Frank Zappa Book,* 84.

68. Hunter S. Thompson, "The 'Hashbury' is the Capital of the Hippies," *New York Times Magazine,* 14 May 1967, reprinted in Hunter S. Thompson, *The Great Shark Hunt: Gonzo Papers,* vol. 1 (New York: Ballantine, 1979), 391. Interestingly enough, Thompson, who was much more overtly interested in politics than Zappa, sees the 1966 elections as the main reason for the hippies turning away from politics. Although Zappa, on *Absolutely Free,* does make references to the president being sick (a veiled attempt, perhaps, to acknowledge Lyndon Johnson's declining ability to run the country), Thompson argues that "One of the most obvious causalities of the 1966 elections was the New Left's illusion of its own [political] leverage" (391). So, although Zappa viewed many of the hippies as lazy, Thompson sees them as classically disenfranchised. It is an interesting disagreement.

69. Quoted in Gitlin, *Sixties,* 217.

70. There have always been kids this age, but this was only the second generation to be unable to work because of post-Depression child labor laws and able to spend money somewhat independently of their parents because of the postwar economic boom.

71. Manchester, *Glory and the Dream,* 1115.

72. Ibid.

73. Watson, *Negative Dialectics,* 116. Watson cites Jonathan Jones, "A World of Secret Hungers," *Eonta* 2, no. 2 (July/August, 1993).

74. The album *Playground Psychotics* is made up, primarily, of tapes of the band on the road.

75. Courrier, *Dangerous Kitchen,* 138.

76. Karl Dallas, "What Did You Do in the Revolution, Dada." *Let It Rock.* June, 1975. Quoted in Watson, *Negative Dialectics,* 117.

77. Zappa commentator Valdimir Sovetov writes,

In fact this line "Don't come in me" derived from one of the most known Lenny Bruce so-called dirty routines. It's the only survivor of the original idea of this album, which supposed to be a mix of Mothers' music and Lenny's materials. It was to be called "Our Man in Nirvana" after the best-selling book of the epoch, Graham Green's *Our Man in Havana.*

See http://www.arf.ru/Notes/Woiftm/harry.html. Zappa's displeasure with MGM would lead to a significant delay in the release of the album as well as a failure on MGM's part to pick up the Mothers' contract.

78. Zappa and Hendrix knew each other a bit, but this never stopped Zappa from making fun of someone.

79. Zappa, *Real Frank Zappa Book,* 84.

80. For a nice example of how the songs changed according to bands, see the versions on *Ahead of Their Time, You Can't Do That on Stage Anymore, Vol. 1,* and *Make a Jazz Noise Here.*

81. Most of the biographies as well as Zappa's autobiography cover this relationship ad nauseam.

82. As is discussed in a number of places in the book, one of the most interesting and entertaining parts of listening to Zappa's work is to start comparing different versions of the same song. Not only for conceptual continuity clues but also to see where Zappa the arranger was at; you can hear at various times Zappa's jazz, rock, blues, doo-wop, and classical influences move to the forefront as his arrangements change according to either Zappa's predilections or due to the makeup of a particular band. The songs are also interesting contextual and historical clues. Certain songs, "Dinah-Moe-Hum" comes to mind, are played with an almost willful disregard for the audience (the version on *You Can't Do That on Stage Anymore, Vol. 6* is performed quickly, as if they are trying to get through it), whereas others are stretched out and given almost complete makeovers; a good example of this is the extended version of "Stevie's Spanking" on *You Can't Do That on Stage Anymore, Vol. 4.*

83. The *ARF* Web site at http://www.arf.ru / Notes / Woiftm / takeoff.html reports that Zappa quotes the old fifties standard "True Love, True Love," which was recorded by, among others, the Drifters. I have not been able to verify this fact anywhere else.

84. Courrier, *Dangerous Kitchen,* 140.

85. Ibid., 141.

86. There is a hilarious story about the title: Courrier quotes Zappa as telling Kurt Loder in a *Rolling Stone* interview that

> Before they started making dolls with sexual organs, the only data you could get from your doll was looking between its legs and seeing that little chrome nozzle—if you squeezed the doll, it made a kind of whistling sound, that was the chrome plated megaphone of destiny.

Quoted in Courrier, *Dangerous Kitchen,* 142.

87. Quoted in Roger Scruton, "Programme Music," in *Grove Music Online,* ed. L. Macy, http://www.grovemusic.com.

88. Liner Notes, *We're Only in It for the Money.*

89. Watson, *Negative Dialectics,* 118.

90. Graff, *Musichound Rock,* 757.

91. Andrew Boscardan, "Review: *We're Only in It for the Money,*" http://www.amazon.com.

92. Courrier, *Dangerous Kitchen,* 138.

93. *Lumpy Gray* is also available as a two-for-the-price-of-one CD set with *We're Only in It for the Money;* however, the version of *Money* on this set is the reedited version with new drum and bass parts recorded in the nineties.

94. Spoken as an introduction to the album.

95. Courrier, *Dangerous Kitchen,* 130.

96. Watson, *Negative Dialectics,* 93. Watson takes great pains to debate whether or not this album is representative of postmodernism. It is an interesting argument. This album, in particular, has some of the easily identifiable elements of postmodernism, but it does not seem to indicate the kind of exhaustion with late capitalism that much postmodern art seems to indicate. I disagree with Watson about the usefulness of postmodernism as a critical tool; I tend to find it more optimistic than Watson does. In many ways, postmodernism is seen as cynical because it represents a historical inevitability and a relative exhaustion with current / contemporary modes of artistic expression. To place a value judgment on this kind of art (i.e., to make it cynical or bad) is, I think, beside the point.

97. Quoted in Miles, *Zappa: A Biography,* 140.

98. Watson, *Negative Dialectics,* 99–100.

99. Courrier, *Dangerous Kitchen,* 131. The Kempton piece has been transcribed and is archived at "Zappa and the Mothers: Ugly Can Be Beautiful," http://www.science.uva.nl / ~robbert / zappa / interviews / Kempton.html. I am unsure, however, of what sorts of copyright violations this article might be subject to.

100. Courrier, *Dangerous Kitchen,* 132.

101. Brackett and Hoard, eds. *The New Rolling Stone Album Guide,* 903.

102. Francois Couture, "Review: *Lumpy Gravy,*" *All Music Guide,* http://www.allmusic.com.

103. There are disagreements as to when this album was originally released. Russo has it released in December 1968, Watson in August 1968, and others tell us it was released in November. This is the only CD for which Zappa remastered and changed the drum and bass parts that has not been reissued in its original format. Zappa argues that the original tapes are in terrible shape and could not be remastered, whereas many of the original band members are unsure as to the truth of this statement; see James, *Necessity Is,* 92–93, for band member reactions. Zappa addresses this specifically in the magazine *Goldmine,* a record collector's trade publication.

104. On the front cover of *Cruising with Ruben & the Jets.*

105. John Rockwell, "Doo-Wop," in *Grove Music Online,* ed. L. Macy, http://www.grovemusic.com.

106. James, *Necessity Is,* 86.

107. Michael Gray, *Mother! The Frank Zappa Story* (London: Plexus, 1993), 110.

108. This is especially interesting in that it prefigures the great fifties revival of the mid-seventies, from *American Graffiti* to *Happy Days* to the incredible popularity of revival band Sha Na Na.

109. Arnold Whittall, "Neo-Classicism," in *Grove Music Online,* ed. L. Macy, http://www.grovemusic.com.

110. Quoted in Miles, *Zappa: A Biography,* 173.

111. I know it is not politically correct to like the remasters, but the bass work on *Cruising* is pretty solid throughout.

112. For a stunning performance of this song, listen to the version on *Tinsel Town Rebellion.* Bob Harris, who sings the high tenor part, is truly gifted.

113. Miles, *Zappa: A Biography,* 172.

114. Ibid., 172–73.

115. Watson, *Negative Dialectics,* 125.

116. Jonathan Bernard, "Listening to Zappa," *Contemporary Music Review* 18, no. 4 (2000): 70.

117. Both Courrier, *Dangerous Kitchen,* and *ARF,* at http://www.arf. ru/Notes/Ruben/flove.html, debate these issues.

118. *Cruising,* http://www.allmusic.com.

119. It is also courageous. Zappa did something, an entire record of homage, that very few bands would have had the courage to try; another band that tried to pull this off was Todd Rundgren's band Utopia who, on their album *Deface the Music,* did an entire album of original songs written and recorded to sound like early Beatles songs.

120. It was originally released as a double album; the CD features dialogue from the film *Uncle Meat.* The comments in this section are about the two-CD set.

121. Lowell George, who would soon leave, along with Roy Estrada, to form Little Feat, did not play on the album, although he was playing live with the Mothers at the time. He is listed in the album's credits (he does end up on at least one song on *Weasels Ripped My Flesh*). Ray Collins sings on the album but was no longer playing with the Mothers. There were many guests on the album, the most important of whom is Ruth Komanoff (soon to be Ruth Underwood), a classically trained percussionist who would tour extensively with Zappa in the late sixties and early seventies.

122. Comments attributed to Zappa during a speech given at the London School of Economics in May 1969.

123. James, *Necessity Is,* 92.

124. Ibid., 91.

125. Ibid., 95.

126. Liner Notes, *Uncle Meat.*

127. Although this book is not the place for this discussion, it is an interesting idea. For more information, see Jean-François Lyotard, *The Postmodern Condition: A Report on Knowledge,* trans. Geoff Bennington and Brian Massumi (Minneapolis: University of Minnesota Press, 1984), or Fredric Jameson, *Postmodernism; Or, The Cultural Logic of Late Capitalism* (Durham, NC: Duke University Press, 1991).

128. The piece was significantly reworked and rearranged in 1977 and revised again in 1983 for ensemble; it was extended to more than twice its length, and one can hear in the newer version some real overtones of Stravinsky. The outcome can be heard on the album *The Yellow Shark.* Another version, arranged by Olli Virtaperko and scored for baroque instruments, can be found on *The Zappa Album* by Ensemble Ambrosius.

129. Miles, *Frank Zappa: In His Own Words,* 53.

130. Liner Notes, *The Yellow Shark.*

131. Barry Miles, *Frank Zappa: A Visual Documentary* (London: Omnibus Press, 1993), 42.

132. For a far more interesting argument about this same idea, one must read *Radical Chic and Mau—Mauing the Flak Catchers* by journalist and novelist Tom Wolfe (New York: Bantam, 1999). Another answer/response is that this kind of racism, especially in the late sixties, was a white response to the rise of black nationalism, something that began in 1965 with the Student Nonviolent Coordinating Committee splintering between hippies, feminists, and black nationalists, a good indication of where things, politically, were headed for the Left (see Gitlin, *Sixties,* 168–69, for more).

133. Sherwood was an old friend of Zappa's whose main job was roadie and who parlayed some of this into a regular gig with the band.

134. For Gardner's comments, see James, *Necessity Is*, 107. For the claim that the solo is on electric sax, see Courrier, *Dangerous Kitchen*, 160, for instance.

135. James, *Necessity Is*, 44–45.

136. I will add, however, that when I started hanging around with some real Zappa fans in college, they were all convinced that Zappa was the son of Mr. Green Jeans. And these were sophisticated guys from Philadelphia—what was I to think?

137. Graff, *Musichound Rock*, 757.

138. Brackett and Hoard, eds. *The New Rolling Stone Album Guide*, 903.

139. Steve Huey, "Review: *Uncle Meat,*" *All Music Guide*, www.allmusic.com.

140. Brackett and Hoard, eds. *The New Rolling Stone Album Guide*, 903.

141. Slaven, *Electric Don Quixote*, 115. For an extensive discussion of song differences from album to album as well as differences between the U.S. versions and international versions, see *A Completist's Guide to Regular Frank Zappa Records*, at http://www.lukpac.org/~handmade/patio/vinylvscds/mothermania.html.

CHAPTER 4

1. Frank Zappa with Peter Occhiogrosso, *The Real Frank Zappa Book* (New York: Poseidon Press, 1989), 109.

2. Ibid.

3. This is one of the few Zappa songs you will still occasionally hear on the radio.

4. Zappa would return again and again to "Peaches en Regalia," most famously on the *Tinsel Town Rebellion* album with a wildly different arrangement. It also shows up on the Ensemble Modern album *Plays Frank Zappa* (RCA Red Seal 82876-59842-2).

5. Zappa, *Real Frank Zappa Book*, 109.

6. "*Hot Rats:* Little Umbrellas—Notes and Comments," *ARF*, http://www.arf.ru/Notes/Hrats/lumbr.html.

7. This is something that drives many fans up a tree. According to a number of sources, including Courrier and Russo, the recorder solo was added for the CD release and was not on the album. It is one of the few questionable musical decisions Zappa made. If I had to guess, I would say that Zappa was trying to radically alter the perception of the album. The recorder solo gives the song a much softer, mellower tone and really pushes it toward the lame sort of smooth jazz that is the bastard stepchild of fusion, which is, perhaps, Zappa's reply to those who blame *Hot Rats* for fusion in the first place.

8. It is almost four minutes longer on CD than it was on the original album release. The CD version contains an increased amount of sax soloing from Ian Underwood.

9. Right after *Hot Rats*, Zappa would work as composer and arranger on Ponty's album *King Kong*, which features several older Zappa songs radically redone in a much more traditional jazz fashion (the version of "King Kong" has to be heard to be believed). It is an odd album, one that many critics spend a lot of time writing about, in part because working with a number of hard-core jazz players gave Zappa a respect many felt he was not getting from the rock press.

10. Nathan Brackett with Christian Hoard, eds. *The New Rolling Stone Album Guide: Completely Revised and Updated Fourth Edition* (New York: Simon & Schuster, 2004), 309.

11. Steve Huey, "Review: *Hot Rats*," *All Music Guide*, www.allmusic.com.

12. Billy James, *Necessity Is: The Early Years of Frank Zappa and the Mothers of Invention* (London: SAF, 2005), 134.

13. Ibid., 133.

14. Ben Watson, *Frank Zappa: The Negative Dialectics of Poodle Play* (New York: St. Martin's, 1995), 169.

15. Barry Miles, *Zappa: A Biography* (New York: Grove Press, 2004), 195–96.

16. Translation available in Kevin Courrier, *The Dangerous Kitchen: The Subversive World of Frank Zappa* (Toronto: ECW Press, 2002), 203. Complete translation available at "*Burnt Weeny Sandwich:* WPLJ (Dobard/McDaniels)—Notes and Comments," *ARF,* http://www.arf.ru/Notes/Burnt/wplj.html.

17. Stephan Walsh, "Igor Stravinsky," in *Grove Music Online*, ed. L. Macy, http://www.grovemusic.com.

18. For complete lyrics, see "*Burnt Weeny Sandwich:* Overture to Holiday in Berlin—Notes and Comments," *ARF,* http://www.arf.ru/Notes/Burnt/ovberl.html.

19. For an interesting peek at the development of the song, check out "The Return of the Hunch Back Duke" on *You Can't Do That on Stage Anymore, Vol. 5.* The song also kicks off the *Fillmore East, 1971* album to be discussed later.

20. For the entire analysis, see "Burnt Weeny Sandwich: The Little House I Used to Live In," *Information Is Not Knowledge,* http://globalia.net/donlope/fz/lyrics/Burnt_Weeny_Sandwich.html#Little.

21. Barry Kernfeld, "Eric Dolphy," in *Grove Music Online*, ed. L. Macy, http://www.grovemusic.com.

22. From an interview in *Downbeat* magazine, quoted in Courrier, *Dangerous Kitchen,* 210.

23. Michael Gray, *Mother! The Frank Zappa Story* (London: Plexus, 1993), 137.

24. Courrier, *Dangerous Kitchen,* 211.

25. An interesting argument because neither of these albums contains new material; all of it was material from some years back.

26. Gary Graff, ed., *Musichound Rock: The Essential Album Guide* (Detroit: Visible Ink Press, 1996), 757.

27. "Samhot," "Weasles Ripped My Mind," review of *Weasles Ripped My Flesh,* www.amazon.com.

28. Steve Huey, "Review: *Burnt Weeny* Sandwich," *All Music Guide*, www.allmusic.com.

29. Barry Miles, *Frank Zappa: In His Own Words* (London: Omnibus Press, 1993), 58.

30. James, *Necessity Is,* 140.

31. If it seems that there were always bits and pieces of music left over from other projects, it is important to remember that the average length of a vinyl LP was about 40 minutes, whereas a CD can hold upward of 70 minutes.

32. Art Tripp and John Guerin should be considered jazz drummers. Dunbar would go on, after Zappa, to play for Journey and Jefferson Starship.

33. James, *Necessity Is,* 142.

34. Kent, Ohio, is less than 30 miles from where this book is being written.

35. William Manchester, *The Glory and the Dream: A Narrative History of America: 1932–1972* (New York: Bantam, 1975), 1224.

36. Quoted in ibid., 1193.

37. Ibid., 1194.

38. Ibid.

39. Ibid.

40. Ibid., 1195–96.

41. One interesting critical note: Nearly all of Zappa's biographers and critics cite accusations of sexism against Zappa; not one comes up with a reference or a direct quote to this effect.

42. The song also shows up on Jean-Luc Ponty's album, arranged by Zappa, *King Kong.*

43. Watson, *Negative Dialectics,* 182.

44. For a good example of how subsequent bands really expanded upon this piece, listen to the more than 15-minute version on *FZ:OZ.*

45. Zappa's arguments about unions, which he makes on a number of songs—including "Lonesome Cowboy Burt" on *200 Motels,* "Flakes" on *Sheik Yerbouti,* "Stick Together" on *Man from Utopia,* and "Yo Cats" on *Frank Zappa Meets the Mothers of Prevention*—are fairly consistent. I will look at this subject again when I discuss *Man from Utopia,* specifically in response to Ben Watson's interesting discussion of Zappa's supposed antiunion stance.

46. The song would be rerecorded or released four other times: on *Playground Psychotics, Them or Us, You Can't Do That on Stage Anymore, Vol. 3* (featuring a solo by the then unknown Dweezil Zappa), and *The Lost Episodes* (where the listener gets to hear the original 11-minute demo with Sugarcane Harris on vocals, a decidedly different take).

47. Steve Huey, "Review: *Chunga's Revenge,*" *All Music Guide,* www.allmusic. com.

48. Biographers have it listed variously as June 4, 5, or 6.

49. Parts of the concert ended up on Lennon's album *Some Time in New York City,* and some ended up under the titles "Scumbag" and "A Small Eternity with Yoko Ono" on the Zappa album *Playground Psychotics.*

50. Quoted in Miles, *Zappa: A Biography,* 212.

51. For Watson's argument, see Watson, *Negative Dialectics,* 190–91.

52. Quoted in Miles, *Zappa: A Biography,* 203.

53. In his biography of Led Zeppelin, Stephen Davis claims that it was Zeppelin, not the Fudge, who were responsible for the Mud Shark incident. He quotes Richard Cole, who was an employee of Zeppelin's, as saying it was mainly something that he and drummer John Bonham cooked up in Seattle. See Stephen Davis, *Hammer of the Gods: The Led Zeppelin Saga* (New York: Berkley Publishing Group, 2001), 78–80.

54. For more commentary on the dance, see "*Fillmore East, June 1971:* The Mud Shark—Notes and Comments, *ARF,* http://www.arf.ru / Notes / Fillmore / mshark.html.

55. Watson, *Negative Dialectics,* 190.

56. Michel Foucault, *The History of Sexuality: An Introduction,* vol. 1, trans. Robert Hurley (New York: Vintage, 1990), 3.

57. Ibid.

58. Or lie about it happening. When televangelist Jimmy Swaggart was caught lying about paying a prostitute for sexual favors, Zappa rewrote "What Kind of Girl Do You Think We Are" to specifically refer to particulars in the Swaggart incident.

59. Zappa, *Real Frank Zappa Book,* 266.

60. "Where Is Our Zappa," www.cbsnews.com / stories / 2005 / 10 / 06 / tech / gamecore / main924513.shtml.

61. The double entendre *member* will go unremarked upon.

62. Parts of "Latex Solar Beef" would show up again in the fade out of the song "Stick it Out" on *Joe's Garage.*

63. The song was initially released as a single credited to "Billy Dexter." Apparently, much like with *Cruising with Ruben and the Jets,* the public was upset that Zappa was trying to pull something over on them, so the single was rereleased and credited to Frank Zappa and the Mothers of Invention. For more, see Greg Russo, *Cosmik Debris: The Collected History and Improvisations of Frank Zappa (The Son of Revised)* (Floral Park, NY: Crossfire Publications, 2003), 109–10.

64. Courrier, *Dangerous Kitchen,* 235.

65. Steve Huey, "Review: *Fillmore East, 1971.*" *All Music Guide,* http://www.allmusic.com.

66. Bill Holdship, "*200 Motels:* Amazon.com Essential Recording," http://www.amazon.com.

67. Like most of Zappa's projects, many things were happening simultaneously: *200 Motels* was shot, and many of the songs were written and recorded before *Fillmore East, 1971;* however, due in part to Zappa's inexperience as a film editor and due in part to the length of time it take to get a movie to the public, *Fillmore East, 1971* came out before *200 Motels.*

68. When I checked, there were 24 used copies on VHS available from Amazon.com.

69. Peter Evans, "Frank Zappa's *200 Motels* and the Theater of the Absurd," *Sapaan: Explorations in Music and Sound,* 2 (2003).

70. Courrier, *Dangerous Kitchen,* 226.

71. Bradford Robinson, "Kurt Weill," in *Grove Music Online,* ed. L. Macy, http://www.grovemusic.com.

72. Courrier, *Dangerous Kitchen,* 227.

73. Watson, *Negative Dialectics,* 187. Watson's discussion of *200 Motels* is one of the few places that he slips into outright hyperbole, arguing that the album shows "the sort of contrast no other twentieth-century musical force has been able to achieve" (188). This is a pretty broad and sweeping statement that needs much more development.

74. In part, this may be indicative of Zappa's political and ideological maturity; Zappa was 30 in 1970 when he did *200 Motels* and 40 when he did *Joe's Garage,* 10 years that can make a huge difference.

75. Many of the short pieces were collected under the name "Bogus Pomp" and can be found on the album *London Symphony Orchestra Vol. II.*

76. Richie Unterberger, "Review: *200 Motels,*" *All Music Guide,* www.allmusic.com.

77. Jerry McCulley, "Review: *Soundtrack to 200 Motels,*" www.amazon.com.

78. Zappa sued Albert Hall and lost. Parts of the trial are excerpted in Zappa, *Real Frank Zappa Book,* 119–37. The transcripts also give great insight into how Zappa thought about his own lyrics.

79. This is the incident referred to in the lyrics to the Deep Purple song "Smoke on the Water": "Frank Zappa & the Mothers were at the best place around / But some stupid with a flare gun burned the place to the ground."

80. All of the biographies and Zappa's own autobiography cover this event.

81. Don Preston, who had played on one song on *Fillmore East, June 1971* was by this time back in the band on a more or less permanent basis.

82. Miles, *Zappa: A Biography*, 215.

83. Watson, *Negative Dialectics*, 192–93; Watson also brings in chaos theory, detective fiction, and leftist politics.

84. Courrier, *Dangerous Kitchen*, 239.

85. Francois Couture, "Review: *Just Another Band from L.A.*," *All Music Guide*, http://www.allmusic.com.

86. Both of these albums were recorded with a tremendous number of studio and session musicians, along with a few regulars, including George Duke, Aynsley Dunbar, and Jeff Simmons and newcomers Sal Marquez, Tony Duran, and Alex "Erroneous" Dmochowski.

87. Neil Slaven, *Electric Don Quixote: The Definitive Story of Frank Zappa* (London: Omnibus Press, 1997), 154.

88. Miles, *Zappa: A Biography*, 225.

89. Courrier, *Dangerous Kitchen*, 245.

90. A number of critics cite Zappa's accident in London as the beginning of a more violent period in his lyrics. I tend to disagree; Zappa's growing disenchantment seems to parallel that of many critics of U.S. culture who saw the earlier seventies as a much harder and meaner era.

91. Dominique Chevalier, *Viva! Zappa*, trans. Matthew Screech (London: Omnibus Press, 1986), 99.

92. Courrier, *Dangerous Kitchen*, 247.

93. Brackett with Hoard, eds. *The New Rolling Stone Album Guide*, 903.

94. Francois Couture, "Review: *Waka / Jawaka* and *The Grand Wazoo*," *All Music Guide*, www.allmusic.com.

95. Andrew Boscardan, "Review: *Waka / Jawaka*," www.amazon.com.

96. Ironically, a September 24, 1972, review of *The Grand Wazoo* touring orchestra by Don Meckman in the *New York Times* compares Zappa to Bernstein. Meckman writes that, "Like Bernstein, Zappa has mastered the elements of one musical discipline . . . and attempts to ally them with elements from another." There is no mention of the fact that both Bernstein and Zappa were sort of depressed by the fact that fans seemed uninterested in their musical experiments.

CHAPTER 5

1. The two were originally available as a two-for-one disc RCD 400025. The Web site *Over-Nite Sensation* http://www.lukpac.org/~handmade/patio/vinyl-vscds/over-nite_sensation.html#1995cd does a nice job of comparing the various releases.

2. Ben Watson, *Frank Zappa: The Negative Dialectics of Poodle Play* (New York: St. Martin's, 1995), 213.

3. Ibid., 210.

4. As late as 1982, "Don't Eat That Yellow Snow" was being used as an advertisement for Zappa's concerts. Although Zappa's fans may well claim that it was and is a sellout, Zappa himself seemed to have little difficulty using its popularity to bring people to his shows. The song (and the other three songs in the suite that starts *Apostrophe (')*) was a staple of Zappa's live shows for years. Zappa acknowledges this in a

number of places, arguing that it was playing these songs live that finally afforded him the ability to have symphonic music played and recorded.

5. In Frank Zappa with Peter Occhiogrosso, *The Real Frank Zappa Book* (New York: Poseidon Press, 1989), Zappa writes that one of his greatest influences was Spike Jones and that he is terrifically fond of what he calls "Archetypal American Musical Icons" (166–68). Much of the music on *Over-Nite* and *Apostrophe (')* comes out of the same U.S. song genre that gave us musical theater and advertising jingles.

6. In his autobiography, Zappa relates that he also suffered a crushed larynx that resulted in his voice being lowered by a third, which he seems to have appreciated, although, as he writes, "I would have preferred some other means of acquiring it" (Zappa, *Real Frank Zappa Book,* 115).

7. Francois Couture, "Review: *Waka/Jawka* and *The Grand Wazoo*," *All Music Guide,* http://www.allmusic.com.

8. *Rolling Stone.* December 20, 1973, quoted in Neil Slaven, *Electric Don Quixote: The Definitive Story of Frank Zappa* (London: Omnibus Press, 1997), 163.

9. Charles Shanmurry, review in *New Music Express* as quoted in Slaven, *Electric Don Quixote,* 164.

10. For good summaries of reviews, see Slaven, *Electric Don Quixote.*

11. Brackett, Nathan, with Christian Hoard, eds., *The New Rolling Stone Album Guide: Completely Revised and Updated Fourth Edition* (New York: Simon & Schuster, 2004), 903–4.

12. Steve Huey, "Allmusic.com Review"

13. Ibid.

14. See especially, Zappa, *Real Frank Zappa Book,* 182–84.

15. It would not be the only time this would happen. Songs from "I Ain't Got No Heart" on the first album to "Any Kind of Pain" on his final album of original music *(Broadway the Hard Way)* all revisit this theme.

16. A number of interviews with Zappa indicate that he viewed being on the road as sort of an endless ethnography of what people would do to and with one another.

17. David Walley, *No Commercial Potential: The Saga of Frank Zappa,* rev. ed. (Cambridge, MA: Da Capo, 1996), 161.

18. Barry Miles, *Zappa: A Biography* (New York: Grove Press, 2004), 233.

19. Slaven, *Electric Don Quixote,* 163. For a more complete discourse on poodle-human relations, see "The Poodle Lecture" on the *Baby Snakes* DVD and *You Can't Do That on Stage Anymore.*

20. James Woods, *The Irresponsible Self: On Laughter and the Novel* (New York: Farrar Straus and Giroux, 2004), 6.

21. Of course, this irony gets even worse if you consider that—at least until *Sheik Yerbouti*—*Over-Nite Sensation* and *Apostrophe (')* were very conscious attempts to make commercial music. In other words, what do you do with an artist who writes an accessible pop song about an industry that will not support him because he writes inaccessible pseudopop songs?

22. Interestingly, when the song was played live, there were many more stylistic differences: on the live albums *FZ:OZ* (1976 band) and *You Can't Do That on Stage Anymore, Vol. 6* (1984 band), the song is played at more than twice the speed of the studio version, except for the last verse, which is slowed into a parody of a big, heavy-metal finale that often segued into the song "Muffin Man."

23. Kevin Courrier, *The Dangerous Kitchen: The Subversive World of Frank Zappa* (Toronto: ECW Press, 2002), 253.

24. For some reason, this seems to be the song most often remembered by people who are not really Zappa fans.

25. Watson, *Negative Dialectics,* 242.

26. Courrier, *Dangerous Kitchen,* 265.

27. For a truly wonderful piece of exegesis, one must read Watson's comparison of the "Yellow Snow" songs to *King Lear* and "Stink Foot" to Plato's dialogue *Phaedo.* It is an interesting concept, and if I could be convinced that Zappa had actually read the *Phaedo,* I would be inclined to go along with it, but it seems fairly far-fetched that Zappa would have read one of Plato's more obscure dialogues and then absorbed it enough to work it into his music.

28. This is an oft-cited Zappa-ism, although no one seems to have an original source for it.

29. Watson, *Negative Dialectics,* 261.

30. Ibid.

31. Courrier, *Dangerous Kitchen,* 261.

32. The recording of "Dickie" from the Roxy shows is included on *You Can't Do That on Stage Anymore, Vol. 3;* the song was also included in the 1988 tour as Zappa made comparisons between Nixon and Ronald Reagan (and it is included on the album *Broadway the Hard Way*).

33. Francois Couture, "Review: *Roxy & Elsewhere,*" *All Music Guide,* http://www.allmusic.com.

34. Andrew Boscardan, "Review: *Roxy & Elsewhere,*" http://www.amazon.com.

35. Courrier, *Dangerous Kitchen,* 274.

36. It is about this time that the United States first started experiencing gasoline lines. I can remember sitting in my parents' brand new Buick Century for more than an hour waiting for gas in Chicago. If memory serves, gas at that time was only available on certain days of the week. It was not a happy time for middle-class America.

37. The "Sofa Suite," as performed by Flo & Eddie, consisted of the two versions of "Sofa" along with "Stick It Out," "Divan" (available on *Playground Psychotics*), and "Once Upon a Time," which leads off *You Can't Do That on Stage Anymore, Vol. 1.* For an explanation of how the songs all fit together, see "The Sofa Suite," *Information Is Not Knowledge,* http://globalia.net/donlope/fz/lyrics/translations/OSFA.html.

38. Francois Couture, "Review: *One Size Fits All,*" *All Music Guide,* http://www.allmusic.com.

39. Andrew Boscardan, "Review: *One Size Fits All,*" http://www.amazon.com.

40. Watson, *Negative Dialectics,* 286.

41. Miles, *Zappa: A Biography,* 247.

42. "Muffin Man," *Information Is Not Knowledge,* http://globalia.net/donlope/fz/songs/Muffin_Man.html.

43. Lindsey Planer, "Review: *Bongo Fury,*" *All Music Guide,* http://www.allmusic.com.

44. Andrew Boscardan, "Review: *Bongo Fury,*" http://www.amazon.com.

45. Brackett with Hoard, eds., *The New Rolling Stone Album Guide,* 904.

46. Courrier, *Dangerous Kitchen,* 285.

47. Greg Russo, *Cosmik Debris: The Collected History and Improvisations of Frank Zappa (The Son of Revised)* (Floral Park, NY: Crossfire Publications, 2003), 127.

48. The song has a final verse in which the singer adopts a German accent. For a really far-out explanation of that, including the argument that the song is about working in a concentration camp, see Watson, *Negative Dialectics,* 305.

49. *Frank Zappa Plays the Music of Frank Zappa: A Memorial Tribute.*

50. To give Watson credit, he goes to great lengths to make the argument that "The Torture Never Stops" is about the German concentration camps. It is a compelling argument, but one on which I am not completely sold (Watson, *Negative Dialectics,* 304–6).

51. Francois Couture, "Review: *Zoot Allures,*" *All Music Guide,* http://www.allmusic.com.

52. Courrier, *Dangerous Kitchen,* 292.

53. Miles, *Zappa: A Biography,* 267.

54. Ibid., 263.

55. Much of what Miles seems to object to is the way the song was performed live. See ibid., 262.

56. Kyle Gann, "Conlon Nancarrow," in *Grove Music Online,* ed. L. Macy, http://www.grovemusic.com.

57. Watson, *Negative Dialectics,* 344.

58. Miles, *Zappa: A Biography,* 267.

59. For lots of collected information about *Hunchentoot* in all of its various incarnations, see "*Sleep Dirt:* Introduction 1—Hunchentoot or Spider of Destiny," *ARF,* http://www.arf.ru / Notes / Sdirt / intro1.html.

60. Francois Couture, "Review: *Sleep Dirt,*" *All Music Guide,* http://www.allmusic.com.

61. Drummer Terry Bozzio, recorded for posterity, on the *Sheik Yerbouti* cut "Wait a Minute."

62. Watson, *Negative Dialectics,* 357.

63. This was true of kids in my generation who would gleefully cite Richard Pryor routines as a way, apparently, to say the word *nigger* in semipolite conversation.

64. Several Web sites bring up the fact that in concert the song would segue into a long set of solos from all of the band members but that the solos were all edited out of the album release.

65. Even though I lived through it, I can not do it justice. Rent *Saturday Night Fever* and *Thank God It's Friday* for a more-than-fair picture of the disco lifestyle.

66. As a teenager in Columbus, Ohio, I can distinctly remember a number of hip discotheques, including roller discos, movie theaters with discos in the lobby, discos in grocery stores, discos everywhere.

67. Steve Huey, "Review: *Sheik Yerbouti,*" *All Music Guide,* http://www.allmusic.com.

68. Andrew Boscardan, "Review: *Sheik Yerbouti,*" http://www.amazon.com.

CHAPTER 6

1. Frank Zappa, Liner Notes, *Joe's Garage, Acts I, II & III.*

2. Barry Miles, *Zappa: A Biography* (New York: Grove Press, 2004), 277.

3. For an excellent investigation of the behavior of contemporary groupies, especially groupies who have migrated from rock stars to athletes, see Lisa Olson, "Making a Play for Players," *New York Daily News*, 30 August 2003, reprinted in *The Best American Sports Writing: 2004*, ed. Richard Ben Cramer (New York: Houghton Mifflin, 2004), 162–66. Olson's piece compares the women who are athlete groupies to "predators . . . dreamers" but also indicts the entire groupie scene as part of male entitlement.

4. For more on this, see John Krakauer's investigation of radical fundamentalism, *Under the Banner of Heaven: A Story of Violent Faith* (New York: Anchor, 2004). In this text, Krakauer argues that, among other things, Elizabeth Smart may well have been predisposed to follow the orders of her captor because of her upbringing as a Mormon.

5. Kevin Courrier, *The Dangerous Kitchen: The Subversive World of Frank Zappa* (Toronto: ECW Press, 2002), 334.

6. There are a large number of Ruth Underwood / Chester Thompson fans, too. And everyone loves Terry Bozzio.

7. With all due respect to Tom Cruise, Zappa saw through this a long time ago.

8. *Scientology,* http://www.scientology.org / en_US / l-ron-hubbard / index.html.

9. For an interesting look at the genesis of the song, listen to the 5:28 version on *Guitar* entitled "Outside Now (Original Solo)." Apparently this song had its origins inside the extended "City of Tiny Lights" solo; Zappa would slow the band down and they would play what is largely the instrumental section of "Outside Now" and then return to "City." For a more extended discussion, see "Outside Now," *Information Is Not Knowledge,* http://globalia.net / donlope /fz / songs / Outside_Now.html.

10. "Easy Meat," which was actually written and performed in 1970, would show up on the next album (*Tinsel Town Rebellion*) and would be a venue for extended soloing for a number of bands.

11. Zappa, quoted in Courrier, *Dangerous Kitchen,* 339.

12. There is a fantastic live version of the song on *Guitar.* Check out the two versions for a good idea of how Zappa approached the song as both a studio construction and a performance piece.

13. Steve Huey, "Review: *Joe's Garage, Acts I, II & III*," *All Music Guide,* http:// www.allmusic.com.

14. Andrew Boscardan, "Review: *Joe's Garage, Acts I, II & III*," http://www. amazon.com.

15. Nathan Brackett with Christian Hoard, eds. *The New Rolling Stone Album Guide: Completely Revised and Updated Fourth Edition* (New York: Simon & Schuster, 2004), 904.

16. Jean Elshtain, "The New Porn Wars: The Undecent Choice between Censorship and Civil Libertarianism," *The New Republic,* 25 June 1984. *The Eighties: A Reader,* ed. Gilbert Sewall, 70–81 (Reading, MA: Perseus Books, 1997, reprint).

17. The song ends up on *You Are What You Is* and will be discussed there.

18. Courrier, *Dangerous Kitchen,* 351.

19. Miles, *Zappa: A Biography,* 284.

20. Randy Newman, "Christmas in Capetown," *Trouble in Paradise* (Reprise / Warner Brothers Records, 1983).

21. Miles, *Zappa: A Biography,* 284.

22. Courrier, *Dangerous Kitchen*, 351.

23. Ben Watson, *The Negative Dialectics of Poodle Play* (New York: St. Martin's, 1995), 382.

24. You can see the finished project at "*Tinsel Town Rebellion* Panty Quilt," *ARF*, http://www.arf.ru / Misc / Quilt /.

25. Miles, *Zappa: A Biography*, 285.

26. Quoted in Courrier, *Dangerous Kitchen*, 353.

27. Many of these can be heard on the version of "Tinsel Town Rebellion" included on *Does Humor Belong in Music?*

28. Miles, *Zappa: A Biography*, 285. I wonder what Miles thinks of the Dixie Chicks' song "Goodbye Earl"?

29. Steve Huey, "Review: *Tinsel Town Rebellion*," *All Music Guide*, http://www.allmusic.com.

30. Dominique Chevalier, *Viva! Zappa*, trans. Matthew Screech (London: Omnibus Press, 1986), 75.

31. This is one of two Zappa CDs (the other is *Tinsel Town Rebellion*) that has been rereleased at least three times. Experts say you will want to get the 1998 CD reissue approved by the Zappa Family Trust and remastered by Spencer Chrislu.

32. Frank Zappa, Liner Notes, *You Are What You Is*.

33. The Web site *FortuneCity*, http://www.fortunecity.com / victorian / churchmews / 503 / intro.htm, has an incredibly detailed essay on the complete *Sinister Footwear* by A. J. Wilkes.

34. C. Vann Woodward, "The Fall of the American Adam," in *The Future of the Past*, ed. Gilbert Sewall (New York: Oxford University Press, 1989); *The Eighties: A Reader* (Reading, MA: Perseus Books, 1997, reprint), 228.

35. Watson, *Negative Dialectics*, 390.

36. Courrier, *Dangerous Kitchen*, 359.

37. "Mudd Club, *Wikipedia*, http://en.wikipedia.org / wiki / Mudd_Club.

38. It is important to keep in mind that Zappa wrote this song more than 20 years before the September 11, 2001, tragedy that woke up many Americans to the idea that other people in other countries have vastly different ideas about the ways we all ought to be living our lives. It is scary to think that Zappa saw so clearly what might happen when Christianity and Islam clash in a technologically advanced world.

39. Zappa, quoted in an interview with CBC radio host Vicki Gabereau; Courrier, *Dangerous Kitchen*, 363.

40. It is one of the few places that Watson is critical of Zappa, even going so far as to bring the song up in an interview with Zappa right before his (Zappa's) death. See Watson, *Negative Dialectics*, 548–49. Courrier calls it "the only truly crass number on the album" (Courrier, *Dangerous Kitchen*, 362).

41. Quoted in Courrier, *Dangerous Kitchen*, 363.

42. Watson, *Negative Dialectics*, 395.

43. Steve Huey, "Review: *You Are What You Is*," *All Music Guide*, http://www.allmusic.com.

44. Andrew Boscardan, "Review: *You Are What You Is*," http://www.amazon.com.

45. Brackett, *New Rolling Stone Album Guide*, 904.

46. Quoted in Courrier, *Dangerous Kitchen*, 368.

47. A moment of personal reflection: I was 14 in 1982 and remember the song being on just about every pop and rock radio station several times a day. You could not escape it if you tried. Soon there was a *Valley Girl* film (not related to the song and pretty good in its own right), lunch boxes, coloring books, and so forth. Zappa had suddenly become ubiquitous.

48. Watson claims that the singer is Bob Harris. There is no corroboration from Zappa on either case. Both Courrier and the completist Web site "Ship Arriving Too Late to Save a Drowning Witch," *Information Is Not Knowledge,* http://globalia. net / donlope / fz / lyrics / Ship_Arriving_Too_Late_To_Save_A_Drowning_Witch. html#Top, credit it to Roy Estrada.

49. Francois Couture, "Review: *Ship Arriving Too Late to Save a Drowning Witch,*" *All Music Guide,* http://www.allmusic.com.

50. Lyrics from "The Jazz Discharge Party Hats."

51. In discussing this album, I am using the Barking Pumpkin CD from the late eighties. This is an album that has been remixed and rereleased at least three times. The CD that I have is resequenced and has an extra song that the vinyl album does not have. It is the only album for which I disagree with the decisions Zappa made. On the original vinyl album, the song "The Jazz Discharge Party Hats" segues immediately into "We Are Not Alone," a sax-drenched instrumental. Now "Jazz" segues into "Luigi & the Wise Guys," an inferior song that makes for a vastly different emotional experience.

52. See Watson, *Negative Dialectics,* 405–7.

53. Neil Slaven, *Electric Don Quixote: The Definitive Story of Frank Zappa* (London: Omnibus Press, 1997), 261.

54. Francois Couture, "Review: *The Man from Utopia,*" *All Music Guide,* http://www.allmusic.com.

55. For an extended discussion of this incident, see Frank Zappa with Peter Occhiogrosso, *The Real Frank Zappa Book* (New York: Poseidon Press, 1989), 214.

56. Although this is not the place for an essay on MTV, it is important to remember that, for a few golden years at the beginning—from 1980–83, for instance—MTV really was a place to discover new and different bands. As the record companies began to discover MTV's marketing potential, they took over the creation and distribution of videos, and MTV had no problem filling up the airwaves and thus could get pickier about what they chose to put on the air.

57. Francois Couture, "Review: *Them or Us,*" *All Music Guide,* http://www. allmusic.com.

58. Rhonda questioning Harry's choice of Broadway entertainment from the album *Thing-Fish.*

59. Charles Dickens, *The Life and Adventures of Nicholas Nickleby* (New York: Penguin, 1999), quoted in Frank Rich, *Hot Seat: Theater Criticism for The New York Times, 1980–1993* (New York: Random House, 1998), 120.

60. Rich, *Hot Seat,* 120.

61. Ibid., 141.

62. Patricia Turner, *Ceramic Uncles & Celluloid Mammies: Black Images and Their Influence on Culture* (New York: Anchor Books, 1994), 24–25.

63. Susan Faludi, *Backlash: The Undeclared War against American Women* (New York: Crown, 1991), 230.

64. I can not do it justice in this space, but Susan Faludi's book *Backlash* fairly directly addresses the manner in which conservatives, starting in the early eighties, worked pretty actively to fight the growing women's movement.

65. Faludi, *Backlash*, 202.

66. For more on Reagan's AIDS policy, see Alan White, "Reagan's AIDS Legacy: Silence Equals Death," *San Francisco Chronicle Online*, 8 June 2004, http://www.sfgate.com.

67. "Abstract of the Syphilis Study Legacy Committee: Final Report of May 20, 1996," http://www.med.virginia.edu/hs-library/historical/apology/report.html.

68. Watson, *Negative Dialectics*, 445.

69. Andrew Boscardan, "Review: *Thing-Fish*," http://www.amazon.com.

70. Francois Couture, "Review: *Thing-Fish*," *All Music Guide*, http://www.allmusic.com.

71. Frank Zappa, letter to President Ronald Reagan; reprinted in Zappa, *Real Frank Zappa Book*, 266–67.

72. For an extended discussion of what he likes and does not like about the Synclavier, see Zappa's comments in ibid., 172–74.

73. Miles, *Zappa: A Biography*, 339.

74. Slaven, *Electronic Don Quixote*, 284.

75. For a list of alumni, see "Prominent Alumni," *Berklee College of Music*, http://www.berklee.edu/about/alumni.html.

76. Francois Couture, "Review: *Frank Zappa Meets the Mothers of Prevention*," *All Music Guide*, http://www.allmusic.com.

77. Frank Zappa, as quoted in Courrier, *Dangerous Kitchen*, 446.

78. A great example of the new arrangements is the horn chart on "Eat That Question" on *Make a Jazz Noise Here*. It must be heard to be believed.

79. *Mike Keneally's Audio Diaries from the '88 Zappa Tour*, http://www.keneally.com/198834.html.

80. As I write this chapter, Robertson, who is still around in 2005, has just publicly called for the assassination of a foreign head of state. Some things never change.

81. Steve Huey, "Review: *Broadway the Hard Way*," *All Music Guide*, http://www.allmusic.com.

DISCOGRAPHY

1. Originally released in May 1981 as three separate albums—*Shut Up 'N Play Yer Guitar, Shut Up 'N Play Yer Guitar Some More,* and *Return of the Son of Shut Up 'N Play Yer Guitar*—the three albums were released as a boxed set in May 1982.

2. Originally released as two separate albums.

Bibliographic Essay

In lieu of a standard annotated bibliography, what follows is a subjective essay on the major pieces of writing on the life and works of Frank Zappa. The reasons for doing this are, I hope, fairy simple: the state of Zappa scholarship is, with perhaps one or two exceptions, pretty sad. In general, most of the existing books about Zappa are biographical in nature, and many of the authors appear either to have some sort of ideological or moral axe to grind or base much of their work on one or two sources who themselves have the aforementioned ideological or moral agenda. The other issue with Zappa scholarship is the tendency of some writers to feel that in order to write a book about Zappa they must somehow be like Zappa. Many of the books sacrifice quality and scholarship for intentional weirdness. Making it through these books becomes a trial.

What I hope to do here is present readers with enough information to judge for themselves if the work in question is worth reading for either personal or professional reasons.

This essay is not exhaustive. I am mainly interested in discussing the various books purporting to be about Zappa. I will not discuss the few significant pieces of musico-logical scholarship because, for the most part, that kind of work is written for other musicologists (please see the list of references for these works). I have made a judg-ment call in terms of some books: Zappa was a figure of such prominence that a few folks have sought their own fame by appending his name to the title or by discussing tangential or inconsequential meetings with Zappa. Both Suzannah Harris's memoir *Under the Same Moon: My Life with Frank Zappa, Steve Vai, Bob Harris and a Commu-nity of Other Artistic Souls* (New Castle, Co: Mastahna Publishing, 1999) and Nigey Lennon's *Being Frank: My Time with Frank Zappa* (Los Angeles: California Classics Books, 1995) are in this category. Harris's book, although competently written, only briefly touches on her husband's involvement with Zappa (he played keyboards, trum-pet, and sang in a few of Zappa's early eighties bands) and even less upon her own (she added vocals to a number of songs on *Sleep Dirt*). Lennon's book is an odder sort— a scandalous recounting of Lennon's affair with Zappa that seems to serve the higher purpose of selling Lennon's records. There is little original in either of these books about Zappa the musician and nothing a scholar or serious fan of Zappa's works is going to take away that they could not learn in other contexts.

The best place to start when researching or writing about Zappa is his autobiography *The Real Frank Zappa Book* (New York: Poseidon Press, 1989). It is very informative about his early years, especially the time he spent in California as a teenager. The book runs chronologically through the Flo & Eddie years and then becomes a series of essays on certain subjects that were dear to Zappa's heart: orchestras, musicians, marriage, church and state, politics, and record companies. If it has a fault it is that it seems, like many of the books about Zappa, to find the work he did in the sixties and seventies much more interesting than the work he did in the eighties. As well, as with any autobiography, the book tends to want to set the record straight. Although I do not deal much with Zappa's biography, several critics, most notably Ben Watson and Barry Miles, raise serious challenges to Zappa's own telling of his life story.

After Zappa's autobiography, the serious scholar must examine Ben Watson's *Frank Zappa: The Negative Dialects of Poodle Play* (New York: St. Martin's, 1995). This book is a big and messy piece of writing that is as close to all over the place as serious scholarship gets. It must be applauded for being the first book to attempt to offer an academic or scholarly study of Zappa. Watson looks at Zappa through a framework that is informed by the work of a number of nineteenth- and twentieth-century philosophers and theorists, including Theodor Adorno, Karl Marx, and Sigmund Freud. Watson offers up a detailed reading of most of Zappa's works as well as a concurrent narrative of Zappa's biography. It is an interesting book (more so, perhaps, if one is familiar with the theorists and philosophers he refers to). There are only two minor drawbacks to the book: the first is that Watson repeatedly uses the book to attack what he dislikes (especially postmodernism, art rock, and people he knows who have disagreed with him in the past), which takes away from the narrative; second, there are places that Watson, a British Marxist, fails to fully understand U.S. history and culture, and his readings of certain Zappa lyrics are affected by his own cultural grounding. Neither of these are particularly problems, and the book is so full of wonderful ideas and insights that it is, for now, the book to be reckoned with for those doing serious scholarship on Zappa.

The Frank Zappa Companion (New York: Schirmer Books, 1997) edited by Richard Kostelanetz is interesting because it tries to collect some important essays and articles on and about Zappa from a number of scholarly and popular sources. Like many books, however, it seems to make the tacit assumption that Zappa's best work was behind him by the end of the sixties. It does, however, include a number of pieces on Zappa that come from the classical music world.

Kevin Courrier's *The Dangerous Kitchen: The Subversive World of Frank Zappa* (Toronto: ECW Press, 2002) is a very readable book that works as a nice companion to Watson's book (it takes a number of ideas and themes from Watson's book and often expands upon them). Courrier's book offers up very detailed examinations of each of the albums and has a lot of good information about their recording histories as well as information on band members. In many ways it works best as a sort of annotated Zappa; if one is looking for a collection of conceptual continuity clues or general readings of certain songs, this book is an interesting place to start.

Greg Russo's *Cosmik Debris: The Collected History and Improvisations of Frank Zappa (The Son of Revised)* (Floral Park, NY: Crossfire Publications, 2003), is the best collection of data about Zappa available in book form. It is an exhaustive collection of lists: record release dates, CD release dates, song composition dates, tour dates, and so forth. It is also interesting for its collection of conceptual continuity clues included in the discussion of each album. Although it does present a biographical narrative to go along with the discussion of the albums, its main value is as a reference work.

Beyond the four aforementioned books, all of which are invaluable to someone considering Zappa scholarship, there are a number of other biographies that are worth mentioning, although all seem to be flawed in some manner.

Michael Gray's *Mother! The Frank Zappa Story* (London: Plexus, 1993) is especially detailed and interesting in dealing with the early Mothers of Invention and their struggle to succeed. The book is marred, however, by the amount of space given to rumor and innuendo supplied by, it would seem, an uncredited Pamala Zarubica, an early fan / groupie / hanger-on who seemed resentful of Zappa's treatment of her. It seems fairly obvious that Gray bases a lot of his information about the early days on interviews with her, and her own bias seems to show up in much of the work. The book also gets some details wrong (the most glaring being the assumption that the Bob Harris who plays on an early Zappa album is the same Bob Harris who plays on *Tinsel Town Rebellion*), which makes much of its attendant research suspect.

Billy James's *Necessity Is: The Early Years of Frank Zappa and the Mothers of Invention* (London: SAF, 2005) works well because it gives a number of people who were there at the time a voice in Zappa mythology. It is not entirely unsympathetic to Zappa, but it does paint a picture that is much more negative than other books, in large part because of the continued bitterness of many former band members.

Neil Slaven's *Electronic Don Quixote: The Definitive Story of Frank Zappa* (London: Omnibus Press, 1997) is a fairly straightforward (and well written) biography that does a good job of covering the early years through the *Läther* controversies. It fades out toward the end, rushing through the last 15 years of Zappa's life in only a few pages.

Dominique Chevalier's *Viva! Zappa* (translated by Matthew Screech; London: Omnibus Press, 1986) is an interesting book written by a fan who has some good information on various band members and breakdowns and minireviews of each album. It is a very subjective work but one that approaches Zappa from a necessary European perspective due to his enormous popularity there.

The first edition of David Walley's *No Commercial Potential: The Saga of Frank Zappa* (Cambridge, MA: Da Capo, 1996) was the first book about Zappa to be released and one that Zappa often spoke about (negatively, to be sure). The revised and updated edition does a good job of describing the early genesis of the Mothers and has a number of interesting interviews and quotes. It is marred, however, by its insistence on the adoption of a number of personas that attempt to make the book Zappa-like in execution. Although these voices and personas offer interesting arguments (and would make the book more valuable if they had been an internal argument with each other over the meaning or value of Zappa), they are distracting and, occasionally, annoying. That said, the book is often cited as a trailblazing book in Zappa scholarship and should be read.

The most recent, and difficult, book on Zappa is Barry Miles's *Zappa: A Biography* (New York: Grove Press, 2004). Miles is a longtime journalist and fan; he has

published two other works on Zappa, including *Frank Zappa: A Visual Documentary* (London: Omnibus Press, 1993) and *Frank Zappa: In His Own Words* (London: Omnibus Press, 1993), and interviewed Zappa a number of times throughout his life. That said, the second half of the book becomes an increasingly acid attack on Zappa the person. Miles, who seems to admire Zappa's music, becomes increasingly disgusted with Zappa's personal life. This becomes especially apparent in the chapter "Orchestral Maneouvres," in which Miles stops being a biographer and becomes an amateur psychologist, writing of Zappa's work habits: "Clinically, these are the symptoms of someone who has immunized himself against loneliness" and "Zappa had become a confirmed misanthrope who treated the outside world with extreme cynicism and scorn" (298–99). After reading this, one is left with an extraordinarily sour taste in the mouth. The question becomes why, 10 years after the death of Zappa, is this necessary? Although the book is useful to scholars (Miles's numerous interviews with Zappa are alone worth the effort) one must be careful to separate Miles's agenda from the scholarship.

One thing that makes Zappa scholarship unique (especially to someone trained in a rather conservative method of literary / cultural scholarship) is the number of excellent, thorough, and specific Web sites devoted to some or another aspect of Zappa scholarship. The problem with Web sites, as my old friend Cort Bishop once reminded me, is that anyone with $9.95 a month can put one up: there are, in general, no editors, publishers, or librarians to make sure that the information is accurate. As well, there is little evidence that the site designers have attempted to attain rights and permissions to use copyrighted materials. That said, there are a few Web sites that are incredibly important: for a complete set of transcribed Zappa lyrics as well as links to various sites that discuss the lyrics (especially in terms of cultural meaning and conceptual continuity), the site *Information Is Not Knowledge* at http://globalia. net / donlope / fz / is unparalleled. Although it is kind of messy, the site *Friendly Little Finger* at http://home.online.no / ~corneliu / zappa.htm contains links to many Zappa fan sites that all have lots of interesting stuff related to the study of Zappa. Finally, the Zappa Family Trust Web site at http://www.zappa.com has some interesting information and, at times, links to sites where one can purchase the more recently released albums. As of the writing of this book, however, the site was being updated only occasionally and the Barfko-Swill online store was closed, thus making the purchase of any recent Zappa releases impossible.

Bibliography

"Abstract of the Syphilis Study Legacy Committee: Final Report of May 20, 1996."
    http://www.med.virginia.edu / hs-library / historical / apology / report.html.

Anastasio, Trey. "Frank Zappa." *Rolling Stone,* 21 April 2005, 78.

Bangs, Lester. *Psychotic Reactions and Carburetor Dung.* Edited by Greil Marcus.
    New York: Vintage, 1988.

Bernard, Jonathan. "Listening to Zappa." *Contemporary Music Review* 18, no. 4
    (2000): 63–103.

Boscardan, Andrew. "Review: *Bongo Fury.*" http://www.amazon.com.

———. "Review: *Freak Out!*" http://www.amazon.com.

———. "Review: *Joe's Garage, Acts I, II & III.*" http://www.amazon.com.

———. "Review: *One Size Fits All.*" http://www.amazon.com.

———. "Review: *Roxy & Elsewhere.*" http://www.amazon.com.

———. "Review: *Sheik Yerbouti.*" http://www.amazon.com.

———. "Review: *Thing Fish.*" http://www.amazon.com.

———. "Review: *Waka/Jawka.*" http://www.amazon.com.

———. "Review: *We're Only in It for the Money.*" www.amazon.com.

———. "Review: *You Are What You Is.*" http://www.amazon.com.

Brackett, Nathan, with Christian Hoard, eds. *The New Rolling Stone Album Guide:
    Completely Revised and Updated Fourth Edition.* New York: Simon & Schuster,
    2004.

Bruce, Lenny. *How to Talk Dirty and Influence People.* New York: Quality Paperback
    Books, 1996.

Brummett, Barry. *Rhetoric in Popular Culture.* New York: St. Martin's, 1994.

Bullitt, John. *Jonathan Swift and the Art of Satire: A Study of Satiric Technique.*
    Cambridge: Harvard University Press, 1953.

Chevalier, Dominique. *Viva! Zappa.* Translated by Matthew Screech. London: Omni-
    bus Press, 1986.

Courrier, Kevin. *The Dangerous Kitchen: The Subversive World of Frank Zappa.* Toronto: ECW Press, 2002.

Couture, Francois. "Review: *Cruising.*" *All Music Guide.* http://www.allmusic.com.

———. "Review: *Frank Zappa Meets the Mothers of Prevention.*" *All Music Guide.* http://www.allmusic.com.

———. "Review: *Just Another Band from L.A.*" *All Music Guide.* http://www.allmusic.com.

———. "Review: *Lumpy Gravy.*" *All Music Guide.* http://www.allmusic.com.

———. "Review: *The Man from Utopia.*" *All Music Guide.* http://www.allmusic.com.

———. "Review: *One Size Fits All.*" *All Music Guide.* http://www.allmusic.com.

———. "Review: *Roxy & Elsewhere.*" *All Music Guide.* http://www.allmusic.com.

———. "Review: *Ship Arriving Too Late to Save a Drowning Witch.*" *All Music Guide.* http://www.allmusic.com.

———. "Review: *Sleep Dirt.*" *All Music Guide.* http://www.allmusic.com.

———. "Review: *Them or Us.*" *All Music Guide.* http://www.allmusic.com.

———. "Review: *Thing Fish.*" *All music Guide.* http://www.allmusic.com.

———. "Review: *Waka/Jawka* and *The Grand Wazoo.*" *All Music Guide.* http://www.allmusic.com.

———. "Review: *Zoot Allures.*" *All Music Guide.* http://www.allmusic.com.

Covach, John, and Walter Everett. "Preface." Special issue, *Contemporary Music Review* 18, no. 4 (2000): 1–3.

Dallas, Karl. "What Did You Do in the Revolution, Dada." *Let It Rock,* June 1975, 33–36.

Davis, Stephen. *Hammer of the Gods: The Led Zeppelin Saga.* New York: Berkley Publishing Group, 2001.

De Certeau, Michel. *The Practice of Everyday Life.* Translated by Steven Randall. Berkeley: University of California Press, 1984.

Dickens, Charles. *The Life and Adventures of Nicholas Nickleby.* New York: Penguin, 1999.

Didion, Joan. *The White Album.* New York: Noonday, 1990.

Elshtain, Jean. "The New Porn Wars: The Undecent Choice between Censorship and Civil Libertarianism." *The New Republic,* 25 June 1984. Reprinted in *The Eighties: A Reader,* ed. Gilbert Sewall, 70–81. Reading, MA: Perseus Books, 1997.

Emerson, Simon, and Denis Smalley. "Electro-Acoustic Music." In *Grove Music Online.* Edited by L. Macy. http://www.grovemusic.com.

Ensemble Ambrosius. *The Zappa Album.* Northern Lights, 2000.

Ensemble Modern. *Plays Frank Zappa: Greggery Peccary & Other Persuasions.* RCA Red Seal, 2004.

Evans, Peter. "Frank Zappa's *200 Motels* and the Theater of the Absurd." In *Sapaan: Explorations in Music and Sound,* 2 (2003).

Faludi, Susan. *Backlash: The Undeclared War against American Women.* New York: Crown, 1991.

Foucault, Michel. *The History of Sexuality: An Introduction.* Vol. 1. Translated by Robert Hurley. New York: Vintage, 1990.

Frampton, Peter. "I'm in You." *I'm in You.* A & M Records, 1977.

Gann, Kyle. "Conlon Nancarrow." In *Grove Music Online.* Edited by L. Macy. http://www.grovemusic.com.

Gans, Herbert. *Popular Culture and High Culture,* rev. and updated ed. New York: Basic Books, 1999.

Gitlin, Todd. *Sixties: Years of Hope, Days of Rage,* rev. ed. New York: Bantam, 1993.

Gowers, Emily. "Satire." In *The Oxford Companion to Classical Civilization.* Edited by Simon Hornblower and Antony Spawforth. Oxford Reference Online. Oxford University Press. http://oxfordreference.com.

Graff, Gary, ed. *Musichound Rock: The Essential Album Guide.* Detroit: Visible Ink Press, 1996.

Gray, Michael. *Mother! The Frank Zappa Story.* London: Plexus, 1993.

Hall, Stuart, and Paddy Whannel. "The Young Audience." In *On the Record: Rock. Pop & the Written Word,* edited by Simon Firth and Andrew Goodwin, 27–37. New York: Pantheon, 1990.

Holdship, Bill. "*200 Motels:* Amazon.com Essential Recording." http://www.amazon.com.

Holm-Hudson, Kevin. "Introduction." In *Progressive Rock Reconsidered,* edited by Kevin Holm-Hudson, 1–18. New York: Routledge, 2002.

Horton, Donald. "The Dialogue of Courtship in Popular Song." In *On the Record: Rock, Pop & the Written Word,* edited by Simon Firth and Andrew Goodwin, 14–26. New York: Pantheon, 1990.

Huey, Steve. "Review: *Absolutely Free.*" *All Music Guide.* http://www.allmusic.com.

———. "Review: *Broadway the Hard Way.*" *All Music Guide.* http://www.allmusic.com.

———. "Review: *Burnt Weeny Sandwich.*" *All Music Guide.* http://www.allmusic.com.

———. "Review: *Chunga's Revenge.*" *All Music Guide.* http://www.allmusic.com.

———. "Review: *Fillmore East, 1971.*" *All Music Guide.* http://www.allmusic.com.

———. "Review: *Freak Out!*" *All Music Guide.* http://www.allmusic.com.

———. "Review: *Hot Rats.*" *All Music Guide.* http://www.allmusic.com.

———. "Review: *Joe's Garage, Acts I, II & III.*" *All Music Guide.* http://www.allmusic.com.

———. "Review: *Sheik Yerbouti.*" *All Music Guide.* http://www.allmusic.com.

———. "Review: *Tinsel Town Rebellion.*" *All Music Guide.* http://www.allmusic.com.

———. "Review: *Uncle Meat.*" *All Music Guide.* http://www.allmusic.com.

———. "Review: *You Are What You Is.*" *All Music Guide.* http://www.allmusic.com.

James, Billy. *Necessity Is: The Early Years of Frank Zappa and the Mothers of Invention.* London: SAF, 2005.

Jameson, Fredric. *Postmodernism; Or, The Cultural Logic of Late Capitalism.* Durham, NC: Duke University Press, 1991.

Kernfeld, Barry. "Eric Dolphy." In *Grove Music Online.* Edited by L. Macy. http://www.grovemusic.com.

Krakauer, John. *Under the Banner of Heaven: A Story of Violent Faith.* New York: Anchor, 2004.

Loder, Kurt. "Interview: Frank Zappa." *Bat Chain Puller: Rock & Roll in the Age of Celebrity,* 107–18. New York: St. Martin's, 1990.

Lyotard, Jean-François. *The Postmodern Condition: A Report on Knowledge.* Translated by Geoff Bennington and Brian Massumi. Minneapolis: University of Minnesota Press, 1984.

Manchester, William. *The Glory and the Dream: A Narrative History of America: 1932–1972.* New York: Bantam, 1975.

McCulley, Jerry. "Review: *Soundtrack to 200 Motels.*" http://www.amazon.com.

Meckman, Don. "Zappa Creates Musical Magic." *New York Times,* 24 September 1972. Reprinted in Greg Russo, *Cosmik Debris,* 116.

Miles, Barry. *Frank Zappa: In His Own Words.* London: Omnibus Press, 1993.

———. *Frank Zappa: A Visual Documentary.* London: Omnibus Press, 1993.

———. *Zappa: A Biography.* New York: Grove Press, 2004.

Newman, Randy. "Christmas in Capetown." *Trouble in Paradise.* Reprise/Warner Brothers Records, 1983.

Olson, Lisa. "Making a Play for Players." *New York Daily News,* 30 August 2003. Reprinted in *The Best American Sports Writing: 2004,* edited by Richard Ben Cramer, 162–66. New York: Houghton Mifflin, 2004.

Planer, Lindsey. "Review: *Bongo Fury.*" *All Music Guide.* http://www.allmusic.com.

Ponty, Jean-Luc. *King Kong: Jean-Luc Ponty Plays the Music of Frank Zappa.* Blue Note Records, 1993.

Prince & The Revolution. *Music from the Motion Picture* Purple Rain. Los Angeles: Warner Brothers Records, 1984.

Rich, Frank. *Hot Seat: Theater Criticism for The New York Times, 1980–1993.* New York: Random House, 1998.

Robinson, Bradford. "Kurt Weill." In *Grove Music Online.* Edited by L. Macy. http://www.grovemusic.com.

Rockwell, John. "Doo-Wop." In *Grove Music Online.* Edited by L. Macy. http://www.grovemusic.com.

Rosenheim, Edward. *Swift and the Satirist's Art.* Chicago: University of Chicago Press, 1963.

Russo, Greg. *Cosmik Debris: The Collected History and Improvisations of Frank Zappa (The Son of Revised).* Floral Park, NY: Crossfire Publications, 2003.

Scribner, Charles, Jr. "Ernest Hemingway: A Publisher's Assessment." In *The Only Thing That Counts: The Ernest Hemingway-Maxwell Perkins Correspondence,* edited by Matthew J. Bruccoli. New York: Scribner, 1996.

Scruton, Roger. "Programme Music." In *Grove Music Online.* Edited by L. Macy. http://www.grovemusic.com.

Shilts, Randy. *And the Band Played On: Politics, People and the AIDS Epidemic.* New York: Stonewall, 2000.

Simon, David, and Edward Burns. *The Corner: A Year in the Life of an Inner-City Neighborhood.* New York: Broadway Books, 1977.

Sinclair, Upton. "How to Be Obscene." In *Fierce Pajamas: An Anthology of Humor Writing from The New Yorker,* edited by David Remnick and Henry Finder, 337–39. New York: Random House, 2001.

Sischy, Ingrid. "Where's Mae West When We Need Her?: An Interview with Camille Paglia." *Interview,* July 2003. Report in *The Best American Sex Writing: 2004,* edited by Daniel O'Connor, 9–12. New York: Thunder's Mouth, 2004.

Slaven, Neil. *Electric Don Quixote: The Definitive Story of Frank Zappa.* London: Omnibus Press, 1997.

Smith, Christopher. "'Broadway the Hard Way': Techniques of Allusion in the Music of Frank Zappa." *College Music Symposium* 35 (1995): 34–60.

Sutton, Paul. "'Bogus Pomp' and Bourdieu's Paradox: Zappa & Resentment." International Conference of Esemplastic Zappology. London, 16 January 2004. http://www.militantesthetix.co.uk/ice-z/paul.htm.

Thompson, Hunter S. *Fear and Loathing in Las Vegas.* New York, Vintage Books, 1989.

———. *The Great Shark Hunt: Gonzo Papers.* Vol. 1. New York: Ballantine, 1979.

Turner, Patricia. *Ceramic Uncles & Celluloid Mammies: Black Images and Their Influence on Culture.* New York: Anchor Books, 1994.

Unterberger, Ritchie. "Review: *200 Motels.*" *All Music Guide.* http://www.allmusic.com.

Utopia. *Deface the Music.* Rhino Records, 1990.

Vai, Steve. "Frank Zappa: Musical Pioneer." *Pro Sound News,* 1 January 2004, 98.

Volpacchio, F. "The Mother of All Interviews: Frank Zappa." *Telos* 87 (1991): 124–137.

Von der Horst, Dirk. "Precarious Pleasures: Situating 'Close to the Edge' in Conflicting Male Desires." In *Progressive Rock Reconsidered,* edited by Kevin Holm-Hudson, 167–82. New York: Routledge, 2002.

Walley, David. *No Commercial Potential: The Saga of Frank Zappa,* rev. ed. Cambridge, MA: Da Capo, 1996.

Walsh, Stephan: "Igor Stravinsky," In *Grove Music Online.* Edited by L. Macy. http://www.grovemusic.com.

Watson, Ben. *Frank Zappa: The Negative Dialectics of Poodle Play.* New York: St. Martin's, 1995.

White, Alan. "Reagan's AIDS Legacy: Silence Equals Death." *San Francisco Chronicle Online,* 8 June 2004. http://www.sfgate.com.

Whittall, Arnold. "Neo-Classicism." In *Grove Music Online.* Edited by L. Macy. http://www.grovemusic.com.

Who, The. *Join Together.* New York: MCA, 1990.

Woods, James. *The Irresponsible Self: On Laughter and the Novel.* New York: Farrar Straus and Giroux, 2004.

Woodward, C. Vann. "The Fall of the American Adam." In *The Future of the Past,* ed. Gilbery Sewall. New York: Oxford University Press, 1989. Reprinted in Gilbert Sewall, *The Eighties: A Reader.* Reading, MA: Perseus Books, 1997.

Zappa, Frank. Liner Notes. *Chunga's Revenge.* Rykodisc, 1995.

———. Liner Notes. *Civilization, Phase III.* Zappa Records, 1994.

———. Liner Notes. *Cruising with Ruben & the Jets.* Rykodisc, 1995.

———. Liner Notes. *Freak Out!* Rykodisc, 1995.

———. Liner Notes. *The Grand Wazoo.* Rykodisc, 1995.

———. Liner Notes. *Guitar.* Rykodisc, 1995.

———. Liner Notes. *Joe's Garage, Acts I, II & III.* Rykodisc, 1995.

———. Liner Notes. *Sheik Yerbouti.* Rykodisc, 1995.

———. Liner Notes. *Uncle Meat.* Rykodisc, 1995.
———. Liner Notes. *The Yellow Shark.* Barking Pumpkin, 1993.
———. Liner Notes. *You Are What You Is.* Rykodisc, 1995.
———. Liner Notes. *You Can't Do That on Stage Anymore, Vol. 1.* Barking Pumpkin, 1988.
———. Liner Notes. *You Can't Do That on Stage Anymore, Vol. 3.* Barking Pumpkin, 1989.
———. Liner Notes. *Zappa in New York.* Rykodisc, 1995.
———. *Them or Us (The Book).* North Hollywood, CA: Barfko-Swill, 1984.
Zappa, Frank, with Peter Occhiogrosso. *The Real Frank Zappa Book.* New York: Poseidon Press, 1989.

Index